G000141021

The Code Of Alabama, Adopted By Act Of The General Assembly Approved February 28, 1887, With Such Statutes Passed At The Session Of 1886-87, As Are Required To Be Incorporated Therein By Act Approved February 21, 1887, And With Citations Of The

THE

CODE OF ALABAMA,

ADOPTED BY ACT OF THE GENERAL ASSEMBLY APPROVED

FEBRUARY 28, 1887;

WITH SUCH STATUTES PASSED AT THE SESSION OF 1886-87, AS ARE RE-
QUIRED TO BE INCORPORATED THEREIN BY ACT APPROVED
FEBRUARY 21, 1887; AND WITH CITATIONS OF THE
DECISIONS OF THE SUPREME COURT OF
THE STATE CONSTRUING THE
STATUTES.

IN TWO VOLUMES.

VOL. II.

PREPARED BY

ROBERT C. BRICKELL, PETER HAMILTON AND JOHN P. TILLMAN,

COMMISSIONERS.

NASHVILLE, TENN.:
MARSHALL & BRUCE, PRINTERS.
1887.

CERTIFICATE OF COMMISSIONER.

I, JOHN P. TILLMAN, Commissioner having in charge the publication of the Code of Alabama, adopted by act of the General Assembly, approved February 28th, 1887, do hereby certify that I have compared the Code, as printed, with the original, as adopted by the General Assembly; and that the Code, as printed, and as corrected by the Tables of Errata appended to the two volumes, is the same as adopted by the act of the General Assembly above noted.   JOHN P. TILLMAN,
                                                            Commissioner.

TABLE OF CONTENTS.

VOLUME II.

PART FIFTH.

CRIMES AND THEIR PUNISHMENT; PROCEDURE IN CRIMINAL CASES; SPECIAL
QUASI-CRIMINAL PROCEEDINGS.

TITLE I.

GENERAL PROVISIONS.

TITLE II.

THE SEVERAL CLASSES OF OFFENSES, WITH THEIR RESPECTIVE PUNISHMENTS.

TITLE III.

TITLE IV.

SPECIAL PROCEEDINGS.

TITLE V.

FEES, COSTS AND DISPOSITION OF FINES, FORFEITURES AND PROCEEDS OF HARD LABOR.

TITLE VI.

PART FIFTH.

CRIMES AND THEIR PUNISHMENT; PROCEDURE IN CRIMINAL CASES;
SPECIAL QUASI-CRIMINAL PROCEEDINGS.

TITLE I.

GENERAL PROVISIONS.

CHAPTER 1.

OFFENSES DEFINED AND GRADED.

3699 (4094). **Public offenses defined.**—A public offense is an act or omission forbidden by law, and punishable as hereinafter provided.

3700 (4097). **What penal acts or omissions not public offenses.**—Acts or omissions to which a pecuniary penalty is attached, recoverable by action by a person for his own use, or for the use, in whole or in part, of the state, or of a county, or corporation, are not public offenses within the meaning of this Code.

3701 (4095, 4096). **Felonies and misdemeanors defined.** A felony, within the meaning of this Code, is a public offense which may be punished by death, or by imprisonment in the penitentiary; all other public offenses are called misdemeanors.

Section construed as to felonies.—Clifton's case, 73 Ala. 473. Misdemeanor defined.—Hunter's case, 67 Ala. 83. Attempt to commit misdemeanor or felony is misdemeanor.—Wolf's case, 41 Ala. 412; Berdeaux v. Davis, 58 Ala. 611.

3702 (4781). **Indictable offenses.**—All felonies and all misdemeanors, originally prosecuted in the circuit or city court, are indictable offenses.

2—VOL. II.

CHAPTER 2.

PERSONS PUNISHABLE UNDER THIS CODE.

3703 (4631). **All persons amenable, except for offenses exclusively cognizable in United States courts.**—Every person, whether an inhabitant of this state, or of any other state or country, is liable to punishment by the laws of this state for an offense committed therein, except when it is by law exclusively cognizable in the United States courts.

CHAPTER 3.

PRINCIPALS AND ACCESSORIES.

3704 (4802). **Accessories before the fact; principals in first and second degrees; distinction abolished.**—The distinction between an accessory before the fact and a principal, and between principals in the first and second degree, in cases of felony, is abolished; and all persons concerned in the commission of a felony, whether they directly commit the act constituting the offense, or aid or abet in its commission, though not present, must hereafter be indicted, tried and punished as principals, as in the case of misdemeanors.

Participants equally guilty.—Wick's case, 44 Ala. 398; Scott's case, 30 Ala. 507. See Hughes' case, 75 Ala. 31.

CHAPTER 4.

WHEN PENAL LAWS TAKE EFFECT.

3705 (4448). **When penal acts take effect.**—No penal act shall take effect until thirty days after the adjournment of the general assembly at which such act may be passed, unless otherwise specially provided in the act.

See Henback's case, 53 Ala. 523; Taylor's case, 31 Ala. 383. Common-law rule.—Click's case, 2 Ala. 26. Statute fixing time of its effect repeals above section as to such statute.—Henback's case, supra. What is a penal statute.—Ex parte Diggs, 52 Ala. 381. Penal statutes strictly construed, but not to defeat intention of legislature.—Reese's case, 73 Ala. 18; Walton's case, 62 Ala. 197. Legislature presumed to use words in their proper signification.—Thurman's case, 18 Ala. 276. Courts look less at words than at substance.—Thompson's case, 20 Ala. 54. Literal interpretation defeating purpose of statute, not adopted.—Ib. In construing repugnant statutes in Code, original statute consulted to ascertain legislative intent.—Steele's case, 61 Ala. 213. Enrolled bills control errors.—Marshall's case, 14 Ala. 411; Washington's case, 68 Ala. 85. Language, and not punctuation or technical grammatical construction, must control.—Danzey's case, 68 Ala. 296. Where words and terms have changed in meaning since the enactment.—Sike's case, 67 Ala. 80. When part only of statute unconstitutional: and when all fails because of defective part.--Vine's case, 67 Ala. 76; Powell's case, 69 Ala. 10; Walker's case, 49 Ala. 329; Ex parte Pollard, 40 Ala. 77. Rules for interpreting statutes.—See Huffman's case, 29 Ala. 40; O'Byrnes' case, 51 Ala. 25; Wetmore's case, 55 Ala. 198; Reese's case, 73 Ala. 18.

CHAPTER 5.

EFFECT OF REPEAL OR CHANGE OF LAW.

3706 (4449). **Repeal or change of law; what does not affect; election of new penalty.**—No repeal, revision, amendment, or alteration of any law shall in any manner affect any prosecution for an offense committed under the law so repealed, revised, amended, or altered, unless the repealing, revising, amending, or altering law shall otherwise expressly provide; but every such prosecution, whether begun before or after the enactment of such repealing, revising, amending, or altering law, is governed by the law under which the offense may be committed; but in cases where the penalty for the offense may have been altered, the defendant may elect to take the new penalty, but such election must be made before the case is submitted to the jury; nor shall the prosecution for the recovery of any penalty, or the enforcement of any forfeiture, be in any manner affected by the repeal of a statute, but such prosecution shall be carried on to final judgment in all respects as if such statute had not been repealed.

Amendatory statutes, their construction and effect under the constitution, and with reference to the original statute.—Bradley's case, 69 Ala. 318. Repeal and amendment by implication.—Washington's case, 72 Ala. 272; Jackson's case, 76 Ala. 26; Lyman's case, 45 Ala. 78. When statute merely changing mode of punishment will not repeal, by implication, the former statute in its operation on offenses committed prior to the new statute.—Miles' case. 40 Ala. 39; Moore's case, Ib. 49; Miller's case, Ib. 54; Stephen's case, Ib. 67; Wade's case, Ib. 74; Magruder's case, Ib. 347. Statute is repealed by a subsequent repugnant statute; also by a subsequent statute clearly intended to create the only rule that should govern. George's case, 39 Ala. 675. Without the above enactment, the repeal of a statute exonerated from subsequent prosecution.—Freeman's case, 6 Port. 372; Allaire's case, 14 Ala. 435; Jordan's case. 15 Ala. 746; Griffin's case, 39 Ala. 541; George's case, Ib. 677; Burt's case, Ib. 618.

CHAPTER 6.

LIMITATION OF PROSECUTIONS.

3707 (4640). **Offenses as to which there is no limitation.** There is no limitation of time within which a prosecution must be commenced for any public offense which may be punished capitally, or for murder in the second degree, manslaughter in the first degree, arson, forgery, counterfeiting, or any offense expressly punishable, under the provisions of this Code, as forgery or counterfeiting.

No limitation in bastardy proceedings.—Hunter's case, 74 Ala. 83.

3708 (4641). **Six years in conversion of state or county revenue.**—A prosecution for conversion of the state or county revenue must be commenced within six years next after the conversion.

3709 (4642). **Five years in perjury and subornation of perjury.**—A prosecution for perjury, or subornation of perjury, must be commenced within five years next after the commission of the offense.

3710 (4643). Three years in other felonies.—The prosecution of all felonies, except those specified in the preceding sections, must be commenced within three years next after the commission of the offense.

Applies to burglary.—Hurt's case, 55 Ala. 214.

3711 (4644). Twelve months in misdemeanors before circuit or county court.—The prosecution of all misdemeanors before the circuit, city, or county court, unless otherwise provided, must be commenced within twelve months next after the commission of the offense.

3712 (4645). Sixty days in prosecution before justice. Prosecutions before a justice of the peace for offenses within his jurisdiction, unless otherwise provided, must be commenced within sixty days next after the commission of the offense.

Feb. 5, 1879, p. 163, sec. 3.

3713. Thirty days in using temporarily personal property of another. — A prosecution for unlawfully taking or using temporarily the property of another must be commenced within thirty days after the commission of the offense.

3714 (4646). Commencement of prosecution.—A prosecution may be commenced, within the meaning of this chapter, by finding an indictment, the issuing of a warrant, or by binding over the offender.

Ross' case, 55 Ala. 177; Molett's case, 33 Ala. 408; Foster's case, 38 Ala 425.

3715 (4820). Statute suspended in certain cases.—When an indictment is lost, mislaid, or destroyed, or when the judgment is arrested, or the indictment quashed for any defect therein, or for the reason that it was not found by a grand jury regularly organized, or because it charged no offense, or for any other cause, or when the prosecution is dismissed because of a variance between the allegations of the indictment and the evidence, and a new indictment is ordered to be preferred, the time elapsing between the preferring of the first charge or indictment and the subsequent indictment must be deducted from the time limited for the prosecution of the offense last charged.

Molett's case, 33 Ala. 408; Foster's case, 38 Ala. 425; Weston's case, 63 Ala. 155; Coleman's case, 71 Ala. 312.

CHAPTER 7.

LOCAL JURISDICTION OF OFFENSES.

3716 (4632). Generally, in county where committed.—The local jurisdiction of all public offenses, unless it is otherwise provided by law, is in the county in which the offense was committed.

3717 (4633). Offense commenced elsewhere, but consummated here.—When the commission of an offense, commenced elsewhere, is consummated within the boundaries of this state, the offender is liable to punishment here, although he was out of the state at the commission of the offense charged, if he con-

summated it in this state through the intervention of an innocent or guilty agent, or by any other means proceeding directly
from himself; and the jurisdiction in such case, unless otherwise provided by law, is in the county in which the offense was
consummated.

Crow's case, 18 Ala. 545.

3718 (4634). **Offense commenced here, but consummated
elsewhere.**—When the commission of an offense, commenced
here, is consummated without the boundaries of this state, the
offender is liable to punishment therefor; and the jurisdiction
in such case, unless otherwise provided by law, is in the county
in which the offense was commenced.

Green's case, 66 Ala 40.

3719 (4635). **Offense committed partly in different counties.**—When an offense is committed partly in one county and
partly in another, or the acts, or effects thereof, constituting, or
requisite to the consummation of the offense, occur in two or
more counties, the jurisdiction is in either county.

3720 (4636). **Offense committed on or near county boundary.**—When an offense is committed on the boundary of two
or more counties, or within a quarter of a mile thereof, or
when it is committed so near the boundary of two counties as
to render it doubtful in which the offense was committed, the
jurisdiction is in either county.

Dickey's case, 68 Ala. 508.

3721 (4637). **Forcible marriage, decoying child, kidnapping, etc.**—For the offenses specified in sections 3743 (4309),
3744 (4310), 3745 (4322), and 3746 (4323) of this Code, the jurisdiction is in the county in which the offense was committed, or
in any other county into or through which, in the commission of
the offense, the person upon whom it was committed may have
been carried.

3722 (4638). **Bringing stolen property into this state.**
When property is stolen elsewhere and brought into this state,
the jurisdiction is in any county into which the property is
brought.

3723 (4639). **Carrying stolen property into another county.**
When property is stolen in one county, and carried into another,
the jurisdiction is in either county.

Aaron's case, 39 Ala. 684; Whizenant's case, 71 Ala. 383. This statute only an
affirmation, not an enlargement of the common law.—Smith's case, 55 Ala. 59;
Crow's case, 18 Ala. 545. Hence, statutory offense of stealing from a store or
dwelling cannot be prosecuted in county where goods carried, though offense may
be there prosecuted as a simple larceny.—Smith's case. 55 Ala. 59. To authorize
conviction in county where goods carried, thief must have had control of property
in such county.—Lucas' case, 62 Ala. 26; Whizenant's case, supra.

TITLE II.

THE SEVERAL CLASSES OF OFFENSES, WITH THEIR RESPECTIVE PUN-
ISHMENTS.

CHAPTER 1.

OFFENSES AGAINST STATE SOVEREIGNTY.

3724 (4100). **Punishment of treason.**—Every one who commits the crime of treason against the state must, on conviction,
suffer death, or imprisonment in the penitentiary for life, at the
discretion of the jury trying the same.

CHAPTER 2.

OFFENSES AGAINST THE PERSON.

ARTICLE I.

HOMICIDE.

3725 (4295). **Murder; different degrees of.** —Every homicide, perpetrated by poison, lying in wait, or any other kind of
willful, deliberate, malicious and premeditated killing; or com-

mitted in the perpetration of, or the attempt to perpetrate, any
arson, rape, robbery, or burglary, or perpetrated from a premeditated design unlawfully and maliciously to effect the death
of any human being other than him who is killed; or perpetrated by any act greatly dangerous to the lives of others, and
evidencing a depraved mind regardless of human life, although
without any preconceived purpose to deprive any particular
person of life, is murder in the first degree; and every other
homicide, committed under such circumstances as would have
constituted murder at common law, is murder in the second
degree.

Murder, and manslaughter generally.—The different degrees of homicide stated,
where there was evidence of previous difficulty and a fight, in which one party was
slain.—Myer's case, 62 Ala. 599.   Statutes have classified, but not reduced offense of
common-law murder.—Mitchell's case, 60 Ala. 28; Judge's case, 58 Ala. 406; Ex parte
Nettles, Ib. 268.   Homicide by poisoning, lying in wait, etc.   See Johnson's case,
17 Ala. 618; Mitchell's case, 60 Ala. 28.   Killing in attempting felonies mentioned,
is murder in the first degree, regardless of malice or specific intent to kill.—Kilgore's case, 74 Ala. 1.   Definition of the words *willful, deliberate, malicious,* and
premeditated, as used in the statute, all grouped under the phrase, *formed design.*
Mitchell's case, 60 Ala 28.   What is deliberation and premeditation.—Ex parte
Brown, 65 Ala. 447.   Meaning of the word malice in the statute.—Holley's case, 75
Ala. 14.   Murder is not always willful, nor is every willful killing murder.—Bob's
case, 29 Ala. 24.   Killing one person by a blow aimed at another; intent of assault
material inquiry in fixing character of homicide; might be murder or involuntary
manslaughter.—Ib. 24.   Killing a person other than the one assaulted or sought
to be killed.—Tidwell's case, 70 Ala. 33.   Attempt to commit felony resulting in un-
intended homicide, is murder.—Isham's case, 38 Ala. 213.   Constituent elements
of murder in first degree.—Smith's case, 68 Ala. 424.   Homicide with malice aforethought not necessarily murder in the first degree; when murder in second degree.
Ib. 424.   Killing to prevent a mere larceny or trespass, is murder.—Jones' case, 76
Ala. 9; Harrison's case, 24 Ala. 67; Simpson's case, 59 Ala. 1; Carroll's case, 23
Ala. 28; Harrison's case, 24 Ala. 67.   A homicide perpetrated by any act greatly
dange ous to the lives of others. etc., when murder under the statute.—Mitchell's
case, 60 Ala. 20.   As to throw cars from the track, etc.—Ib. 26; Presley's case, 59
Ala. 98.   To fire pistol at night through window of a lighted room.—Washington's
case, 60 Ala. 10.   When murder to kill in a fight, though mutual blows pass.—Ex
parte Nettles, 58 Ala. 268.   To kill voluntarily party accused of misdemeanor, because he flies from arrest, is murder.—Williams' case, 44 Ala. 41; Clements' case,
50 Ala. 117.   Also to kill one who interferes to prevent a felony.—Dill's case, 25
Ala. 15.   Murder in second degree committed without an intent to kill.—Nutt's case,
63 Ala. 180.   See Field's case, 52 Ala. 348.   The intent to kill is not negatived by
drunkenness, beyond determining degree.—Tidwell's case, 70 Ala. 33. "Homicide
committed by direct force, cannot be murder in first degree unless there was intention to kill."—Mitchell's case, 60 Ala. 31.   Death caused by excessive resistance of
an assault, when murder.—Judge's case, 58 Ala. 406.   Homicide committed on
sudden provocation, when murder; mere abusive or insulting words will not reduce offense, if at all, below murder in second degree —Ex parte Brown, 65
Ala. 447; Mitchell's case, 60 Ala. 33; Judge's case, 58 Ala. 406; Nutt's case,
63 Ala. 180.   When killing manslaughter, and when murder.—Ex parte Warrick, 73 Ala. 57.   Charge incorrectly defining murder.—Perry's case, 43 Ala.
21.   Correct charge defining murder in second degree.—Field's case, 52 Ala.
348.   Purpose of section 3727.—Ex parte Brown, 65 Ala. 447.   Where two persons fight by mutual consent, or willingly.—See Brown's case, 74 Ala. 478; Cates'
case, 50 Ala. 166; McNeezer's case, 63 Ala. 169.   Where third parties interfere in
the combat of others, and kill or get killed.—Dill's case, 25 Ala. 15; Frank's case,
27 Ala. 37; Will's case, 74 Ala. 21.   **Manslaughter in the first degree** is the result
of passion, suddenly engendered, and without premeditation, from present provocation, which must, in no case. be less than an assault —Mitchell's case, 60 Ala.
33; Cates' case, 50 Ala. 166; McNeezer's case, 63 Ala. 169.   And the killing must
be unlawful as well as voluntary.—Smith's case, 68 Ala. 424.   There must be a
criminal intent, or negligence so gross as to imply it, to constitute manslaughter.
Hampton's case, 45 Ala. 82.   There need be no specific intention to kill, if death
ensues from the intentional application of unlawful force.—McManus' case, 36
Ala. 285.   See Collier's case, 69 Ala. 247; Will's case, 74 Ala. 21; Ex parte Brown,
65 Ala. 446; Cross' case, 68 Ala. 476.   The statute, without regard to circumstances
of provocation, fixes the grade of manslaughter in the first degree, if the act be
voluntarily committed; presumption that the act was voluntary.—Oliver's case, 17
Ala. 587.   Manslaughter in first degree by party stricken or engaged in combat.

Ex parte Brown, 65 Ala. 447. See, also, Brown's case, 74 Ala. 478; Cates' case, 50 Ala. 166. Killing to resist an unlawful arrest, when manslaughter.—See Noles' case, 26 Ala. 31. If resistance of an assault be excessive, and the fatal blow be inflicted in the heat of blood, although with a deadly weapon, and there be no evidence of previous malice, formed design, or of such deliberation as to show that reason held sway, it is manslaughter; but if inflicted pursuant to a formed design, if there be other satisfactory evidence of premeditation, then it is murder.—Judge's case, 58 Ala. 406. Provocation necessary to reduce homicide to manslaughter. Flanagan's case, 46 Ala. 703; Mitchell's case, 60 Ala. 33. Misleading charges as to sufficient provocation to justify homicide.—Smith's case, 68 Ala. 424. Insufficient provocation, such as mere words, however insulting. — Morris' case, 25 Ala. 57; Taylor's case, 48 Ala. 180; Felix's case, 18 Ala. 720; Collier's case, 69 Ala. 247; Judge's case, 58 Ala. 406; Mitchell's case, 60 Ala. 33; Nutt's case, 63 Ala. 180. Evidence of opprobrious words or abusive language not permissible. Taylor's case, 48 Ala. 180. **Manslaughter in second degree** may occur in a case where the evidence showed a fight in which one party was slain, if the circumstances fail to show murder or manslaughter in the first degree, and yet show that the killing is done without legal provocation and not in self-defense.—Myer's case, 62 Ala. 599. See Evans' case, 62 Ala. 6; McNeezer's case, 62 Ala. 169; Bob's case, 29 Ala. 24. Also, when the killing is through recklessly pointing a loaded gun at another. Cross' case, 68 Ala. 476. **Malice**, either expressed or implied, is not an ingredient . of manslaughter.—Jackson's case, 74 Ala. 26. **Malice aforethought** is the criterion distinguishing murder from all other homicides.—See Roberts' case, 68 Ala. 166 ; Morris' case, 25 Ala. 57. Every unexplained homicide is presumptively malicious. Clements' case, 50 Ala. 117. When a homicide is committed with a deadly weapon, malice is presumed, and the burden is on the defendant to rebut the inference of malice, unless the evidence which proves the killing proves also justification or extenuation.—Ex parte Warrick, 73 Ala. 57; De Arman's case, 71 Ala. 351; Sylvester's case, 71 Ala. 17; s. c., 72 Ala. 201; Murphy's case, 37 Ala. 142; Eiland's case, 52 Ala. 322; Roberts' case, 68 Ala. 156; Wharton's case, 73 Ala. 366; Dills' case, 25 Ala. 15. When malice not implied.—Tempe's case, 40 Ala. 350; Clements' case, 50 Ala. 117; Grant's case, 62 Ala. 234. Deadly weapon defined. Sylvester's case, 72 Ala. 201. Former difficulty, ill-will, and **motive** as proof of malice.—Garrett's case, 76 Ala. 18; McAnally's case, 74 Ala. 9; Marler's case; 68 Ala. 580; Faire's case, 58 Ala. 74. Failure to prove motive is not a circumstance in favor of accused.—Cross' case, 68 Ala. 476. And the proof of motive is not indispensable.—Clifton's case, 73 Ala. 473. As to what facts admissible as tending to prove motive, see Flanagan's case, 46 Ala. 703; Ex parte Nettles, 58 Ala. 268; Childs' case, 55 Ala. 25; Commander's case, 60 Ala. 1; Noles' case, 26 Ala. 31; Hall's case, 40 Ala. 698; Kelsoe's case, 47 Ala. 573; Baalam's case, 17 Ala. 451; Phillips' case, 68 Ala. 469; Garrett's case, 76 Ala. 18. What not admissible evidence for prisoner as showing motive.—Dupree's case, 33 Ala. 380; Hadley's case, 55 Ala. 31. Motive to get rid of a witness.—Marler's case, 67 Ala. 66; s. c., 68 Ala. 580. **Justifiable homicide and self-defense**, by an officer when resisted in making an arrest.—Clements' case, 50 Ala. 117. Killing a felon who resists or flies from arrest.—Williams' case, 44 Ala. 41. Right to kill to prevent forcible and atrocious felonies (Dill's case, 25 Ala. 15) does not extend to right to prevent secret or fraudulent felonies.—Storey's case, 71 Ala. 338. Killing by misfortune or misadventure, while in the performance of a lawful act, may be excusable, when. Tidwell's case, 70 Ala. 33. Killing upon chance medley.—Green's case, 69 Ala 6. The right to kill in **self-defense**.—Oliver's case, 17 Ala. 587; Holme's case. 23 Ala. 17; Dupree's case, 33 Ala. 380; Harrison's case, 24 Ala. 67; Lewis' case, 51 Ala. 1; Tidwell's case, 70 Ala. 33; De Arman's case, 71 Ala. 351; Storey's case, 71 Ala 330; Holley's case, 75 Ala. 14; Jones' case, 76 Ala. 9; McDaniel's case, 76 Ala. 1; Cross' case, 63 Ala. 40; McNeezer's case, Ib. 169; Judge's case. 58 Ala. 406; Mitchell's case, 60 Ala. 26; Eiland's case, 52 Ala. 322; Rogers' case, 62 Ala. 170; Myers' case, Ib. 599; Taylor's case, 48 Ala. 180; Simpson's case, 59 Ala. 1. To make out a case of justifiable self-defense, the evidence must show that the difficulty was not provoked or encouraged by the defendant; that he was, or appeared to be so menaced at the time as to create a reasonable apprehension of danger to his life, or of grievous bodily harm, and that there was no other reasonable hope of escape from such present impending peril.—Cross' case, 63 Ala. 40. Party claiming self-defense must be wholly without fault; must not have brought the necessity upon himself by his own misconduct.—Eiland's case, 52 Ala. 322. The slayer must have neither provoked nor encouraged the difficulty.—Bain's case, 70 Ala. 4; Ex parte Brown, 65 Ala. 446; Leonard's case, 66 Ala. 461; Lewis' case, 51 Ala. 1; Eiland's case, 52 Ala. 322; Kimbrough's case, 62 Ala. 248; Myers' case, Ib. 599. The danger or necessity need not be actual, but must reasonably appear to be so.—Oliver's case, 17 Ala. 587; Roberts' case, 68 Ala. 156; De Arman's case, 71 Ala. 351; Brown's case, 74 Ala. 478; Ex parte Brown, 65 Ala. 446; Bain's case, 70 Ala. 4; Ingram's case, 67 Ala. 67. Peril of mere indignity or of a battery, not endangering life or limb, will not justify killing.—Eiland's case, 52 Ala. 322. Bare fear. however well grounded, will not justify killing.—Harrison's case, 24 Ala. 67; Oliver's case, 17

Ala. 587; Holmes' case, 23 Ala. 17; Dupree's case, 33 Ala. 380; Dill's case, 25 Ala. 15; Jones' case, 76 Ala. 9. When one not in fault he may anticipate the other, and draw and fire first, though the other party is in fact unarmed.—De Arman's case, 71 Ala. 351. If the deceased struck first in self-defense, the slayer cannot for himself invoke the doctrine of self-defense so as to excuse or mitigate the killing.—Myers' case, 62 Ala. 599; Lewis' case, 51 Ala. 1. When doctrine of self-defense is inapplicable and unavailing, and charges on self-defense are properly refused.—Mills' case, 73 Ala. 362; De Arman's case, 71 Ala. 351; Holley's case, 75 Ala. 14; Taylor's case, 48 Ala. 180; Allen's case, 60 Ala. 19. Charge ignoring self-defense, when there is evidence tending to show it, is erroneous.—Martin's case, 47 Ala. 564. **Theory of retreat.** Same as common law of England.—Pierson's case, 12 Ala. 149; Eiland's case, 52 Ala. 322. Need not retreat in one's own house. Robert's case, 68 Ala. 156; Cary's case, 76 Ala. 78; Jones' case, Ib. 8. One's place of business is pro hac vice his dwelling-house within this principle.—Cary's case, 76 Ala. 78; Jones' case, 76 Ala 8. And the principle applies as between partners, and joint tenants, and tenants in common.—Jones' case, 76 Ala. 8. When one not required to retreat.—De Arman's case, 71 Ala. 351. Charges ignoring the principle of retreat erroneous.—Ingram's case, 67 Ala. 67. **Threats made by the accused** to kill somebody admissible, and for jury to decide whether they were intended against the deceased.—Jones' case, 76 Ala. 9; Ford's case, 71 Ala. 385. Threats to kill deceased made at different times for two years back, admissible to show feeling.—Redd's case, 68 Ala. 492. Threats against deceased made by accomplice, who is a witness, admissible as showing malice in the witness himself.—Marler's case, 67 Ala. 66. Threats made by accused after a blow resulting in death, when admissible.—McManus' case, 36 Ala. 285. Mere threats made by the deceased to take life, will not justify homicide.—Hughey's case, 47 Ala. 97; Roberts' case 68 Ala. 515. **Communicated threats** by deceased, admissible as tending to create a belief that accused had reason to apprehend danger to life or limb from the acts and motives of deceased.—Pritchett's case, 22 Ala. 39; De Arman's case, 71 Ala. 352; Dupree's case, 33 Ala. 380; Powell's case, 52 Ala. 1; Myers' case, 62 Ala. 599. Such evidence inadmissible, however, unless there be some act or demonstration by deceased at time of killing, indicating intention to carry out threats. Hughey's case, 47 Ala. 97; Green's case, 69 Ala 6; Payne's case, 60 Ala. 80. **Uncommunicated threats** by deceased, as a general rule, inadmissible, unless part of res gestæ.—Burns' case, 49 Ala. 370. Nor are they admissible for defense when the homicide is proved by direct evidence.—Rogers' case, 62 Ala 170. But they are sometimes admissible, in cases of doubt, as tending to show the animus of the deceased, and ascertain who was the aggressor.—Green's case, 69 Ala. 6; Roberts' case, 68 Ala. 163; Burns' case, 49 Ala. 370; Powell's case, 19 Ala. 577; Carroll's case, 23 Ala. 28. Also admissible to corroborate evidence of communicated threats.—Roberts' case, 68 Ala. 156. When inadmissible.—Carroll's case, 23 Ala. 28. Defendant cannot prove **threats made by third persons** against deceased.—Alston's case, 63 Ala. 178. **Indictment**, under forms in Code sufficient.—Noles' case, 24 Ala. 672; Aikin's case. 35 Ala. 399; Phillips' case, 68 Ala. 469; Billingslea's case, Ib. 486. Also analogous forms.—Redd's case, 68 Ala. 492; s. c., 69 Ala. 255. For murder by administering poison.—Ben's case, 22 Ala. 9; Anthony's case, 29 Ala. 27. May allege different means and instruments in different counts.—Tempe's case, 40 Ala. 350. Indictment framed under the common law, good for statutory offense of murder.—Flanagan's case, 5 Ala. 477. **Presumptions;** of death being cause of unskillful treatment.—See Phillips' case, 68 Ala. 469; McDaniel's case, 76 Ala. 1. Shooting by one person and subsequent blow by another hastening death.—Tidwell's case, 70 Ala. 33. Of life when death is a material issue.—Howard's case, 75 Ala. 27. Death must ensue within a year and a day; hastening death by acts.—See Parsons' case, 21 Ala. 300; Morea's case, 2 Ala. 275. When burden of proof not on defendant to negative presumptions of malice, etc. McDaniel's case, 76 Ala. 1. **Jurisdiction** in this state if blow struck here, although death ensues elsewhere.—Green's case, 66 Ala. 40. **Dying declarations** are admissible only in cases of homicide, when made by the person injured while under a sense of impending death; and are restricted to the circumstances immediately attending the act, showing the transactions from which the death results, and forming a part of the res gestæ, and to the identification of the party or parties to the killing. — Reynolds' case, 68 Ala. 502; Green's case, 66 Ala 40; Kilgore's case, 74 Ala. 1; Wills' case, 74 Ala. 21; West's case, 76 Ala. 98; Johnson's case, 50 Ala. 456; Walker's case, 52 Ala. 192; Johnson's case, 47 Ala. 9; Mose's case, 35 Ala. 421; Ben's case, 37 Ala. 103; McLean's case, 16 Ala. 672; Oliver's case, 17 Ala 587; Johnson's case, Ib. 618; May's case, 55 Ala. 39; Faire's case, 58 Ala. 74; Ex parte Nettles, Ib. 268. Direct evidence of sense of impending death not required; may be inferred from conduct and circumstances.—Johnson's case, 47 Ala. 9; McLean's case, 16 Ala. 672; Moore's case, 12 Ala. 764; McHugh's case, 31 Ala. 317. Not admissible when the charge is rape or carnal knowledge, though death results.—Johnson's case, 50 Ala. 456. Not rendered inadmissible because death ensues after a considerable time.—Reynolds' case, 68 Ala. 502. Their admissibility not violative of constitutional right to be "confronted by witnesses."—Green's case, 66 Ala. 40. Not impaired because the family thought deceased would recover.—Sylvester's case, 72 Ala. 201. Admissible though made in response to questions asked.—Ingram's case, 67 Ala. 71, citing McHugh's case, 31 Ala. 317; Moore's case, 12 Ala. 764. Inadmissible to show state of feeling between deceased and prisoner.—Ben's case, 37 Ala. 103; Mose's case, 35 Ala. 421; Reynolds' case, 68 Ala 502; Brown's case, 74 Ala. 483 May be proved by oral evidence, although they were reduced to writing when made.—Kelly's case, 52 Ala. 361; McHugh's case, 31 Ala. 317. Admissible if made by husband against wife.—Moore's case, 12 Ala. 764. Admissible as well for as against the accused.—Ib. May be discredited.—Ib.; Sylvester's case, 71 Ala. 17; Green's case, 66 Ala. 40. But contradictory declarations of third parties in presence of, and not denied or affirmed by, deceased, inadmissible.—Sylvester's case, 71 Ala. 17. Admissible as identifying accused, though he be spoken of at different times by different names.—Ib. Inconsistent declarations admissible, and their credibility for the jury.—Moore's case, 12 Ala. 764; Faire's case, 58 Ala. 74. Not excluded because other evidence exists to the same effect. Reynolds' case, 68 Ala. 502. General objection to dying declarations, as a whole, may be overruled, although a part may be illegal.—Ib. As to the theory on which dying declarations are admitted in evidence, see Sylvester's case, 71 Ala. 17; Reynolds' case, 68 Ala. 502; Green's case, 66 Ala. 40. **Character of defendant for peace and quiet** admissible in connection with other facts of the case.—Felix's case, 18 Ala. 720; Harrison's case, 37 Ala. 154; Dupree's case, 33 Ala. 380; Hall's case, 40 Ala. 698; Field's case, 47 Ala. 603. **Character of deceased for turbulence, violence and revengefulness,** when and for what admissible—Williams' case, 74 Ala. 18; Brown's case. Ib. 42; De Arman's case, 71 Ala. 351; Storey's case, 71 Ala. 331; Roberts' case, 68 Ala. 156; Eiland's case, 52 Ala. 323; Field's case, 47 Ala. 607; Franklin's case, 29 Ala. 14; Dupree's case, 33 Ala. 380; Pritchett's case, 22 Ala. 39; Quesenberry's case, 3 Stew. & Port., 308. Also held admissible to determine degree of murder.—Field's case, 47 Ala. 607. The conduct of deceased held admissible to be considered in determining degree or grade of the homicide. Green's case, 69 Ala. 6. Prosecution cannot introduce evidence of peaceable character of deceased, unless his character is first assailed by the defense.—Ben's case, 37 Ala. 103. **Admissibility of certain circumstances,** such as proximity of prisoner to scene of crime.—Johnson's case, 17 Ala. 618. Appearance of prisoner.—Campbell's case, 23 Ala. 44. Object of deceased in going to prisoner's house.—Noles' case, 26 Ala 31. Correspondence between shoes of accused and tracks near body of deceased.—Campbell's case, 23 Ala. 44; Young's case, 68 Ala. 569. Flight of accused. Sylvester's case, 72 Ala. 201; Kelsoe's case, 47 Ala. 573. Letter written by accused found near place of killing.—Aiken's case, 35 Ala. 399. Clothing worn by deceased, and perforated by shot.—Holley's case, 75 Ala. 14. Absence of blood on clothing, when not a material fact for prisoner.—Sylvester's case, 72 Ala. 201. Facts having no tendency to influence the conduct of deceased, or to mitigate act of prisoner, inadmissible.—Steele's case, 61 Ala. 213 Fact that prisoner made complaint of being hurt himself, not part of res gestæ, inadmissible.—Ib. 213. History of prisoner's acts during the day, and any circumstances, if not foreign to the inquiry, admissible.—Campbell's case, 23 Ala. 44. Preparations of deceased to kill the accused, when and what admissible.—Ford's case, 71 Ala. 385. That the prisoner wiped his knife after the homicide.—Pierson's case, 12 Ala. 149. Fierceness of defendant's dog, connected with other circumstances.—Mattison's case, 55 Ala. 224. **Res gestæ;** what declarations of accused and third person held admissible as.—Lile's case, 30 Ala. 24. What declarations of deceased.—Wesley's case, 52 Ala. 182. Declaration of by-stander at difficulty three hours before killing, held too remote to form part of.—Garrett's case, 76 Ala. 18. Proposal by accused to deceased, on day of killing, to go and commit a robbery, not part of.—Birdsong's case, 47 Ala. 68. Declarations by deceased while walking to church, where he was killed, as to why he had not killed the prisoner in a previous difficulty, held inadmissible against prisoner.—Jackson's case, 52 Ala. 305. Declarations of defendant not connected with the killing.—Redd's case, 68 Ala. 492. Declarations before killing of husband charged with killing his wife, as to troubles between them.—Billingslea's case, 68 Ala. 486. Declarations are admissible only when part of res gestæ, or as dying declarations.—Birdsong's case, 47 Ala. 68. Declarations are not governed by the rules of admitting confessions, only when voluntary, etc.—Allen's case, 60 Ala. 19. **Judicial knowledge** of a dangerous or deadly wound.—McDaniel's case, 76 Ala. 1. **Variance** between allegations and proof, as to the kind of instrument and manner of using it.—Rodgers' case, 50 Ala. 102; Phillips' case. 68 Ala. 469. As to the part taken by persons jointly charged, what immaterial; conviction for striking blow had under evidence for aiding and abetting.—Brister's case, 26 Ala. 107. **Charge of court,** on different aspects of case; questions for court and jury.—Smith's case, 68 Ala. 424; Bland's case, 75 Ala. 574. A charge "that upon the evidence the defendant is guilty of murder in first degree or nothing," is a charge on the effect of the evidence, and, if given without request of either side, is erroneous.—Beaseley's case, 50 Ala. 149. Also erroneous to charge that "defendant cannot be convicted of murder in first degree unless he had murder in his heart."—Holley's case, 75 Ala.

14. When failure to instruct jury as to constituents of manslaughter, not error. De Arman's case, 71 Ala. 351. When charge ignoring self-defense not erroneous. Taylor's case, 48 Ala. 180; Beasley's case, 50 Ala. 149. When there is some evidence of accidental killing, to charge that malice may be inferred from fact of killing, is erroneous.—Hampton's case, 45 Ala. 82. Also, a charge ignoring suicide, or death from conflict, when these circumstances might exist.—Hall's case, 40 Ala. 698. Also, a charge asserting unreasonable beliefs of accused as reasons why he should be acquitted, where there was no evidence of insanity.—Flanagan's case, 46 Ala. 703. Proper charge as to presumptions of intent and consequences of an act.—McElroy's case, 75 Ala. 9. **Verdict of jury** must ascertain degree of murder, else erroneous.—Murphy's case, 45 Ala. 32; Hall's case, 40 Ala. 698; Cobia's case, 16 Ala. 781; Johnson's case, 17 Ala. 618; Robertson's case, 42 Ala. 509; Kendall's case, 65 Ala. 492; Dover's case, 75 Ala. 40; Field's case, 47 Ala. 603; Levison's case, 54 Ala. 520. Yet verdict not ascertaining degree will not authorize discharge on habeas corpus.—Dover's case, 75 Ala. 40. Verdict, though irregular in form, may be sufficient to sustain judgment and sentence.—Lewis' case, 51 Ala. 1; Noles' case, 24 Ala. 672; Bramlett's case, 31 Ala. 376; Harrall's case, 26 Ala. 52; Noles' case, Ib. 31. Verdict must determine character and extent of punishment.—Field's case, 47 Ala. 603. For murder in second degree, jury may affix any number of years in penitentiary, not less than ten.—Miller's case, 54 Ala. 155. Conviction of lower degree is acquittal of higher.—Field's case, 52 Ala. 348; Lewis' case, 51 Ala. 1; Nutt's case, 63 Ala. 180; Berry's case, 65 Ala. 117; Smith's case, 68 Ala. 424; Sylvester's case, 72 Ala. 201; De Arman's case, 71 Ala. 351. Yet on a second trial, a conviction may be had for the lower, although proof shows higher degree.—De Arman's case, 71 Ala. 351; Sylvester's case, 72 Ala. 201. **Judgment and sentence** cannot be rendered unless the degree found.—Hall's case, 40 Ala. 698; Cobia's case, 16 Ala. 781; Johnson's case, 17 Ala. 618; Robertson's case, 42 Ala. 509; Murphy's case. 45 Ala. 32. Sentencing two prisoners "during their natural lifetime," equivalent to sentencing each for life.—White's case. 30 Ala. 518. A sentence to death, without specifying the day of execution, supreme court, on affirmance, will fix a day.—Russell's case, 33 Ala. 366.

3726 (4297). **Same; killing in duel; degree.**—Killing by fight in single combat, commonly called a duel, with deadly weapons, is murder in the second degree.

3727 (4298). **Same; killing in sudden rencounter with concealed weapon.**—When the killing in any sudden rencounter or affray is caused by the assailant by the use of a deadly weapon, which was concealed before the commencement of the fight, his adversary having no deadly weapon drawn, such killing is murder in the second degree, and may, according to the circumstances, be murder in the first degree.

3728 (4299). **Same; degree to be found by jury.**—When the jury find the defendant guilty under an indictment for murder, they must ascertain, by their verdict, whether it is murder in the first or second degree; but if the defendant on arraignment confesses his guilt, the court must proceed to determine the degree of the crime, by the verdict of a jury, upon an examination of the testimony, and pass sentence accordingly.

See note to section 3725.

3729 (4296). **Same; p u n i s h m e n t .**—Any person, who is guilty of murder in the first degree, must, on conviction, suffer death, or imprisonment in the penitentiary for life, at the discretion of the jury; and any person, who is guilty of murder in the second degree, must, on conviction, be imprisoned in the penitentiary for not less than ten years, at the discretion of the jury.

3730 (4598). **Same; punishment when committed by convict.**—Any convict sentenced to imprisonment for life, who commits murder in the first degree, while such sentence remains in force against him, must, on conviction, suffer death.

3731 (4301). **Manslaughter; different degrees of.**—Manslaughter, by voluntarily depriving a human being of life, is manslaughter in the first degree; and manslaughter committed under any other circumstances is manslaughter in the second degree.

See note to section 3725.

3732 (4302). **Same; by engineer of steamboat, and employer.**—In case of the loss of life from the explosion of a boiler, or any apparatus connected therewith, on any steamboat navigating the waters of this state, and the person acting thereon as engineer has not obtained a certificate to act as such engineer, or is acting out of the grade therein specified, or is knowingly employed after the revocation of his certificate, the captain or owner employing such person, and the person so employed or acting are guilty of manslaughter in the first degree.

3733 (4303). **Same; punishment.**—Any person who is convicted of manslaughter in the first degree must, at the discretion of the jury, be imprisoned in the penitentiary for not less than one, nor more than ten years, and any person who is convicted of manslaughter in the second degree must, at the discretion of the jury, be imprisoned in the county jail, or sentenced to hard labor for the county, for not more than one year, and may also be fined not more than five hundred dollars.

3734 (4300). **Same; punishment when committed with bowie-knife.**—Any person, who, being armed with a razor, bowie-knife, or other knife of the like kind or description, commits manslaughter therewith in a sudden rencounter, must, on conviction, be imprisoned in the penitentiary for not less than five, nor more than ten years.

ARTICLE II.

MAYHEM.

3735 (4312). **Mayhem defined.**—Any person, who unlawfully, maliciously and intentionally cuts out or disables the tongue; puts out or destroys an eye; cuts, bites, or strikes off an ear; cuts, bites off, slits, mutilates, or destroys the nose or lip; or cuts, bites, tears, strikes off, or disables a limb, or member, of any other person, must, on conviction, be imprisoned in the penitentiary for not less than two, nor more than twenty years.

Must be unlawfully, intentionally, and with malice.—Abram's case, 10 Ala. 928. Design or intent need not have been formed previous to conflict.—Simmons' case, 3 Ala. 497. What no defense: erroneous charges as to specific design.—Molett's case, 49 Ala. 18. And on question of instruction or self-defense, or animal nature prompting act.—Ib. Under joint indictment, one may be guilty of beating and the other of mayhem.—Absence's case, 4 Port. 397. Injury must be permanent. Briley's case, 8 Port. 472. But there need not be an entire mutilation of the member, yet must be sufficient to disfigure.—Abram's case, 10 Ala. 928. Where injury was by shooting, jury may look to character of wound to determine with what view gun was fired.—Eskridge's case, 25 Ala. 30.

ARTICLE III.

RAPE AND FORCIBLE CARNAL KNOWLEDGE.

3736 (4304). **Punishment of rape.**—Any person, who is guilty of the crime of rape, must, on conviction, be punished,

/

at the discretion of the jury, by death, or by imprisonment in the penitentiary for life.

Rape may be joined in indictment with "carnal knowledge of female child under ten years."—Beason's case, 72 Ala. 91.   Form in Code sufficient.—Ib. 91; Leoni's case, 44 Ala. 110.   What sufficient proof of actual penetration.—Waller's case, 40 Ala. 325.   There must be force, actual or constructive.—McNair's case, 53 Ala. 453; Lewis' case, 30 Ala. 54; Murphy's case, 6 Ala. 765.   Constructive force may be by use of drugs, intoxicants, or where female is idiotic.—Lewis' case, 30 Ala. 54.   Common strumpet, or concubine or ravisher, under protection of law, and cannot be forced.—Boddie's case, 52 Ala. 395.   Amount of force or duress necessary may depend on age, state of health, temper, disposition, and other circumstances.—Smith's case, 47 Ala. 540; Waller's case, 40 Ala. 325.   The woman is a competent witness, and her testimony alone, if believed, is sufficient, although of ill-fame for chastity. Boddie's case, 52 Ala. 395; Leoni's case, 44 Ala. 110.   Charge where prosecutrix was only witness, when misleading —Ib.   Evidence of complaint made immediately, or within reasonable time, but not of particulars, admissible.—Lacy's case, 45 Ala. 80; Johnson's case, 50 Ala. 456; Leoni's case, 44 Ala. 110; Smith's case, 47 Ala. 540.   Evidence impeaching and sustaining prosecutrix as to her complaint. Griffin's case, 76 Ala. 29.   Precaution to be observed in trial of rape cases. Leoni's case, 44 Ala. 110.   Conviction may be had for assault to commit rape, or simple assault, or assault and battery.—Richardson's case, 54 Ala. 158; Lewis' case, 30 Ala. 54.

3737 (4896). **Proof of rape.**—To sustain an indictment for rape, proof of actual penetration is sufficient, when the act is shown to have been committed forcibly and against the consent of the person on whom the offense was committed.

See note to preceding section.

3738 (4305). **Carnal knowledge of women by administering drug, etc.**—Any person, who has carnal knowledge of any female above ten years of age, without her consent, by administering to her any drug or other substance which produces such stupor, imbecility of mind, or weakness of body, as to prevent effectual resistance, must, on conviction, be punished, at the discretion of the jury, by death, or by imprisonment in the penitentiary for life.

Lewis' case, 30 Ala. 54.

3739 (4306). **Carnal knowledge of female under ten years of age.**—Any person, who has carnal knowledge of any female under ten years of age, or abuses such female in the attempt to have carnal knowledge of her, must, on conviction, be punished, at the discretion of the jury, either by death, or by imprisonment in the penitentiary for life.

Distinguished from rape, though a kindred offense.—Vasser's case, 55 Ala. 264. Meaning of the word "abuse" in the statute.—Dawkins' case, 58 Ala. 376.   When indictment insufficient as to describing child abused.—Nugent's case, 19 Ala. 540. Child under eight years a competent witness under discretion of court.—Wade's case, 50 Ala. 164.   See Carter's case, 63 Ala. 52.   An infant adjudged incompetent to testify on a former trial may be old enough to testify on a second trial of same case.—Kelly's case, 75 Ala. 21.   Evidence that child had venereal disease may be rebutted by proof of her sexual intercourse with other persons about the time alleged.—Nugent's case, 18 Ala. 521.   Dying declarations of child, identifying prisoner, incompetent.—Johnson's case, 50 Ala. 456.   Indictment in Code form sufficient.—Beason's case, 72 Ala. 191.   May be joined with rape, and prosecution need not elect, though child proved over ten.—Ib. 191.   But a conviction cannot be had for this offense under indictment for rape.—Vasser's case, 55 Ala. 264. Verdict of guilty, under disjunctive indictment, sufficient.—Johnson's case, 50 Ala. 456.

3740 (4307). **Carnal knowledge of married women by falsely personating husband.**—Any person, who falsely personates the husband of any married women, and thereby deceives her and, by means of such deception, gains access to her, and has carnal knowledge of her, must, on conviction, be punished, at the discretion of the jury, by death, or by imprisonment in the penitentiary for not less than ten years; but no conviction must be had under this section on the unsupported evidence of the woman.

3741 (4308). **Attempt to have carnal knowledge of married woman by such deception.**—Any person, who falsely personates the husband of any married woman, and thereby gains access to her with the intent to have carnal knowledge of her, must, on conviction, be fined not less than five hundred dollars, and may also be imprisoned in the county jail, or sentenced to hard labor for the county, for not more than twelve months.

ARTICLE IV.

ROBBERY.

3742 (4311). **Punishment of robbery.**—Any person who is convicted of robbery must be punished, at the discretion of the jury, by death, or by imprisonment in the penitentiary for not less than five years.

Some property must be taken by violence from person robbed.—James' case, 53 Ala. 380; Jackson's case, 69 Ala. 249. Taking in presence of owner or possessor, same as taking from his person.—Cracker's case, 47 Ala. 53; James' case, 53 Ala. 380. A person entrusted to help carry goods along with the owner, and by violence carries them off, may be guilty of robbery, his possession before the violence being constructive possession of owner.—Ib. While unexpectedly snatching goods is not robbery, yet if there be resistance overcome by force, or threats of actual violence creating reasonable apprehension, it is robbery.—Jackson's case, 69 Ala. 249. Indictment may follow Code form; omission to charge felonious intent is fatal.—Chappel's case, 52 Ala. 359. Must contain distinct averment of value of property taken; what sufficient.—Jackson's case, 69 Ala. 249; Wesley's case, 61 Ala. 282. What insufficient description of money, bank notes, etc.—Cracker's case, 47 Ala. 53; Wesley's case, 61 Ala. 282. Proof that property had a specific value immaterial; sufficient if of value to owner, and not worthless.—Jackson's case, 69 Ala. 249. See James' case, 53 Ala. 380; Wesley's case, 61 Ala. 282. May be a conviction of larceny under such indictment. Allen's case, 58 Ala. 98.

ARTICLE V.

ABDUCTION AND KIDNAPPING.

3743 (4309). **Forcible marriage, etc., of woman.**—Any person, who unlawfully takes any woman against her will, and, by menace, force, or duress, compels her to marry him or any other person, or to be defiled, or who unlawfully takes any woman against her will with the intent to compel her, by menace, force, or duress, to marry him or any other person, or to be defiled, must, on conviction, be imprisoned in the penitentiary for not less than five years.

3744 (4310). **Taking girl under fourteen from father, etc., for prostitution or marriage.**—Any person, who takes any girl under fourteen years of age from her father, mother, guardian, or other person having the legal charge of her, for the purpose of prostitution, concubinage, or marriage, must, on conviction, be imprisoned in the penitentiary for not less than two years.

3745 (4322). **Decoying off children.**—Any person, who unlawfully takes or decoys away any child under the age of twelve years, with intent to detain or conceal it from its parents, guardian, or other person having the lawful charge of it, must, on conviction, be imprisoned in the county jail, or sentenced to hard labor for the county, for not more than two years.

3746 (4323). **Kidnapping.**—Any person, who forcibly or unlawfully confines, inveigles, or entices away another, with the intent to cause him to be secretly confined or imprisoned against his will, or to be sent out of the state against his will, must, on conviction, be imprisoned in the penitentiary for not less than two, nor more than ten years.

Article VI.

ASSAULT AND BATTERY; LYNCHING.

3747 (4318). **Punishment of assaults, and assaults and batteries.**—Any person, who commits an assault, or an assault and battery on another, must, on conviction, be fined not more than five hundred dollars, and may also be imprisoned in the county, jail, or sentenced to hard labor for the county, for not more than six months.

To constitute an assault, there must be an attempt, though interrupted, to inflict personal violence.—Blackwell's case, 9 Ala. 79; Johnson's case, 35 Ala. 363; Shaw's case, 18 Ala. 547.   Held, an assault to cause a person to give up his gun through fear of bodily harm.—Balkum's case, 40 Ala. 671. Also raising a stick near enough and intending to strike, causing the party to strike in self-defense.—Johnson's case, 35 Ala 363. Also to attempt to strike in striking distance, or to shoot in shooting distance.—Gray's case, 63 Ala. 66. **An assault and battery,** to unlawfully take and detain another without his consent.—Long v. Rogers, 17 Ala. 540. Also for hirer to chastise convict.—Prewitt's case, 51 Ala. 33. Also to maltreat a convict.—Sanders' case, 55 Ala. 43. Also for husband to whip his wife.—Robbins' case, 20 Ala. 36. Husband no authority to inflict moderate correction on his wife; the authority for "wife-whipping" is a relict of barbarism.—Fulgham's case, 46 Ala. 143. citing Turner v. Turner. 44 Ala, 437; Goodrich v. Goodrich. Ib. 670. **To constitute assault with gun or pistol,** it must be presented within a dangerous distance.—Tarver's case, 43 Ala. 354; Lawson's case, 30 Ala. 14. **Justice of the peace no jurisdiction** of assault with weapon, and a conviction by him is void. Danzey's case, 68 Ala. 296. **No defense,** if person assaulted struck first blow, if retaliation disproportionate or excessive.—Mooney's case, 33 Ala. 419; Riddle's case, 49 Ala. 389. Self-defense cannot be invoked if accused provoked the difficulty. Johnson's case, 69 Ala. 253; Page's case, 1b. 229. No excuse that person assaulted had possession, and refused to surrender defendant's property, which had been stolen.—Hendrix's case, 50 Ala. 148. Violent character of person assaulted inadmissible.—Brown's case. 74 Ala. 42. Husband may prove wife's conduct in mitigation.—Robbins' case, 20 Ala. 36. A pending civil action may be proved in mitigation.—Autery's case, 1 Stew. 399. Also remark of accused at the time, as part of res gestæ.—Riddle's case, 49 Ala. 389; Blackwell's case, 9 Ala. 79; Johnson's case, 35 Ala. 363. An owner of goods may, after notice, employ **reasonable force** to prevent an unlawful levy. Johnson's case, 12 Ala. 840. **As to what circumstances inadmissible to justify or mitigate.**—Rosenbaum's case, 33 Ala. 354; Ward's case, 28 Ala. 53; Prewett's case, 51 Ala. 33; Hendrix's case, 50 Ala. 148. Code form of **indictment** sufficient.—Thompson's case. 25 Ala. 41. Means used may be alleged in alternative.—Murdock's case, 65 Ala. 520. Specific intent or circumstances of aggravation may be alleged.—Ib. 520. Allegation of assault with a weapon must be proved, else **variance** is fatal.—Johnson's case, 35 Ala, 363; Walker's case, 73 Ala. 17. Indictment charging assault with both a stick and a knife; when prosecutor need not **elect.**—Johnson's case, 35 Ala. 363. Conviction for assault and battery may be had under indictment for rape.—Richardson's case, 54 Ala. 158.

3748 (4315). **Assault and battery with cowhide, etc., having pistol, etc., to intimidate.**—Any person, who assaults and beats another with a cowhide, stick, or whip, having in his possession at the time a pistol, or other deadly weapon, with intent to intimidate and prevent the person assaulted from defending himself, must, on conviction, at the discretion of the jury, be fined not more than two thousand dollars, or be imprisoned in the county jail, or sentenced to hard labor for the county, for not more than twelve months.

When indictment, insufficient for this offense, held good for a simple assault and battery.—Higginbotham's case, 50 Ala. 133.

3749 (4900). **Evidence of abusive words to extenuate or justify.**—On the trial of any person for an assault, an assault and battery, or an affray, he may give in evidence any opprobious words or abusive language used by the person assaulted or beaten at or near the time of the assault or affray; and such evidence shall be good in extenuation or justification, as the jury may determine.

Brown v. State, 74 Ala. 42.

3750 (4317). **Abusing or beating accused person, or lynching.**—Any two or more persons, who abuse, whip, or beat any person, upon any accusation, real or pretended, to force such person to confess himself guilty of any offense, or to make any disclosures, or to consent to leave the neighborhood, county, or state, must, on conviction, each be fined not less than five hundred dollars, and may be imprisoned in the county jail, or sentenced to hard labor for the county, for not more than twelve months.

Underwood's case, 25 Ala. 70; Higginbotham's case, 50 Ala. 133.

— — ——

ARTICLE VII.

ASSAULTS TO COMMIT A FELONY.

3751 (4314). **What assaults or attempts felonies.**—Any person, who commits an assault on another, with intent to murder, maim, rob, ravish, or commit the crime against nature, or who attempts to poison any human being, or to commit murder by any means not amounting to an assault, must, on conviction, be punished by imprisonment in the penitentiary for not less than two, nor more than twenty years.

Assault to murder; is with the intent, unlawfully and maliciously, to kill the *person assaulted.* —Washington's case, 53 Ala. 29; Burns' case, 8 Ala. 313; Moore's case, 18 Ala. 532; Tarver's case, 43 Ala. 354; Ogletree's case, 28 Ala. 693; Meredith's case, 60 Ala 441; Simpson's case, 59 Ala. 1; Washington's case, 53 Ala. 29. Is a common-law offense, statute merely changing the punishment.—Meredith's case, 60 Ala. 441. *Attempt* not equivalent to *intent.*—Marshall's case, 14 Ala. 411. Need not be a specific intent, as contradistinguished from the intent to be implied by the jury from the attendant circumstances.—Meredith's case. 60 Ala. 441. Party may be guilty without knowing the person assaulted.—Washington's case, 53 Ala. 29. That the offense would be murder had death ensued, is not sufficient evidence of intent.—Morris' case, 18 Ala. 532. Immaterial as to which degree of murder intended.—Meredith's case, 60 Ala. 441. The means to accomplish the intent need not exist; as the absence of a cap from a gun would not matter, if the accused supposed it was on the gun.—Mullen's case, 45 Ala. 43. The facts must raise presumption of intent to murder.—Morgan's case, 33 Ala. 413. Evidence of malice and intent.—Ogletree's case, 28 Ala. 693; Cabbell's case, 46 Ala. 195; Tarver's case, 43 Ala. 354; Allen's case, 52 Ala. 391; Moore's case, 18 Ala. 532; Simpson's case. 59 Ala. 1; Ross' case, 62 Ala. 224; Gray's case, 63 Ala. 66; Meredith's case, 60 Ala. 441. Intent is question for jury.—Washington's case, 63 Ala. 135; Simpson's case, 59 Ala. 1. Deprived of felonious character under same provocation as homicide.—Ogletree's case, 28 Ala. 693; Allen's case, 52 Ala. 391; Robinson's case, 54 Ala. 86. **Aiding and abetting,** and encouraging a mob by words to commit this offense; must be shown that the mob heard the words. Cabbell's case, 46 Ala. 195. Admissible to show malice and intention by previous threats made by defendant against the accused.—Henderson's case, 70 Ala. 29; Ogletree's case, 28 Ala. 693. Admissibility of subsequent threats to prove malice and hostile intent.—Henderson's case, 70 Ala. 29. The **indictment**, when defective, yet good for simple assault.—Wood's case, 50 Ala. 144; Bullock's case, 13 Ala. 413. Formerly held necessary to allege the facts which constitute the offense.—(Clay s Digest, 442, §26); Beasley's case, 18 Ala. 539; Trexler's case, 19 Ala. 22. Where a weapon is alleged, **a plea of guilty** of simple assault is admission of assault with the weapon, without the intent.—Adams' case, 48 Ala. 421. And if the intent to murder is not proved, **verdict** may be for simple assault. Turbaville's case, 40 Ala. 715; Mooney's case, 33 Ala. 419. When held to be for simple assault.—Burns' case, 8 Ala. 313. **Assault to maim**; the intent, whether deliberate or formed on the instant. whether specific or general, if directed against the person assaulted, is the criminal intent meant in the statute.—Allen's case, 52 Ala. 393. **Indictment**, when good only for simple assault.—Murdock's case, 65 Ala. 520. An **attempt** should be accompanied by an intent to maim.—Allen's case, 52 Ala. 393. **Assault to ravish** must be forcible attempt to cohabit against female's consent.—Lewis' case, 30 Ala. 54. An intent to do a thing implies a purpose only, while an attempt to do a thing implies both a purpose and an actual effort to carry that purpose into execution.—Witherby's case, 39 Ala. 703, citing on this point Prince's case, 35 Ala. 367. Hence, an "assault with intent to commit a rape," is of itself an attempt to commit a rape.—Ib. 702. Indecent advancement or importunity not sufficient, unless accompanied by acts evidencing intent. and creating terror; subsequent abandonment of purpose. no excuse.—Lewis' case, 35 Ala. 380. The mere fact of **complaint** admissible.—Scott's case, 48 Ala. 420. See note to section 3736. Prosecutrix cannot give opinion, and state that defendant "attempted to ravish her, but did not accomplish his purpose."—Scott's case, 48 Ala. 420. Physical inability of defendant may be considered.—Nugent's case, 18 Ala. 521. An indictment in Code form sufficient.—Bradford's case, 54 Ala. 230.

3752 (4599). **Assaults to kill or maim and conspiracies by convicts.**—Any convict, who assaults an inspector of convicts, or an officer or other person having the charge of, or superintendence over convicts, with intent to kill or maim him, or conspires with any other person for the purpose of killing or maiming any such officer or person, must, on conviction thereof, if his former sentence was for life, suffer death; and, if his former sentence was for a term less than life, be imprisoned for an additional term, not less than five, nor more than twenty years.

ARTICLE VIII.

MALTREATMENT OF CONVICTS.

3753 (4319). **Maltreatment of convicts by officer.**—Any superintendent, guard, or other officer having charge of convicts, who overworks or maltreats any convict, or inflicts upon him any other or greater punishment than he is authorized by law to inflict, must, on conviction, be fined not less than fifty, nor more than five hundred dollars, and may also be imprisoned in the county jail, or sentenced to hard labor for the county, for not more than six months.

3754 (4320). **Maltreatment of convicts by hirer.**—Any hirer of a convict, who overworks or maltreats such convict, or fails to supply him with a sufficiency of good and wholesome food, or with necessary medicines and medical attention, or with warm and comfortable clothing, or with comfortable shelter in inclement weather, must, on conviction, be fined not less than fifty, nor more than five hundred dollars, and may also be imprisoned in the county jail, or sentenced to hard labor for the county, for not more than six months.

Sufficiency of indictment.—Sanders' case, 55 Ala. 184. For hirer to chastise convict, may be assault and battery.—Prewitt's case, 51 Ala. 33.

3755 (4321). **Imprisoning together white and colored prisoners before conviction.**—Any jailer or sheriff, having the charge of white and colored prisoners before conviction, who imprisons them permanently together in the same apartment of any jail, or other place of safe keeping, if there is a sufficient number of apartments to keep them separate, must, on conviction, be fined not less than fifty, nor more than one hundred dollars.

ARTICLE IX.

OFFENSES CONCERNING SERVANTS, APPRENTICES, IMMIGRANTS, AND OTHER EMPLOYES.

3756 (4324). **Enticing away servants or apprentices.**—Any person, who entices, decoys, or persuades any apprentice or servant to leave the service or employment of his master, must, on conviction, be fined not less than twenty, nor more than one hundred dollars; and may also be imprisoned in the county jail, or sentenced to hard labor for the county, for not more than three months.

Owen's case, 48 Ala. 281.

As amended,
Feb. 15, 1881,
p. 42.

3757 (4325). **Enticing away servants or laborers under written contract, etc.**—Any person, who knowingly interferes with, hires, employs, entices away, or induces to leave the service of another, or attempts to hire, employ, entice away, or induce to leave the service of another, any laborer or servant who has contracted in writing to serve such other person for any given time, not to exceed one year, before the expiration of the time so contracted for, or who knowingly interferes with, hires, employs, entices away, or induces any minor to leave the service of any person to whom such service is lawfully due, without the consent of the party employing, or to whom such service is due, given in writing, or in the presence of some credible person, must, on conviction, be fined not less than fifty, nor more than five hundred dollars, at the discretion of the jury, and in no case less than double the damages sustained by the party whom such laborer or servant was induced to leave; one-half to the party sustaining such damage, and the other half to the county.

Not in violation of law of congress known as "civil rights bill."—Murrell's case, 44 Ala. 367. If contract in writing legally dissolved, laborer can make another. Ib. 368. Prior verbal contract with accused, good defense.—Turner's case, 48 Ala. 549. Infant's contract voidable, and, when disaffirmed, he may be hired by another. Langham's case, 55 Ala. 114 (overruling on this point Murrell's case, supra). Contract must be in writing.—Murrell's case, 44 Ala. 367. Must be mutual.—Ib. 367. Knowledge of previous subsisting contract not essential to conviction; but, with such knowledge, refusal to discharge laborer is sufficient.—Murrell's case, Ib. 368. No conviction, if defendant's agent did the enticing.—Roseberry's case, 50 Ala. 160. Indictment may follow language of statute, and charge in alternative.—Murrell's case, 44 Ala. 367. And must allege christian name of laborer, or that it is unknown.—Roseberry's case, 50 Ala. 160.

3758 (4327). **Same; evidence of enticement.**—When any laborer or servant, having contracted as provided in the preceding section, is afterwards found in the service or employment of another before the termination of such contract, that fact is prima facie evidence that such person is guilty of a violation of that section, if he fail and refuse to forthwith discharge such laborer or servant, after being notified and informed of such former contract or employment.

3759 (4328). **Master violating duty to apprentice.**—A master violating any duty to his apprentice, as prescribed by section 1479 (1735) of the Code, must, on conviction, be fined not less than fifty dollars.

Cockran's case, 46 Ala. 714.

3760 (4329). **Enticing away, and giving supplies, etc., to apprentice.**—Any person, who entices away any apprentice from his master, or knowingly employs an apprentice, or furnishes him food and clothing, without the written consent of his master, or gives or sells such apprentice ardent spirits without such consent, must, on conviction, be fined not exceeding five hundred dollars.

3761 (4330). **Enticing away immigrant from employer.** Any person, who employs any immigrant, or otherwise entices him from his employer, in violation of the contract of such immigrant, must, on conviction, be fined in a sum not less than the amount of wages for the unexpired term of the contract, and may be imprisoned in the county jail, or sentenced to hard labor for the county, at the discretion of the jury, for not more than three months.

3762 (4331). **Immigrant leaving service without payment of advances.**—Any immigrant, who abandons or leaves the service of an employer without repaying all passage money and all other advances, must, on conviction, be fined in a sum not more than double the amount of wages for the unexpired term of service, and imprisoned not longer than three months, or sentenced to hard labor for the county for not more than three months, at the discretion of the jury.

3763. Preventing persons from engaging in peaceful work or lawful industry.—Any person, who, by force or threats of violence to person or property, prevents, or seeks to prevent another from doing work or furnishing materials, or from contracting to do work or furnish materials, for or to any person engaged in any lawful business, or who disturbs, interferes with, or prevents the peaceable exercise of any lawful industry, business, or calling by any other person, must, on conviction, be fined not less than ten, nor more than five hundred dollars, and may also be imprisoned in the county jail, or sentenced to hard labor for the county, for not more than twelve months.* Feb. 17, 1885, p. 143.

---

* On February 28, 1887 (Pamp. Acts 1886-7, p. 90), an act was approved, providing: " That whoever compels a child under eighteen years of age, or a woman, to labor in a mechanical or manufacturing business more than eight hours in any day, or permits a child under the age of fourteen years to labor, for more than eight hours in any day, in any factory, workshop, or other place used for mechanical or manufacturing purposes, of which he has control, or whoever shall work, or permit to be worked. in a coal or iron mine or mines, children under the age of fifteen years, shall be fined not more than fifty dollars, nor less than five dollars."

CHAPTER 3.

OFFENSES AGAINST THE PUBLIC PEACE.

ARTICLE 1.—Affrays.

    2.—Riots, routs and unlawful assemblies.

    3.—Challenging to fight a duel, publishing another as a coward for not fighting or accepting challenge, and sending threatening or abusive letters.

    4.—Prize-fighting.

    5.—Libel and defamation.

    6.—Carrying concealed weapons.

ARTICLE I.

AFFRAYS.

3764 (4101). **Punishment of affray.**—All persons guilty of an affray must, on conviction, be fined not more than five hundred dollars, and may also be imprisoned in the county jail, or sentenced to hard labor for the county, for not more than six months.

Defined to be "the fighting of two or more persons in a public place to the terror of the people."—McClelland's case, 53 Ala. 640. Mere words do not constitute, though party using them is assaulted.—O'Neill's case, 16 Ala. 65. What is a "public place."—Carwile's case, 35 Ala. 392; Taylor's case, 22 Ala. 15. "Terror of the people," may be actual or presumed.—Carwile's case, 35 Ala. 392. Distinguishing characteristics are the actual or presumable terror to the people and the number of persons engaged and the place in which it occurs.—Ib.; McClelland's case, 53 Ala. 640. Includes, of necessity, an assault and battery.—Thompson's case, 70 Ala. 26. Of which some may be convicted, and some of the affray.—Ib. Sufficient. if those indicted fought against others not indicted.—Ib.; Thompson's case, 70 Ala. 26. Proof of previous affray inadmissible, unless connected.—Skain's case, 21 Ala. 218. Court cannot take away from jury their discretion as to amount of fine.—Ib.

ARTICLE II.

RIOTS, ROUTS AND UNLAWFUL ASSEMBLIES.

3765 (4102). **Unlawful assemblies.**—If three or more persons meet together to commit a breach of the peace, or to do any other unlawful act, each of them must, on conviction, be punished, at the discretion of the jury, by fine and imprisonment in the county jail, or hard labor for the county, for not more than six months.

3766 (4103). **Riots and routs.**—If any persons, unlawfully assembled, demolish, pull down, or destroy, or begin to demolish, pull down, or destroy, any dwelling-house or other building, or any ship or vessel, they must each be punished, on conviction, at the discretion of the jury, by fine and imprisonment in the county jail, or by imprisonment in the penitentiary, for not less than two, nor more than five years.

Article III.

CHALLENGING TO FIGHT A DUEL, PUBLISHING ANOTHER AS A COWARD FOR NOT
FIGHTING OR ACCEPTING CHALLENGE, AND SENDING THREATENING
OR ABUSIVE LETTERS.

3767 (4104). **Challenge to fight duel.**—Any person, who gives, accepts, or knowingly carries a challenge, in writing or otherwise, to fight in single combat, with any deadly weapon, either in or out of this state, must be punished, on conviction, at the discretion of the jury, by imprisonment in the penitentiary for two years.

Ivey's case, 12 Ala. 276.

3768 (4105). **Publishing another as a coward for not fighting or accepting challenge to fight.**—Any person, who, in any newspaper, handbill, or other advertisement, written or printed, publishes or proclaims another person as a coward, or uses any other opprobious or abusive language, for not accepting a challenge to fight a duel, or for not fighting a duel, must be punished, on conviction, by a fine of not less than two hundred, nor more than five hundred dollars, and by imprisonment in the county jail, or hard labor for the county, for not less than six, nor more than twelve months.

3769 (4106). **Sending threatening or abusive letters.**—Any person, who sends to another a threatening or abusive letter, which may tend to provoke a breach of the peace, must be punished, on conviction, by fine and imprisonment in the county jail, or hard labor for the county; the fine not to exceed in any case five hundred dollars, and the imprisonment or hard labor not to exceed six months.

Graves' case, 9 Ala. 447; Crow's case, 18 Ala. 546; Reid's case, 53 Ala. 402.

Article IV.

PRIZE-FIGHTING.

3770 (4313). **Prize-fighting.**—Any person, who, as principal, engages in any prize-fight or pugilistic encounter for a money reward to the victor, must, on conviction, be imprisoned in the penitentiary for not less than one, nor more than three years.

Article V.

LIBEL AND DEFAMATION.

3771 (4106). **Libel.**—Any person, who publishes a libel of another which may tend to provoke a breach of the peace, must be punished, on conviction, by fine and imprisonment in the county jail, or hard labor for the county; the fine not to exceed in any case five hundred dollars, and the imprisonment or hard labor not to exceed six months.

See citations to section 3769.

3772 (4805). **Indictment for libel.**—An indictment for a libel need not set forth any extrinsic facts for the purpose of showing the application to the party libeled of the defamatory matter on which the indictment is founded; it is sufficient to state generally that the same was published concerning him, and the fact that it was so published must be proved on the trial.

Reid's case, 53 Ala. 402.

3773 (4107). **Defamation.**—Any person, who writes, prints, or speaks of and concerning any woman, falsely and maliciously imputing to her a want of chastity; and any person who speaks, writes, or prints of and concerning another any accusation, falsely and maliciously importing the commission by such person of a felony, or any other indictable offense involving moral turpitude, must, on conviction, be punished by fine not exceeding five hundred dollars, and imprisonment in the county jail, or sentenced to hard labor for the county, not exceeding six months; one or both, at the discretion of the jury.

Haley's case, 63 Ala. 83.

3774 (4108). **Refusal to testify by printer of libel or defamation.**—The printer or proprietor of any newspaper, handbill, advertisement, or libel, the publication of which is punishable under the preceding sections, who refuses, when summoned, to appear and testify before either the grand or petit jury, respecting the publication of such newspaper, handbill, advertisement, or libel (not having a good excuse, to be determined by the court), is guilty of a contempt, and also of a misdemeanor; and, on conviction for such misdemeanor, must be fined not less than twenty, nor more than three hundred dollars, and may also be imprisoned in the county jail, or sentenced to hard labor for the county, for not more than six months.

Article VI.

CARRYING CONCEALED WEAPONS.

As amended, Feb. 19, 188', p. 38.

3775 (4109). **Carrying concealed weapons.**—Anyone, who carries concealed about his person a bowie-knife, or knife or instrument of like kind or description, or a pistol, or fire-arms of any other kind or description, or an air-gun, must, on conviction, be fined not less than fifty, nor more than five hundred dollars, and may also be imprisoned in the county jail, or sentenced to hard labor for the county, for not more than six months. But the defendant may give evidence that, at the time of carrying the weapon concealed, he had good reason to apprehend an attack, which the jury may consider in mitigation of the punishment, or justification of the offense.

Statute **not unconstitutional**; it does not prohibit, but merely regulates the carrying of arms.—Reid's case, 1 Ala. 612. **Weapon**; the "pistol" or "fire-arm" may be imperfect, and yet be a "fire-arm."—Atwood's case, 53 Ala. 508. See Evins' case, 46 Ala. 88. What imperfections in the pistol will exclude it from the purview of the statute.—Ib. Sufficient weapon, if all the separated pieces of a pistol which can be readily put together, are carried.—Hutchinson's case, 62 Ala. 3. Also a knife, if not unlike a bowie-knife in all, but only in some essential particulars. Sears' case 33 Ala. 347. It is sufficient **concealment** if the weapon be hidden from ordinary observation, although it may be seen on closer examination; to be determined by the jury.—Jones' case, 51 Ala. 16. As to concealment, see also Street's case, 67 Ala. 88. Concealment in one's saddle-bags on horse-back, is not concealment about his person.—Cunningham's case, 76 Ala. 88. Unlawful to carry pistol concealed within the curtilage of one's abode.—Harman s case, 69 Ala. 248. Or in the room of another person.—Owen's case, 31 Ala. 387. Juries may be, and often are convinced beyond reasonable doubt, that the pistol was previously concealed, where proof shows that defendant was afterwards seen with a pistol, although no witness can testify that he had previously looked to see whether defendant had a pistol.—Farley's case, 72 Ala. 170.   The **right to carry a pistol concealed** is co-extensive only with the particular necessity, and ceases when that necessity ceases. Eslava's case, 49 Ala. 355.   Having reason to apprehend attack not sufficient; there must be "good reason to apprehend an attack."—Baker's case, Ib. 350.   As to having good reason to apprehend an attack, see Collier's case, 68 Ala. 499; Berney's case, 69 Ala. 233; Shorter's case, 63 Ala. 129; Hardin's case, Ib. 38.   Proper charge when this is the only defense.—Hogg's case, 52 Ala. 2.   Good reason to apprehend an attack at a dangerous time or place will not excuse casual carrying weapon at safer time and place.—Chatteaux' case, Ib. 388.   Must be carried for **defensive**, not **offensive** purposes.—Shorter's case, 63 Ala. 129; Stroud's case, 55 Ala. 77.   Defendant **cannot prove that he was advised to arm himself.**—Berney's case, 69 Ala. 233.   Nor an offer by him to borrow five dollars to buy a pistol.—Ib. **No excuse** that defendant carried pistol **to take part in a piece at school exhibition.** Preston's case, 63 Ala. 127.   Court may charge jury **to assess such a fine** as they may deem necessary to suppress the evil.—Shorter's case, 63 Ala. 130.   See Chatteaux' case, 52 Ala. 388; McManus' case, 36 Ala. 293; Sullivan's case, 68 Ala. 525; Farley's case, 72 Ala. 170.

3776 (4110). Same; brass knuckles and slung-shot.—Any one, who carries concealed about his person brass knuckles, slung-shot, or other weapon of like kind or description, must, on conviction, be fined not less than fifty, nor more than five hundred dollars, and may also be imprisoned in the county jail, or sentenced to hard labor for the county, for not more than six months.

3777 (4111). Carrying rifle or shot-gun walking-cane. Any person, who carries a rifle or shot-gun walking-cane, must, on conviction, be fined not less than five hundred, nor more than one thousand dollars, and be imprisoned in the penitentiary not less than two years.

3778. Given in special charge to grand jury; their duty. The three preceding sections must be given in special charge to the grand jury; and it is their duty, if the evidence justifies it, to find and present an indictment.

Feb. 19. 1881. p. 38, secs. 2, 3

3779 (4809). Indictment for carrying concealed weapons; proof.—In an indictment for carrying concealed weapons, it is sufficient to charge that the defendant "carried concealed about his person a pistol, or other description of fire-arms," or a "bowie-knife, or other knife or instrument of the like kind or description," or other forbidden weapon, describing it, as the case may be ; and the excuse, if any, must be proved by the defendant, on the trial, to the satisfaction of the jury.

CHAPTER 4.

OFFENSES AGAINST PROPERTY.

ARTICLE I.

ARSON.

As amended.
Jan 30, 188 .
p 105, sec. 1.

3780 (4346). **Arson in the first degree.**—Any person, who willfully sets fire to, or burns any steamboat or vessel in which there is at the time any human being, or any prison or jail, or any other house or building which is occupied by a person lodged therein, or any inhabited dwelling-house, or any house adjoining such dwelling-house, whether there is at the time in such dwelling-house any human being or not, is guilty of arson in the first degree, and must, on conviction, be punished, at the discretion of the jury, by death, or by imprisonment in the penitentiary for not less than ten years.

The **setting fire to, or burning,** must be actual burning of the house or some part thereof, within the meaning of the word burn, at common law.—Graham's case, 40 Ala. 659. Setting fire to one house with the intent to communicate to another deemed a burning of the latter.—Grimes' case, 63 Ala. 166. Also by placing matches with unginned cotton, with intention to have matches ignited by handling of the cotton.—Overstreet's case, 46 Ala. 30. Setting fire to a jail to burn a hole to escape, is sufficient—Luke's case, 49 Ala. 30; Lockett's case, 63 Ala. 5. Indictments under which they are held, best evidence of the charge against them, and of their intent in setting fire to jail.—Luke's case, 49 Ala. 30. When one may be guilty, though he did not personally set fire to the house or "assist" any other person in so doing.—Hughes' case, 75 Ala. 31. The act must be willfull; no negligence or mischance can make one guilty of arson.—Pairo's case, 49 Ala. 27. To burn a "**cotton-house**" is arson in **second degree**, whether it contains cotton or not. Washington's case, 68 Ala. 85. **Value of buildings and contents** not an essential element of **arson in third degree.**—Brown's case, 52 Ala. 345. **Indictment in Code**

form sufficient.—Boles' case, 46 Ala. 207; Miller's case, 45 Ala. 24.   Should aver
the ownership.—Martha's case, 26 Ala. 72; Miller's case, 45 Ala 24; Davis' case,
52 Ala. 357; Boles' case, 46 Ala. 204.   Unless it is a public building; what sufficient averment of public building.—Lockett's case, 63 Ala. 5.   Different house and
different ownership may be alleged in different counts.—Miller's case, 45 Ala. 24;
Martha's case, 26 Ala. 72.   Ownership sufficiently laid in a servant in possession,
dwelling in the house under contract to do so.—Davis' case, 52 Ala. 357.   Indictment intending to charge arson in first or second degree, when good only in third
degree.—Brown's case, 52 Ala. 345; Cheatham's cases, 59 Ala. 40.   Ownership
properly laid in a co-tenant in possession.—Adams' case, 62 Ala. 177.   **Evidence**;
ownership must be proved as laid.—Martha's case, 26 Ala. 72; Graham's case, 40
Ala. 659.—What sufficient prima facie proof of corpus delicti to render defendant's
confession admissible.—Winslow's case, 76 Ala. 42.   Hostility and other circumstances admissible to show intent.—Hinds' case 55 Ala. 145; Overstreet's case, 46
Ala. 30; Balaam's case, 17 Ala. 451.   Proof of collateral fact to show motive.
Winslow's case, 76 Ala. 42.   Previous request by defendant of witness to burn the
house, admissible —Martin's case, 28 Ala. 71.   But evidence that another house
belonging to prosecutor was subsequently burned, inadmissible —Brock's case, 26
Ala. 104.   Admissibility of promises and threats made by a third person to state
witness to leave the state; evidence connecting defendant.—Martin's case, 28 Ala.
71.   Evidence under indictment for arson in third degree as to contents of building admissible.—Brown's case, 52 Ala. 345.   **Verdict** for arson in first degree, need
not state the degree.—Davis' case, 52 Ala. 357.

3781 (4347). **Arson in the second degree.**—Any person, who
willfully sets fire to, or burns any church, meeting-house, court-
house, town-house, college, academy, jail, or other building
erected for public use, or any banking-house, warehouse, cotton-house, gin-house, store, manufactory, or mill, which, with
the property therein contained, is of the value of five hundred
dollars or more, or any car, car-shed, cotton-house, or cotton-
pen containing cotton, or corn-crib, or corn-pen containing corn,
or any barn, stable, shop, or office, within the curtilage of any
dwelling-house, or other building by the burning whereof any
building hereinbefore specified in this section is burned, or who
willfully sets fire to, or burns any uninhabited dwelling-house,
or any steamboat or vessel in which there is at the time no human being, is guilty of arson in the second degree, and must,
on conviction, be punished by imprisonment in the penitentiary
for not less than two, nor more than ten years.

As amended,
Jan. 30, 1885,
p. 105, sec. 2.

See note to preceding section.

3782. Attempts to commit arson.—An attempt to commit
arson, in either the first or second degree, is a felony punishable, on conviction, by imprisonment in the penitentiary for not
less than two, nor more than five years.

3783. Same; sufficiency of indictment.—An indictment
for an attempt to commit arson is sufficient, if it alleges that the
person charged "did attempt to willfully set fire to or burn a
steamboat or vessel in which there was at the time a human
being," or "did attempt to willfully set fire to or burn a church
or meeting-house, erected for public use," as the case may be,
without alleging the particular acts constituting the attempt.

3784 (4348). **Arson in third degree.**—Any person, who willfully sets fire to, or burns any house, building, boat, or vessel,
or any bridge, causeway, turnpike-gate, or toll-gate, by law
erected or authorized, under such circumstances as do not constitute arson in the first or second degree, is guilty of arson in
the third degree, and must, on conviction, be imprisoned in the
county jail, or sentenced to hard labor for the county, for not
more than twelve months, and may also be fined not more than
two thousand dollars, at the discretion of the jury.

See note to section 3780.

3785 (4349). **Burning insured house, vessel, etc., or casting away or destroying boat or vessel.**—Any person, who, with intent to charge, injure, or defraud the insurer, willfully burns, or, with intent to burn, sets fire to any building or property which is at the time insured against fire; or who willfully burns, or sets fire to, with intent to burn, or sinks, casts away, or otherwise destroys any boat, ship, or vessel, with intent to charge, injure, or defraud the owner of such boat, ship, or vessel, or of any property on board of the same, or the insurer of such boat, vessel, or property; or any person who attempts to commit the offense defined by this section, must, on conviction, be punished by imprisonment in the county jail, or hard labor for the county, for not more than twelve months; and may also be fined not more than two thousand dollars, at the discretion of the jury.

Martin's case, 29 Ala. 30; s. c., 28 Ala. 71.

ARTICLE II.

BURGLARY AND BURGLARIOUS INSTRUMENTS.

3786 (4348). **Burglary in a dwelling-house, shop, storehouse, building, enclosure, etc.**—Any person, who, either in the night or day-time, with intent to steal, or to commit a felony, breaks into and enters a dwelling-house, or any building, structure, or enclosure within the curtilage of a dwelling-house, though not forming a part thereof, or into any shop, store, warehouse, or other building, structure, or enclosure, in which any goods, merchandise, or other valuable thing, is kept for use, sale, or deposit, provided such structure or enclosure, other than a shop, store, warehouse, or building, is specially constructed or made to keep such goods, merchandise, or other valuable thing, is guilty of burglary, and must, on conviction, be imprisoned in the penitentiary for not less than one, nor more than twenty years.

"**Dwelling-house;**" same meaning as at common law.—Ex parte Vincent, 26 Ala. 145. **Curtilage** includes smoke-house, part in yard and part outside; and breaking, etc. from without sufficient.—Fisher's case, 43 Ala. 17. House used as store in front and where clerk slept in rear, held a **dwelling-house.**—Ex parte Vincent, 26 Ala. 145. Sufficient **breaking and entering.**—Donohoo's case, 36 Ala. 281; Carter's case, 68 Ala. 96; Pines' case, 50 Ala. 153. Going down an open chimney sufficient; or even getting into a chimney and no further, with intent to steal.—Donohoo's case, 36 Ala. 381; Walkers' case, 52 Ala. 376. Breaking outside shutters and protruding hand, without breaking inside window, not sufficient entering.—McCall's case, 4 Ala. 643. Entering open window, and opening door to let in accomplices, not burglary, unless accomplices enter, though may be attempt to commit burglary.—Ray's case, 66 Ala. 281. Boring a hole through floor of corn-crib, and letting corn run out, is sufficient, the use of the instrument constituting both the breaking and entering.—Walker's case, 63 Ala. 49. Employe left in charge of house may commit burglary in room where he had no right to enter.—Hild's case, 67 Ala. 39. A servant having the key and right to enter office in day-time, may commit burglary by unlocking and entering to steal at night; but not if in the habit of sleeping there at night, and forms intent to steal after entering.—Lowder's case, 63 Ala. 143. Constructive breaking, by servant prearranged to capture thief, held not burglary, when.—Allen's case, 40 Ala. 334. Two persons owning adjoining rooms, not burglary for either to unlock his own door with intent to enter an opening left between the rooms and steal in other's room.—Stone's case, 63 Ala. 115. **Indictment** must aver an entrance.—Pine's case, 50 Ala. 153. Also that party committed theft or felony, or broke and entered with such intent.—Bell's case, 48 Ala. 684. And if to commit arson, must allege with intent willfully to set fire to, etc.—Pairo's case, 49 Ala. 25. Where the larceny is charged without alleging the intent in breaking, etc., it is necessary to prove the larceny; but if the intent to steal is alleged, and the larceny added, conviction may be had for the burglary, though acquitted of larceny.—Bell's case, 48 Ala. 684; Murray's case, 48 Ala. 675; Wolf's case, 49 Ala. 359. May allege the consummation of the intent by an actual larceny of the goods.—Murray's case, 48 Ala. 675; Wolf's case, 49 Ala. 359. What is an averment of grand larceny, and not of burglary.—Bell's case, 48 Ala. 684. When count charges burglary only, and when both burglary and grand larceny.—Ib. May be joined with grand larceny, but not subject to doctrine of merger.—Bell's case, Ib. 694. May be joined with petit larceny in same count.—Snow's case, 54 Ala. 138; Gordon's case, 71 Ala. 315; Borum's case, 66 Ala. 468. But not in different counts.—Adam's case, 55 Ala. 143. Ownership must be precisely laid and proved.—Beall's case, 53 Ala. 460. Properly laid in person having undisputed occupancy and possession.—Matthew's case, 55 Ala. 65. Also may be jointly laid in owner and occupier, if erected for their joint use.—Webb's case, 52 Ala. 422. But may, under the statute, be laid in any one or more of several partners, joint owners, or tenants in common.—White's case, 72 Ala. 195; Williams' case, 67 Ala. 183. Insufficient to allege in a firm name, without naming individuals of the firm.—Davis' case, 54 Ala. 88. Also insufficient to allege ownership in the estate of a deceased person, though named.—Beall's case, 53 Ala. 460 (overruling, on this point, Murray's case, 48 Ala. 675, and Anderson's case. Ib. 665). May allege, in disjunctive, "dwelling-house, or a building within the curtilage of the dwelling-house, or shop, store, warehouse, or other building," etc.—Ward's case, 50 Ala. 120; Williams' case, 67 Ala. 183. But cannot describe the building as "a barn or stable," or as "a barn, house, or building."—Horton's case. 60 Ala. 72. And for burglary in "shop," or "store," or "other building," the "other valuable things" must be described generally, and alleged to be ." of value." Neal's case, 53 Ala. 465; Williams' case, 67 Ala. 183; Kelly's case, 72 Ala. 244; Henderson's case, 70 Ala. 23; Norris' case, 50 Ala. 126; Robinson's case, 52 Ala. 587; Webb's case. Ib. 422; Rowland's case, 55 Ala. 210; Matthews' case, Ib. 65; Hurt's case, Ib. 214; Stone's case, 63 Ala. 115; Pickett's case, 60 Ala. 77; Davis' case, 54 Ala. 88; Crawford's case, 44 Ala. 382. Strict correspondence as to proof of value not essential.—Robinson's case, 52 Ala. 587. But "goods and merchandise" need not be averred to be valuable things.—Wicks' case, 44 Ala. 398. Averment that goods, etc., "were kept for use," etc., sufficiently means that they were so kept at the time.—Henderson's case, 70 Ala. 23; Pond's case, 55 Ala. 196. Only structures of a temporary character require additional descriptive averment of being "specially constructed or made to keep such goods," etc.—Stone's case, 63 Ala. 115. **Evidence** of ownership proved as laid.—Beall's case, 53 Ala. 460. If alleged in two jointly; sufficient, if proof shows one was owner, and both occupied it as a store.—White's case, 49 Ala. 344. Must show that some one lived in a dwelling-house, though not actually there when offense committed.—Fuller's case, 48 Ala. 273. Must be proof of a breaking, or that house had been closed.—Green's case. 68 Ala. 539. Of other distinct burglaries, incompetent.—Mason's case, 42 Ala. 532. **Recent unexplained possession of stolen goods,** sufficient to authorize conviction, if larceny was committed at time of the burglary.—Neal's case, 53 Ala. 465; Crawford's case, 44 Ala. 45. See, also, Murray's case, 48 Ala. 675. Explanation of possession made at time, as part of res gestæ, admissible.—Henderson's case, 70 Ala. 23. Admissibility and weight of **confessions** and acts of prisoner.—Mountain's case, 40 Ala. 344; White's case, 49 Ala. 344; Ward's case, 50 Ala. 120; Murdock's case, 68 Ala. 567. Uncorroborated confessions sufficient to convict.—White's case, 49 Ala. 344. Refusal by accused to permit his house to be searched without a warrant, inadmissible against him.—Murdock's case, 68 Ala. 567. **Verdict** may be general, when burglary and grand larceny charged in same or different counts, though only one punishment imposed.—Gordon's case, 71 Ala. 315; Bell's case, 48 Ala. 694. May be verdict for petit larceny, if alleged in same count with burglary.—Borum's case, 66 Ala. 468; Gordon's case, 71 Ala. 315 And a conviction of one offense is an acquittal of the other.—Bell's case, 48 Ala. 694; Fisher's case, 46 Ala. 717. **Sentence** may be imprisonment in penitentiary or hard labor for two years, on verdict of guilty.—Washington's case, 63 Ala. 189.

3787 (4344). **Burglary in railroad car.**—Any person, who, in the night or day-time, with the intent to steal, or to commit a felony, breaks into and enters any railroad car upon or connected with any railroad in this state, in which any goods, merchandise, or other valuable thing is kept for use, deposit, or transportation, is guilty of burglary, and must, on conviction, be imprisoned in the penitentiary for not less than one, nor more than four years.

Johnson's case, 73 Ala. 483.

3788 (4345). **Possession of burglarious instruments, etc.** Any person, who has in his possession any implement or instru-

ment designed and intended by him to aid in the commission
of burglary or larceny in this state, or elsewhere, must, on conviction, be fined not less than one hundred dollars, and may
also be imprisoned in the county jail, or sentenced to hard labor
for the county, for not more than twelve months.

ARTICLE III.

LARCENY, RECEIVING STOLEN GOODS, AND BRINGING STOLEN PROPERTY INTO THIS STATE.

3789 (4358, 4359, 4360). **Grand larceny.**—Any person, who
steals any horse, mare, gelding, colt, filly, mule, jack, jenny, cow,
or animal of the cow kind, hog, sheep, goat, or any part of any
outstanding crop of corn or cotton; and any person, who steals
any personal property of any value from the person of another,
or from or in any building on fire, or which was removed in
consequence of an alarm of fire, or from or in any dwelling-
house, or from or in any store-house, warehouse, shop, railroad
car, steamboat, ship, vessel, or boat used for carrying freight or
passengers; and any person who steals any personal property,
other than hereinbefore enumerated, of the value of twenty-
five dollars, or more; and any person who knowingly, willfully,
and without the consent of the owner thereof, enters upon the
land of another and cuts and carries off any timber or rails of
the value of twenty-five dollars, or more, with the intent to
convert the same to his own use, is guilty of grand larceny,
and, on conviction, must be imprisoned in the penitentiary for
not less than one, nor more than ten years.

Meaning of terms, and subjects of larceny; meaning of "corn" and "outstanding crop."—Sullins' case, 53 Ala. 474.   Purpose of the statute.—Ib.   Unknown to
common law.—Ib.; Gregg's case, 55 Ala. 116.   Not subject of petit larceny.
Smitherman's case, 63 Ala. 21.   Larceny of animals; stealing carcass under
twenty-five dollars in value, is petit larceny.—Hunt's case, 55 Ala. 138.   Dogs not
subjects of larceny.—Ward's case, 48 Ala. 161.   But a box of matches may be.
Mitchum's case, 45 Ala. 29.   Outstanding or growing crops not subject of petit
larceny, unless severed from the freehold.—Gregg's case, 55 Ala. 116; Pinkard's
case, 62 Ala. 167.   Choses in action.—Corbett's case, 31 Ala. 329; Sallie's case, 39
Ala. 691; Wilson's case, 1 Port. 118.   What structure may constitute a "warehouse," within the statute.—Hagan's case, 52 Ala. 373.   Stealing from warehouse
or dwelling is statutory offense.—Smith's case, 55 Ala. 59.   A "steer" is "an animal of the cow kind," within the statute.—Watson's case, 55 Ala. 150.   A "pig"
is a "hog."—Washington's case, 58 Ala. 355; Lavender's case, 60 Ala. 60.   The
taking or possession must be complete.—Wisdom's case, 8 Port. 511.   And taking
of an animal by operating on its volition, assuming dominion over it, and getting
it once under control, is sufficient.—Ib.   Taking by party who has only the bare
charge or custody of the goods.—Oxford's case, 33 Ala. 416.   Where the possession
is obtained fraudulently, with the intent ab initio to steal.—Wilson's case, 1 Port.
118; Case's case, 26 Ala. 17.   Taking by a bailee.—Spivey's case, 26 Ala. 90.
Taking by joint tenants, tenants in common, or partners.—Bonham's case, 65 Ala.
457; McCall's case, 69 Ala. 227; Holcombe's case, Ib. 218; Jones' case, 76 Ala. 8.
Taking one's own goods to charge bailee.—Kirksey v. Fike, 29 Ala. 206; Holcombe's case, 69 Ala. 218   Taking lost goods, or larceny by finding.—Griggs' case,
58 Ala. 425; Rountree's case, Ib. 381.   Taking money paid by mistake.—Bailey's
case, Ib. 414.   Taking of goods mislaid, or left by mistake.—Griggs' case, 58 Ala.
425.   Taking must be against the will of the owner.—Spivey's case, 26 Ala. 90.
To constitute **larceny from a dwelling-house**, there must be an entry against the
consent of the owner, unless the crime be meditated at the time of a permissive entry.
Chambers' case, 6 Ala. 855.   Held immaterial if thief be in house by invitation of
owner.—Point's case, 37 Ala. 148.   Or if a servant is thief.—Case's case, 26 Ala. 17.
Stealing from banisters or piazza of dwelling-house is not larceny in a dwelling-
house.—Henry's case, 39 Ala. 679.   See Moore's case, 40 Ala. 49.   The **intent**
must be *animus furandi*, wrongful and fraudulent, to deprive the owner of his
property; and must be formed at the time, or before possession is acquired.—Spivey's case, 26 Ala. 90; Williams' case, 44 Ala. 396; McMullen's case, 53 Ala. 531;

Hawkins' case, 8 Port. 461; Griggs' case, 58 Ala. 425; Lyon's case 61 Ala. 224.
Need not be for the sake of gain.—Williams' case, 52 Ala. 413. No benefit to the
guilty agent may be sought, but only injury to the owner.—Ib. 413. Not larceny
for one to take property honestly believing it to be his.—Bonham's case, 65 Ala.
457; Randle's case, 49 Ala. 14. Or if he had a claim to it, honestly entertained,
though he knows of another's adverse claim.—Morningstar's case, 55 Ala. 148.
Or where the taking is open, without concealment or denial, but an avowal of the
taking.—McMullen's case, 53 Ala. 531. Following case held not larceny.—Johnson's case, 73 Ala. 523. If the taking is without a felonious intent, the act is but
a civil wrong.—Rountree's case, 58 Ala. 381; Bailey's case, Ib. 414; Griggs' case,
Ib. 426. **Indictment** for stealing any of the animals mentioned in the statute, or
outstanding crops, need not allege value or the time of the larceny. — Maynard's case, 46 Ala. 85; Sheppard's case, 42 Ala. 531; Adam's case, 60 Ala. 52;
Harris' case, Ib. 50; Gregg's case, 55 Ala. 116. A "heifer" may be described as
a "cow."—Parker's case, 39 Ala. 365. An "animal of the cow kind," as a "steer."
Watson's case, 55 Ala. 150. A "pig" as a "hog."—Washington's case, 58 Ala.
355; Lavender's case, 60 Ala. 60. "A yearling of the value of six dollars," not
sufficient description.—Stollenwork's case, 55 Ala. 142. Insufficient allegation of
larceny of outstanding crop.—Smitherman's case, 63 Ala. 24; Holly's case, 54
Ala. 238. What need not be averred; word "portion" may be used instead of word
"part," as in statute.—Ib. Sufficiency of indictment for larceny from one's person.
Dubois' case, 50 Ala. 139. Sufficiency of description of promissory notes, bank-bills,
treasury notes, currency, U. S coin, money, etc.—Ib.; Sallie's case, 39 Ala. 691;
Williams' case, 19 Ala. 15; Culps' case, 1 Port. 33; Grant's case, 55 Ala. 201;
Chisholm's case, 45 Ala. 66. Must allege name of owner, or that it is unknown.
Morningstar's case, 52 Ala. 405; Underwood's case, 72 Ala. 220. In case of bailment or possession.—Jones' case, 13 Ala. 153 Sufficient to lay ownership in railroad company having goods for transportation.—Rountree's case, 58 Ala. 381.
Ownership of timber properly laid in one having possession, asserting title.—Morningstar's case, 52 Ala. 405. But not in a plantation superintendent who is the
servant of the employer.—Heygood's case, 59 Ala. 49. Property of wife may be
laid in husband.—Davis' case, 17 Ala. 415; Lavender's case, 60 Ala. 60; Ellis'
case, 76 Ala. 90. Averment of aggregate value of several articles, sufficient.
Grant's case, 55 Ala. 201. Allegation of value necessary.—Williams' case, 44 Ala.
396. Except where the statute fixes the offense without reference to value.—Sheppard's case, 42 Ala. 531. But not of U S. coin, and national currency notes, if
described, the value of which is fixed by law.—See Duval's case, 63 Ala. 12;
Grant's case, 55 Ala. 201. Allegation of value, when necessary, must not be indefinite or uncertain.—Williams' case, 44 Ala. 396. Joinder of counts and offenses.
Gabriel's case, 40 Ala. 357; Bonham's case, 65 Ala. 456 May be joined with
burglary.—(See note to §3786.) With receiving stolen goods.—(See note to §3794.)
With false pretenses.—(See note to §3811.) Two counts of grand larceny may
be joined alleging ownership differently. — Maynard's case, 46 Ala. 86. When
prosecutor required to elect as to one of two larcenies. — Bonham's case, 65
Ala. 456. **Evidence** of the taking and carrying away, though open and not denied, may be rebutted, and a charge to acquit improper.—McMullen's case, 53
Ala. 531. What not evidence of larceny. — Green's case, 68 Ala. 539; Rountree's case, 58 Ala. 381; Bailey's case, Ib. 414 Sufficiency of **asportavit** in larceny
of an animal.—Johnson's case, 47 Ala 62; Wolf's case, 41 Ala. 412; Edmond's
case, 70 Ala. 8; Croom's case, 71 Ala. 14; Hunt's case, 55 Ala. 138. Of outstanding crop.—Lyon's case, 61 Ala. 224; Sullin's case, 53 Ala. 474. **Variance** as to
number, quantity, and value of articles stolen not fatal to whole indictment.
Kreps' case, 8 Ala. 951. Owner may state value to him, though not conclusive.
Cohen's case, 50 Ala. 108. Genuineness and value of bank-bills, money, etc.,
proved by evidence of their circulation as money.—Corbett's case, 31 Ala. 329.
Value of American gold and silver coin, and of "national currency" notes, "treasury notes," or "national bank-notes" being fixed by law at what their face im-
ports, no proof of value necessary.—Grant's case, 55 Ala. 201; Duval's case, 63
Ala. 12. Proof of value to fix the grade of the offense.—Dubois' case, 50 Ala.
139. **Ownership** must be proved as alleged.—Underwood's case, 72 Ala. 220. Not
necessary to produce title to land.—Morningstar's case, 52 Ala. 405. Proof where
ownership transferred.—Wilson's case, 1 Port. 118. Proof of possession may be
sufficient proof of ownership.—Morningstar's case, 52 Ala. 405; Miller's case, 40
Ala. 54. Proof of ownership by an accomplice sufficient, though uncorroborated.
Smith's case, 59 Ala. 104. Evidence of third person that prosecutor identified article stolen as his property, mere hearsay and inadmissible.—Johnson's case, 59
Ala. 37. Proving fewer owners than is alleged is fatal variance.—Partner's case,
41 Ala. 416. Alleging J. H. Dargin and proving John H. Dargin as owner is sufficient, if shown to be same person.—Thompson's case, 48 Ala. 165. What competent to prove possession or ownership.—Oakley's case, 40 Ala. 372; Sayre's case,
30 Ala. 15. The dispossession or taking should be proved by the rightful possessor
if possible.—Chisolm's case, 45 Ala. 66. But no presumption favorable to defendant's innocence arises from failure to examine as witness last rightful possessor.

White's case, 72 Ala. 195. **Felonious intent** presumed from circumstances arising out of the evidence, as secrecy in acquiring goods, attempts at concealment, false denial of possession, etc.—Rountree's case, 58 Ala. 381; Bailey's case, Ib. 414; McMullen's case, 53 Ala. 531. See, also, Durrett's case, 62 Ala. 434; Morningstar's case, 59 Ala. 30; Lyon's case, 61 Ala. 224. When felonious intent a question for court and when for jury.—Johnson's case, 73 Ala. 523 (overruling on this point McMullen's case, 53 Ala. 551). Presumption of innocent intent when taking is open.—Ib. 523. Or when taking is by mistake.—Randle's case, 49 Ala. 14; Bonham's case, 65 Ala. 456. **Recent unexplained possession** of stolen goods as evidence of guilt —Henderson's case, 70 Ala. 23; White's case, 72 Ala. 195; Fuller's case, 48 Ala. 273; Murray's case, Ib. 675; Underwood's case, 72 Ala. 220; Neal's case, 53 Ala. 465; Maynard's case, 46 Ala. 85; Fisher's case, Ib. 717. Possession of such articles not named in indictment admissible.—Grant's case, 55 Ala. 201. Sufficiency of such evidence question for the jury.—Underwood's case, 72 Ala. 220. Question of being **recent** is generally for the jury, though there may be cases in which it may be a matter of law for the court.—White's case, 72 Ala. 195 (overruling on this point Maynard's case, 40 Ala. 85). Contradictory declarations made to different persons, with a view of accounting for such possession, are not subject to rules for admitting confessions.—Harrison's case, 55 Ala. 239. Declarations explanatory of recent possession admissible for accused **if part of res gestæ.**—Henderson's case, 70 Ala. 23; Crawford's case, 44 Ala. 45; Allen's case, 73 Ala. 23; Allen's case, 71 Ala. 5. But declarations of ownership by prisoner or third party not admissible.—Allen's case, 71 Ala. 5; Sayre's case, 30 Ala. 15. When a statement by defendant that the money was given to him is not admissible as part of **res gestæ.**—Cooper's case, 63 Ala. 80. The corpus delicti must be established before accepting evidence of recent possession.—Fuller's case, 48 Ala. 273. But this can be shown circumstantially.—Colquitt's case, 61 Ala. 48; Robert's case, Ib. 401. And it is not necessary to call all of the clerks of a store to prove that the goods were not sold to accused.—Roberts' case, 61 Ala. 401. Identification of money or article, such as wheat, alleged to have been stolen.—Grant's case. 55 Ala. 201; Walker's case, 58 Ala. 393. Improper charge by defendant as to explanation of possession.—Grant's case, 55 Ala. 201; Dubois' case, 50 Ala. 139. Proper charge for defendant when evidence chiefly circumstantial.—Moorer's case, 44 Ala. 15. **Election by prosecutor** to proceed as to one of three larcenies; what is not.—Peacher's case, 61 Ala. 22. **Verdict,** when joined with burglary.—See note to § 3786. When indictment charges burglary only, verdict for larceny is void, and defendant not thereby put in jeopardy for larceny.—Fisher's case, 46 Ala. 717. May be convicted of larceny under indictment for robbery.—Allen's case, 58 Ala. 98. May be for an "attempt to commit larceny" if **asportavit** not proved.—Wolf's case, 41 Ala. 412; Edmond's case. 70 Ala. 8. See Berdeaux v. Davis, 58 Ala 611. Cannot be for the offense of "fraudulently disposing of property of tenants in common." Holcombe's case, 69 Ala. 218. **Punishment** imposed according to value of article stolen.—Cohen's case, 55 Ala. 109. **Value** need not be assessed of each article or at all.—Dubois' case, 50 Ala. 139; Jones' case, 13 Ala. 153; Yarbrough's case, 41 Ala. 405. On conviction of grand larceny, court has no power to sentence to county jail.—De Bardelaben's case, 50 Ala. 179; Cohen's case, Ib. 108.

3790 (4360, 4361). **Petit larceny.**—Any person, who steals any personal property under any other circumstances than are specified in the preceding section, if the value of the property is less than twenty-five dollars; and any person, who knowingly, willfully, and without the consent of the owner thereof, enters upon the land of another, and cuts and carries off any timber or rails, with intent to convert the same to his own use, if the value of the property is less than twenty-five dollars, is guilty of petit larceny, and, on conviction, must be imprisoned in the county jail, or sentenced to hard labor for the county, for not more than twelve months, and may also be fined not more than five hundred dollars, at the discretion of the jury.

See note to preceding section.

3791 (4812). **Description of animal stolen.**—In an indictment for the larceny of any animal, it is sufficient to describe the animal by such name as, in the common understanding, embraces it, without designating its sex.

As amended,
Feb. 28, 1887,
p. 148.

3792 (4362). **Judgment for value of property on conviction of larceny, and like offenses.**—When the defendant is found guilty of larceny, obtaining property under false pretenses, embezzlement, and all offenses punishable like larceny, the court, justice, or jury trying the issue, unless the property has been returned, or the value thereof paid to the owner, must assess the value of each article, and such assessed value shall be made an item of costs in the case; and whenever the costs in such cases, including the value of the property stolen, obtained under false pretenses, or embezzled, are paid or worked out at hard labor, the court of county commissioners must, upon a proper showing, allow and draw a warrant on the county treasury, in favor of the owner of such property, for the value thereof, to be paid out of the fund arising from the proceeds of such labor.

3793 (4368). **Bringing stolen property into this state.**—Any person, who brings into this state any personal property which he has stolen elsewhere, must, on conviction, be punished as if he had stolen it in this state.

Statute does not propose to punish for larceny in another state, but for bringing such property into this state.—Adam's case, 14 Ala. 490; Seay's case, 3 Stewart 123. Taking must be such as to constitute larceny here; immaterial whether larceny or not in other state.—Spencer's case, 20 Ala. 24; Murray's case, 18 Ala. 727; Ham's case, 17 Ala. 188. And the larceny must be charged as if committed here.—Ham's case, 17 Ala. 188. Sufficiency of indictment.—Alsey's case, 39 Ala. 664. Must be framed under the statute creating this offense, and not in form for larceny.—La Vaul's case, 40 Ala. 44.

3794 (4365, 4367). **Buying, receiving, concealing, etc., stolen property.**—Any person, who buys, receives, conceals, or aids in concealing any personal property whatever, knowing that it has been stolen, and not having the intent to restore it to the owner, must, on conviction, be punished as if he had stolen it; and such offender may be tried and convicted, although the person who stole the property has not been tried and convicted.

Circumstances constituting the offense, and from which jury may justly infer guilt.—Adam's case, 52 Ala. 379. Indictment may charge conjunctively "receive and conceal," as well as disjunctively "riceive or conceal.".—Murphy's case, 6 Ala. 845. Must allege "not having the intent to restore" the goods, etc.—Sellers' case, 49 Ala. 357. Must allege name of owner with same certainty as in larceny, but need not allege whether thief has been prosecuted, or his name.—Murphy's case. 6 Ala. 845. Joinder of several counts, and with larceny.—See Oxford's case, 33 Ala. 416. A sufficient form of indictment in Seller's case, 49 Ala. 357. Evidence of receiving stolen goods.—Adam's case, 52 Ala. 379. The owner a competent witness.—Gassenheimer's case, 52 Ala. 313. And may testify what the value was to him.—Cohen's case, 50 Ala. 108. Proof of guilty knowledge.—Gassenheimer's case, 52 Ala. 313; Collins' case, 33 Ala. 434. Proper charge as to what may authorize conviction.—Ib. Possession of stolen goods, when sufficient to infer guilt of receiving, etc.—Adam's case, 52 Ala. 379. Punishment according to assessed value of property.—Cohen's case, 50 Ala. 109; DeBardelaben's case, Ib. 179.

ARTICLE IV.

EMBEZZLEMENT, RECEIVING EMBEZZLED PROPERTY, FRAUDULENT CONVERSIONS, AND LIKE OFFENSES.

3795 (4377). **Embezzlement by officer, clerk, agent, servant, or apprentice.**—Any officer, agent, or clerk of any incorporated company, or municipal corporation, or clerk, agent, servant, or apprentice of any private person or persons, who embezzles or fraudulently converts to his own use, or fraudulently secretes with intent to convert to his own use, any money or property which has come into his possession by virtue of his

As amended, Nov. 26, 1880, p. 43.

office or employment, must be punished, on conviction, as if he had stolen it.

This section (and sections 3796 and 3797) embraces same acts which were larceny at common law, as well as acts which were breaches of trust.—Insurance Co. v. Tunstall, 72 Ala. 142. When embezzlement under this section a felony. and when a misdemeanor.—Washington's case, 72 Ala. 272. The gist of this offense.—Ib. 276. A wrongful conversion is an unauthorized assumption and exercise of the right of ownership over goods and personal chattels belonging to another, to the alteration of their condition, or the exclusion of the owner's rights.—Noble's case, 59 Ala. 79. Indictment should allege agent, or servant, etc., of some named principal; and it is well, though not required, to allege ownership of property.—Washington's case, 72 Ala. 272. May be joined with larceny in separate count.—Mayo's case, 30 Ala. 32. When prosecutor required to elect, and when not.—Ib. Sufficiency of description of articles embezzled.—Ib. Code form sufficient.—Ib.; Lowenthal's case, 32 Ala. 589. Who is an agent within the meaning of the statute.—Hinderer's case, 38 Ala. 415. What proof sufficient to convict clerk —Lowenthal's case, 32 Ala. 589; Washington's case, 72 Ala. 272.

3796 (4383). **Embezzlement or fraudulent secretion by officer, etc., of incorporated bank.**—Any officer, agent, clerk, or servant of any bank incorporated under any law of this state, who embezzles or fraudulently converts to his own use, or fraudulently secretes with intent to convert to his own use, any money, property, or effects belonging to, or in the possession of such bank, or deposited therein, must be punished, on conviction, as if he had stolen it.

See note to preceding section.

3797 (4384). **Embezzlement or fraudulent secretion by banker, factor, attorney, or other agent.**—Any private banker. commission merchant, factor, broker, attorney, bailee, or other agent, who embezzles, or fraudulently converts to his own use, or fraudulently secretes with intent to convert to his own use, any money, property, or effects deposited with him, or the proceeds of any property sold by him for another, must be punished, on conviction, as if he had stolen it.

This section applies only to bailments in which the parties stand to each other in a fiduciary relation. the bailee having the possession wholly and exclusively for the benefit of the bailor, and not against hirer of domestic animal, who sells animal during term of bailment.—Watson's case, 70 Ala. 13. See note to section 3795.

3798 (4379). **Embezzlement by common carrier.**—Any common carrier or other person, to whom any money or property has been delivered to be carried for hire, and who embezzles or fraudulently converts to his own use, or fraudulently secretes with intent to convert to his own use, such money or property, or any part thereof, must be punished, on conviction, as if he had stolen it.

As amended, Feb. 7, 1879, p. 140.

3799 (4381). **Embezzlement by county superintendent of education.**—Any county superintendent of education, to whom any money or property has been delivered as county superintendent of education, who embezzles or fraudulently converts to his own use such money or property, or any part thereof. must be punished, on conviction, as if he had stolen it, and shall forfeit his office.

As amended, Feb. 7, 1879, p. 140.

3800 (4382). **Embezzlement by using school money for other than school purposes.**—Any person, into whose hands, or under whose control, any of the public school money may come, who uses or permits the use of the same, or any part thereof, except for purposes of the public schools, and in accordance with the law regulating the public schools, and pro-

viding for the disbursement of the public school money, is
guilty of embezzlement, and, on conviction, must be punished
as if he had stolen it.

3801 (4261). **Embezzlement by state treasurer, or person
employed in his office.**—If the state treasurer, or any other
person employed in his office, embezzles, or fraudulently converts to his own use, or fraudulently secretes with intent to convert to his own use, any money, property, or effects belonging
to the state, and which has come to his possession by virtue of
his office or employment, he must be punished, on conviction,
as if he had stolen it.

Noble's case, 59 Ala. 73.

3802 (4266). **Embezzlement by tax-collector in failing to
make returns and forward tax money.**—Any tax-collector,
who fails to make returns and forward the tax money in his
hands, from time to time, to the proper authorities, as provided
by law, except for good cause, is guilty of embezzlement of
public funds, and is liable, on conviction, to a fine of not exceeding ten thousand dollars, and imprisonment in the penitentiary
not exceeding two years.

3803 (4275). **Embezzlement of state or county revenue.**
Any officer or person, who knowingly converts or applies any of
the revenue of the state, or of any county thereof, to his own use,
or to the use of any other person, must, on conviction, be punished as if he had stolen it.

Noble's case, 59 Ala. 73.

3804. **Embezzlement by collector of municipal taxes.** Feb. 12, 1879,
Any officer or person charged with the collection of taxes, gen-   p. 179.
eral or special, for any city, town, or municipal corporation,
who embezzles, or fraudulently converts to his own ·use, or
fraudulently secretes with intent to convert to his own use, such
taxes, or any portion thereof, must, on conviction, be punished
as if he had stolen the same.

3805 (4389.) **Conversion of money by certain public officers.**
Any probate judge, clerk of a court of record, register in chancery, sheriff, coroner, tax-collector, county treasurer, trustee of
public schools, notary public, justice of the peace, or constable,
who knowingly converts to his own use, or permits another to
use any money paid into his office, or received by him in his
official capacity, is liable to indictment, and, on conviction, must
be punished as if he had stolen it.

3806. **Prima facie evidence of embezzlement by tax-col-** Feb. 17. 1885,
lector under preceding section.—The failure of any tax-col-   p. 48, sec. 76.
lector to pay over or produce any money collected by him, either
as state or county taxes, after demand by the state or county
treasurer, shall be prima facie evidence against such tax-collector of embezzlement by him.

3807 (4387). **Failure of private banker, broker, etc., to pay
over money on demand.**—Any private banker, commission
merchant, factor, broker, attorney, or other agent, who sells or
disposes of property for another, and refuses, for three days
after demand made by the person entitled to the same, his agent,
or attorney, to pay the amount to which such person is entitled,
must, on conviction, be fined not more than one thousand dol-

lars, and may also be imprisoned in the county jail, or sentenced to hard labor for the county, for not more than six months.

3808 (4385). **Receiving embezzled property.**—Any person, who buys or receives property, knowing that it has been embezzled, or fraudulently converted, or fraudulently secreted, with intent to prevent the recovery thereof, or to defraud the rightful owner, must be punished, on conviction, as if he had stolen it.

3809 (4386). **Conviction of receiver before embezzler.**—An offender may be tried and convicted under the preceding section, although the person who embezzled the property has not been tried and convicted.

3810 (4811). **Description of property in indictments.**—In an indictment for embezzlement, or other offense under this article, it is sufficient to describe the property in general terms, as "money," "bank-notes," "checks," "bills of exchange," or other evidences of debt, of or about a certain amount.

ARTICLE V.

FALSE PRETENSES, FRAUDS, CHEATS, ACTS TO INJURE, AND THE LIKE.

3811 (4370). **Obtaining property by false pretenses.**—Any person, who, by any false pretense or token, and with the intent to injure or defraud, obtains from another any money, or other personal property, must, on conviction, be punished as if he had stolen it.

False pretense must be of an existing or past fact; mere promise, though false, not sufficient.—Colly's case, 55 Ala. 85.   Must be of material fact, calculated to deceive and defraud, and not absurd or irrational; yet, if party is imposed upon, his want of prudence no defense.—Woodbury's case, 69 Ala. 242; Beasley's case, 59 Ala. 20.   Every pretense made need not be false.—Ib.   And the false pretense need not be the sole, but must be the controlling inducement to part with the property.—Woodbury's case, 69 Ala. 242.   And not necessary that the money obtained should be paid directly to defendant, but may be paid to another at his request.—Sandy's case, 60 Ala. 58.   The same false pretense, repeated on different days, is but one transaction, and no ground to require prosecutor to elect.—Beasley's case, 59 Ala. 20.   The word "injure" means what is implied in the word "defraud."—Carlisle's case, 76 Ala. 75.   Goods may be obtained from bailee.—Mack's case, 63 Ala. 138.   **Indictment** in the Code form, sufficient.—Sandy's case, 60 Ala. 58; O'Connor's case, 30 Ala. 9.   Allegation that "he had one small black mule," means that he had the mule as owner.—Franklin's case, 52 Ala. 414.   Must aver an intent to injure or defraud.—Mack's case, 63 Ala. 138.   May allege in different counts that pretense was made to different persons.—Oliver's case, 37 Ala. 134.   Need not allege all the pretense made.—Beasley's case, 59 Ala. 20.   The description "sixty-five dollars in money," is sufficient; also, of a certain instrument as "a deed of trust.—Oliver's case, 37 Ala. 134.   **Evidence** as to the pretense alleged, what a material variance.—O'Conner's case, 30 Ala. 9.   Allegation that pretense was to H. B. Clark and proof to Hiram B. Clark, if same person, is immaterial variance.—Franklin's case, 52 Ala. 415.   Not necessary to prove all pretenses alleged.   Beasley' case, 59 Ala. 20.   Evidence showing use of goods by defendant, admissible to prove intent.—Mack's case, 63 Ala. 138.   Sufficiency of proof of intent to injure or defraud.—Ib.; Carlisle's case, 76 Ala. 75; O'Conner's case, 30 Ala. 9; Johnson's case, 29 Ala. 62.

Feb. 17, 1885, p. 142.
3812. Same; under contract for performance of act or service.—Any person, who, with intent to injure or defraud his employer, enters into a contract in writing for the performance of any act or service, and thereby obtains money or other personal property from such employer, and with like intent, and without just cause, and without refunding such money, or pay-

ing for such property, refuses to perform such act or service, must, on conviction, be punished as if he had stolen it.

3813 (4374). **Obtaining signature by false pretenses.**—Any person, who, by any false pretense or token, and with the intent to injure or defraud, obtains from another his signature to any written instrument, the false making of which is forgery, must, on conviction, be punished as if he had forged the instrument.

Langford's case, 45 Ala. 26.

3814 (4376). **Obtaining property by false personation.**—Any person, who, by falsely personating another, and with the intent to injure or defraud, obtains or receives any property intended to be delivered to the individual personated, must, on convicton, be punished as if he had stolen it.

3815 (4371). **Obtaining building material by false pretenses.**—Any original contractor, or sub-contractor, who, having contracted to do or perform any work or labor upon, or to furnish any material, fixtures, engine, boiler, or machinery for any building or improvement upon land, or for repairing the same, purchases materials from any person on credit, and, at the time of the purchase, represents that the same are to be used in a designated building or improvement, and thereafter, without first giving to such person due notice of his intention to so use the same, and, with intent to defraud, uses such material for any other purpose; or any such original contractor, who, when required, makes to the owner or proprietor of any land upon which such building or improvement is situated, a false and fraudulent list of material-men, laborers and employes, who have furnished any material or thing, or have done any labor, or performed any service, or may be under any contract or engagement to furnish any material or thing, or to do any labor, or perform any service for such contractor, or for or on such building or improvement, must, on conviction, be fined not less than fifty dollars.

3816 (4372). **Same; by false representation of contract with owner of building.**—Any person, who, with intent to injure or defraud, obtains any material for any building or other improvement, or procures any labor to be done on such building or improvement upon any false representation of or touching any contract or agreement with the owner or proprietor thereof, or of any lot or parcel of land, whereby sufficient money would be obtained to pay for such material or labor, and afterwards refuses to pay therefor, and such material or labor is lost by reason of such representation, must, on conviction, be punished as if he had stolen the same.

3817 (4373). **Fraudulently obtaining money or goods on credit, or bringing into state money or goods so obtained.**—Any person, who, by false representation of his pecuniary condition, or under the false color and pretense of carrying on business, and dealing in the ordinary course of trade, obtains on credit from any person money, goods, or chattels, with the intent to defraud, or brings, or causes to be brought, into this state any money, goods, or chattels so obtained in any other state, must, on conviction, be punished as if he had stolen the same; and any person violating the provisions of this section may be

As amended, Feb. 14, 1885, p. 117.

indicted and tried in the county in which he resides, or in any county into which he brings, or causes to be brought, any of such money, goods, or chattels.

Feb. 13, 1879, p. 170.

3818. Bringing into state property obtained elsewhere by false pretense.—Any person, who brings or causes to be brought into this state any money or other personal property obtained from another by any false pretense, with intent to defraud, must, on conviction, be punished as if he had stolen the same.

3819 (4375). **Keeping false books or accounts by officers or agents of corporations.**—Any officer, agent, or servant of any private or municipal corporation organized under the laws of this state, who keeps false books or accounts, or makes false entries therein, with the intent to deceive, injure, or defraud such corporation, or the officers or agents thereof, or, if a private corporation, the stockholders therein, must, on conviction, be fined not less than one hundred, nor more than one thousand dollars, and may also be sentenced to hard labor for the county for not more than two years, one or both, at the discretion of the jury.

Nov. 29, 1880, p. 127.

3820. Issuing false receipts for merchandise, produce, or article of value.—Any warehouseman, or agent or employe of any warehouseman, or any person engaged in the storage or safe-keeping of goods, wares, merchandise, lime, or lumber, or cotton, grain, hay, or other produce, or any article of value, or any agent or employe of such person, or any officer or agent of any corporation engaged in such business, who, with an intent to injure or defraud, issues any false receipt for any goods, wares, merchandise, lime, or lumber, cotton, grain, hay, or other produce, or any article of value, must, on conviction, be fined not more than two thousand dollars, and sentenced to hard labor for the county for not more than two years, one or both, at the discretion of the jury.

Feb. 28, 1881, p. 134, sec. 7.

3821. Issuing false receipt or delivering goods without surrender of receipt.—Any warehouseman, wharfinger, agent of a vessel or railroad, or other person, who violates any of the provisions of —— sections of this Code, must, on conviction, be fined not more than one thousand dollars, or imprisoned in the penitentiary for not more than five years.*

3822 (2082). **Fraud by partner in limited partnership.** A partner in a limited partnership, who commits a fraud in the affairs of the partnership, is guilty of a misdemeanor.

Dec. 6, 1882, p. 7, sec. 1.

3823. Taking rebate or gratuity by state officer, or person employed by state government.—Any officer, agent, or person, who may be empowered or authorized to purchase for the state, or any department of the state government, any property or thing of value, and who asks for, bargains for, demands, agrees to take, or receives, or takes from the seller of such property, directly or indirectly, any rebate, return compensation, discount, or drawback, in money or anything of value, must, on conviction, be punished as if he had stolen it.

Ib. sec. 2.

3824. Same; by officer, agent, or servant of state institution.—Any officer, agent, or servant of the University of Ala-

---

* The omission to state sections referred to, is in the original manuscript; but on the margin are these words, written in pencil: "Insert proper sections of new Civil Code." The sections referred to are evidently sections 1175, 1177, 1178 and 1179.

bama, the Agricultural and Mechanical College, the Alabama Insane Hospital, the Alabama Institution for the Deaf and Dumb and the Blind, or of any other corporation to which is appropriated any of the public funds of the state, who shall be authorized to buy any property of any kind for any of such corporations, and who asks for, bargains for, demands, takes, or receives, directly or indirectly, from the seller of such property, any rebate, discount, drawback, return commission, gift, or gratuity, must, on conviction, be punished as if he had stolen it.

3825. Same; by officer, agent, employe, or contractor of county, city, or town.—Any officer, agent, or person of any county, city, or town, who may be authorized or employed to buy for such county, city, or town, or any department or office thereof, or who may be authorized, empowered, or employed to contract for, or let out any work, contract, or employment, and who asks for, bargains for, demands, or who takes or receives, directly or indirectly, from the seller of such property, or the contractor for such work, or the person who may be employed, any rebate, discount, drawback, return commission, gift, or gratuity, or a part or percentage of the profits of such contract or employment, must, on conviction, be punished as if he had stolen it.

3826. Same; by officer, agent, or servant of railroad, manufacturing, or mining corporation.—Any officer, agent, or servant of any railroad, manufacturing, or mining corporation, who is authorized or employed to buy any property for such corporation, and who demands, asks for, bargains for, agrees to take, takes, or receives, directly or indirectly, from the seller of such property, any rebate, discount, drawback, return commission, gift, or gratuity, must, on conviction, be punished as if he had stolen it.

3827. Same; by factor, commission merchant, broker, attorney, auctioneer, or agent.—Any factor, commission merchant, broker, attorney, auctioneer, or agent, who is employed or authorized to sell the property of another, and who demands, asks for, bargains for, agrees to take, takes, or receives, directly or indirectly, from the purchaser or any person who is employed to store, move, handle, transport, insure, repair, or do any act or service in or about the taking care of, preserving, and marketing such property, any rebate, discount, drawback, return commission, gift, or gratuity, or who charges his principal on account of any one or more of the above enumerated services more than he actually paid therefor, or who buys any property or thing for his principal, and charges his principal more than he actually paid therefor, must, on conviction, be punished as if he had stolen it.

3828 (4350). False affidavit, etc., to defraud insurer.—Any person, who, being the master, or an officer, or mariner of any vessel, makes, or causes to be made, or swears to any false affidavit, or protest; or, being the owner, or other person concerned in such vessel, or in any property laden on board the same, procures any such false affidavit or protest to be made, or exhibits the same, with the intent to injure, deceive, or defraud the insurer of such vessel or property, must, on conviction, be

Ib. sec. 3.

Ib. sec. 4.

Ib. sec. 5.

imprisoned in the county jail, or sentenced to hard labor for the county, for not more than one year, and may also be fined not more than two thousand dollars, at the discretion of the jury.

3829 (4351). **False estimate, etc., to defraud insurer.**—Any person, who, being the owner, or part owner of any steamboat, or vessel, or of any property laden, or pretended to be laden on board thereof, or being concerned in the lading or fitting out of such steamboat or vessel, makes out and exhibits any false or fraudulent estimate of any property, laden or pretended to be laden, on board of such steamboat or vessel, with intent to injure, deceive, or defraud the insurer of such steamboat, vessel, or property, must. on conviction, be imprisoned in the county jail, or sentenced to hard labor for the county, for not more than one year, and may also be fined not more than two thousand dollars, at the discretion of the jury.

3830 (4366). **Taking, destroying, or concealing deed to injure or defraud.**—Any person, who, with intent to injure or defraud, takes or destroys any will, deed, or conveyance of real or personal property, belonging to another, or receives, conceals, or aids in concealing such deed or conveyance, knowing it to have been taken with the intention to injure or defraud, must, on conviction, be punished as if he were guilty of grand larceny.

3831 (4404). **Marking, or altering or defacing brands of domestic animals with intent to defraud.**—Any person, who, with intent to defraud, marks or brands any unmarked horse, mule, cow, hog, sheep, goat, or other domestic animal, the property of another, or alters or defaces the mark or brand of such animal. must, on conviction, be punished as if he had stolen it.*

Feb. 23, 1883,
p. 166.

3832. Failure of defendant to perform contract with surety confessing judgment for fine and cost.—Any defendant, on whom a fine is imposed on conviction for a misdemeanor, who in open court signs a written contract, approved in writing by the judge of the court in which the conviction is had, whereby, in consideration of another becoming his surety on a confession of judgment for the fine and costs, agrees to do any act, or perform any service for such person, and who, after being released on such confession of judgment, fails or refuses, without a good and sufficient excuse, to be determined by the jury, to do the act, or perform the service, which in such contract he promised or agreed to do or perform, must, on conviction, be fined not less than the amount of the damages which the party contracting with him has suffered by such failure or refusal, and not more than five hundred dollars; and the jury shall assess the amount of such damages; but no conviction shall be had under this section, unless it is shown on the trial that such contract was filed for record in the office of the judge of probate of the county in which the confession of judgment was had, within ten days after the date of the execution thereof.

Lee's case. 75 Ala. 29: Leach's case, Ib. 36.

Ib.

3833. Damages paid to injured party out of fine imposed. From the fine imposed under the preceding section, when col-

---

* See act, entitled "An act to define and punish the obtaining registrations of cattle and other animals by false representations as to their breeding," approved February 10, 1887. Pamph. Acts 1886–7, p. 125.

lected, the damages sustained by the party contracting with such defendant must be paid to such person by the officer collecting the same.

ARTICLE VI.

FRAUDULENT CONVEYANCES, AND ILLEGAL DISPOSITION OF PROPERTY ON WHICH ANOTHER HAS A CLAIM.

3834 (4352). **Fraudulent conveyances.**—Any person, who, with intent to hinder, delay, or defraud creditors, makes or receives any conveyance of property, must, on conviction, be fined not less than one hundred, nor more than one thousand dollars; and may also be imprisoned in the county jail, or sentenced to hard labor for the county, for not more than six months.

3835 (4353). **Removing, selling, or buying property to which others have claim.**—Any person, who removes or sells any personal property for the purpose of hindering, delaying, or defrauding any person who has a claim thereto, under any written instrument, lien created by law for rent or advances, or any other lawful or valid claim, verbal or written, with a knowledge of the existence thereof; or who, with like intent, buys, receives, or conceals any such property, with knowledge of the existence of any such claim, must, on conviction, be punished as if he had stolen the same.

3836 (4354). **Selling mortgaged property.** — Any person, who sells or conveys any personal property, upon which he has given a written mortgage, lien, or deed of trust, and which is then unsatisfied, in whole or in part, without first obtaining the consent of the lawful holder thereof to such sale or conveyance, must, on conviction, be fined not more than five hundred dollars, and may also be imprisoned in the county jail, or sentenced to hard labor for the county, for not more than six months, one or both, at the discretion of the jury.

Walker's case, 49 Ala. 329; Johnson's case, 69 Ala. 593.

3837 (4355). **Disposing of property of tenants in common, or in which another has an interest.**—Any tenant in common, or any person in any other way interested in any personal property or outstanding crop in which any other person has an interest, who, with intent to defraud his co-tenant, or such other person, sells, gives way, or otherwise disposes of, or conceals, or removes such personal property or outstanding crop, or any part thereof; or any person who, with such intent, aids or assists in removing or concealing the same, must, on conviction, be punished as if he had stolen personal property of the value of the interest of such co-tenant, or other person having an interest therein.   As amended, Feb. 23, 1883, p. 187.

Holcombe's case, 69 Ala. 218; McCall's case, Ib. 227.

3838 (4356). **Disposing of mare or jenny before price for foaling is paid.**—Any person, who, with a knowledge of the lien, sells, or otherwise disposes of any mare or jenny before the stipulated price for the service of any stallion or jack, for which a lien is given by law, is paid, must, on conviction, be fined not more than one hundred dollars.

3839. Selling or exchanging "choking" horse or mule.
Any person, by himself or another, or as agent for another, who shall knowingly sell or exchange any horse or mule subject to the disease or affection known as "choking," must, on conviction, be fined not less than one hundred, nor more than five hundred dollars, and may also be sentenced to hard labor for the county for not less than three, nor more than six months; one-half of the fine shall go to the party injured. For each conviction under this section the solicitor shall be entitled to a fee of fifty dollars. Justices of the peace shall have concurrent jurisdiction with the circuit and city court of offenses arising under this section, and shall have power, in such cases, to sentence the defendant to hard labor for the county for fine and costs.*

ARTICLE VII.

FRAUDS AND OTHER OFFENSES CONCERNING COTTON.

Feb. 19, 1883, p. 59, sec. 1.

3840. Mutilating or changing marks, brands, or numbers on cotton, or concealing cotton.—Any warehouse proprietor, common carrier, officer, agent, clerk, or employe of such common carrier or person, or any other person, who, for the purpose of preventing, delaying, or hindering the rightful owner, or person having a lien thereon, from recognizing, finding and recovering his cotton (whether the same has been sold to the warehouse proprietor, or to other parties), changes or mutilates the marks, brands, or numbers on such cotton, or conceals any cotton delivered to such warehouse, common carrier, or to such other person for sale or storage, must, on conviction, be fined not less than ten, nor more than one hundred dollars.

3841 (4391). **Taking cotton from bale by factor, etc., with intent to defraud, etc.**—Any factor, commission merchant, consignee, or agent, having the control of any cotton, who, with intent to defraud the owner, appropriates to his own use any cotton taken from any bale under his control, or authorizes, or knowingly permits any other person to take from any such bale any part thereof, and to retain the same to his own use, must, on conviction, be fined not less than fifty, nor more than one thousand dollars, and may also be imprisoned in the county jail, or sentenced to hard labor for the county, for not more than twelve months.

3842 (4392). **Taking cotton from bale by person without authority.**—Any person, who knowingly and unlawfully takes from any bale of cotton any part thereof, without the authority of the owner, consignee, or agent, must, on conviction, be fined not less than fifty, nor more than five hundred dollars, and may also be imprisoned in the county jail, or sentenced to hard labor for the county, for not more than six months.

3843 (4393). **Fraudulent conversion of cotton samples.**
Any person who is authorized to sample cotton, and who, with

---

*Added by joint committee.

intent to defraud, converts such samples to his own use, or refuses to deliver them on demand to the owner, consignee, or agent, within thirty days after they are taken, unless they have, in the meantime, been destroyed or stolen without his agency, or taken out of his possession by legal process, must, on conviction, be fined not less than fifty, nor more than five hundred dollars, and may also be imprisoned in the county jail, or sentenced to hard labor for the county, for not more than six months.

3844 (4394). **Buying cotton taken from bale without authority, etc.**—Any person, who knowingly and with intent to defraud, buys or receives any cotton taken from the bale without the authority of the owner, consignee, or agent, must, on conviction, be fined not less than fifty, nor more than five hundred dollars, and may also be imprisoned in the county jail, or sentenced to hard labor for the county, for not more than six months.

3845 (4395). **Injuring cotton bales by cutting, etc.**—Any person, who, without the authority of the owner, consignee, or agent, willfully cuts, tears, or otherwise opens any bale of cotton, must, on conviction, be fined not more than five hundred dollars, and may also be imprisoned in the county jail, or sentenced to hard labor for the county, for not more than six months.

3846 (4396). **Penalty on broker purchasing cotton for failure to pay for same.**—Any cotton broker, engaged in the business of buying cotton, either on his own account, or for others, who buys, or engages to buy from a planter or commission merchant any cotton, and fails or refuses to pay for the same at the time agreed upon, and makes way with or disposes of any cotton purchased and not paid for, is guilty of fraud and embezzlement, and, on conviction, must be imprisoned in the penitentiary not less than one, nor more than five years, at the discretion of the jury.

3847 (4397). **Unlawful sampling or removing of cotton, or illegal consideration for sampling.**—Any person violating any of the provisions of sections 1189 (1421), 1190 (1422), or 1191 (1423) of the Code, on conviction, must be fined not less than fifty, nor more than one hundred dollars for each offense, one-half of which shall go to the informer; and in prosecutions under this section, the ownership of the cotton need not be alleged or proved.

3848 (4398). **Frauds in packing cotton.**—Any person, who fraudulently packs or bales any cotton, by plating or otherwise, must, on conviction, be fined not less than fifty, nor more than five hundred dollars, and may also be imprisoned in the county jail, or sentenced to hard labor for the county, for not more than six months.

Daniels' case, 61 Ala. 4.

3849 (4399). **Fraudulently exhibiting false samples.**—Any person, who fraudulently exhibits any false samples of any cotton, or of any other article or commodity, by means whereof any person is injured, must, on conviction, be fined not less than fifty dollars, and may also be imprisoned in the county jail, or sentenced to hard labor for the county, for not more than six months.*

Cowles' case, 50 Ala. 454.

3850 (4357). **Removing cotton subject to lien from state.** Any person, who removes, or aids in removing from this state, any cotton subject to the lien given by law for the purchase-money, with intent to prevent, hinder, or delay the enforcement of such lien, must, on conviction, be imprisoned in the penitentiary for not less than one, nor more than five years, at the discretion of the jury.

ARTICLE VIII.

FORGERY AND COUNTERFEITING.

3851 (4332, 4333). **Forgery in first degree.**—Any person, who, with intent to injure or defraud any person, corporation, state, or government, alters, forges, or counterfeits any bill, note, draft, check, certificate, or other evidence of debt, issued by any incorporated bank or banking company of this or any other state, or by authority of any law of the United States, or private bank, or by any officer authorized to issue the same, or drawn on any incorporated bank or banking company, or on the treasurer of this state; or who, with such intent, utters and publishes as true any falsely altered, forged, or counterfeited bill, note, draft, check, certificate, or other evidence of debt, so issued or drawn, knowing the same to be altered, forged, or counterfeited, is guilty of forgery in the first degree.

Forgery defined.—Rembert's case, 53 Ala. 468.   What need not be alleged in forgery of bank bill.—Bostick's case, 34 Ala. 266.   Expert opinion of genuine and counterfeit bank bills.—Johnson's case, 35 Ala. 370.

As amended, Jan. 27, 1883, p. 33.

3852 (4340). **Forgery in second degree; of will deed, note, bond, bill, order, etc.**—Any person, who, with intent to injure or defraud, falsely makes, alters, forges, counterfeits, or totally obliterates any will of real or personal property, or any deed, conveyance, or other instrument, being or purporting to be the act of another, by which any right or interest in property is, or purports to be transferred, conveyed, or in any way changed or affected; or any bond, bill-single, bill of exchange, promissory note, or any indorsement thereof, the forgery of which does not constitute forgery in the first degree; or any cotton receipt, or receipt for the payment of money, or any instrument or writing, being or purporting to be the act of another; or any entry in any book account, by which any pecuniary demand or obligation is or purports to be created, increased, discharged, or diminished; or who, with such intent, utters and publishes as true any falsely made, altered, forged, or counterfeited instrument, writing, indorsement, or entry, specified or included in this section, is guilty of forgery in the second degree.

What instrument subject of forgery under this section.—Jones' case, 50 Ala. 161; Horton's case, 53 Ala. 489; Anderson's case, 65 Ala. 553; Allen's case, 74 Ala. 557; Hobbs' case, 75 Ala. 1: Butler's case, 22 Ala. 43; Givens' case, 5 Ala. 747; Thompson's case, 49 Ala. 16; Rembert's case, 53 Ala. 469; Gooden's case, 55

* See act, entitled "An act to prohibit the docking or deducting from the actual weights of baled cotton by the purchaser thereof," approved February 28, 1887. Pamph. Acts 1886–7, p. 72.

Ala. 178; Williams' case, 61 Ala. 33. Writing void on its face is not subject of forgery.—Hobbs' case, 75 Ala. 1; McGuire's case, 37 Ala. 161; Rembert's case, 53 Ala. 467. But otherwise, if validity can be imparted to it by extrinsic facts alleged.—Ib. 467. Defendant need not have written the instrument himself; sufficient if he procured another to write it.—Gooden's case, 55 Ala. 178. May be forgery of check, though no funds in bank.—Thompson's case, 49 Ala. 16. Also of a check drawn in name of fictitious person.—Ib. Intent to injure or defraud is material ingredient.—Gooden's case, 55 Ala. 178. One making an instrument in one county is indictable for forgery in another county where he has an agent (though innocent) to utter or publish it as true.—Bishop's case, 30 Ala. 34; Scully's case, 39 Ala. 240. See, also, McGuire's case, 37 Ala. 161; Harrison's case, 36 Ala. 248. Indictment must aver extrinsic facts when the instrument is unintelligible or obscure.—Rembert's case, 53 Ala. 469; Hobbs' case, 75 Ala. 1. Sufficiency of indictment in following cases.—Johnson's case, 35 Ala. 370; Horton's case, 53 Ala. 488; Rembert's case, Ib. 467; Thompson's case, 49 Ala. 16; Jones' case, 50 Ala. 161; Anderson's case, 65 Ala. 553; Allen's case, 74 Ala. 557. Sufficient, if analogous to forms prescribed by the Code in other cases.—Jones' case, 50 Ala. 161; Johnson's case, 35 Ala. 370; Thompson's case, 49 Ala. 16. Evidence of genuine papers and money of same kind admissible, when and for what.—Manaway's case, 44 Ala. 375; Johnson's case, 35 Ala. 370. That the defendant knowingly uttered and published a forged instrument as true, may be sufficient proof that he committed the forgery.—McGuire's case, 37 Ala. 161; Harrison's case, 36 Ala. 248; Allen's case, 74 Ala. 560. Also unexplained possession of forged instrument. Hobbs' case, 75 Ala. 1; Allen's case, 74 Ala. 560; Johnson's case, 35 Ala. 370. Proof of handwriting by comparison not permitted.—Givens' case, 5 Ala. 747; Bishop's case, 30 Ala. 34; Williams' case, 61 Ala. 33. Forged instrument must be produced or accounted for.—Manaway's case, 44 Ala. 375. Secondary evidence when instrument mutilated, lost, or destroyed.—Thompson's case, 30 Ala. 28; Morton's case, Ib. 527. That the supposed drawer refused to pay, inadmissible as hearsay.—Horton's case, 53 Ala. 488. Agent of company defrauded competent to prove his agency.—Manaway's case, 44 Ala. 375. Court must explain ambiguity apparent in face of forged note.—Butler's case, 22 Ala. 43. Verdict need not specify degree of forgery.—Anderson's case, 65 Ala. 553.

3853 (4337). **Same; public seal, or seal of incorporated bank.**—Any person, who, with intent to defraud, counterfeits or forges the seal of this state, or of any public office authorized by law, or of any court of record, or of any bank or banking company, or any corporation incorporated under the authority of this state, or falsely makes, forges, or counterfeits any impression purporting to be the impression of any such seal, is guilty of forgery in the second degree.

3854 (4338). **Same; by forging, destroying, or falsifying records, return to process, etc.**—Any person, who, with intent to defraud, falsely alters, forges, destroys, or falsifies the record of any judgment or decree of any court of record, either of law or equity, or of any will, conveyance, or other instrument, which is by law required or authorized to be recorded, or the return of any officer to any writ or process of any court, is guilty of forgery in the second degree.

3855 (4339). **Same; by forging official certificate.** — Any person, who, with intent to defraud, counterfeits, forges, or falsely alters any certificate or indorsement, made, or purporting to have been made, by any officer authorized by law to make such certificate or indorsement, of the acknowledgment by any person of any deed or other instrument by law authorized or required to be acknowledged and recorded, or any certificate, made or purporting to have been made by any court or officer authorized by law to make such certificate, of the proof of any deed, will, or other instrument, which is by law authorized or required to be recorded on proof, is guilty of forgery in the second degree.

3856 (4334). **Same; by counterfeiting gold or silver coin, etc.**—Any person, who counterfeits any gold, silver, or other coin, which is at the time current by law, usage, or custom, in this state, or who has in his possession any counterfeit gold, silver, or other coin, which is at the time current in this state, knowing the same to be counterfeit, and with intent to defraud or injure by uttering the same as true, or by causing the same to be so uttered, or who utters and publishes as true such counterfeit coin, knowing the same to be counterfeit, and with intent to injure or defraud, is guilty of forgery in the second degree.

Nicholson's case, 18 Ala. 529.

3857 (4335, 4336). **Same; by counterfeiting engraved plate of bank-note, check, etc.** — Any person, who makes or engraves, or causes or procures to be made or engraved, any plate in the form or similitude of a promissory note, bill of exchange, draft, check, certificate of deposit, or other evidence of debt, issued by any incorporated bank or banking company within this or any other state, without the authority of such bank or banking company; or who has in his custody or possession, without the authority of such bank, any impression taken from any such plate, with the intent to have the same filled up and completed for the purpose of being passed, sold, or uttered; or who makes, or causes or procures to be made, or has in his custody or possession any plate on which are engraved any words or figures which may be used for falsely uttering any evidence of debt issued by any such bank or banking company, with intent to use the same for that purpose, is guilty of forgery in the second degree; and every plate, the engraving on which resembles or conforms to such parts of the genuine instrument as are engraved, must be deemed to be in the form or similitude of the instrument imitated, within the meaning of this section.

3858 (4341). **Forgery in the third degree.**—Any forgery which, under the provisions of this Code, does not amount to forgery in the first or second degree, must be adjudged forgery in the third degree.

3859 (4804). **Indictment for forgery of instrument destroyed or withheld.**—In an indictment for the forgery of an instrument which has been destroyed, or is withheld by the act or procurement of the defendant, if that fact is alleged in the indictment, a misdescription of the instrument is immaterial.

3860 (4342). **Punishment of forgery and counterfeiting.** Forgery in the first degree is punished by imprisonment in the penitentiary for not less than ten, nor more than twenty years; in the second degree, by imprisonment in the penitentiary for not less than two, nor more than ten years; and in the third degree, by imprisonment in the county jail, or hard labor for the county, for not more than twelve months.

ARTICLE IX.

TAKING OR USING TEMPORARILY PROPERTY OF ANOTHER.

Feb. 5, 1879, p. 165.

3861. Taking or using temporarily any animal or vehicle of another without authority.—Any person, who unlawfully takes for temporary use, or uses temporarily any animal or vehicle, without the consent of the owner, or person having control thereof, and without a bona fide claim of title thereto, must, on conviction, be fined not more than one hundred dollars, and may also be imprisoned in the county jail, or sentenced to hard labor for the county, for not more than six months; but no prosecution shall be commenced, or indictment found under this section, except upon complaint of the owner, or person having control of such animal or vehicle.

Article X.

OFFENSES CONCERNING FLOATING LOGS OR TIMBER, AND PROPERTY ADRIFT.

3862. Cutting loose or floating off logs or timber without authority.—Any person, who, without authority of the owner, cuts loose and sets adrift any log or timber fastened to the bank of any navigable stream, or who runs or floats any log or timber of another into any creek, bayou, lagoon, or lake, with the intention of concealing or appropriating the same, must, on conviction, be fined not less than one hundred, nor more than two hundred dollars, and may also be imprisoned in the county jail, or sentenced to hard labor for the county, not more than one year. *Feb. 17, 1885, p. 165, sec. 1.*

3863. Selling or disposing of floating logs or timber taken up unlawfully.—Any person, who takes up any floating logs or timber which are branded or marked, and sells or disposes of the same, without the consent of the owner, or his agent, and without a compliance with the law touching the salvage of property taken adrift, must, on conviction, be fined not less than one hundred, nor more than two hundred dollars, and may also be imprisoned in the county jail, or sentenced to hard labor for the county, not more than one year. *Ib. sec. 2.*

3864 (4364). **Concealing, etc., property taken up adrift.** Any person, who conceals, destroys, injures, obliterates, or defaces any mark upon, or sells, or disposes of, or carries beyond the state, any property taken up adrift, before the expiration of the time allowed for the owner to prove his property, must, on conviction, be fined not less than one hundred dollars.

Article XI.

TAKING FISH AND OYSTERS FROM PRIVATE PREMISES.

3865 (4363). **Taking fish, without owner's consent, from artificial pond, lake, or trap.**—Any person, who takes or catches any fish from a private artificial fish-pond or lake, or fish trap, without the consent of the owner, must, on conviction, be fined not less than five, nor more than fifty dollars.

3866 (4440). **Taking and carrying away oysters without consent of owner of bed.**—Any person, who takes or carries away from any oyster bed any oysters, without the written consent of the owner, must, on conviction, be fined not more than five hundred dollars, and imprisoned in the county jail, or sentenced to hard labor for the county, for not more than one year; one or both, at the discretion of the jury.

ARTICLE XII.

CONCERNING MILITARY PROPERTY.

March 1, 1881,
p. 112, sec. 29.
3867. Disposing of, or retaining without right, military property belonging to state.—Any person, who sells, purchases, retains, or has in his possession or custody, without right, any military property belonging to this state or any regiment or company of Alabama State Troops, or who, after proper demand, refuses to deliver the same to any officer entitled to take possession thereof, is guilty of a misdemeanor; and any person belonging to the Alabama State Troops, who, contrary to the lawful orders of the proper officer, retains in his possession or control any military property of the state, is guilty of a misdemeanor; and any commanding officer may take possession of such military property mentioned in this section, wherever the same may be found.

ARTICLE XIII.

ILLEGALLY REMOVING AND IMPOUNDING ANIMALS.

Feb 13, 1879.
p. 168.
3868. Driving animal from lawful into an unlawful district, to be impounded.—Any person, who knowingly and willfully drives or carries any animal running at large in any district where it is lawful for such animal to run at large, into any other district where it is not lawful for such animal to run at large, with the intention that such animal shall be impounded, must, on conviction, be fined not less than ten, nor more than one hundred dollars, and may also be imprisoned in the county jail, or sentenced to hard labor for the county, for not more than six months.

ARTICLE XIV.

MALICIOUS MISCHIEF, AND INJURY AND CRUELTY TO ANIMALS.

3869 (4408, 4420). **Malicious injury to animals or other article of value.**—Any person, who unlawfully and maliciously kills, disables, disfigures, destroys, or injures any animal, or article or commodity of value, the property of another, must, on conviction, be fined not less than twenty, nor more than five hundred dollars, and may also be imprisoned in the county jail, or sentenced to hard labor for the county, for not more than six months; and the fine goes to the party injured.

Malice towards owner essential ingredient; else mere trespass.—Northcot's case, 43 Ala. 330; Hobson's case, 44 Ala. 380. Malice inferred from instrument used, and circumstances attending injury inflicted, etc.—Ib. 380; Hill's case, 43 Ala. 335. Malice to son of owner not sufficient.—Northcot's case, Ib. 330. Indictment must allege name of owner, or that it is unknown.—Pierce's case, 7 Ala. 728. Value need not be averred.—Caldwell's case, 49 Ala. 34. Alleging injury of two animals conjointly, proof must show that both were injured at same time; but otherwise, if charged in different counts or disjunctively in same count.—Burgess' case, 44 Ala. 190. If proof fails to show a known proprietor, killing cannot be malicious mischief.—Pierce's case, 7 Ala. 728. Party injured held incompetent witness in Northcot's case, 43 Ala. 330. But Northcot's case overruled on this point by Daniels' case, 60 Ala. 561; Bohanon's case, 73 Ala. 49.

3870 (4409, 4410). **Unlawful or wanton killing, disabling, etc., certain domestic animals.**—Any person, who unlawfully or wantonly kills, disables, disfigures, destroys, or injures any horse, mare, gelding, colt, filly, mule, jack, jenny, bull, ox, cow, calf, heifer, hog, goat, or sheep, the property of another, must, on conviction, be fined not less than twice the value of the injury to the animal killed, disabled, disfigured, destroyed, or injured, nor more than five hundred dollars, and may also be imprisoned in the county jail, or sentenced to hard labor for the county, for not more than six months; and one-half of the fine imposed shall go to the owner of the property.

Malice not necessary.—Johnson's case, 37 Ala. 457; Thompson's case, 67 Ala. 106; Tatum's case, 66 Ala. 465. Trespass to pursue and kill with dog animals in one's own field.—Thompson's case, 67 Ala. 106. Specific intent to kill, disable, or injure, unnecessary; sufficient if done unlawfully or wantonly.—Tatum's case, 66 Ala. 465. Indictment may aver ownership of property in different persons or names in different counts; when prosecutor put to an election.—Bass' case, 63 Ala. 108. Value of animal killed no bearing on question of guilt vel non.—Ashworth's case, 63 Ala. 120. When an indictment should aver value of property injured. Garner's case, 8 Port. 447.

3871 (4411). Same; trial and conviction; mitigation or justification.

—Upon the trial, the defendant may prove in mitigation or justification, as the jury may determine, that, at the time of the injury, the stock was trespassing upon a growing crop, inclosed by a lawful fence, or cultivated without a fence where stock laws prevail; and no conviction must be had, if it is shown that, before the commencement of the prosecution, compensation for the injury was made or tendered to the owner.

Name of prosecutor need not appear on indictment, nor the record show that complaint was made by owner; yet, on motion and proof quashed if not shown that was found on necessary complaint.—Ashworth's case, 63 Ala. 120. Judgment rendered for whole amount of fine, in favor of state for use of county as in other cases.—Bass' case, 63 Ala. 108. Justification under verbal license, if language ambiguous, left to jury to determine meaning of authority or license from owner to kill, etc.—Ashworth's case, 63 Ala. 120. Tender of compensation for the damage, what necessary.—Ib. What necessary to be shown as a defense on ground of doing "damage to any growing crop," etc.

3872. Cruelty to animals.

— Any person, who overrides, overdrives, overloads, drives when overloaded, tortures, torments, deprives of necessary sustenance, cruelly beats, mutilates, or cruelly kills, or causes or procures to be overridden, overdriven, overloaded, driven when overloaded, tortured, tormented, deprived of necessary sustenance, cruelly beaten, mutilated, or cruelly killed, any domestic animal, and whoever, having the charge or custody of any such animal, either as owner or otherwise, inflicts unnecessary cruelty upon the same, or fails to provide the same with proper food, drink, or protection from the weather, or cruelly drives the same when unfit for labor, must, on conviction, be fined not less than ten, nor more than one hundred dollars. *Feb. 27, 1883, p. 187.*

3873. Duty of law-officer; lawful for any person to arrest; compensation; penalty.

—It is the duty of any officer of the law, county or municipal, and it is lawful for any other person, to arrest and take before a justice of the peace, any person violating the provisions of the preceding section, and shall, upon conviction of the person arrested, be entitled to the sum of two dollars, which shall be taxed as a part of the cost; and any officer herein named, who fails or neglects to arrest such offender, must, on conviction, be fined not less than ten dollars. *Ib., as amended, Feb. 17, 1885, p. 156*

Article XV.

TRESPASS AND INJURY TO REALTY.

3874 (4419, 4120). **Trespass after warning.**—Any person, who, without legal cause or good excuse, enters into the dwelling-house, or on the premises of another, after having been warned, within six months preceding, not to do so, must, on conviction, be fined not more than one hundred dollars, and may also be imprisoned in the county jail, or sentenced to hard labor for the county, for not more than three months; and the fine goes to the party injured.

What acts covered by the statute.—McLeod v. McLeod, 73 Ala. 42. **Purpose of statute** and constituents of offense.—Watson's case, 63 Ala. 19. **Premises** means any real estate, etc.; includes pasture more than mile from dwelling-house.—Sandy's case, 60 Ala. 18. Prosecutor must have **actual or constructive possession.**—Bohannon's case, 73 Ala. 47; Watson's case, 63 Ala. 19. What is "**legal cause**" or "**good excuse**;" burden of proof on defense.—Owens' case, 74 Ala. 401. **Warning** not to enter may be verbal or written.—Watson's case, 63 Ala. 19. Sufficiency of such warning—Owens' case, 74 Ala. 401. Copy of warning, if in writing, sufficient evidence without notice to produce original.—Watson's case, 63 Ala. 19. When deeds to land **competent evidence.**—Bohannon's case. 73 Ala. 47. **Legal advice** no defense.—Watson's case, 63 Ala. 19. Prosecutor a **competent witness** (overruling, on this point, Northcot's case, 43 Ala. 330).—Daniels' case, 60 Ala. 56; Bohannon's case, 73 Ala. 47. **Indictment** need not particularly describe premises or allege venue.—Watson's case, 63 Ala. 19. Sufficiency of description of premises in notice of warning, and indictment—Owens' case, 74 Ala. 401. **Right to protect property** against trespass; human life cannot be taken.—Simpson's case, 59 Ala. 1.

3875 (4417, 4420). **Trespass on lands by cutting down trees, etc.; severing and taking property from freehold.**—Any person, who willfully and maliciously commits any trespass on the lands of another, by cutting down or destroying any wood or timber growing thereon, or by severing from the freehold any produce thereof, or any property or thing thereto attached; or any person, who severs and carries away from the freehold any property or thing thereto attached under such circumstances as would render the trespass a larceny, if the thing severed and carried away were personal property, must, on conviction, be fined not more than two hundred dollars, and may also be imprisoned in the county jail, or sentenced to hard labor for the county, for not more than six months; and the fine goes to the injured party.

Johnson's case, 61 Ala. 9.

3876 (4425). **Trespass by cutting down shade trees, shrubs, etc.**—Any person, who maliciously, or for the purpose of injuring an individual, or the public, cuts down, destroys, or injures any trees or shrubs, planted or preserved for shade or ornament in any public street or square, or in any yard or grounds, must, on conviction (unless the trees or shrubs cut down or injured belong to him), be fined not less than fifty, nor more than two hundred dollars, and may also be imprisoned in the county jail, or sentenced to hard labor for the county, for not more than three months.

3877 (4416). **Trespass on school lands; disposition of fine.** Every trespasser on school lands must, on conviction, be fined not less than three times the amount of the injury occasioned by such trespass; and the fine shall be added to the principal of the school fund of the township.

3878 (4414). **Trespass by allowing stock to run at large under common fence.** — Any one of several parties occupying or cultivating land under a common fence, who turns stock of any kind into such inclosure, or knowingly suffers such stock to go at large therein, without a sufficient guard to prevent injury to crops, must, on conviction, be fined not less than ten, nor more than fifty dollars, and also the amount of the damages inflicted by the stock, which damages shall be held as a part of the penalty imposed by the court, and shall go to the party injured; but this section shall not apply where there is no growing or outstanding crop on the lands within the inclosure, or in any case from the twenty-fifth day of December to the first day of March succeeding.

Cole's case, 72 Ala. 216.

3879 (4415). **Same; disposition of stock in default of payment of penalty.**—Whenever a conviction shall be had under the preceding section, unless the full amount of the penalty is immediately paid, it shall be the duty of the sheriff, or other officer charged with the execution of the judgment of the court, to seize and hold the stock committing the trespass, and, after giving five days' notice, by posting at three or more public places in the neighborhood, to sell the same, and out of the proceeds to collect the amount of such penalty and costs; and the surplus shall be paid to the owner of such stock.

3880. Trespass on state capitol grounds.—Any person, who turns a horse or other animal of any kind to graze upon the grounds of the state capitol, must, on conviction, be fined not more than twenty dollars. Jan. 17, 1879, p. 201.

3881. Trespass on lands, by cutting or boxing pine trees for turpentine.—Any person, who knowingly and willfully, and without the consent of the owner, enters upon the lands of any person or corporation, or upon the lands belonging to the state, and cuts, girdles, or boxes any pine tree for the purpose of obtaining crude turpentine, must, on conviction, be fined not more than five hundred dollars, and may also be imprisoned in the county jail, or sentenced to hard labor for the county, for not more than six months. Feb. 13, 1879. p. 167.

ARTICLE XVI.

BURNING WOODS AND TURPENTINE FORESTS.

3882 (4426). **Burning woods willfully.**—Any person, who willfully sets fire to the woods or forest on uninclosed lands not belonging to himself, or willfully causes fire to be communicated to such woods or forest (except during the months of February and March), must, on conviction, be fined not less than ten, nor more than two hundred dollars.*

---

* On February 28, 1887 (Pamph. Acts, 1886-7, p. 145), an act was approved, which is as follows: "SECTION 1. *Be it enacted by the General Assembly of Alabama,* That section 4426 of the Code shall be so amended as to read as follows: Any person, who willfully sets fire to the woods or forest on lands not belonging to himself, or willfully causes fire to be communicated to such woods or forest, must, on conviction, be fined not less than ten, nor more than two hundred dollars; *Provided,* The provisions of this bill shall apply only to the counties of Baldwin, Clark, Monroe, Washington, Montgomery, Barbour, Mobile, Marengo, Dallas, Wilcox, Greene, Escambia, Cullman, Autauga, Lauderdale, Bullock, Perry, Hale, Calhoun, Russell and Lowndes."

3883 (4427). **Burning pine forest willfully.**—Any person, who willfully sets fire to any pine forest which is used for the purpose of procuring turpentine, with the intent to injure or destroy the same, must, on conviction, be fined not less than one hundred, nor more than one thousand dollars, and may also be imprisoned in the county jail, or sentenced to hard labor for the county, for not more than twelve months.

As amended,
Feb. 17, 1885,
p. 125.
3884 (4428). **Burning turpentine and other forest negligently.**—Any person, who negligently causes fire to be communicated to any pine forest which is used for the purpose of procuring turpentine, or to any forest belonging to another, and thereby injures or destroys the same, must, on conviction, be fined not less than fifty, nor more than two hundred dollars.

ARTICLE XVII.

INJURING AND DEFACING BUILDINGS, STRUCTURES, FENCES, BOATS, MILL-DAMS, BRIDGES, ETC.; AND OTHER OFFENSES CONCERNING PROPERTY.

3885 (4412, 4420). **Injuring or defacing public or private buildings, or fences thereof.**—Any person, who willfully injures or defaces any church, or building belonging to the state, or to any county, city, town, or private person, or writes or draws figures, letters, or characters on the walls thereof, or on the fences or inclosures thereof, must, on conviction, be fined not less than ten, nor more than one hundred dollars, and may also be imprisoned in the county jail, or sentenced to hard labor for the county, for not more than three months; and the fine goes to the injured party.

3886 (4418, 4420). **Injuring water-dams, bridges, canals, road-gates, etc.**—Any person, who willfully injures any mill-dam, or other dam to create water-power, or any embankment necessary to support such dam, or willfully removes, injures, or destroys any lock, bank, culvert, aqueduct, or water-weir of any canal, or wantonly obstructs or hinders the free use or navigation of any canal, or wantonly opens any lock-gate, puddle-gate, culvert-gate, or water-gate of any canal, or willfully injures or destroys, otherwise than by burning, any public bridge, toll-bridge, causeway, turnpike-gate, or other gate erected on any road by authority of law, must, on conviction, be fined not less than fifty, nor more than five hundred dollars, and may also be imprisoned in the county jail, or sentenced to hard labor for the county, for not more than six months; and the fine goes to the injured party.

Sufficiency of indictment for destroying public bridge under this section. Owens' case, 52 Ala. 400. Destroying a bridge to allow passage of a raft, when admissible as an excuse.—Ib. What no defense.—Ib.

3887 (4424). **Injuring telegraph line or post.**—Any person, who willfully cuts, pulls down, destroys, or in any manner injures any telegraph or telephone line, or any post or part thereof, must, on conviction, be fined not less than fifty, nor more than five hundred dollars, and may also be imprisoned in the county jail, or sentenced to hard labor for the county, for not more than six months.

3888 (4413, 4420). **Maliciously or negligently breaking or destroying fences.**—Any person, who unlawfully, maliciously, or negligently destroys, throws down, or breaks any fence or inclosure of another, and fails immediately to rebuild or repair the same, must, on conviction, be fined not less than twenty, nor more than five hundred dollars, and may also be imprisoned in the county jail, or sentenced to hard labor for the county, for not more than six months; and the fine goes to the injured party.

Brazelton's case, 66 Ala. 96.

3889 (4413). **Injuring, breaking, or taking boat from its mooring.**—Any person, who unlawfully or maliciously injures, breaks, cuts off, or carries away from its mooring or landing any ferry-boat, flat-boat, canoe, or other vessel, the property of another, must, on conviction, be fined not less than twenty, nor more than five hundred dollars, and may also be imprisoned in the county jail, or sentenced to hard labor for the county, for not more than six months; and the fine goes to the injured party.

3890 (4422). **Removing or destroying boundary marks, monuments, etc.**—Any person, who willfully removes or destroys any monument or post, or cuts down, removes, or destroys any tree, or defaces, or alters the marks made on such monument, post, or tree, which monument, post, or tree was erected or used to designate the corner, or any other point on the boundary of any lot or tract of land, must, on conviction, be fined not less than fifty, nor more than five hundred dollars, and may also be imprisoned in the county jail, or sentenced to hard labor for the county, for not more than twelve months.

3891 (4423). **Removing or defacing mile-post, guide-board, etc.**—Any person, who willfully destroys or removes any milestone, post, board, or guide-board, set upon any road or highway, or willfully defaces, alters, or destroys any letters or figures thereon, must, on conviction, be fined not less than ten, nor more than fifty dollars, and may also be imprisoned in the county jail, or sentenced to hard labor for the county, for not more than thirty days.

CHAPTER 5.

OFFENSES AGAINST THE PUBLIC REVENUE.

3892 (4274). **Engaging in or carrying on business without license.**—Any person, who, after the fifteenth day of January in any year, engages in or carries on any business for which a license is required, without having taken out such license, must, on conviction, be fined three times the amount of the state license.

License to sell intoxicating liquors is a permit which may be revoked, and not a contract.—Powell's case, 69 Ala. 10; Jones v. Hilliard, Ib. 300. Permission by city to retail does not protect one from indictment by state.—Davis' case, 4 Stew. & Port. 83; Estabrook's case, 6 Ala. 653. Only one license required to sell in two adjoining and communicating rooms of same proprietor.—Hochstadler's case. 73

Ala. 24. Statute exacting license of products of other states and not of this state, unconstitutional.—Vine's case, 67 Ala. 73. Law requiring license for peddling is constitutional.—Seymour's case, 51 Ala. 52. Also for practicing law.—Cousins' case, 50 Ala. 113. Construction of law requiring license on pistols, bowie-knives. etc.—Porter's case, 58 Ala. 66. "**To engage in or carry on any business,**" within the meaning of the revenue law, is to pursue an occupation or employment, as a livelihood, or as a source of profit; but it is not necessary that it should be the party's sole occupation or employment. It is a question of intention for the determination of the jury.—Harris' case, 50 Ala. 127. See, also, Moore's case, 16 Ala. 411; Carter's case, 44 Ala. 29; Johnson's case, Ib. 414; Bryant's case, 46 Ala. 302; Espy's case, 47 Ala. 533; Weil's case, 52 Ala. 19; Grant's case, 73 Ala. 13. And it is immaterial whether such profit was realized or not.—Weil's case, 52 Ala. 19. While a single act pertaining to a business may not be sufficient, a series of such acts will.—Weil's case, 52 Ala. 19; Martin's case, 59 Ala. 34; Sanders' case, 58 Ala. 371; Lawson's case, 55 Ala. 118; McPherson's case, 54 Ala. 221; Ulmer's case, 61 Ala. 208; Bryant's case. 46 Ala. 302; Jackson's case, 50 Ala. 141. When one act of sale or exhibition sufficient proof of engaging in business.—Chamber's case, 26 Ala. 64. To constitute occupation or vocation.—Johnson's case, 44 Ala. 414. What constitutes a "dealer in tobacco."—Carter's case, 44 Ala. 29. "Commission merchant."—Perkins' case, 50 Ala. 154. A "theater."—Gillman's case, 55 Ala. 248. "Exhibition of sleight of hand."—Pike's case, 35 Ala. 419. "Retailing liquor."—Lemon's case, 50 Ala. 130; Lillensteine's case, 46 Ala. 498; Nicrosi's case, 52 Ala. 336; Winter's case, 30 Ala. 22. "Wholesale liquor dealer."—Espy's case. 47 Ala. 533; Hafter's case, 51 Ala. 37. "Sewing machines."—Merritt's case, 59 Ala. 46. "Distilling."—Grant's case, 73 Ala. 13. Intent necessary; and how proved, and for the jury.—Carter's case. 44 Ala. 29; Merritt's case, 59 Ala. 46; Weil's case, 52 Ala. 19. Superintendent, or manager, of corporation without license, indictable.—Elsberry's case, 52 Ala. 8. **Two or more persons jointly indicted** liable to joint or separate fine.—Lemon's case, 50 Ala. 130. Taking out license **subsequent to acts done,** no defense.—Elsberry's case, 52 Ala. 8. **Indictment** may allege in one count, conjunctively, different liquors, "brandy, whisky and gin," just as different articles stolen may be alleged in larceny.—Whitted's case, 3 Ala. 102. For retailing liquor, must allege the place, with sufficient certainty to show amount of license required, so that, on conviction, the proper fine may be imposed.—Harris' case, 50 Ala. 127; Child's case, 52 Ala 14; Hafter's case, 51 Ala. 37. Averment of time fixed by law for taking out license, when held necessary.—McIntyre's case, 55 Ala. 167. When not.—Henback's case, 53 Ala. 525. Indictment must conform to statute describing the offense.—McPherson's case, 54 Ala. 221 Sufficiency of indictment for "selling sewing machines," without license.—Merritt's case, 59 Ala. 46. "Exhibiting feats of sleight of hand."—Pike's case, 35 Ala 419. "Distilling liquors."—Johnson's case, 44 Ala. 414. "Practicing law."—Cousins' case. 50 Ala. 113. "Wholesale liquor dealer."—Koopman's case, 61 Ala. 70. "Retailing liquor."—Harris' case, 50 Ala. 127; Childs' case, 52 Ala. 14. "Keeping a restaurant."—Huttenstein's case, 37 Ala. 157. "Hawking and peddling."—Sterne's case, 20 Ala. 43. "Peddling."—May's case, 9 Ala. 167. **Evidence** for state need not show that there is no license; burden is on defense to prove that a license was taken out.—Porter's case, 58 Ala. 66. **Penalty** is three times amount of annual license.—Weil's case, 52 Ala. 19.

3893 (4272). **Keeping hotel or inn without license.** — Any person, or the agent or manager of any corporation, who engages in or carries on the business of keeping an inn or hotel, without having taken out license as required by law, must, on conviction, be fined three times the amount of the state license.

Dec. 12, 1884, p. 12, sec. 10. **3894. Probate judge must furnish statement of licenses to solicitor.**—The probate judge in each county, on the first day of each circuit or city court, must furnish to the acting solicitor, to be by him laid before the grand jury, a statement in writing, showing the licenses granted and the taxes received thereon, within the last twelve months preceding such court, and to whom and for what such license was granted.

Ib. sec. 15. **3895. Selling lightning rods without license.**—Any person, who sells lightning rods for himself or as agent for another, without payment of the tax required by law, must, on conviction, be fined not less than one hundred, nor more than five hundred dollars.

3896. Engaging in business as mercantile agent for unlicensed agency.—Any agent or correspondent of any unlicensed person, partnership, or corporation, engaged in the business of inquiring into, and reporting upon the credit and standing of persons doing business in this state, who makes any report to, or transacts any business for his principal, must, on conviction, be fined not more than five hundred dollars. Ib. sec. 21.

3897. Acting as agent for unlicensed foreign insurance company.—Any person, who acts as agent of any unlicensed foreign insurance company, must, on conviction, be fined in a sum equal to the state, county and municipal tax required to be paid by such company for license, and five hundred dollars in addition thereto; and, on a second or other conviction, must be fined one thousand dollars, and may be imprisoned in the county jail, or sentenced to hard labor for the county, for six months. Ib. sec. 17.

Jackson's case, 50 Ala. 141.

3898. Non-performance of duty by tax-collector, assessor, or probate judge.—Any tax-collector, assessor, or probate judge, who fails or neglects to perform any duty imposed upon him by the revenue law in regard to the assessment and collection of taxes, if there is no other punishment provided for such failure or neglect, must, on conviction, be fined not less than twenty, nor more than one thousand dollars. Feb. 17, 1885, p. 67, sec. 188.

3899 (4262). **Fraudulently obtaining duplicate warrant on state treasury.**—Any person, who fraudulently obtains from the state auditor any duplicate warrant upon the treasury of the state, must, on conviction, be punished as if he had stolen the amount specified in the warrant.

3900. Failure of assessor or collector to list, etc., persons liable to poll-tax.—Any tax-assessor, who fails to note on each assessment list the township and range in which each person liable for poll-tax resides, or to note the number of each race in each township liable to poll-tax, as required by law, or any tax-collector, who fails to keep a separate account of the amount of poll-tax paid by persons of the respective races in each township, or who fails to furnish a statement thereof to the county superintendent of education, on payment of such poll-tax to him, as required by law. must, on conviction, be fined not less than one hundred dollars. * Feb. 17, 1879, p. 188, sec. 59.

3901 (4271). **Dealing in state securities.**—Any tax-collector, or other person engaged in collecting the revenues of the state, who buys, sells, or otherwise trades in state warrants, state certificates, or other securities of the state, must, on conviction, be imprisoned in the penitentiary for not less than one, nor more than five years, and fined not less than fifty, nor more than one thousand dollars, one or both, at the discretion of the court.

3902 (4273). **Failure of commissioners court to publish semi-annual statements.**—If any court of county commissioners fail to publish semi-annual exhibits of the receipts and expenditures of moneys for and on account of their respective

* See amendment to act of February 7, 1879, authorizing and regulating a system of public instruction, for the State of Alabama, approved February 28, 1887. Pamph. Acts, 1886–7, p. 117.

counties, as required by law, each member of such court must, on conviction, be fined not more than one hundred dollars for each offense.

3903 (4277). **False or fraudulent list by tax-payer.**—Any tax-payer, or other person, whose duty it is to return tax-list, who renders a false or fraudulent tax-list, must, on conviction, be fined not less than fifty, nor more than two hundred dollars, at the discretion of the court; and it is the duty of the assessor to present all persons so offending to the first grand jury thereafter.

3904 (4278). **Failure of assessor to administer oath to tax-payer.**—Any tax-assessor, who fails to administer the oath, as required by law, to any tax-payer before proceeding to list his property, must, on conviction, be fined not more than fifty dollars.

As amended,
Feb. 17, 1885,
p. 69, sec. 141.

3905 (4276). **Failure or neglect of duty under revenue law not otherwise provided.**—Any officer, on whom any duty is imposed by the revenue law, who fails or neglects to perform such duty, if there is no other punishment provided for such failure or neglect, must, on conviction, be fined not less than twenty, nor more than two hundred dollars.

CHAPTER 6.

OFFENSES AGAINST PUBLIC JUSTICE AND OFFICIAL DUTY.

ARTICLE 1.—Perjury.

2.—Bribery.

3.—Misconduct by officers and persons concerned in the administration of justice.

4.—Buying, selling and illegally assuming office.

5.—Disclosing indictment and testimony given before grand jury.

6.—Failure to execute process, or to receive prisoner.

7.—Resisting arrest or process, and refusing to aid officer.

8.—Violating duties concerning convicts and prisoners.

9.—Escapes.

10.—Accessories after the fact.

11.—Compounding felony.

12.—Conspiracy.

13.—Falsely personating another in any legal proceeding.

14.—Prosecuting a suit without legal authority.

15.—Suing out search warrant wrongfully.

ARTICLE I.

PERJURY.

3906 (4112, 4114). **Perjury and subornation of perjury on trial for felony.**—Any person, who willfully and corruptly swears or affirms falsely, or corruptly procures another to so swear or affirm, in regard to any material matter or thing, on the trial of any person under an indictment for felony, must, on

conviction, be imprisoned in the penitentiary for not less than
three, nor more than twenty years.

3907 (4113, 4114). **Perjury and subornation in other cases.**
Any person, who willfully and corruptly swears or affirms
falsely, or corruptly procures another to so swear or affirm, in
regard to any material matter or thing, upon any oath or
affirmation authorized by law, except on the trial of any person
under an indictment for a felony, must, on conviction, be imprisoned in the penitentiary for not less than two, nor more
than five years.

A definition of perjury given in Hood's case, 44 Ala. 81. Oath must be willfully and corruptly false.—Ib.; Green's case, 41 Ala. 419. Effect of taking oath
pursuant to advice of counsel.—Hood's case, 44 Ala. 81. False oath or affidavit to
superfluous or immaterial matter not perjury.—Gibson's case, 44 Ala. 17; Hood's
case, Ib. 81; McMurry's case, 6 Ala. 324. Need not be immediately material; sufficient if it adds weight to, and has direct connection with facts that are material.
Williams' case, 68 Ala. 551; Jacobs' case, 61 Ala. 448. False oath to affidavit in
detinue is perjury.—Jacobs' case, 61 Ala. 448. In affidavit for attachment.—Hood's
case, 44 Ala. 81. On application for habeas corpus.—Gibson' case, 44 Ala. 17.
Evidence of officer's authority to administer oath.—Moore's case, 52 Ala. 424. Proceedings wherein the perjury was committed; what material variance.—Brown's
case, 47 Ala. 47; Jacobs' case, 61 Ala. 448. Proof of substance of matter falsely
sworn to, sufficient.—Taylor's case, 48 Ala. 157. Also of assignment of perjury.
Williams' case, 68 Ala. 551. Materiality of matter sworn to must appear.—Ib.;
Floyd's case, 30 Ala. 511 Falsity of statement proved by two witnesses, or one
witness and strong corroborating circumstances.—Williams' case, 68 Ala. 551;
Peterson's case, 74 Ala. 34. Necessity and admissibility in evidence of original
papers, record, indictment, etc.—McMurry's case, 6 Ala. 324; Williams' case, 68
Ala. 551.

3908 (4813). **Indictment for perjury or subornation.**—In an
indictment for perjury, or subornation of perjury, it is not
necessary to set forth the pleadings, record, or proceedings, with
which the false oath is connected, or the commission or authority of the court or person before whom the perjury was committed; it is sufficient to state the substance of the proceedings,
the name of the court or officer before whom the oath was
taken, and that such court or officer had authority to administer it, with the necessary allegations of the falsity of the matter on which the perjury is assigned.

Statute dispenses with many requirements of common-law indictments, but substance of proceedings must be set forth; and other averments necessary.—Jacobs'
case, 61 Ala. 448. Forms in Code, and analogous forms sufficient; sufficient allegation of false testimony, or assignments of perjury; proof of one assignment sufficient.—Williams' case, 68 Ala. 551; Brown's case, 47 Ala. 47; Peterson's case, 74
Ala. 34; DeBernie's case, 19 Ala. 23; McMurry's case, 6 Ala. 324; Lea's case, 3
Ala. 602.

3909 (4287, 4288). **Perjury of electors.**—Any person, who
willfully, corruptly and falsely takes the registration oath required by law of electors, or willfully, corruptly and falsely
takes any oath required by law at any election, general or
special, or state, county, or municipal, is guilty of perjury, and
must, on conviction, be imprisoned in the penitentiary not less
than two, nor more than five years.

Moore's case, 52 Ala. 424.

3910 (4115). **Perjury by wholesale or retail dealer in violating license oath.**—Any licensed wholesale or retail dealer
in vinous, spirituous, or malt liquors, who, after taking the oath
prescribed by law to be taken by applicants for license to sell
such liquors, willfully and corruptly violates such oath, is guilty
of perjury, and must, on conviction, be imprisoned in the penitentiary for not less than two, nor more than five years.

Feb. 17, 1885, p. 28, sec. 5.

3911. False oath by tax-payer.—Any person, who, having taken the oath required by law to be administered to him by the tax-assessor or his deputy, before proceeding to list property and other subjects for taxation, willfully and corruptly answers falsely any lawful question which such assessor or his deputy may put to him touching the return of property and other subjects of taxation, or willfully and corruptly makes a false return of the property and other subjects of taxation required by law to be by him returned for taxation, is guilty of perjury, and must, on conviction, be imprisoned in the penitentiary for not less than two, nor more than five years.

March 1, 1881, p. 116, sec. 37; Feb. 23, 1883, p. 148.

3912. Perjury by officer of state troops in making false oath claiming allowance.—Any commanding officer of any military company forming a part of the Alabama State Troops, who willfully and corruptly makes any false oath touching any matter required by law to be contained in any statement made by him for the purpose of obtaining for such company any allowance provided by law, is guilty of perjury, and, on conviction, must be imprisoned in the penitentiary for not less than two, nor more than five years. *

ARTICLE II.

BRIBERY.

3913 (4116). **Bribery of executive, legislative, or judicial officers.**—Any person, who corruptly offers, promises, or gives to any executive, legislative or judicial officer, after his election or appointment, either before or after he has been qualified, any gift, gratuity, or thing of value, with intent to influence his act, vote, opinion, decision, or judgment, on any cause, matter, or proceeding, which may be then pending, or which may be by law brought before him in his official capacity, must, on conviction, be imprisoned in the penitentiary for not less than two, nor more than ten years.

3914 (4117). **Accepting bribe by such officer.**—Any executive, legislative, or judicial officer, who corruptly accepts, or agrees to accept, any gift, or gratuity, or other thing of value, or any promise to make any gift, or to do any act beneficial to such officer, under an agreement, or with an understanding that his act, vote, opinion, decision, or judgment is to be given in any particular manner, or upon any particular side of any cause, question, or proceeding, which is pending, or may be by law brought before him in his official capacity, or that he is to make any particular appointment in his official capacity, must, on conviction, be imprisoned in the penitentiary for not less than two, nor more than ten years.

3915 (4118). **Bribery of ministerial officer, juror, or arbitrator.**—Any person, who corruptly offers, promises, or gives to any ministerial officer of any court of law or equity in this state, or to any auditor, juror, arbitrator, umpire, or referee,

---

* See act. entitled "An act to amend an act to amend section 37 of an act entitled 'An act for the organization and discipline of the volunteer forces of Alabama. approved March 1, 1881,' approved February 23, 1883," which was approved 28th February, 1887. Pamph. Acts 1886-7, p. 83.

any gift, gratuity, or thing of value, with intent to bias the mind, or influence the decision of such ministerial officer, auditor, juror, arbitrator, umpire, or referee, in relation to any cause or matter which is pending in any of said courts, or before such arbitrator, umpire, or referee, must, on conviction, be imprisoned in the penitentiary for not less than two, nor more than five years.

Caruthers' case, 74 Ala. 406.

3916 (4119). **Same; juror, if summoned, need not have been sworn.**—To authorize a conviction under the last section for bribing, or offering to bribe a juror, it is not necessary that such juror should have been actually sworn or qualified, but it is sufficient that he had been summoned under legal authority.

3917 (4120). **Accepting bribe by such officer, juror, etc.** Any ministerial officer of any court, or any person summoned as a juror, or appointed an auditor, arbitrator, umpire, or referee, who corruptly takes, or agrees to take any thing to give his verdict, award, or report, or corruptly receives, or agrees to receive, any gift or gratuity whatever, must, on conviction, be imprisoned in the penitentiary for not less than two, nor more than five years.

Diggs' case, 49 Ala. 311.

3918 (4122). **Bribery of officer to stock jury.**—Any person, who gives, offers, or promises to any sheriff or other officer any gift, gratuity, or thing of value, to induce him to summon a jury or juror, with the intent to produce a result favorable to either party in any cause pending in any court, must, on conviction, be imprisoned in the penitentiary for not less than two, nor more than five years.

3919 (4123). **Same; connivance of sheriff at such offense.** Any sheriff, who connives at the commission of the offense prohibited by the preceding section, by any constable, bailiff, or deputy sheriff, must, on conviction, be imprisoned in the penitentiary for not less than two, nor more than five years.

3920 (4124). **Bribery to commit offenses.** — Any person, who corruptly gives, offers, or promises any gift, gratuity, or thing of value, to another person, with intent to induce or influence such person to commit any crime or offense punishable as a felony, must, on conviction, be imprisoned in the penitentiary not less than two, nor more than ten years; and if the offense, for the commission of which such bribe is offered, be less than a felony, then the person giving, offering, or promising such bribe must, on conviction, be punished as if he had committed such offense.

ARTICLE III.

MISCONDUCT BY OFFICERS AND PERSONS CONCERNED IN THE ADMINISTRATION OF JUSTICE.

3921. Willful neglect of duty by jury commissioner or officer.—Any jury commissioner, or other officer, who willfully or negligently fails to discharge any duty required of him by law in the drawing or selecting of a juror or jury, or who draws or selects a juror or jury in any other manner or order than

Feb. 17, 1885, p. 186, sec. 9.

that prescribed by law, must, on conviction, be fined not less than fifty, nor more than one thousand dollars.

Ib. sec. 13.

3922. Corruptly influencing jury commissioner or officer. Any person, who attempts, otherwise than by bribery, to influence any jury commissioner, or any other officer charged with the execution of any duty concerning the selecting, drawing, summoning, impaneling, or organizing of jurors or juries, must, on conviction, be .fined not more than one thousand dollars, and may also be imprisoned in the county jail, or sentenced to hard labor for the county, for not more than twelve months.

3923 (4766). **Drawing jury unfairly; penalty.**—Any person, who does any act calculated to affect the fair drawing of a jury, and with intent to affect the same, must, on conviction, be fined not less than two hundred, nor more than one thousand dollars, and may also be imprisoned in the county jail for not more than six months; and if such person is the judge of probate, sheriff, or clerk of the circuit or city court, or jury commissioner, or a member of a board of revenue, or a county commissioner, his office is thereby vacated, and must be filled as in other cases of vacancy, on such conviction being certified to the appointing power by the presiding judge or the clerk of the court in which it is had.

3924 (4121). **Stocking jury.**—Any sheriff or other officer having a discretion in summoning jurors, who summons any person with intent to produce a result favorable to any party having a cause in the court in which such person is summoned, must, on conviction, be imprisoned in the penitentiary for not less than two, nor more than five years.

3925 (4123). **Same; connivance of sheriff at such offense.** Any sheriff, who connives at the commission of the offense prohibited by the preceding section, by any constable, bailiff, or deputy sheriff, must, on conviction, be imprisoned in the penitentiary for not less than two, nor more than five years.

3926 (4154). **Extortion.**—Any justice of the peace, clerk, sheriff, or other officer, who is by law authorized to receive fees for services rendered by him in his official capacity, and who knowingly takes a fee or fees for any service not actually rendered by him, or knowingly takes any greater fee or fees than are by law allowed for any services actually rendered by him, must, on conviction, be fined not less than twenty, nor more than five hundred dollars, and may also be imprisoned in the county jail, or sentenced to hard labor for the county, for not more than six months.

Collier's case, 55 Ala. 125; Cleaveland's case, 34 Ala. 254.

3927 (5022). **Probate judge corruptly receiving illegal fees.**—Any judge of probate, who corruptly receives any fee or item of costs not authorized by law, must, on conviction, be fined not less than one hundred, nor more than five hundred dollars; and the grand jury must present an indictment, if justified by the evidence. Upon such conviction, the office shall be vacated, and the fact of such conviction shall be certified to the governor by the presiding judge.

Dec. 11, 1882, p. 15, sec. 5.

3928. Failure of sheriff to keep book, etc., showing accounts for feeding prisoners, etc.—Any sheriff, who fails to enter into a book to be kept by him for that purpose any account paid him by the state for feeding prisoners, or to keep such book in his office as one of the public records thereof, or to lay the same before the grand jury at each term of the circuit or city court held in his county, or, upon the expiration of his term of office, to turn the same over to his successor, as required by law, is guilty of a misdemeanor.

3929. Failure of clerk to receipt for and pay over money collected for feeding prisoners.—Any clerk of the circuit or city court, who fails to give to the officer paying to him any money collected for feeding prisoners in jail a receipt in duplicate therefor, or to pay over to the state treasurer any such money so received by him, as required by law, is guilty of a misdemeanor. Ib. sec. 5.

3930. Sheriff receiving unlawful pay for feeding prisoners.—Any sheriff, who knowingly receives from the state for feeding a prisoner or prisoners any sum of money to which he is not lawfully entitled, must, on conviction, be punished as if he had stolen it. Feb. 22, 1881, p. 11, sec. 6; Dec. 11, 1882, p. 15, sec. 5.

3931 (4170). Dealing in county claims by county officers. Any public officer, who, directly or indirectly, by himself or through another, purchases, deals, or traffics, in any manner whatever, in any claim payable out of the county treasury, or out of the fine and forfeiture fund of the county, must, on conviction, be fined for each offense not less than ten, nor more than fifty dollars; but nothing contained in this section prevents any officer from receiving in good faith any county claim in payment of a debt due him. This section must be given in charge to the grand jury; and the solicitor is required to summon the county treasurer before the grand jury to give evidence against any one for a violation of this section.

3932 (4169). County officers interested in county contracts, or hire of county convicts.—Any judge of probate, tax-collector, tax-assessor, sheriff, clerk of the circuit court, solicitor, or county treasurer, members of the court of county commissioners or board of revenue, or any other state or county officer, who takes any contract for work or services of the county, or is employed in any way under such contract, or is interested in any contract for hire of county convicts, or sells any goods or supplies to the county, or is in anywise pecuniarily interested in any such contract or sale, as principal or agent, must, on conviction, be fined not less than fifty, nor more than one thousand dollars, and may be imprisoned in the county jail, or sentenced to hard labor for the county, for not exceeding twelve months; but nothing in this section shall apply to the sale or purchase of drugs or medicines for the use of prisoners or paupers. As amended, Dec. 2, 1880, p. 44.

3933 (4156). False certificate by officer.—Any officer authorized to take proof or acknowledgment of any conveyance of property, real or personal, who, with intent to injure or defraud, or to enable any other person to injure or defraud, willfully certifies that any such conveyance was duly proved or acknowledged, when such proof or acknowledgment was not in fact made, or was not made on the day stated in such certificate, must, on conviction, be imprisoned in the penitentiary for not less than two, nor more than ten years.

3934 (4157). **Refusal of officer to take or certify proof or acknowledgment of deed, etc.**—Any officer authorized by law to take and certify the proof or acknowledgment of any deed, conveyance, or other instrument authorized or required by law to be recorded, who refuses to receive or certify the proof or acknowledgment of any such deed, conveyance, or other instrument, or to record any deed, conveyance, or other instrument, properly proved or acknowledged and certified, which it is his duty to record (his lawful fees for any such services being first tendered to him), must, on conviction, be fined not less than fifty, nor more than one thousand dollars, and may also be imprisoned in the county jail, or sentenced to hard labor for the county, for not more than six months.

3935 (4155). **Officer contracting for, etc., profit or advantage for publication of notice.**—Any officer whose duty it is to give public notice by advertisement in any newspaper, who makes any contract or agreement, whereby any advantage, gain, or profit is to accrue to him, or who demands or receives, directly or indirectly, any consideration whatever in or about such publication, must, on conviction, be fined one hundred dollars.

Feb. 17, 1885,
p. 116, sec. 2. **3936. Failure of sheriff to pay over costs taxed for removing prisoners.**—Any sheriff, who, having collected, on execution or otherwise, from any defendant convicted for a criminal offense the fees or compensation allowed to sheriffs as mileage for themselves, guards and prisoners, on removing such defendant under the order of any court or judge upon a change of venue, or when such defendant is arrested and confined in a county other than that in which he is triable, fails for ninety days after the collection thereof to pay the same to the state treasurer, must, on conviction, be fined not less than fifty, nor more than five hundred dollars.

Feb. 7, 1879.
p. 128, sec. 26. **3937. Failure of county superintendent to make statement of money received and disbursed.**—Any county superintendent of education, who fails to make under oath, and post at the court-house of his county semi-annually, an itemized statement of all moneys received and disbursed by him during the scholastic year, and the balance then on hand, as required by law, must, on conviction, be fined not less than ten, nor more than one hundred dollars.

As amended,
Dec. 6, 1880,
p. 45. **3938** (153). **Exercising duties of office without obtaining commission.**—Any state or county officer required by law to be commissioned, who exercises any of the duties of the office to which he has been elected or appointed, without having first obtained his commission, must, on conviction, be fined not less than five, nor more than twenty dollars.

3939 (4264). **Failure of duty by county treasurer.**—Any county treasurer, who fails to discharge any duty required of him by law, is guilty of a misdemeanor.

3940 (4146). **Solicitor commencing prosecution on his own affidavit.**—Any solicitor, who commences a prosecution for any criminal offense by his own affidavit, except for an offense against his person or property, or for a violation of the revenue law, or unless the affidavit be upon his personal knowledge of the commission of the offense, must, on conviction, be fined not less than fifty dollars.

3941. (4143). **Attorney appearing without authority.** Any attorney appearing for a person without being employed must, on conviction, be fined not less than five hundred dollars, and shall be incompetent to practice in any court of this state.

3942 (4144). **Attorney practicing in court of which he is clerk or employe.**—Any person, who practices law in any court in which he is a clerk, deputy clerk, or regularly employed to perform any of the ministerial duties thereof, must, on conviction, be fined not less than one hundred dollars.

3943. **Certain ministerial officers prohibited from practicing law.**—Any sheriff, coroner, or deputy thereof, or constable, who practices law in any court of this state, must, on conviction, be fined not less than one hundred dollars.

3944. Practicing law by register in chancery, or his partner; when prohibited.—Any register in chancery, who practices law in the court of which he is register, or any partner of such register, who practices in such court, must, on conviction, be fined not less than one hundred, nor more than five hundred dollars; and this section shall be given in special charge to the grand jury. Feb. 14, 1885, p. 119.

3945 (4179). **Judges not to practice law.**—Any judge of a court of record in this state, who practices law in any of the courts of this state, or of the United States, must, on conviction, be fined in such sum as the jury may assess.

3946 (4172). **Appointment by judge of probate of guardian ad litem.**—Any judge of probate, who appoints as guardian ad litem any clerk, employe, or any person connected with his office, or any person related to him by consanguinity or marriage, must, on conviction, be fined fifty dollars.

3947 (4173). **Willful neglect of duty by probate judge.** Any judge of probate, who knowingly and willfully does any act contrary to the duties of his office, or knowingly omits or refuses to perform any duty required of him by law, must, on conviction, be fined not more than two hundred dollars, if there be no other punishment prescribed for such act or omission, and be removed from office.

3948 (4180). **Failure to take, keep and bind newspapers.** Any probate judge, clerk of the circuit court, or register in chancery, who fails to subscribe for, take, file, cause to be bound, and safely keep in his office weekly newspapers, as required by law, must, on conviction, be fined not less than fifty dollars; and one conviction shall not bar a subsequent conviction for a continuing neglect.

3949 (4158). **Refusal of public officer to permit examination of records.**—Any public officer, having charge of any book of record, who shall refuse to allow any person to examine such record free of charge, must, on conviction, be fined not less than fifty dollars.

3950 (4159). **Neglect of duty by clerk or register.**—Any clerk of any court of record, or register in chancery, who fails to perform any duty imposed on him, for the failure to perform which no other punishment is provided, must, on conviction, be fined not exceeding two hundred dollars.

Chapman's case, 73 Ala. 20.

3951 (4160). **Failing to take and file oath.**—Any officer or deputy required by law to take and file an oath of office, who enters upon the duties of his office, without first taking and filing such oath in the proper office, must, on conviction, be fined not less than two hundred dollars.

3952 (4161). **Acting officially before filing bond.**—Any public officer required by law to give bond, who performs any official act before his bond is approved and filed, as required by law, must, on conviction, be fined not less than five hundred dollars.

3953 (4162). **Failure to give notice of omission to file official bonds.**—Any officer, who omits to give the notice of failure by a public officer to file his official bond, as required by law, must, on conviction, be fined not less than one hundred dollars.

3954 (4163). **Failure to indorse date of filing official bond.** Any officer, who fails to indorse the date of the filing of an official bond, as required by law, must, on conviction, be fined not less than fifty dollars.

3955 (4164, 4165). **Failure of officer to file new or additional bond.**—Any officer giving a new or additional bond, who fails to file the same in the proper office within ten days after its approval, must, on conviction, be fined not less than five hundred dollars.

3956 (4166). **Failure to deliver property and papers of office to successor.**—Any person, who fails or refuses on demand to deliver the books, papers, property and money belonging to an office to the qualified successor in office, as required by law, must, on conviction, be fined not less than two hundred dollars.

3957 (4167). **Failure of sheriff to make deed of land.**—Any sheriff, who, having made the sale of real estate, or any interest therein, under legal process, after payment of the purchase-money and on demand of the purchaser, and payment or tender of the proper fees, fails to execute a conveyance to the purchaser, must, on conviction, be fined not less than one hundred dollars.

3958 (4167). **Failure of register in chancery or commissioner to make deed of land.**—Any register in chancery, or commissioner, who, having made sale of any real estate, or any interest therein, under any decree of the chancery or probate court, after the order of the court authorizing it, fails, on demand, to execute a conveyance to the purchaser, must, on conviction, be fined not less than one hundred dollars.

3959 (4175). **Failure to keep direct and reverse indexes.** Any probate judge, clerk of the circuit or city court, or register in chancery, who fails to keep direct and reverse indexes of all books and records in his office, as required by law to be kept, must, on conviction, be fined not more than five hundred dollars.

3960 (4176). **Failure of sheriff, clerk, or register to pay over money to successor.**—Any sheriff, clerk of the circuit or city court, or register in chancery, who, having in his hands, at the expiration of his official term, any money held by him subject to the further order of any court, on demand of his successor in office, fails to pay over to him such money, must, on conviction, be fined not less than fifty, nor more than five hundred dollars.

3961 (4148). **Judicial or ministerial officer becoming bail in certain cases.**—Any judicial, executive, or ministerial officer of any court having criminal jurisdiction, who becomes bail for any prisoner, or other person under any criminal accusation, or signs any bond or other obligation for the release or appearance of such person before himself, or before any other officer or court, must, on conviction, be fined not less than fifty, nor more than five hundred dollars, and may also be imprisoned in the county jail for not more than twelve months.

3962 (4181). **Failure of justice to keep and report docket of criminal cases.**—Any justice of the peace, or notary public having and exercising the jurisdiction of a justice of the peace, who fails to keep or report to the grand jury a docket of criminal cases, as required by law, must, on conviction, be fined not less than twenty, nor more than one hundred dollars.

3963 (4182). **Failure of justice, notary, or constable to report and pay over fines.**—Any justice of the peace, notary public having and exercising the jurisdiction of justice of the peace, or constable, who fails to report to the county treasurer, under oath, on or before the first day of each term of the circuit or city court, the amount of fines and forfeitures collected by him, or who, after deducting therefrom the amount due for fees in cases in which the defendant was acquitted, or insolvent and unable to pay after conviction, fails to pay the balance to the county treasurer, must, on conviction, be fined not less than ten, nor more than one hundred dollars.

3964 (1333). **Failure to deliver notary's register to probate judge on demand.**—Any person, who, after the death, resignation, removal, or expiration of the term of office of any notary public, having in possession the register kept by such notary public, refuses, on demand, to deliver the same to the judge of probate of the county, must, on conviction, be fined not less than one hundred dollars.

3965 (536). **Failure of certain officers to make report as to public arms.**—Any quartermaster-general, brigade-quartermaster, or adjutant-general, who fails to make any report required of him by law concerning public arms and accoutrements, must, on conviction, be fined not less than fifty dollars.

3966 (4178). **Failure of commissioners to levy tax to rebuild jail.**—If any court of county commissioners fail to levy a tax to erect or repair a county jail, when necessary, the persons composing such court are severally guilty of a misdemeanor, and must, on conviction, be fined not less than fifty dollars; but any member thereof may exonerate himself from such fine by proving that he was in favor of levying a tax sufficient for the erection or repair of the county jail, but was overruled by his colleagues.

ARTICLE IV.

BUYING, SELLING, AND ILLEGALLY ASSUMING OFFICE.

3967 (4171). **Bargaining away and bargaining for office or deputation thereof.**—Any person elected or appointed to any office, state, county, or municipal, who bargains away such office, or corruptly bargains away any deputation thereof, or any person bargaining with such officer for such office, or corruptly bargaining with him for any deputation thereof, must, on conviction, be fined not less than one hundred, nor more than one thousand dollars, and may also be imprisoned in the county jail, or sentenced to hard labor for the county, for not less than six, nor more than twelve months.

3968 (4168). **Assuming office by one ineligible.**—Any person, being disqualified by law, who, by election or appointment, enters upon any public office, must, on conviction, be fined not less than one hundred dollars.

ARTICLE V.

DISCLOSING INDICTMENT AND TESTIMONY GIVEN BEFORE GRAND JURY.

3969 (4134). **Disclosure of indictment by officer or grand juror.**—Any judge, solicitor, clerk, or other officer of court, or any grand juror, who discloses the fact that an indictment has been found, before the defendant has been arrested, or has given bail for his appearance to answer thereto, must, on conviction, be fined not less than two hundred dollars, and may also be imprisoned in the county jail, or sentenced to hard labor for the county, for not more than six months.

White's case, 44 Ala. 109.

3970 (4135). **Disclosure of testimony before grand jury by witness.**—Any person who, having been a witness before the grand jury, discloses the name of the person about whom he testified, or any of the facts to which he testified, before the arrest of the person against whom he testified, or before such person has given bail for his appearance to answer the indictment or indictments found against him, must, on conviction, be fined not less than one hundred dollars, and may also be imprisoned in the county jail, or sentenced to hard labor for the county, for not more than six months.

ARTICLE VI.

FAILURE TO EXECUTE PROCESS, OR TO RECEIVE PRISONER.

3971 (4838). **Failure to execute process.**—Any sheriff or other officer, who fails negligently to execute any lawful process which it is his duty to execute, requiring the arrest of any person charged with a public offense, must, on conviction, be fined not less than one hundred dollars.

3972 (4128). **Refusal to execute process, or receive prisoner into jail.**—Any sheriff or other officer, who willfully or corruptly refuses to execute any lawful process which it is his duty to execute, requiring the arrest of any person charged with a public offense, or willfully or corruptly omits to execute such process, or willfully or corruptly refuses to receive into any jail under his charge any offender lawfully committed thereto, and ordered to be confined therein on any criminal charge, conviction, or lawful process whatever, must, on conviction, be fined not less than five hundred, nor more than two thousand dollars.

3973 (4129). **Refusal to receive prisoner into custody.** Any jailer or other officer, who willfully refuses to receive into his custody any person lawfully committed thereto, on any criminal charge or conviction, must, on conviction, be fined not more than five hundred dollars.

Article VII.

RESISTING ARREST OR PROCESS, AND REFUSING TO AID OFFICER.

3974 (4137). **Resisting officer in execution of process.** Any person, who knowingly and willfully opposes or resists any officer of the state in serving, executing, or attempting to serve or execute any legal writ or process whatsoever, must, on conviction, be fined not less than fifty, nor more than one thousand dollars, and may also be imprisoned in the county jail, or sentenced to hard labor for the county, for not more than six months.

An officer de facto, a sufficient officer.—Heath's case, 36 Ala. 273; Cary's case, 76 Ala. 78. What constitutes a de facto officer.—Ib. 273; Ib. 78. When and what resistance allowed to a levy on articles exempt.—Johnson's case, 12 Ala. 840. When resistance a simple assault and battery.—Jones' case, 60 Ala. 99. Indictment alleging offense to be after return day of process, is defective.—McGehee's case, 26 Ala. 154. Sufficient to describe the officer resisted as a constable, or magistrate, or a justice of the peace, without alleging that he was at the time a constable or a justice of the peace.—Murphy's case, 55 Ala. 252. Alternative averments that the warrant was issued by a justice of the peace or a notary public, allowed. Murphy's case, 55 Ala. 252. Conviction of this offense bars indictment for assault. Johnson's case, 12 Ala. 840.

3975 (4138). **Refusal to aid in arrest for breach of the peace.**—Any person, who, being required by any justice or other conservator of the peace, upon view of any breach of the peace, or other offense proper for the cognizance of such officer, to apprehend or assist in apprehending the offender, and bring him before such officer, refuses or neglects to obey the command of such officer, must, on conviction, be fined not less than fifty, nor more than three hundred dollars.

3976 (4139). **Refusal to aid officer in making arrest or executing process.**—Any person, who, having been summoned or commanded by any sheriff, constable, or other officer having authority, to assist such officer in making an arrest, or in executing any other duty devolving upon him under any law in relation to public offenses, refuses or neglects to obey such summons or command, must, on conviction, be fined not less than fifty, nor more than three hundred dollars.

3977 (4140). **Resisting person aiding officer in execution of process.**—Any person, who assaults, beats, or resists a person not an officer, who is acting in obedience to the lawful summons or command of any justice, sheriff, or other officer, with a knowledge of such command or summons, must, on conviction, be punished in the same manner as if he had assaulted or resisted the officer himself.

Article VIII.

OFFENSES CONCERNING CONVICTS AND PRISONERS.

3978 (4183). **Failure to discharge duty as to defendant's performing hard labor before conviction.**—Any officer, who fails to perform any duty imposed upon him by section 4290 (4683), must, on conviction, be fined not less than fifty, nor more than five hundred dollars.

3979 (4177). **Failure of county commissioners to put convicts to hard labor.**—If any court of county commissioners fail or refuse to provide for the carrying out of the provisions of this Code in relation to hard labor for the county, and to put convicts to hard labor, as provided therein, each member of such court who fails or refuses must, on conviction, be fined not more than two hundred dollars.

Dec. 6, 1880, p. 130. **3980. Failure of certain officers to perform duty in reference to jail.**—Any judge of probate, sheriff, clerk of the circuit court, or member of the court of county commissioners, who negligently or willfully fails or refuses to perform any duty imposed upon him by law in reference to the county jail, the construction, examination, or the keeping thereof in the condition required by law, or the making of appropriations for keeping the same in the condition required by law, or any county treasurer failing to pay, in the order prescribed, any warrant of the court of county commissioners drawn for an appropriation for keeping the county jail in the condition required by law, must, on conviction, be fined not more than one hundred dollars.

Feb 22. 1883, p. 140, sec. 22. **3981. Detaining convict after expiration of his sentence.** Any person, who willfully detains, imprisons, or works any convict, state or county, after the termination of the sentence of such convict, must, on conviction, be fined not less than one hundred, nor more than one thousand dollars, and shall also be sentenced to hard labor for the county for not more than twelve months; and one-half of the fine, when paid, or when the fine is not paid, one-half of the amount received from such hard labor, shall go to the convict so illegally detained or imprisoned.

Feb. 17. 1885, p. 198. sec. 25. **3982. Witness refusing to appear or testify concerning treatment of convicts.**—Any person, who fails to obey the summons of any inspector of convicts to appear and testify as a witness, or who appears as a witness and refuses to testify as to any matter concerning the management and treatment of convicts, must, on conviction, be fined not more than one hundred dollars.

3983 (4490). **Failure to deliver jail, etc., to successor.**—Any person in charge of the jail, or having in his possession any paper, or other thing thereto belonging, on the death, resignation, removal from office, or expiration of the term of office, of any sheriff, or of any coroner acting as sheriff, who fails on demand to deliver the same to his successor, or other person authorized by law to take charge thereof, must, on conviction, be fined not less than three hundred dollars.

Ib. sec. 28. **3984. Failure of duty, or violation of law regulating convicts by guard, etc.**—Any inspector, guard, or hirer of convicts, state or county, or any other person having the charge, management, or control of any such convict, who fails to discharge any of the duties imposed upon him by law, or in any other way violates any of the provisions of law regulating or governing the hiring, inspection, treatment, confinement, working, or guarding, or the charge, management, or control of convicts, state or county, when no other punishment is provided for such failure in duty, or violation of law, must, on conviction, be fined not more than one thousand dollars, and may also be imprisoned in the county jail, or sentenced to hard labor for the county, for not more than twelve months.

3985. Sheriff, deputy, or jailer, permitting lynching of prisoner. — Any sheriff, deputy sheriff, or jailer, who negligently, or through cowardice, allows a prisoner to be taken from the jail of his county, or to be taken from his custody and put to death by violence, or to receive bodily harm, must, on conviction, be fined not less than five hundred, nor more than two thousand dollars, and may also be sentenced to hard labor for the county for not more than two years.

Feb. 17, 1885, p. 186.

3986. Convict discharged when term expires; furnished with clothes, etc.—Any person, having in his possession or under his control any state convict, who refuses or fails to discharge such convict at the expiration of his term of penal servitude, or who, upon so discharging such convict, fails to furnish him with transportation to the county-seat where such convict was sentenced, or its equivalent in money, or to furnish such convict with one good suit of clothes, must, on conviction, be fined not more than one thousand dollars, and may also be imprisoned in the county jail, or sentenced to hard labor for the county, for not more than twelve months. *

Feb. 22, 1883, p. 159, secs. 17, 22.

3987 (4583). **Permitting convicts to be furnished with intoxicating liquors.**—Any officer or other person, having the management or control of convicts, who permits any intoxicating liquors to be furnished to any convict, except on the written prescription of a physician, forfeits all wages due him, and must, on conviction, be fined not less than one hundred dollars.

3988 (4494). **Permitting prisoner to receive spirituous or vinous liquors.**—Any jailer, who gives, or knowingly suffers any prisoner to receive any spirituous or vinous liquors on any pretext whatever, except on the written order of a physician, stating that such liquor is necessary for his health, must, on conviction, be fined not less than one hundred dollars.

3989 (4606). **Violation of duty concerning convict in solitary confinement, or allowing conversation with him.**—Any officer or person employed in the penitentiary, who suffers any convict under sentence of solitary confinement to be at large, out of the cell assigned him, unless directed by the physician to remove him to the hospital on account of sickness, or allows any convict to be conversed with contrary to the regulations of the penitentiary, must, on conviction, be fined not less than one hundred, nor more than five hundred dollars.

---

* See act entitled "An act to amend section 17 of an act to regulate the hiring and treatment of state and county convicts; approved February 22, 1883," approved February 28, 1887.—Pamph. Acts 1886-7, p. 90.

ARTICLE IX.

ESCAPES.

3990 (4125). **Voluntary escape by officer.**—Any sheriff, or other officer or person, who has the legal custody of any person charged with, or convicted of an indictable offense, and who voluntarily permits or suffers such person to escape, must, on conviction, be imprisoned in the penitentiary not less than two, nor more than twenty years.

Kavanaugh's case, 41 Ala. 399.

3991 (4603). **Voluntary escape by officer of penitentiary.** Any officer or other person employed in the penitentiary, or who has charge of a convict, who voluntarily suffers any convict imprisoned therein to escape, must, on conviction, be imprisoned in the penitentiary for a period equal to the unexpired term of such convict, but in no case less than two years.

3992. Concealing, harboring, or aiding escaped convict. Any person, who knowingly conceals, harbors, or in any way aids or assists any escaped convict, whether such escaped convict be under sentence to the penitentiary, or to hard labor for the county, must, on conviction, be imprisoned in the penitentiary for not less than one, nor more than five years.

3993 (4126). **Negligent escape.**—Any officer or person, who has the legal custody of any person charged with, or convicted of an indictable offense, and who through negligence suffers such person to escape, must, on conviction, be fined not less than two hundred, nor more than one thousand dollars.

Nall's case, 34 Ala. 262; Kavanaugh's case, 41 Ala. 399; Smith's case, 76 Ala. 69.

3994 (4127). **Same; by hiring convicts contrary to law.** Any officer charged with the duty of hiring convicts, who knowingly hires a convict to any person related to such convict by consanguinity or affinity within the fifth degree, or hostile to such convict, or of inhuman disposition, must, on conviction, be fined not less than two hundred, nor more than one thousand dollars.

Feb. 22, 1883, p. 141, sec. 28. **3995. Same; by hirer permitting convict to go at large, or insufficiently guarded.**—Any hirer of state or county convicts, who suffers or permits any convict under his control to go at large at any time during the term for which such convict was sentenced, or who fails to keep such convict safely confined, or attened by a sufficient guard, must, on conviction, be fined not less than two hundred, nor more than one thousand dollars.

3996 (4133). **Escape of convict from jail or hard labor.** Any convict sentenced to imprisonment in the county jail, or to hard labor for the county, who escapes from such confinement, or departs or runs away from such labor before the expiration of the time for which he was sentenced, must, on conviction, be sentenced to the same punishment for not more than six months.

3997 (4498, 4502). **Escape of prisoner on removal from jail, or from one county to another.** — Any sheriff, jailer, guard, or other person, who, having charge of any prisoner while being removed from any jail on fire, or endangered by the burning of any other building, or on account of his life or health being seriously endangered by longer confinement therein, or while being removed from the jail of one county to that of another, negligently or voluntarily suffers such prisoner to escape, is guilty of an escape, as if such person had escaped from jail, and, on conviction, must be punished accordingly.

3998 (4600). **Escapes and attempts to escape from penitentiary, hirer, or guard.**—Any convict, who escapes, or attempts to escape, from the penitentiary, or from any person to whom he may be hired, or from any person or guard having him in charge under authority of law, either within or outside the walls of the penitentiary, before the expiration of the term for which he was sentenced, must, on conviction, be imprisoned for an additional term of not more than one year.

As amended, Feb. 17, 1835, p. 187.

3999 (4604). **Escapes by United States prisoners from penitentiary.**—If any convict, committed by any court of the United States, escapes, or attempts to escape, out of the penitentiary, he is subject, on conviction, to the same punishment as if he had been committed by virtue of a conviction under the laws of this state; and the officer having charge of such convict is liable to the same penalties and punishment for any neglect or violation of duty in respect to the custody of such convict, as if he had been committed under a conviction, and sentenced under the laws of this state.

4000 (4570). **Escapes or attempts to escape by convict while being conveyed to penitentiary.**—All statutory provisions in regard to escapes and attempts to escape from the penitentiary by convicts are applicable to escapes and attempts to escape by them while being conveyed to the penitentiary.

4001. Escapes not otherwise provided for.—Any prisoner, who escapes from lawful custody, or any officer, or other person, who aids in such escape, if there is no other punishment prescribed by law, must, on conviction, be fined not more than one thousand dollars, and may also be imprisoned in the county jail, or sentenced to hard labor for the county, for not more than six months.

4002 (4130, 4602). **Aiding convicts to escape from place of confinement; rescue.**—Any person, who conveys into the county jail, or into the penitentiary, or into any convict prison, or into any other lawful place of confinement, any disguise, weapon, tool, instrument, or other thing useful to aid any prisoner to escape therefrom, with the intent to facilitate the escape of any prisoner lawfully confined therein under a charge or conviction of felony, or who, by any other act, or in any other way, aids or assists such prisoner to escape, whether such escape be attempted or effected or not, or who rescues, or attempts to rescue, any such prisoner therefrom, or from the lawful custody of any officer or person, must, on conviction, be imprisoned in the penitentiary for not less than two, nor more than ten years.

Two persons aiding each other, by trying to burn a hole and escape, each guilty in assisting the other.—Luke's case, 49 Ala. 30.   This section creates a new and different offense from common-law offense of aiding felon to escape; section construed.—Wilson's case, 61 Ala. 151.   What the indictment must allege —Kyle's case, 10 Ala. 236; Ramsey's case, 43 Ala. 404; Wilson's case, 61 Ala. 151.   Indictment best evidence of cause of imprisonment.—Luke's case, 49 Ala. 30

4003 (4131). **Aiding other prisoner to escape.**—Any person, who, by any of the means specified in the last preceding section, or by any other act, or in any other manner whatsoever, intentionally assists, or attempts to assist, any prisoner to escape from any county jail, or other lawful place of confinement, in which he is lawfully confined under a charge or conviction of misdemeanor, whether such escape be attempted or effected or not, or who rescues, or attempts to rescue, any such prisoner therefrom, or from the lawful custody of any officer or person, must, on conviction, be fined not more than one thousand dollars, and may also be imprisoned in the county jail, or sentenced to hard labor for the county, for not more than twelve months.

4004 (4132). **Aiding prisoner to escape from custody of officer.**—Any person, who does any act with intent to assist any prisoner in escaping, or attempting to escape, from the custody of any officer or person having the lawful charge of him, upon any criminal charge or conviction, must, on conviction, be punished as if he had assisted such prisoner to escape, or attempt to escape, from the county jail.

4005 (4150, 4151). **When concealing felon makes one an accessory after the fact.**—Any person, who, knowing that another has committed a felony, and not occupying the legitimate relation of parent, child, brother, sister, husband, or wife to such offender, conceals, or gives any other aid to such offender, with intent to enable him to avoid or escape from arrest, trial, conviction, or punishment, is an accessory after the fact, and, on conviction, must be fined not more than one thousand dollars, and may also be imprisoned in the county jail, or sentenced to hard labor for the county, for not more than six months; and if the principal felon is dead, or has fled from justice, such accessory may be prosecuted and convicted before the principal; but in such case it shall be necessary to allege in the indictment, and to prove on the trial, the fact that the principal felon is dead or has fled.

ARTICLE X.

COMPOUNDING FELONY.

4006 (4149). **Compounding felony.**—Any person, who, having knowledge of the commission of a felony, takes, receives, or agrees to take or receive from another, any money, property, or other thing of value, to compound or conceal such felony, or to abstain from any prosecution therefor, must, on conviction, be fined not more than one thousand dollars, and may also be imprisoned in the county jail, or sentenced to hard labor for the county, for not more than twelve months. A prosecution and conviction may be had under this section, although the person guilty of the original offense has not been tried.

ARTICLE XI.

CONSPIRACY.

4007 (4152). **Conspiracy to commit felony.**—Any two or more persons, conspiring together to commit a felony, must each, on conviction, be fined not more than one thousand dollars, and may also be imprisoned in the county jail, or sentenced to hard labor for the county, for not more than six months.

See note to succeeding section.

4008 (4153). **Conspiracy to commit misdemeanor.**—Any two or more persons, conspiring together to commit a misdemeanor must each, on conviction, be fined not more than five hundred dollars, and may also be imprisoned in the county jail, or sentenced to hard labor for the county, for not more than three months.

Conspiracy defined.—Murphy's case, 6 Ala. 765. Unlawful agreement is gist of offense, though nothing be done.—Cawood's case, 2 Stew. 360.   To seduce a virtuous female.—Murphy's case, 6 Ala. 765.   Agreement between a man and woman to commit adultery is not a conspiracy.—Miles' case, 58 Ala. 390. To commit misdemeanor is not merged into the offense, but indictment may be framed to convict of either.—Murphy's case, 6 Ala. 765.   May be proved circumstantially without positive agreement or meeting of conspirators.—Johnson's case, 29 Ala. 62; Scott's case, 30 Ala. 503; Marler's case, 67 Ala. 66. Established by testimony of accomplice, if his statement connecting defendant with the offense is corroborated. Marler's case, 67 Ala. 66. What said and done by one in presence of others, while committing the offense, admissible against all.—Smith's case, 52 Ala. 407. Motion in arrest of judgment allowable to one or more, in absence of others.—Covington's case, 4 Ala. 603.

ARTICLE XII.

FALSELY PERSONATING ANOTHER IN ANY LEGAL PROCEEDING.

4009 (4147). **Falsely personating another in any suit, etc.** Any person, who falsely personates another, and, in such assumed character, becomes bail or surety for any party in any proceeding, civil or criminal, before any court, magistrate, or officer authorized to take such bail, or confesses any judgment, acknowledges the execution of any conveyance, or does any act in the course of any suit, prosecution, or proceeding, whereby the person so personated may be made liable for the payment of any debt, damages, costs, or sum of money, or his rights or interest be in any way affected, must, on conviction, be punished by imprisonment in the penitentiary for not less than two, nor more than five years.

ARTICLE XIII.

PROSECUTING SUIT WITHOUT AUTHORITY.

4010 (4142). **Prosecuting suit in name of another without authority.**—Any person, who, without lawful authority, prosecutes a suit in the name of another person, in any court of this state, must, on conviction, be fined not less than one hundred dollars.

ARTICLE XIV.

SUING OUT SEARCH WARRANT ILLEGALLY.

4011 (4141). **Suing out search warrant maliciously and without probable cause.**—Any person, who maliciously, and without probable cause, procures a search warrant to be issued and executed, must, on conviction, be fined not less than twenty, nor more than five hundred dollars, and may also be imprisoned in the county jail, or sentenced to hard labor for the county, for not more than six months.

CHAPTER 7.

OFFENSES AGAINST PUBLIC MORALITY AND DECENCY.

ARTICLE 1.—Adultery and fornication.

2.—Incest.

3.—Seduction.

4.—Bigamy.

5.—Miscegenation.

6.—Crime against nature.

7.—Abortion.

8.—Offenses concerning dead bodies and graves.

9.—Obscene prints and literature.

10.—Abusive and obscene language.

11.—Disturbing females, religious worship, public and school assemblies.

12.—Public drunkenness.

13.—Disposing of liquor illegally, and violating prohibitory laws.

14.—Sunday laws.

15.—Vagrants and tramps.

16.—Gaming and lotteries.

ARTICLE I.

ADULTERY AND FORNICATION.

4012 (4184). **Living in adultery or fornication.**—If any man and woman live together in adultery or fornication, each of them must, on the first conviction of the offense, be fined not less than one hundred dollars, and may also be imprisoned in the county jail, or sentenced to hard labor for the county, for not more than six months; on the second conviction for the offense, with the same person, the offender must be fined not less than three hundred dollars, and may be imprisoned in the county jail, or sentenced to hard labor for the county, for not more than twelve months; and, on a third, or any subsequent conviction, with the same person, must be imprisoned in the penitentiary for two years.

Adultery is illicit connection where either is married, and includes **fornication.** Hinton's case, 6 Ala. 864; White's case, 74 Ala. 31.   Must be a **living together**; one act, or occasional acts, not sufficient; what constitutes living together.—Hall's case, 53 Ala. 463; Smith's case, 39 Ala. 554; Collins' case, 14 Ala. 608; Quartemas' case, 48 Ala. 269.   The question of living together is for the jury.—Hall's ca e, 53 Ala. 463.   **Marriage** of one of the parties is essential to **adultery; fornication,** if neither is married, or in the unmarried party.—Buchanan's case, 55 Ala. 154. Indictment charging adultery implies marriage without further alleging that either was married.—Hinton's case, 6 Ala. 864. Need not allege sex of the parties.—McLeod's case, 35 Ala. 395. Nor a continuendo.—Glaze's case, 9 Ala. 283. But must allege that they lived together, or with each other.—Maull's case, 37 Ala. 160. The averment "did live together in fornication," sufficient.—Lawson's case, 20 Ala. 65. **Evidence** of declarations and conduct, cohabitation and confessions of the parties, but not of general reputation, admissible to prove marriage.—Buchanan's case, 55 Ala. 154; Green's case, 59 Ala. 68; Cameron's case, 14 Ala. 546. Admissibility of evidence of anterior acts.—Lawson's case, 20 Ala. 65; McLeod's case, 35 Ala. 395; Alsabrook's case, 52 Ala. 24. Admissibility of evidence of subsequent acts.—Smitherman's case, 40 Ala. 255; Crowley's case, 13 Ala. 172; Alsabrook's case, 52 Ala. 24; Lawson's case, 20 Ala. 65. Proof of defendants' sex. White's case, 74 Ala. 31. Proof of woman's general reputation for want of chastity; when admissible.—Blackman's case, 36 Ala. 295. When burden of proving death of absent husband, on woman claiming such defense.—Cameron's case, 14 Ala. 546. Confessions and admissions by either party, admissible only against party making them.—Lawson's case. 20 Ala. 65. Unless made in presence of the other.—Gore's case, 58 Ala. 391. Declarations, unconnected with conversations or admissions offered by the state, inadmissible.—Lawson's case, 20 Ala. 65. Conversations during child-birth, in presence of female, in which she took no part, inadmissible against her.—Ib. Direct fact of adultery need not be proved; presumptive or circumstantial evidence sufficient.—Ib.; Collins' case, 14 Ala. 405. See, also, Glaze's case, 9 Ala. 283; Crowley's case, 13 Ala. 172. One party competent witness for the other, to be weighed by the jury.—Crowley's case, 13 Ala. 172. Husband cannot testify against wife, or her paramour, for this offense.—Cotton's case, 62 Ala. 12. If proof shows both parties unmarried, **conviction** cannot be had under indictment charging adultery only.—Smitherman's case, 27 Ala. 23. Misnomer as to one, if known by name charged, will not entitle other to acquittal.—Glaze's case, 9 Ala. 283. Conviction for this offense allowed under indictment charging miscegenation. Bryant's case, 76 Ala. 33.

ARTICLE II.

INCEST.

4013 (4187). **By intermarriage or sexual intercourse.**—If any man and woman, being within the degrees of consangunity or relationship within which marriages are declared by law to be incestuous and void, and knowing of such consanguinty or relationship, intermarry, or have sexual intercourse together, or live together in adultery, each of them must, on conviction, be imprisoned in the penitentiary, for not less than one, nor more than seven years.

Morgan's case, 11 Ala. 289; Baker's case, 30 Ala. 521.

4014 (2673). **On conviction, the marriage annulled.**—On conviction for incest for marrying within the prohibited degrees, the court must declare such marriage null and void, and may require the parties to enter into a recognizance, with sufficient sureties, that they will not thereafter cohabit.

ARTICLE III.

SEDUCTION.

4015 (4188). **Seduction.**—Any man, who, by means of temptation, deception, arts, flattery, or a promise of marriage, seduces any unmarried woman in this state, must, on conviction, be imprisoned in the penitentiary for not less than one, nor more than ten years; but no indictment or conviction shall be had under this section on the uncorroborated testimony of the woman upon whom the seduction is charged; and no conviction shall be had,

As amended, Feb. 25, 1881, p. 48.

if on the trial it is proved that such woman was, at the time of alleged offense, unchaste.

Import of word seduce.—Wilson's case, 73 Ala. 527. A fallen woman *reformed*, may be subject of seduction.—Ib. Chastity an element of the offense, but is presumed, if there is no evidence to the contrary.—Ib. Birth of child as evidence of sexual intercourse.—Cunningham's case, 73 Ala. 51. Sufficiency of corroboration of prosecutrix.—Ib.; Wilson's case, 73 Ala. 527. Prosecutrix cannot testify to motive prompting her to sexual intercourse.—Ib. 527. Proposition by defendant to adjust compromise is not admissible in evidence against him.—Ib. Indictment sufficient.—Ib.

ARTICLE IV.

BIGAMY.

4016 (4185). **Bigamy, and bigamous cohabitation; punishment of.**—If any person, having a former wife or husband living, marries another, or continues to cohabit with such second husband or wife in this state, he or she must, on conviction, be imprisoned in the penitentiary for not less than two, nor more than five years.

Two distinct offenses created by the statute.—Brewer's case, 59 Ala. 101; Beggs' case, 55 Ala. 108. **Bigamy** is committed by illegal second marriage without cohabitation, and is **indictable** only in county of second marriage.--Brewer's case, 59 Ala. 101; Beggs' case, 55 Ala. 108; Williams' case, 44 Ala. 24. While **subsequent cohabitation** is indictable in any county where committed.—Beggs' case, 55 Ala. 108; Brewer's case, 59 Ala. 101. But **conviction of bigamy** is not allowed on proof of subsequent cohabitation only, when second marriage took place in another county or state.—Beggs' case, 55 Ala. 108. **What person guilty of bigamy.**—Jones' case, 67 Ala. 84. **Acquittal of bigamy** no bar to indictment for subsequent cohabitation. Brewer's case, 59 Ala. 101. Intent; what necessary.—Dotson's case, 62 Ala. 141. **Marriage by infant** under age of consent being voidable only, is a marriage in fact until disaffirmed.—Beggs' case, 55 Ala. 108; Cooley's case, Ib. 162. **Marriage under duress or fear** may be void, but not if fear he of prosecution for bastardy.—Williams' case, 44 Ala. 24. Oral **proof of marriage** admissible.—Brewer's case, 59 Ala. 101. Unsworn bill for divorce inadmissible.—Cooley's case, 55 Ala. 162. Certified transcript of marriage license, with certificate of solemnization of marriage, admissible without official seal.—Beggs' case, 55 Ala. 108. First marriage proved by cohabitation and confession without the record or a witness to it.—Langtry's case, 30 Ala. 536; Williams' case 54 Ala. 131. But see Brown's case, 52 Ala. 338. But such proof cannot make a void marriage valid.—Williams' case, 44 Ala. 24. Proof of marriage in another state by confession made there or here.—Williams' case, 54 Ala. 131. **First and lawful wife incompetent witness** against the husband.—Williams' case, 44 Ala. 24. Rumor or belief that former husband or wife is dead, no **defense.**—Jones' case, 67 Ala. 84.

4017 (4186). **Same; exceptions.**—The provisions of the preceding section do not apply to any person who, prior to such second marriage, had procured a decree from a court of competent jurisdiction, dissolving his or her former marriage, and allowing him or her the privilege of marrying again; nor to any person who, at the time of such second marriage, did not know that his or her former husband or wife was living, and whose former husband or wife had remained absent from him or her for the last five years preceding such second marriage.

ARTICLE V.

MISCEGENATION.

4018 (4189). **Marriage, adultery and fornication between white persons and negroes.**—If any white person and any negro, or the descendant of any negro, to the third generation, inclusive, though one ancestor of each generation was a white person, intermarry, or live in adultery or fornication with each other, each of them must, on conviction, be imprisoned in the penitentiary for not less than two, nor more than seven years.

Constitutionality of this section discussed.—Ellis' case, 42 Ala. 525; Burns' case, 48 Ala. 195; Ford's case, 53 Ala. 151; Pace's case, 69 Ala. 231; Green's case, 58 Ala. 190 (overruling Burns' case, 48 Ala. 195). Held not violative of fourteenth amendment to constitution of United States.—Pace's case, 69 Ala. 231. Power of state over marriage.—Green's case, 58 Ala. 190. Marriage between white and negro absolutely void.—Hoover's case, 59 Ala. 57. Sufficient indictment in Pace's case, 69 Ala. 231. Evidence that probate judge told parties they could lawfully marry, inadmissible.—Hoover's case, 59 Ala. 57. On failure to prove averments of race, etc., verdict may be for misdemeanor, which would bar subsequent prosecution for felony.—Bryant's case, 76 Ala. 33.

4019 (4190). **Officer issuing license or performing marriage ceremony.**—Any probate judge, who issues a license for the marriage of any persons who are prohibited by the preceding section from intermarrying, knowing that they are within the provisions of that section; and any justice of the peace, minister of the gospel, or other person by law authorized to solemnize the rites of matrimony, who performs a marriage ceremony for such persons, knowing that they are within the provisions of such section, must each, on conviction, be fined not less than one hundred, nor more than one thousand dollars, and may also be imprisoned in the county jail, or sentenced to hard labor for the county, for not more than six months.

ARTICLE VI.

CRIME AGAINST NATURE.

4020 (4191). **Punishment of crime against nature.**—Any person, who commits a crime against nature, either with mankind or with any beast, must, on conviction, be imprisoned in the penitentiary for not less than two, nor more than ten years.

4021 (4896). **Proof of crime against nature.**—To sustain an indictment for crime against nature, proof of emission is unnecessary.

ARTICLE VII.

ABORTION.

4022 (4192). **Attempts to procure abortion.**—Any person, who willfully administers to any pregnant woman any drug or substance, or uses or employs any instrument, or other means, to procure her miscarriage, unless the same is necessary to preserve her life, and done for that purpose, must, on conviction, be fined not more than five hundred dollars, and may also be imprisoned in the county jail, or sentenced to hard labor for the county, for not less than three, nor more than twelve months.

ARTICLE VIII.

OFFENSES CONCERNING DEAD BODIES AND GRAVES.

4023 (4193). **Removing dead body from grave.**—Any person, who, from wantonness, or for the purpose of dissection or sale, removes the dead body of any human being from its place of interment, must, on conviction, be fined not less- than one hundred, nor more than five hundred dollars, and may also be imprisoned in the county jail, or sentenced to hard labor for the county, for not more than six months.

4024 (4194). **Same; exception as to physicians and surgeons.**—Licensed physicians and surgeons, to whom the bodies of criminals executed for capital offenses are delivered pursuant to law, or to whom the bodies of other persons are delivered by or with the consent of their relatives, are not within the provisions of the preceding section.

4025 (4195). **Buying such dead bodies.**—Any person, who purchases or receives from another the dead body of any human being, knowing that it was disinterred contrary to law, must, on conviction, be fined not less than one hundred, nor more than five hundred dollars.

As amended, Feb. 12, 1879, p. 71.

4026 (4196). **Violating grave with intent to steal or remove dead body, etc.**—Any person, who opens any place of interment, with intent to remove the dead body of any human being for the purpose of selling or dissecting it, or with intent to steal the coffin, or any part thereof, or the vestments, or any other article interred with the body, or for the purpose of obtaining money or any thing of value from the relations or friends of the deceased for the return of the body, or for malice, revenge, or ill-will towards the deceased, or his or her friends, must, on conviction, be imprisoned in the penitentiary for not less than one, nor more than·five years.

4027 (4197). **Mutilating dead bodies.**—Any person, who wantonly mutilates the dead body of any human being, must, on conviction, be fined not more than five hundred dollars, and may also be imprisoned in the county jail, or sentenced to hard labor for the county, for not more than one year; but the provisions of this section do not apply to dissections by physicians and surgeons.

4028 (4198). **Defacing tomb-stone, trees, shrubbery, etc.** Any person, who willfully or maliciously injures, defaces, removes, or destroys any tomb, monument, grave-stone, or other memorial of the dead, or any fence or inclosure about any tomb, monument, grave-stone, or memorial, or who willfully destroys, removes, cuts, breaks, or injures any tree, shrub, or plant, within such inclosure, must, on conviction, be fined not less than one hundred, nor more than five hundred dollars, and may also be imprisoned in the county jail, or sentenced to hard labor for the county, for not more than one year.

ARTICLE IX.

OBSCENE PRINTS AND LITERATURE.

4029 (4201). **Posting or leaving obscene picture, writing, or printing.**—Any person, who willfully posts up or leaves any obscene or vulgar picture, placard, writing, or printed matter about or near to any church, dwelling, school, academy, or a public highway, must, on conviction, be fined not less than ten, nor more than fifty dollars.

4030. Introducing, advertising, or selling obscene litera- Dec. 3, 1884, **ture.**—Any person, who brings, or causes to be brought, into p. 74. this state for sale, or advertises, or prints, or sells, or offers to sell, or receives subscription for any indecent or obscene book, pamphlet, print, picture, or paper, must, on conviction, be fined not less than fifty, nor more than one thousand dollars.

ARTICLE X.

ABUSIVE AND OBSCENE LANGUAGE.

4031 (4203.) **Using obscene or insulting language in pres-** As amended, **ence of females, etc.**—Any person, who enters into, or goes p. 30. sufficiently near to the dwelling-house of another, and, in the presence or hearing of the family of the occupant thereof, or any member of his family, or any person, who, in the presence or hearing of any female, uses abusive, insulting, or obscene language, must, on conviction, be fined not more than two hundred dollars, and may also be imprisoned in the county jail, or sentenced to hard labor for the county, for not more than six months.

Constituents of the offense.—Benson's case, 68 Ala. 513. As to this offense before the present section, see Henderson's case, 63 Ala. 193; Ivey's case, 61 Ala. 58; Comer's case, 62 Ala. 320. Sufficiently near to be heard, regarded as in the presence.—Henderson's case, 63 Ala. 193. The words, "If you don't give up my pistol I'll knock your brains out, by God," held sufficiently insulting.—Benson's case, 68 Ala. 513. Meaning of dwelling-house, whether house of wife or husband. Bragg's case, 69 Ala. 204. Indictment need not set out the words used.—Yancy's case, 63 Ala. 141. Nor is it necessary to prove that the words were actually heard by the females.—Ib. And if the words are alleged, need not prove same words, but sufficient if there is no variance in the sense.—Benson's case, 68 Ala. 544. Offense cannot be committed jointly, unless one person incites other to use the language.—Cox's case, 76 Ala. 66. But an acquittal of one would, on reversal, authorize a nol. pros. against him and trial of the other.—Ib. Witness may testify he was near enough to hear. but did not hear the language imputed to defendant.—Ib.

ARTICLE XI.

DISTURBING FEMALES, RELIGIOUS WORSHIP, PUBLIC AND SCHOOL ASSEMBLIES.

4032 (4200). **Disturbing women at public assembly, etc.** Any person, who, by rude or indecent behavior, or by profane or obscene language, willfully disturbs any woman at a public assembly, met for instruction or recreation, or in a railroad car, steamboat, or in any other public conveyance, or at a depot, landing, or other place frequented by the traveling public, must, on conviction, be fined not more than two hundred dollars, and may also be imprisoned in the county jail, or sentenced to hard labor for the county, for not more than six months.

Smith's case, 63 Ala. 55.

4033 (4199). **Disturbing religious worship.**—Any person, who willfully interrupts or disturbs any assemblage of people met for religious worship, by noise, profane discourse, rude or indecent behavior, or any other act, at or near the place of worship, must, on conviction, be fined not less than twenty, nor more than two hundred dollars, and may also be imprisoned in the county jail, or sentenced to hard labor for the county, for not more than six months.

Act causing disturbance must be willful or intentional; not sufficient if done recklessly or carelessly.—Harrison's case, 37 Ala. 154; Brown's case, 46 Ala. 175;

Lancaster's case, 53 Ala. 398.   Natural tendency of act must be to disturb some, if only one, of the worshipers.—Lancaster's case, 53 Ala. 398.   Sufficient if disturbance made while people assembling or dispersing.—Kinney's case, 38 Ala. 224; Lancaster's case, supra.   Evidence of previous bad character as disturber of public worship not admissible by state, except in rebuttal of good character.—Harrison's case, 37 Ala. 154; Brown's case, 46 Ala 175.   Evidence that others disturbed congregation, without objection by the members, inadmissible.—Harrison's case, supra.   Permission to speak no excuse for violent and insulting discourse, though not called to order.—Lancaster's case, 53 Ala. 398.

Feb. 17, 1879,
p. 144, sec. 82.

4034. Disturbing people met for school purposes or holiday.—Any person, who willfully disturbs any school, or other assembly of people, met for school purposes, or for amusement or recreation on a holiday for a school, must, on conviction, be fined not less than five, nor more than fifty dollars.

ARTICLE XII.

PUBLIC DRUNKENNESS.

Feb. 17, 1885,
p. 142.

1 02, '8.9,

4035. Appearing in public or at private residence while drunk or intoxicated.—Any person, who, while intoxicated or drunk, appears in any public place where one or more persons are present, or at or within the curtilage of any private residence, not his own, where one or more persons are present, and manifests a drunken condition by boisterous or indecent conduct, or rude and profane discourse, must, on conviction, be fined not more than one hundred dollars.

ARTICLE XIII.

DISPOSING OF LIQUOR ILLEGALLY, AND VIOLATING PROHIBITORY LAWS.

As amended,
Dec. 3, 1878,
p. 71.

4036 (4204). **Retailing or selling vinous or spirituous liquors without license.** — Any person, who, without license as a retailer, sells spirituous, vinous, or malt liquors, in any quantity less than one quart, or in any quantity, if the same, or any portion thereof, is drunk on or about his premises, must, on conviction, be fined not less than fifty, nor more than five hundred dollars, and may also be imprisoned in the county jail, or sentenced to hard labor for the county, for not more than six months.

The court will take judicial notice that lager beer is malt liquor.—Adler's case, 55 Ala. 16; Watson's case, Ib. 158.   Statute construed.—Ulmer's case, 61 Ala. 208. This offense is distinguished from engaging in or carrying on business; is not a revenue, but a penal law, and hence not repealed by a revenue law.—Campbell's case, 46 Ala. 116; Lillensteine's case, Ib. 498; McPherson's case, 54 Ala. 221; Sanders' case, 58 Ala. 371.   It is mere police regulation.—McPherson's case, 54 Ala. 221.   One act of sale sufficient, of which prosecutor must elect.—Martin's case, 59 Ala. 34; McPherson's case, 54 Ala. 221; Sanders' case 58 Ala. 371; Lawson's case, 55 Ala. 118.   What is and what is not an election by prosecutor.—Elam's case, 26 Ala. 48; Hughes' case, 35 Ala. 351; Seibert's case, 40 Ala. 60.   License to keep a tavern does not confer the right.—Page's case, 11 Ala. 849.   License to one partner confers no authority on firm or copartners, although a license may be granted to a partnership.—Long's case, 27 Ala. 32.   Mere removal to another county does not abrogate license, or make clerk indictable for continuing business.—Thompson's case, 37 Ala. 151.   Agent of unlicensed corporation indictable.—Martin's case, 59 Ala. 34.   Conviction of husband for sale by wife in his presence.—Hensly's case, 52 Ala. 10.   Statute contains no exception of sale for medicinal purposes.—Thomason's case, 70 Ala. 20.   When drinking must be " on or about the premises."—Hafter's case, 51 Ala. 37.   See Ulmer's case, 61 Ala. 208.   "What constitutes on or about the premises."—Swan's case, 12 Ala 594; Downman's case, 14 Ala. 242; Easterling's case, 30 Ala. 46; Brown's case, 31 Ala, 353; Pearce's case, 40 Ala 720; Christian's case, Ib. 376 ; Patterson's case, 36 Ala. 297. A sale from jug in a field one mile from house, sufficient.—Powell's case, 63 Ala. 177 ; Pearce's case, 40 Ala. 720. The fact "on or about the premises," sometimes a question for the jury, and sometimes for the court.—Brown's case, 31 Ala. 353 ; Easterling's case, 30 Ala. 46 ; Daly's case, 33 Ala. 431.

4037 (4806). **Forms of indictment for retailing, and violating special prohibitory laws; proof of retailing.**—In an indictment for retailing spirituous, vinous, or malt liquors without license, it is sufficient to charge that the defendant sold spirituous, vinous, or malt liquors without a license, and contrary to law ; and on the trial, any act of retailing in violation of the law may be proved ; and for any violation of any special and local laws regulating or prohibiting the sale of spirituous, vinous, or malt liquors within the place specified, such form shall be held good and sufficient.

Indictment for retailing, etc., in form prescribed by the Code, is sufficient. Bryan's case, 45 Ala. 86 ; Sills' case, 76 Ala. 92 ; McCreary's case, 73 Ala. 480. When defective.—Raisler's case, 55 Ala. 64. Indictment charging that defendant " did sell vinous or spirituous liquors without a license and contrary to law," sufficient for offense of violating local prohibitory laws.—Powell's case, 69 Ala. 10 ; Boon's case, Ib. 226 ; McCreary's case, 73 Ala. 480.

4038 (4205). **Liquor to minor or person of intemperate habits; false statement as to age.**—Any person, who sells or gives spirituous, vinous, or malt liquors to a minor, without the consent of the parent or guardian, or person having the management or control of such minor, unless it be upon the prescription of a physician ; or who sells or gives spirituous, vinous, or malt liquors to a person of known intemperate habits, unless it be upon the prescription of a physician, must, on conviction, be fined not less than fifty, nor more than five hundred dollars ; and any minor, who obtains any such liquor by means of a false representation as to his age, must, on conviction, be fined not more than fifty dollars. *

As amended, Feb. 26, 1881, p. 50.

Punishes sale with or without license.—Ulmer's case, 61 Ala. 208. The actual seller, whether owner of saloon, or employe, indictable.—Marshall's case, 49 Ala. 21. The requisition must be a verbal or written application or request to sell by the physician himself.—Bain's case, 61 Ala. 75. Proof of infancy, based upon recollection of witness as to former appearance of alleged minor.—Weed's case, 55 Ala. 13. Defendant permitted to prove that minor was mature-looking person ; but witness cannot be asked if he would not take him to be twenty-one years old.— Marshall's case, 49 Ala. 21. Charge asserting fact of minority is conclusive of defendant's intention, is erroneous.—Ib. Immaterial who owns liquor given to minor or intemperate person.—Hill's case, 62 Ala. 168. Sale made under honest, though mistaken, belief that minor was twenty-one years old, is excusable ; but whether so made is a question for jury.—Adler's case, 55 Ala. 16. Voluntary drunkenness of defendant no defense or excuse.—Hill's case, 62 Ala. 168. Specific intent not necessary ; gift or sale is evidence of intention.—Bain's case, 61 Ala. 75. Bar-keeper selling to one who divides with or treats an intemperate person at the bar is guilty of selling to such intemperate person.—Walton's case, 62 Ala. 197. Burden of proving consent of minor's parent or guardian is on defendant.—Farrall's case, 32 Ala. 557. Also to prove requisition of physician.—Atkins' case, 60 Ala. 45. Formerly, consent of minor's father was no excuse.—Adler's case, 55 Ala. 16 Court may charge jury as to evil consequences of this offense.—Weed's case, 55 Ala. 13. Indictment in form "A. B. did sell or give spirituous, vinous, or malt liquor to C. D., a minor," etc., is sufficient.—Spigener's case, 62 Ala. 383. As to indictments under former law, see Weed's case, 55 Ala. 13 (overruling Bryan's case, 45 Ala. 86). Jury need not find whether liquor, if averred

* By act approved December 4, 1886 (Pamph. Acts 1886-7, p. 121), it is provided : (1). " That it shall be unlawful for any person to employ any minor to sell vinous, spirituous, or malt liquors in this state ; and any person violating the provision of this act shall be deemed guilty of a misdemeanor." (2). " That any person, who is guilty of a violation of the first section of this act, upon conviction thereof, shall be fined not less than fifty, nor more than five hundred dollars."

in alternative, was vinous or malt; and a charge to the contrary is erroneous.—Adler's case, 55 Ala. 16.   When witness may express opinion that lager beer is fermented liquor.—Merkle's case, 37 Ala. 139.   What must be proved under indictment for selling liquor to "person of known intemperate habits."—Tatum's case, 63 Ala. 147.   What does not constitute either "selling or giving."—Young's case, 58 Ala. 358.   Aiding and abetting sale is sufficient.—Walton's case, 62 Ala. 197.   Knowledge by defendant of one's intemperate habits necessary; but may be inferred by jury from notoriety.—Smith's case, 55 Ala. 1; Stalling's case, 33 Ala. 425 (overruling on this point Stanley's case, 26 Ala. 26); Tatum's case, 63 Ala. 147.   But the fact of intemperate habits or the sale of the liquor cannot be proved by notoriety.—Ib.   Proof of fact of intemperate habits.—Atkins' case, 60 Ala. 45.   Intemperate habits is a collective fact to which the intemperate person or a witness may testify.—Tatum's case, 63 Ala. 147; Smith's case, 55 Ala. 1.   What constitutes intemperate habits.—Tatum's case, 63 Ala. 147; Smith's case, 55 Ala. 1.   Whether a person of such known habits, is a question of fact for the jury.—Elam's case, 25 Ala. 53; Smith's case, 53 Ala. 1.   Burden is on defendant to show he had requisition of a physician.—Atkins' case, 60 Ala. 45.   Indictment in Code form sufficient, without negativing requisition of a physician.—Tatum's case, 63 Ala. 147.   See Elam's case, 25 Ala. 53.   Need not allege specific time.—Atkins' case, 60 Ala. 45.

4039 (4206). Giving or selling liquor to person of unsound mind.

—Any person, who sells or gives spirituous, vinous, or malt liquors to a person known or reputed to be of unsound mind, unless it be upon the prescription of a physician, or with the consent of the parent, guardian, husband, or wife of such person, must, on conviction, be fined not less than fifty, nor more than five hundred dollars.

4040 (4202). Prohibiting disposition of liquors near place of religious worship, etc.

—Any person, who sells, gives away, or otherwise disposes of any spirituous, vinous, or malt liquors, within one mile of any church, or other place of religious worship, not in any incorporated town or city, on any day on which there is public preaching at such place, must, on conviction, be fined not less than twenty, nor more than fifty dollars, and be imprisoned in the county jail, or sentenced to hard labor for the county, one or both, at the discretion of the jury.

Special prohibitory liquor laws not unconstitutional.—Barnes' case, 49 Ala. 342; Dorman's case. 34 Ala. 216.   Retail license not operative within special prohibited limits.—Barnes' case, 49 Ala. 342; Hudgin's case, 46 Ala. 208.

Feb. 17, 1885, p. 159, sec. 1.

4041. Evasion of prohibitory liquor laws.

—Any person, who conceals himself in any house, room, booth, inclosure, or other place, and sells, gives away, or otherwise disposes of spirituous, vinous, or malt liquors, or intoxicating beverage, in violation or evasion of law, or, by any device or subterfuge, sells, gives away, or otherwise disposes of any spirituous, vinous, or malt liquors, or intoxicating beverage, in violation or evasion of law, must, on conviction, be fined not less than two hundred and fifty, nor more than one thousand dollars, and may also be imprisoned in the county jail, or sentenced to hard labor for the county, for not more than twelve months.

Ib. sec. 2.

4042. Permitting such evasion.

—Any person, being the owner or proprietor, or having the control or possession of any house. room, booth, inclosure, or other place, who knowingly permits any person to conceal himself therein, and to sell, give away, or otherwise dispose of spirituous, vinous, or malt liquors, or intoxicating beverage, in violation or evasion of law, or knowingly permits any person to use therein any device or subterfuge in selling, giving away, or otherwise disposing of such liquors or beverage, in violation or evasion of law, must, on conviction, be fined not less than fifty, nor more than one thousand dollars, and may also be imprisoned in the county jail, or sentenced to hard labor for the county, for not more than twelve months.

4043 Same; duty of justice, etc.; warrant for arrest of all persons on premises, issued when.—If any person violates the provisions of section 4041, and so conceals himself that he is not known, upon complaint being made on oath before a justice of the peace, or judge of the county court, that spirituous, vinous, or malt liquors, or intoxicating beverage, have been sold, given away, or otherwise disposed of, in violation or evasion of law, and that the person committing such offense conceals himself in a house, room, booth, inclosure, or other place, or is using therein a device or subterfuge in selling, giving away, or otherwise disposing of such liquors or beverage, and that such person is unknown to the person making the complaint, it is the duty of such justice or judge to issue forthwith a warrant of arrest for such unknown person for the offense charged in the complaint, and immediately place such warrant in the hands of a constable or sheriff, who shall proceed at once to the house, room, booth, inclosure, or other place, in which such violation of law is alleged to have occurred, and arrest all persons therein; and if such constable or sheriff is refused admittance, he shall force an entrance into such house, room, booth, inclosure, or other place, and, if necessary, break in the door, or other part thereof, and arrest all persons found therein, and carry them before the officer before whom the warrant is returnable; and thereupon such proceedings shall be had as if such warrant contained the. name of each person so arrested.

4044. Same; forfeiture of lease, etc.—Any lessee of any house, room, booth, inclosure, or other place, who uses or permits the use of the same in violation of sections 4041, and 4042, thereby forfeits his lease.

ARTICLE XIV.

SUNDAY LAWS.

4045 (4443). Certain acts prohibited on Sunday; punishment.—Any person, who compels his child, apprentice, or servant to perform any labor on Sunday, except the customary domestic duties of daily necessity or comfort, or works of charity; or who engages in shooting, hunting, gaming, card-playing, or racing on that day; or who, being a merchant or shopkeeper, druggist excepted, keeps open store on that day, must, for the first offense, be fined not less than ten, nor more than twenty dollars, and, for the second, or any subsequent offense, must be fined not less than twenty, nor more than one hundred dollars, and may also be imprisoned in the county jail, or sentenced to hard labor for the county, for not more than three months; but the provisions of this section do not apply to the running of railroads, stages, or steamboats, or other vessels navigating the waters of this state, or any manufacturing establishment which requires to be kept in constant operation.

All unnecessary shooting prohibited; such as to shoot at a dog in wantonness and mischief.—Smith's case, 50 Ala. 159. Constituents and proof of the offense of

keeping open store.—Dixon's case, 76 Ala. 89.   Evidence explaining a sale.—Ib.
Store or shop must be kept open for purpose of traffic.—Snider's case, 59 Ala. 64.
Word "shop" not equivalent to word "store."—Sparrenberger's case, 53 Ala. 481.
Different sales are merely evidences of intent; do not require election by state.
Snider's case, 59 Ala. 64.   Purpose for which store kept open, question for jury.—Ib.

4046 (4444). **Holding public markets and trading therein on Sunday.**—Any person, who opens, or causes to be opened, for the purpose of selling or trading, any public market-house or place on Sunday, or opens, or causes to be opened, any stall or shop therein, or connected therewith, or brings any thing for sale or barter to such market or place, or offers the same for sale therein on that day, or buys or sells therein on that day (including live stock or cattle), must, on conviction, be punished as prescribed in the preceding section.   Any place where people assemble for the purchase and sale of goods, wares and merchandise, provisions, cattle, or other articles, is a market-house or place, within the meaning of this section.

ARTICLE XV.

VAGRANTS AND TRAMPS.

4047 (4218). **Vagrancy; punishment of.**—Any person, who, having no visible means, of support, or, being dependent on his labor, lives without employment, or habitually neglects his employment; or who abandons his family and leaves them in danger of becoming a burden to the public; or who, being an able-bodied person, is found begging; or who is a common drunkard, or a common gambler, or goes from place to place for the purpose of gambling; or who is a prostitute, or the keeper of a house of prostitution, and has no honest employment whereby to maintain herself, must, on conviction, for the first offense, be fined not less than ten, nor more than fifty dollars; and, on a second conviction within six months after the first, must be fined not less than fifty, nor more than one hundred dollars, and may be imprisoned in the county jail, or sentenced to hard labor for the county, for not more than six months.

Abandonment of wife or family, what constitutes.—Boulo's case, 49 Ala. 22. Personal dislike no excuse.—Ib. A common prostitute, to be vagrant, must have "no honest employment."—Ex parte Birchfield, 52 Ala. 377. A lewd woman, if a minor and supported by parents who have honest occupation, is not a vagrant. Taylor's case, 59 Ala. 19.   Common-law offense of keeping bawdy-house not repealed by this section.—Ex parte Birchfield, 52 Ala. 377. Sufficiency of indictment for abandoning family, etc.—Boulo's case, 49 Ala. 24. Of being common prostitute, etc.—Toney's case, 60 Ala. 97. Proof of character of female of bawdy-house.—Ib.

March 1, 1881, p. 142, secs. 1, 5. **4048. Being tramp; definition and punishment.**—Any person, other than one who is blind or visibly unable to do manual labor, or other than one asking charity within the county in which he has had a known place of residence for six months next preceding, who goes from place to place, or house to house, begging or demanding food, raiment, or other thing, is a tramp, and must, on conviction of being such tramp, be fined, for the first offense, not less than fifty, nor more than two hundred dollars, and imprisoned in the county jail, or sentenced to hard labor for the county, for not less than six, nor more than twelve months; and, for each subsequent conviction, must be fined not less than one hundred, nor more than five hundred dollars, and imprisoned in the county jail, or sentenced to hard labor for the county, for not less than one, nor more than two years.

4049. Tramp entering dwelling-house or threatening injury to person or property.—Any tramp, who enters any dwelling-house or other building, without the consent of the occupant thereof, or who willfully or maliciously injures or threatens to injure any person therein, or who injures or threatens to do an injury to the real or personal property of another, or who demands of, or orders any person to deliver or surrender to him any thing of value, must, on conviction, be fined not less than five hundred dollars, and imprisoned in the county jail, or sentenced to hard labor for the county, for not more than two years.

4050. Tramp released on the payment of fine and costs. Any person convicted under either of the two preceding sections, who pays in full the fine and costs of conviction, shall forthwith be released from the sentence, and discharged from custody.

4051. Prima facie evidence of being a tramp.—Acts of begging, vagabondage, or vagrancy, by one having no known residence within the county, are prima facie evidence that he is a tramp.

Article XVI.

GAMING AND LOTTERIES.

4052 (4207). **Card and dice-playing at public houses and other public places.**—Any person, who plays at any game with cards or dice, or any device or substitute therefor, at any tavern, inn, store-house for selling or retailing spirituous, vinous, or malt liquors, or house or place where spirituous, vinous, or malt liquors are retailed, sold, or given away, or in any public house, highway, or in any other public place, or any out-house where people resort, must, on conviction, be fined not less than twenty, nor more than fifty dollars.

The game **backgammon** not prohibited.—Wetmore's case, 55 Ala. 198. **Raffling with dice** prohibited.—McInnis' case, 51 Ala. 23. **Throwing dice** for money or drinks sufficient.—Jones' case, 26 Ala. 155. **Playing once,** sufficient.—Cameron's case, 15 Ala. 383; Swallow's case, 20 Ala. 30. Words "**device**" and "**substitute**" not of same meaning.—Henderson's case, 59 Ala. 89. **Dominoes** as a substitute for cards in playing euchre.—See Harris' case, 31 Ala. 362; s. c., 33 Ala. 373. No matter what **secrecy** observed, if playing done at public house, or other place specially mentioned.—Windham's case, 26 Ala. 69. A **public place** is, in general, any place which, for the time being, is made public by the assemblage of people.—Campbell's case, 17 Ala. 369. Any place, house, or room, even a bed-room, may become a public place from the use of it, generally, or at the time.—Smith's case, 52 Ala. 384; Coleman's case, 20 Ala. 51; Russell's case, 72 Ala. 222; Johnson's case, 75 Ala. 7. Also a steamboat.—Coleman's case, 13 Ala. 602. Or an infirmary. Flake's case, 19 Ala. 551. Or a ferry-boat in the middle of a navigable river. Dickey's case, 68 Ala. 508. Or a place in the bushes in the edge of an old field. Henderson's case, 59 Ala. 89. In the following cases, the places were held not to be public on account of circumstances of privacy attaching at the time: A private house or room.—Coleman's case, 20 Ala. 51. A deep hollow in a piece of woods. Bythwood's case, 20 Ala. 47. A physician's office.—Clarke's case, 12 Ala. 492; Sherrod's case, 25 Ala. 78. A lawyer's office.—Burdine's case, 25 Ala. 60. A back-room occupied by a register in chancery as a bed-room.—Roquemore's case, 19 Ala. 528. The term **public place** does not include **public house,** or other place specially mentioned. — Windham's case, 26 Ala. 69; Brown's case, 27 Ala. 47; Sweeney's case, 28 Ala. 47; Huffman's case, 28 Ala. 48; Smith's case, 37 Ala. 472; Burdine's case, 25 Ala. 60; Sherrod's case, 25 Ala. 78; Roquemore's case,

19 Ala. 528; Clarke's case. 12 Ala. 492; McCauley's case, 26 Ala. 135. But a contrary rule is laid down in decisions on **betting** in a public place, etc. — See Napier's case, 50 Ala. 168. **Bed-room or dwelling-house** may, from use of it, become one of the **prohibited places.**--Johnson's case, 75 Ala. 7. Held to be **public house** in each of the following cases: A room in a warehouse on river bank. Windham's case, 26 Ala. 69. Also a room belonging to a hotel or tavern, although in a lot separate and distant from the hotel. — Russell's case, 72 Ala. 222. A "lawyer's office."—McCauley's case, 26 Ala. 135. The office of a justice of the peace, or a back-room thereto.--Burnett's case, 30 Ala. 19. A store-house for selling dry goods.—Skinner's case, 30 Ala. 524. A "barber-shop" and "rooms above." Moore's case, Ib. 550; Cochran's case, Ib 542. A broker's office and connected sleeping-room.—Wilson's case, 31 Ala. 371. Building where saddle and harness business carried on, and connected rooms.—Bentley's case, 32 Ala. 596. A toll-bridge house, unless used exclusively as a private residence.—Arnold's case, 29 Ala. 46. **Store-house for sale of liquors, or house or place where liquors are sold, etc.**; held to be within the statute in the following cases: Johnson's case, 19 Ala. 527; Huffman's case, 29 Ala. 40; s. c., 30 Ala. 532. But the following cases held not to be within the statute: Dale's case, 27 Ala. 31; Philips' case, 51 Ala. 20. **Meaning of the statutory term "at" the house, etc.**—Ray's case, 50 Ala. 168 **Out-house where people resort, etc.**; what held to be.—Swallow's case, 20 Ala. 30. What held not to be.—Cain's case, 30 Ala. 534; McDaniel's case, 35 Ala. 390. **Highway** means a public road, as distinguished from a private way.—Mills' case, 20 Ala. 86. A navigable river is not a highway within this statute.—Glass' case, 30 Ala. 529; Dickey's case, 68 Ala. 508. But it may become a public place.—Dickey's case, 68 Ala. 508. Meaning of word **tavern**, generally.—Cloud's case, 6 Ala. 628.

As amended,
Feb. 18, 1879,
p. 48.

4053 (4207). **Same; exceptions; burden of proof.**—A conviction must not be had under the preceding section, if it is shown on the trial that the playing occurred at any house, room, or building attached to a public watering-place, and under the control of the owner or lessee of such watering-place, or at a house, room, or building in the use and occupancy of any social club or literary society incorporated under the laws of this state, and that in the room in which such playing occurred spirituous, vinous, or malt liquors were not kept, retailed, sold, or given away, and that nothing of value was bet on such playing.

4054 (4807). **Indictment and proof of gaming.**—In an indictment for gaming under the second preceding section, it is not necessary to state the name of the game played; it is sufficient to charge that the defendant "played at a game with cards, or dice, or some device or substitute therefor," in one or more of the places enumerated in that section, or in a public place; and it is not necessary to prove on the trial what the game was called.

The statute dispenses with the necessity of alleging or proving the kind of game. McInnis' case, 51 Ala. 23; citing Holland's case, 3 Port. 292. Design of statute was to dispense with technicalities.—Atkyns' case, 1 Ala. 180. Form in Code sufficient; not unconstitutional.—Burdine's case, 25 Ala. 60; Burnett's case, 30 Ala. 19; Harris' case, 31 Ala. 362. Alleging a game "of" cards, etc., instead of "with" cards, etc., sufficient.—Cochran's case, 30 Ala. 542. Also sufficient to allege "played at cards," instead of "at a game with cards."—Coggins' case, 7 Port. 263; Holland's case, 3 Port 292. Need not allege ownership of public house.—Atkyns' case, 1 Ala. 180. Cannot join different persons in same indictment, unless they played at same game; variance on proof of a separate game.—Lindsey's case, 48 Ala. 169. Election by prosecutor, when is, and when not required.—Smith's case, 52 Ala. 384; Elam's case, 26 Ala. 48; Cochran's case, 30 Ala. 542. Proof must show the character of the house at the time of playing.—Logan's case, 24 Ala. 182; Mitchell's case, 55 Ala. 160. See, also, Coleman's case, 3 Ala. 14. Defendant's want of knowledge of character of place, no excuse; it is duty of persons to see that they do not play at a prohibited place.—Johnson's case, 75 Ala. 7. Witness may testify to card-playing without giving a particular description of the game.—Johnson's case, 74 Ala. 537. When witness not an accomplice.—Smith's case, 37 Ala. 472. When defendant was seen with cards in hand with others, question for jury to say whether he was playing.—Henderson's case, 59 Ala. 89.

As amended,
Feb. 10, 1887.
p. 142.

4055 (4208). **Keeping gaming table.**—Any person, who keeps, exhibits, or is interested or concerned in keeping or exhibiting any table for gaming, of whatsoever name, kind, or description, not regularly licensed under the laws of this state, shall be guilty of a felony, and, on conviction thereof, must be fined not less than one hundred, nor more than five hundred dollars, and shall also be imprisoned in the penitentiary for not less than six months, nor more than two years; and, on a second or any subsequent conviction, shall be imprisoned in the penitentiary for not less than two, nor more than five years.

The kind of table is not confined to banking tables, such as faro, roulette, etc., but includes tables for games of cards, such as "draw poker," etc.—Wren's case, 70 Ala. 1. **Any table,** even a plank, kept and used for gaming, although without any particular device or appliance, and though not used for any particular game, is a "table for gaming" within the statute.—Toney's case, 61 Ala. 1. **Game of "keno"** is within the statute.—Miller's case, 48 Ala. 122. What does not show a sufficient violation of the statute, as to the use of the table.—Owens' case, 52 Ala. 213. What constitutes the **keeping** or "**being interested or concerned** in keeping," etc.—Miller's case, 48 Ala. 122; Wren's case, 70 Ala. 1. **Indictment** need not allege, nor need it be proved, that any money was bet at the table.—Whitworth's case, 8 Port. 434. Two or more persons may be joined, and only one convicted.—Covy's case, 4 Port. 186.

4056 (4808). **Indictment for, and proof of keeping or exhibiting gaming tables, etc.**—In an indictment for keeping or exhibiting a gaming table under the preceding section, it is sufficient to charge, in general terms, that the defendant kept, exhibited, or was interested or concerned in keeping or exhibiting, a gaming table for gaming, without describing the table more particularly, or alleging in what manner the defendant was interested or concerned in keeping or exhibiting it; nor is it necessary to allege or prove that any money was bet at the table.

4057 (4209). **Betting at cards, dice, etc.**—Any person, who bets or hazards any money, bank-notes, or other thing of value, at any gaming table prohibited by section 4055 (4208), or at any game prohibited by section 4052 (4207), or at a game called keno, or at any game of hazard or skill played on any steamboat while engaged in plying any of the navigable waters of this state, must, on conviction, be fined not less than fifty, nor more than three hundred dollars.

Betting defined; when a bet is complete.—Welch's case, 7 Port. 463. **Betting at keno.**—Schuster's case, 48 Ala. 199. **Prohibited places.**—See note to section 4052. **Indictment** need not specify the thing bet, nor its value; form in Code sufficient.—Collins' case, 70 Ala. 19; Jacobson's case, 55 Ala. 151; Mitchell's case, Ib. 160; Johnson's case, 75 Ala. 7. But such form in Code, literally followed, is sufficient only for betting at gaming table, or keno; other words necessary for betting at prohibited places.—Johnson's case, 75 Ala. 7. See the following cases as to sufficiency of indictment.—Napier's case, 50 Ala. 168; Ray's case, Ib. 172; Rodger's case, 26 Ala. 76; Clark's case, 19 Ala. 552. Joinder in same count of betting, and being concerned in betting under former statute.—Ward's case, 22 Ala. 16. Two or more persons may be joined.—Ib.; Swallow's case, Ib. 20. Allegation of betting at "public place" sustained by proof of betting "at a house where spirituous liquors were retailed."—Ray's case, 50 Ala. 172; Napier's case, Ib. 168. Whether place played at sufficiently proved to be public place, is a question for the jury.—Johnson's case, 75 Ala. 7.

4058 (4210). **Betting at billiards, ten-pins, etc.**—Any person, who bets or hazards any money, bank-notes, or other thing of value, except for charge for the use of the table or alley, at billiards, ten-pins, or any other game, at any table or any alley regularly licensed, must, on conviction, be fined not less than fifty, nor more than one hundred dollars.

License to keep billiard table does not authorize its use for the game of pool. Rodger's case, 26 Ala. 76.—What constitutes offense of betting at ten-pins.—Bass'

case, 37 Ala. 469.   What proof required under this section.—Bone's case, 63 Ala.
185

4059 (4211). **Betting with minor or apprentice.**—Any person, who, being of full age, bets or hazards any money, bank-notes, or other thing of value, with a minor, or with an apprentice, or who allows any minor or apprentice to bet or hazard any thing of value at any gaming table kept or exhibited by him, or in which he is interested or concerned, must, on conviction, be fined not less than one hundred, nor more than five hundred dollars, and may also be imprisoned in the county jail, or sentenced to hard labor for the county, for not more than six months.

Dec. 4, 1878, p. 164.

4060. Betting on election in this state.—Any person, who bets or hazards any money, bank-notes, or other thing of value, on any general or special election authorized by law to be held in this state, must, on conviction, be fined not less than twenty, nor more than five hundred dollars.

4061 (4212). **Proprietors of liquor saloons and other public houses permitting gaming.**—Any person, who, being a licensed retailer, or the keeper, proprietor, owner, or superintendent of any tavern, inn, or other public house, or of any house where spirituous, vinous, or malt liquors are sold, retailed, or given away, or of any out-house where people resort, or the captain or other commanding officer of any steamboat engaged in plying any of the navigable waters of this state, knowingly suffers any of the offenses prohibited by sections 4052 (4207), 4055 (4208), 4057 (4209), 4058 (4210) and 4059 (4211) to be committed in his house, or on his premises, or on his boat, must, on conviction, be fined not less than one hundred, nor more than five hundred dollars, and may also be imprisoned in the county jail, or sentenced to hard labor for the county, for not more than six months.

Retailers, etc., must be diligent, and use all proper means to prevent gaming on premises.—Wilcox' case, 50 Ala. 142; Campbell's case, 55 Ala. 89.   Party indicted must have control of premises.—Perez' case, 48 Ala. 357.   Agent or servant superintending may be responsible, although his principal knew of and did not prevent the gaming.—Wilcox' case, 50 Ala. 142.   Lessee of two-story house, who retails below, and knows that a room of his tenant shows in second story is used for gaming purposes, may be convicted, unless he affirmatively shows such a separation from the lower story as will exonerate him from liability; question for jury. Campbell's case, 55 Ala. 89.   When manager of social club indictable.—Jacobi's case, 59 Ala. 71.   Mobile Bay not a river, and hence not included in the term "any of the rivers of this state."—Johnson's case, 74 Ala. 537.   [But the statute has been changed by substituting "waters" for "rivers.")   Indictment against retailer must allege that he was a licensed retailer.—Kenedy's case, 1 Ala. 31. Need not allege name of person permitted to keep or exhibit gaming table. Clarke's case, 19 Ala. 552.   When indictment defective.—Perez' case, 48 Ala. 336.

4062 (4212). **Same; exceptions.** — A conviction must not be had under the preceding section for suffering to be played at any house or place therein designated any game mentioned in section 4052 (4207), if it is shown on the trial that such playing was at any house, room, or building attached to a public watering-place, and under the control of the owner or lessee of such watering-place, and that in the room in which such playing occurred spirituous, vinous, or malt liquors were not kept, retailed, sold, or given away, and that nothing of value was bet on such playing.

4063 (4213). **Keeper of liquor saloons permitting minors to play billiards or pool.**—Any person, who is the owner or keeper of a saloon in which vinous, spirituous, or other intoxicating liquors are kept for sale, having a billiard or pool table connected therewith, whether under the same roof or not, on which the public can play, whether for pay or not, who knowingly permits any minor to play thereon, must, on conviction, be fined not less than fifty dollars.

Sikes' case, 67 Ala. 80.

4064 (4214). **Renting room, booth, etc., to be used for gaming purposes.**—Any person, who, being the owner or proprietor of any house, room, booth, or tent, rents or leases the same to be used for gaming purposes, or for the exhibition of any gaming table, or knowingly permits the same to be used for any such purpose, must, on conviction, be fined not less than one hundred, nor more than five hundred dollars, and may also be imprisoned in the county jail, or sentenced to hard labor for the county, for not more than six months.

Poteete's case, 72 Ala. 558.

4065 (4216). **Examination of witnesses before grand jury in gaming and lottery cases.**—Witnesses before the grand jury, summoned to give evidence of any violation of the laws against gaming or lotteries, may be required to answer generally as to any such offense, within their knowledge, committed within the twelve months next preceding, without being first specially interrogated as to any particular offense; but no witness must be prosecuted for any offense, as to which he testified before the grand jury, and any member of the grand jury may be a witness to prove that fact.

4066 (4136). **Refusal of witness to testify before grand jury as to gaming or lottery.**—Any person, who is summoned as a witness before the grand jury to answer as to any gaming or lottery within his knowledge, and who fails or refuses to attend and testify in obedience to such summons, without a good excuse, to be determined by the court, is guilty of a contempt, and also of a misdemeanor; and, on conviction for such misdemeanor, must be fined not less than twenty, nor more than three hundred dollars, and may also be imprisoned in the county jail, or sentenced to hard labor for the county, for not more than three months.

Drake's case, 60 Ala. 62.

4067 (4217). **Judicial and executive officers' authority and duty in gaming cases.**—Judges of the circuit, city and county courts, justices of the peace, sheriffs, constables, and the judicial and executive officers of any incorporated city or town, have authority, and it is their duty, on receiving information, or having good cause to believe, that any person is violating, or has violated the provisions of section 4055 (4208), to cause such person to be arrested and carried before some judicial officer having jurisdiction of the offense; and the officer before whom he is carried, if it appears from the evidence that he is guilty, must require him to give bail for his appearance at the next term of the court having jurisdiction of the offense, and, on his failure to do so, must commit him to the county jail.

4068 (4445). **Setting up or carrying on, or selling tickets or shares in lotteries.**—Any person, who sets up, carries on, or is concerned in setting up or carrying on any lottery or device of the like kind, or who sells, or is interested or concerned in selling, any tickets or shares in such lottery, must, on conviction, be fined not less than one hundred, nor more than two thousand dollars.

Constitution prohibits legislature from authorizing lotteries or similar schemes. Const. art. 4, sec. 26; Boyd's case, 61 Ala. 177.   Lottery defined.—Buckalew's case, 62 Ala. 334.   Game of "keno" not a lottery.—Eslava's case, 44 Ala. 406.   What is a "device of like kind."—Chavannah's case, 49 Ala. 396.   Selling lottery tickets is being "concerned in carrying on" a lottery.—Salomon's case, 27 Ala. 26.   Re-sale of lottery ticket by one entirely disconnected with lottery, is no violation of statute; but otherwise, if connected with the lottery.—Salomon's case, 28 Ala. 83. Evidence tending to prove being "concerned in," etc.—Ib.   Selling tickets in foreign lottery as proof of being concerned in such lottery; when burden on de-fendant to disprove charge.—Ib.   Not necessary to prove that party himself sold lottery ticket; may be through an agent.—Mark's case, 45 Ala. 38.   Insufficient description of "being concerned in" lottery, in undertaking of bail.—Keipp's case, 49 Ala. 337.   Indictment in Code form sufficient —Salomon's case, 27 Ala. 261.

4069 (4446). **Selling lottery tickets, or gift-enterprise tickets.**—Any person, who sells or disposes of any lottery or gift-enterprise tickets, or tickets in any scheme in the nature of a lottery, or who receives money or takes an order for any lottery or gift-enterprise ticket, or for any ticket in any scheme in the nature of a lottery, or who acts for, or represents any other person in selling or disposing of any such ticket, must, on conviction, be fined not less than one hundred, nor more than two thousand dollars.

Ex parte Thompkins, 58 Ala. 71.

CHAPTER 8.

OFFENSES AGAINST PUBLIC HEALTH, PUBLIC SAFETY AND CONVENIENCE.

ARTICLE I.

UNWHOLESOME FOOD AND ADULTERATED LIQUORS.

4070 (4219). **Selling or exposing for sale tainted or dis-eased meat.**—Any butcher, or other person, who sells, or offers or exposes for sale, or suffers his apprentice, servant, agent, or other person for him, to sell, offer, or expose for sale, any tainted, putrid, or unwholesome fish or flesh, or the flesh of any animal dying otherwise than by slaughter, or slaughtered when dis-eased, for the purpose of being sold or offered for sale, must, on conviction, be fined not less than twenty, nor more than two hundred dollars, and may also be imprisoned in the county jail, or sentenced to hard labor for the county, for not more than six months.

4071 (4220). **Selling or exposing for sale unwholesome bread.**—Any baker, or other person, who sells, or offers or exposes for sale, or suffers his servant, apprentice, agent, or other person for him, to sell, offer, or expose for sale, any bread made from sour or unwholesome flour, must, on conviction, be fined not less than twenty, nor more than two hundred dollars, and may also be imprisoned in the county jail, or sentenced to hard labor for the county, for not more than six months.

4072 (1602). **Selling bread without baker's name stamped thereon.**—Any person, who sells or exposes for sale any bread, biscuit, or cracker, without having the name, or the initials of the christian and surname of the baker legibly marked on each biscuit, cracker, or loaf of bread, must, on conviction, be fined not more than twenty dollars.

4073 (1603). **Counterfeiting, or using another's name on bread.**—Any person, who counterfeits the name or initials of another on any bread, biscuit, or cracker, or who marks any bread, biscuit, or cracker with any other initials or name than his own, must, on conviction, be fined not less than twenty, nor more than fifty dollars.

4074 (4221). **Adulterating sugar and other articles of food.**—Any merchant, grocer, or other person, who mixes any foreign matter or substance with sugar, syrup, or molasses, lard or butter, or other article of food, so as to deteriorate or change the quality thereof, or sells, or offers or exposes for sale, such adulterated sugar, syrup, or molasses, lard or butter, or other article of food, or who suffers his servant, agent, apprentice, or other person for him, so to adulterate, or to sell, offer, or expose for sale, such adulterated sugar, syrup, or molasses, lard or butter, or other article of food, or who sells, offers, or exposes for sale any oleomargarine, cotton-seed oil, or fatarine butter, without having the same designated by name or brand, and to inform each and every purchaser thereof of the name, class and kind of butter, or other article of food, at the time of purchase, must, on conviction, be fined not less than fifty, nor more than five hundred dollars, and may also be imprisoned in the county jail, or sentenced to hard labor for the county, for not more than six months. *As amended, Feb. 28, 1887, p. 150.*

4075 (4222). **Adulterating liquors and selling same.**—Any manufacturer, brewer, distiller, grocer, tavern-keeper, retailer of spirituous, vinous, or malt liquors, or wholesale dealer of spirituous, vinous, or malt liquors, or any other person, who makes, distills, sells, or offers to sell, or exposes for sale, or permits his servant, apprentice, clerk, or agent, or other person for him, to sell, offer, or expose for sale, any such liquors which have been adulterated by the mixture or addition of any poisonous, unwholesome substances, or which are composed or compounded, in whole or in part, of any drug or oil, must, on conviction, be fined not less than two hundred and fifty, and not more than one thousand dollars. *As amended, Feb. 17, 1885, p. 139.*

ARTICLE II.

POISONING SPRINGS AND WELLS.

4076 (4240). **Poisoning springs, wells, etc.**—Any person, who willfully or wantonly poisons any spring, fountain, well, or reservoir of water, must, on conviction, be imprisoned in the penitentiary for not less than ten, nor more than twenty years.

ARTICLE III.

SELLING POISONS WITHOUT PRECAUTION.

4077 (4242). **Selling poisons without precautions to prevent accidents.**—Any druggist, apothecary, or other person, who sells and delivers any poison, or poisonous substance, not having the word "poison" written or printed on a label attached to the vial, box, or parcel, in which the same is sold, or sells and delivers any tartar emetic, laudanum, or morphine, not having the common name thereof written or printed on a label attached to the vial, box, or parcel containing the same, or sells or delivers any poison or poisonous drug or substance to any apprentice, or to any child under ten years of age, without the written order of the master of such apprentice, or the parent, guardian, or person having the legal charge of such child, must, on conviction, be fined not less than fifty, nor more than three hundred dollars.

ARTICLE IV.

CONCERNING DRUGGISTS, PHYSICIANS AND DENTISTS.

4078 (4243). **Dealing in drugs, or practicing medicine without license from medical board.**—Any person practicing medicine or surgery, or engaging in the business of a druggist, or dealer in drugs or medicines, without having first obtained a license, or diploma, or certificate of qualification, or not being a regular graduate of a medical college of this state, having had his diploma legally recorded, must, on conviction, be fined not more than one hundred dollars.*

As amended,
Feb. 11, 1881,
p. 84, secs. 8, 9.

4079 (4244). **Practicing dentistry without license from dental examiners.**—Any person practicing dentistry, not having obtained license from the board of dental examiners, must, on conviction, be fined not less than fifty, nor more than three hundred dollars; but the extraction of teeth only must not be considered a violation of this section.†

* See act entitled "An act to regulate the practice of pharmacy and the sale of poisons in cities and towns of more than one thousand inhabitants in the State of Alabama," approved February 28, 1887.—Pamph. Acts 1886-7, p. 106.

† See amendment to act of February 11, 1881, approved February 28, 1877. Pamph. Acts 1886-7, p. 97.

ARTICLE V.

HEALTH AND QUARANTINE LAWS.

4080. Failure of head of family to report pestilential or infectious disease.—Any head of a family, or any other person, upon whose premises a case of pestilential or infectious disease occurs, which is not under the charge of a physician, who refuses or willfully fails to report the same to the county health-officer, must, on conviction, be fined not less than five, nor more than twenty-five dollars. Feb. 28, 1881, p. 81, secs. 5, 8.

4081. Failure of midwife to report birth. — Any midwife attending a child-birth, who refuses or willfully fails to make to the county health-officer, within the time prescribed by the county board of health, a full report, specifying the name of the parents, if known, the date of the birth, and the sex and color of the child, with such other details as are required by the board of health, must, on conviction, be fined not less than five, nor more than twenty-five dollars. Ib.

4082. Failure of midwife to report death.—Any midwife, having charge of a patient at the time of death, who refuses or willfully fails to make to the county health-officer, within such time as may be prescribed by the county board of health, a full report of the name, age, sex, color, date, place, and cause of the death of such patient, so far as known, together with such other details as may be required by the county board of health, must, on conviction, be fined not less than five, nor more than twenty-five dollars. Ib.

4083. Failure of physician to report pestilential or infectious diseases.—Any physician, or person practicing medicine, being called upon to treat a case of pestilential or infectious disease in the limits of the county, who refuses or willfully fails, to make to the county health-officer, within such time as may be prescribed by the county board of health, a full report of the same, specifying the character of the disease, the name and locality of the patient, together with such other details as may be required by the county board of health, must, on conviction, be fined not less than ten, nor more than fifty dollars. Ib.

4084. Failure of physician to report birth.—Any physician, or person practicing medicine or surgery, attending a child-birth, who refuses or willfully fails to make to the county health-officer, within the time prescribed by the county board of health, a full report, specifying the name of the parent, if known, the date of the birth, and the sex and color of the child, with such other details as are required by the board of health, must, on conviction, be fined not less than ten, nor more than fifty dollars. Ib.

4085. Failure of physician to report death.—Any physician, or person practicing medicine or surgery, having charge of a patient at the time of death, who refuses or willfully fails to make to the county health-officer, within such time as may be prescribed by the county board of health, a full report of the name, age, sex, color, date, place, and cause of the death of such patient, so far as is known, together with such other details as may be required by the county board of health, must, on conviction, be fined not less than ten, nor more than fifty dollars. Ib.

Feb. 17, 1885,
p. 134, sec. 4.

4086. Failure of health-officer, etc., of Escambia county to report yellow fever in Florida.—If the health-officer or probate judge of the county of Escambia has good cause of suspicion or of belief that yellow fever exists in either of the counties of Santa Rosa or Escambia, in the State of Florida, and fails to report the same to the governor of this state, he must, on conviction, be fined not less than five hundred dollars.

Ib.

4087. Failure of judge of probate to act upon notice from governor.—If the judge of probate of Escambia county, upon being notified by the governor of this state that there is good cause for suspicion or belief that yellow fever exists in either or both of the counties of Santa Rosa or Escambia, in the State of Florida, fails to take such steps as he is by law authorized to take to prevent the introduction or spread of contagious or infectious diseases, or to establish such hospitals, or to appoint such guards, as are necessary and suitable for that purpose, must, on conviction, be fined not less than five hundred dollars.

4088 (4223). **Penalty for violation of quarantine regulations of ships and vessels.**—Any person, who violates the regulations prescribed by the corporate authorities of any town or city, or by the court of county commissioners of any county in relation to vessels arriving in the harbor, or in the vicinity of such town or city, after notice thereof has been given for five days in some newspaper printed in such town or city, or when there is none, by notice posted up at some public place therein for the same length of time, must, on conviction, be fined not less than fifty dollars.

4089 (4224). **Refusal of information to health-officer; penalty.**—Any master, seaman, or passenger, belonging to any vessel supposed to have any infection on board, or from a port where any dangerous infectious disease prevails, who refuses to answer on oath such inquiries as are made by any health-officer relating to any infection or disease, must, on conviction, be fined not less than one hundred dollars.

4090 (4225). **Breach of quarantine; penalty.**—The master of any vessel, ordered to perform quarantine, must deliver to the officer appointed to see it performed his bill of health, and manifest, log-book and journal; if he fails so to do, or to repair, in proper time after notice, to the quarantine ground, or departs thence without authority, he must, on conviction, be fined not less than two hundred dollars.

4091 (4226). **Travelers from infected district compelled to perform quarantine; breach and penalty.**—Any person, coming into a city or town by land from a place infected with a contagious disease, may be compelled to perform quarantine by the health-officer, and restrained from traveling until discharged; and any person thus restrained, traveling before he is discharged, must, on conviction, be fined not less than one hundred dollars.

4092 (4227). **Disposition of fines.**—All fines recovered under the three preceding sections must be paid into the city or town treasury.*

---

*See act entitled "An act for the prevention and suppression of infectious and contagious diseases of horses and other animals," approved February 28, 1887. Pamph. Acts, 1886-7, p. 95.

Article VI.

STORING GUNPOWDER IN TOWN LIMITS.

4093 (4236). **Storing gunpowder in city or town.**—Any person, who keeps on hand, at any one time, within the limits of any incorporated city or town, for sale or for use, more than fifty pounds of gunpowder, must, on conviction, be fined not less than one hundred dollars.

Article VII.

USING FIRE-ARMS IN PUBLIC PLACES, AND SELLING WEAPONS TO MINORS.

4094 (4228). **Using fire-arms while fighting in public place.**—Any person, who, while fighting in the streets of any city or town, or at a militia muster, or at any public place, whether public in itself, or made public at the time by an assemblage of persons, uses, or attempts to use, except in self-defense, any kind of fire-arms, must, on conviction, be fined not less than two hundred, nor more than five hundred dollars, and may also be imprisoned in the county jail, or sentenced to hard labor for the county, for not more than six months.

4095 (4229). **Shooting along or across public road.**—Any person, who discharges a gun, or any other kind of fire-arms, along or across any public road, must, on conviction, be fined not less than ten, nor more than fifty dollars.

4096 (4230). **Selling, etc., pistol or bowie-knife to boy under eighteen.**—Any person, who sells, gives, or lends to any boy under eighteen years of age any pistol or bowie-knife, or other knife of like kind or description, must, on conviction, be fined not less than fifty, nor more than five hundred dollars. |
Coleman's case, 32 Ala. 581.

Article VIII.

HORSE-RACING ON PUBLIC ROAD.

4097 (4229). **Engaging in horse-race on public road.**—Any person, who engages in a horse-race on any public road, must, on conviction, be fined not less than ten, nor more than fifty dollars.
Redman's case, 33 Ala. 428.

Article IX.

CONCERNING RAILROADS, STEAMBOATS AND PILOTS.

4098. Throwing or shooting deadly missile into locomotive or car.—Any person, who wantonly or maliciously throws or casts a missile, calculated to produce death or great bodily harm, or shoots at or into any locomotive or car of any railroad train, in or on which there is any human being, or at or into any passenger car forming part of a railroad train, whether there is in or on such passenger car any human being or not, must, on conviction, be imprisoned in the penitentiary for not less than two, nor more than twenty years.   Feb. 18, 1879, p. 175, sec. 1.

Ib.

4099. Throwing or casting other missile into locomotive or car.—Any person, who wantonly or maliciously throws or casts any missile, other than that mentioned in the preceding section, at or into any locomotive or car of any railroad train, in or on which there is any human being, or at or into any passenger car forming part of a railroad train, whether there is in or on such passenger car any human being or not, must, on conviction, be fined not more than one thousand dollars, and may also be sentenced to hard labor for the county for not more than two years.

Ib. sec. 2.

4100. Injuring or obstructing railroad bridge, trestle, etc., or salting track.—Any person, who wantonly or maliciously injures any railroad, or any bridge, trestle, or culvert, cattle-guard, stock-gap, or other superstructure of such railroad, or places any impediment or obstruction on such railroad, or removes or destroys any portion thereof, in such manner as to render liable any engine, car, or other vehicle to diverge or to be thrown from the track thereof, or who salts the track of such railroad for the purpose of attracting cattle thereon, must, on conviction, be fined not more than one thousand dollars, and imprisoned in the penitentiary for not more than five years.

4101 (4238). Obstructing railroad maliciously, and throwing car from track, etc.—Any person who wantonly or maliciously injures any railroad, or places any impediment or obstruction thereon, by means of which injury, impediment, or obstruction any engine, car, or other vehicle diverges or is thrown from the track thereof, must, on conviction, be imprisoned in the penitentiary for not less than two, nor more than ten years.

Feb. 23, 1883, p. 154, sec. 2.

4102. Failure to comply with order of railroad commissioners to provide depot conveniences.—Any person, or corporation operating a railroad, which fails for more than ninety days after its receipt to comply with a legal order of the railroad commissioners regarding the erection of a depot, or providing other conveniences for travelers at stations, must, on conviction, be fined not less than one hundred, nor more than five hundred dollars.

March 1, 1881, p. 98, sec. 6.

4103. Violating chancery decree upon railroad commissioners' award.—Any officer or agent of a person or corporation operating a railroad, who knowingly violates a chancery decree confirming railroad commissioners' award, regulating such railroad's business with any connecting line, must, on conviction, be fined not less than ten, nor more than five hundred dollars.

4104 (1703). Failure of chief superintendent to instruct engineers and conductors.—Any superintendent of a railroad, who fails to instruct the engineers and conductors thereof, as to the provisions of this Code in regard to blowing the whistle, ringing the bell, and stopping and handling the train, and order them to comply therewith, must, on conviction, be fined not less than one thousand dollars, and may be imprisoned in the county jail, or sentenced to hard labor for the county, for not more than twelve months, at the discretion of the jury.

4105 (4258). Railroads must keep lights and drinking water; conductor punishable for neglect.—Railroad companies must keep good lights on their night trains, and a sufficiency of good drinking water on all trains; and every conductor, who runs any train without lights or water, as required by this section, must, on conviction, be fined not less than one hundred, nor more than five hundred dollars.

4106 (4256). **Failing to ring bell and blow whistle on trains.**—Any engineer, or other person, having the control of the running of a locomotive on any railroad, who shall fail to perform any of the duties required of him by section 1144 (1699), must, on conviction, be fined not less than fifty, nor more than one thousand dollars, and imprisoned in the county jail for not more than twelve months, one or both, at the discretion of the jury.

4107. Failure to stop at railroad crossings for passengers or freight.—Any conductor, engineer, or other person, in charge of any railroad train passing within two hundred feet of a station of an intersecting railroad located within two hundred yards of the intersection, who fails to stop such train opposite such station, take on or let off passengers, or their baggage, or to receive or deliver the freight of such station, on receipt of the usual charges for such passenger or freight transportation, must, on conviction, be fined not less than fifty, nor more than five hundred dollars. Feb. 19, 1881
p. 96, sec. 2.

4108 (4257). **Failing to stop at railroad crossing.**—Any conductor, or any other person, in charge of any locomotive or train, who fails to cause it to come to a full stop within one hundred feet from the place at which one railroad crosses another, or, after such stop, allows such train to proceed before he knows the way to be clear, must, on conviction, be fined not less than one hundred, nor more than one thousand dollars, and may be imprisoned in the county jail, or sentenced to hard labor for the county, for not more than twelve months, one or both, at the discretion of the jury.

4109 (4234). **Negligence of railroad conductors, etc.**—Any engineer, conductor, or other person, who, having the control or management of any steam engine running on any railroad in this state, fails to use proper precautions to prevent accidents, by ringing the bell, blowing the whistle, or checking the speed of his engine, on approaching any curve in the road, or any depot, station, or crossing of any public road, or on leaving any depot or station, must, on conviction, be fined not less than one hundred, nor more than one thousand dollars, and may also be imprisoned in the county jail, or sentenced to hard labor for the county, for not more than six months.

4110 (4235). **Endangering life by railroad accident.**—If, from the negligence, carelessness, or want of proper skill of any engineer or conductor having the control or management of any steam engine running on any railroad in this state, or any brakeman, the engine or cars are thrown off the track, or any other accident occurs, and the life of any human being is thereby endangered, such engineer, conductor, or brakeman must, on conviction, be fined not less than five hundred, nor more than two thousand dollars, and may also be imprisoned in the county jail, or sentenced to hard labor for the county, for not more than twelve months.

4111 (4237). **Failing to attach bell-cord.**—Any conductor

on any passenger train on any railroad in this state, who fails
at any time, when his train is in motion, to have a cord attached
to the bell on the engine, and passing through each passenger
car attached to his train, must, on conviction, be fined not less
than one hundred, nor more than five hundred dollars; one-half
the fine to go to the informer, the other half to the state; and
for such offense an indictment may be found and trial had in
any county through which the road passes.*

Feb. 26, 1881,
p. 92, sec. 24. **4112. Wantonly or willfully injuring railroad fences.**—Any
person, who wantonly, willfully, or intentionally disturbs, breaks,
throws down, or destroys any railroad fence, or any part thereof,
must, on conviction, be fined not less than ten, nor more than
five hundred dollars, or imprisoned in the county jail, or sentenced to hard labor for the county, for not less than ten days,
nor more than twelve months.

4113 (4231). **Endangering life by bursting boiler of steamboat.**—If the captain of any steamboat used for the conveyance
of passengers or freight, or any other officer or person having
charge thereof, or the engineer having charge of the machinery, or of any part of the apparatus for the generation of steam,
from gross negligence, or from ignorance, creates, or allows to
be created, such an undue quantity of steam as to burst the
boiler, or other apparatus in which such steam is generated, or
any apparatus or machinery therewith connected, and human
life is thereby endangered, such captain, engineer, or other officer, or person, must, on conviction, be imprisoned in the penitentiary for not less than two years.

4114 (4232). **Endangering life by steamboat-racing.**
Whenever any steamboat, while racing with another boat, or
attempting to excel her in speed, bursts its boiler, or any apparatus or machinery therewith connected, and the life of any
person is thereby endangered, the captain and engineer of such
boat must each, on conviction, be imprisoned in the penitentiary for not less than two years.

4115 (4233). **Endangering life by overloading vessel.**—Any
person navigating any boat or vessel for gain, who willfully
receives on board thereof so many passengers, or such a quantity of freight, that by means thereof such boat or vessel sinks,
or overturns, and the life of any human being is thereby endangered, must, on conviction, be fined not less than one hundred, nor more than one thousand dollars, and may also be imprisoned in the county jail, or sentenced to hard labor for the
county, for not more than six months.

---

* See act, entitled "An act to provide for the comfort and accommodation of
passengers at each of the passenger stations along the line of every railroad oper-
ated by any railroad company or person in this state," approved February 28, 1887.
Pamph. Acts 1886–7, p. 74.

Also, an act, entitled "An act to require railroads in Alabama to keep a register
of marks and brands of stock killed or injured by trains or locomotives of such
roads," approved February 28, 1887.—Pamph. Acts 1886–7, p. 78.

Also, an act, entitled "An act to require locomotive engineers in this state to be
examined and licensed by a board to be appointed by the governor for that purpose," approved February 28, 1887.—Pamph. Acts 1886–7, p. 100.

Also, an act, entitled "An act to prevent the obstruction by railroad employes
in charge of trains of public roads outside of incorporated towns in this state," approved December 11, 1886.—Pamph. Acts 1886–7, p. 763.

4116 (4316). **Loss of life or injury on steamboat from negligence, etc.**—Whenever any loss of human life, or any injury to any human being occurs on board of any steamboat navigating any of the waters of this state, from negligence or want of skill on the part of the captain, engineer, or other officer or person engaged in the management of such boat, or any part of the machinery thereof, the officer or person from whose negligence or want of skill such loss of life or injury occurred, must, on conviction, be imprisoned in the penitentiary for not less than two, nor more than ten years.

4117 (4260). **Piloting without license.**—Any person, who acts as pilot in the bay or harbor of Mobile, without a license from the commissioners of pilotage, or after he knows that they have revoked his license, must, on conviction, be fined not less than one hundred dollars. ^{As amended,}

As amended, Dec. 12, 1882, p. 16, sec. 4.

Article X.

CONCERNING PUBLIC STREETS, ROADS AND WATER-COURSES.

4118 (4248). **Streets of town out of order for more than ten days; penalty.**—In all towns or cities incorporated under any law of this state, if the inhabitants are exempt from working on the public roads within the limits thereof, and any of the streets therein are out of repair for more than ten days at any one time, without a reasonable excuse therefor, to be determined by the court, the corporate officers of such town, or any one or more of them, are guilty of a misdemeanor.

Nowlin's case, 49 Ala. 41.

4119 (4245). **Failure of corporation, etc., to keep road or bridge in good order.**—If any corporation or person, authorized by any law of the state to charge toll on any turnpike, plank, or macadamized road, water-course, or bridge, allows the same to be out of the repair or order contemplated by its charter or such law, for ten days at any one time, without a sufficient excuse, to be determined by the court, the president and directors of such corporation, or the person so authorized, are guilty of a misdemeanor; and on the trial, proof that such road, bridge, or water-course has been out of such order for ten days at any one time, and that such corporation or person, or any one on the part thereof, charged toll for such road, bridge, or water-course, and that such president and directors act, or claim to act in that capacity, is presumptive evidence of the existence of such corporation, of a charter or law authorizing toll to be charged, and that the persons so acting, or claiming to act, are the president and directors of such corporation.

4120 (4246). **Permitting bridge to remain out of repair.** When a bridge or causeway has been erected by contract with the county commissioners, with a guarantee by bond or otherwise, that it shall continue safe for the passage of travelers and other persons for a stipulated time, and the contractor knowingly suffers any such bridge or causeway to remain out of repair and unsafe for the passage of travelers and other persons for more than ten days at any one time, during the period stipulated for its safety by the terms of his contract, must, on conviction, be fined for the use of the county in a sum not less than double the value of the materials and labor necessary to put such bridge or causeway in the state of safety required by the terms of his contract.

4121 (4247). **Neglecting or obstructing fords.**—Any overseer of roads, who fails to keep open and in good condition the existing fords of water-courses at crossings where toll-bridges on public roads are constructed, and the land entrance thereto on either side, or any person who places obstructions in such fords, or in any manner intentionally interferes with travel through such fords, on conviction, is subject to such penalties as are imposed by law upon defaulting overseers of public roads.

4122 (4249). **Changing, obstructing and injuring public roads.**—To change a public road, except by order of the court of county commissioners, founded on a report of viewers appointed by the court, unless it straightens the same through inclosures, or renders it more convenient for the public; to obstruct a public road by a fence, bar, or other impediment, except by gates erected across the same by leave of the court of county commissioners, obtained as provided by law; to cut or place a tree, brush, or other obstacle across or along a public road, so as to impede travel, and not remove the same within six hours; willfully to deface, injure, or destroy any mile-post, index-board, bridge, or causeway; or willfully to injure or obstruct any public road in any way, is a misdemeanor.

When road can be lawfully changed.—James v. Hendree, 34 Ala. 488.   When not indictable for straightening and rendering road more convenient.—Ib.   Failure to repair bridge not indictable under this section as "an obstruction of public road."—Malone's case, 51 Ala. 55.   Obstruction caused by mill-dam must be willfully done.—Prim's case, 36 Ala. 244.   Sufficiency of indictment.--Thompson's case, 20 Ala. 54; Johnson's case, 32 Ala. 583.   What no defense to obstructing road opened by an overseer de facto.—Thompson's case, 21 Ala. 48.

4123 (4250). **Overseers permitting obstructions to remain on public roads; when hands defaulters.**—Any overseer permitting a fallen tree, dead animal, or such quantity of brushwood as obstructs travel to remain in or across a public road for three days after notice thereof, without a good excuse, to be determined by the court, is guilty of a misdemeanor; and all hands warned by such overseer for the purpose of removing such tree or brushwood are bound to attend, notwithstanding they may have worked ten days; and, failing so to do, must be proceeded against by such overseer as other defaulters.

4124 (4251). **Failure to open new road or neglect to repair.** Any overseer, who fails to open any new road which he has been appointed to open, or allows his precinct, or any part of the same, to be out of repair more than ten days at any one time, without good excuse, to be determined by the court, is guilty of a misdemeanor.

4125 (4252). **Neglect of duties imposed as to public roads.** Any apportioner, or other officer, on whom any duty is imposed as to public roads, who neglects to perform the same, in case no other provision has been made for the punishment of such neglect, is guilty of a misdemeanor.

Appointment of person under twenty-one as road overseer not void; but his minority is personal exemption which he may claim or waive.—Allison's case, 60 Ala. 54.   Regularly appointed overseer can only relieve himself by excuse or resignation, as prescribed by statute.—Ib. 54.   Sufficiency of indictment.—Malone's case, 51 Ala. 55; McCullough's case, 63 Ala. 75.   Overseer neglecting to repair for ten days; what an excuse.—McCullough's case, 63 Ala. 75.   Apportioners of roads not required to report overseer to grand jury unless overseer has neglected his duty. Williams' case, 45 Ala. 55.

4126 (4253). **Failure to work on public road after legal notice.**—Any person, liable to road duty, who willfully fails or refuses, after legal notice, to work the public roads, either in person or by substitute, without a sufficient excuse therefor, must, on conviction, be fined not less than one dollar, nor more than three dollars, for each day for which he is so in default, and may also be imprisoned in the county jail, or put to hard labor for the county, for not more than twenty days.

Brown's case, 63 Ala. 97.

4127 (4174). **Failure of judge of probate as to duty concerning public roads.**—Any judge of probate, who fails, on the establishment of a new road, the division of the same into precincts, and the appointment of the overseers therefor, to issue to such overseers an order directing the opening thereof, or who fails, for ten days after the appointment of overseers and apportioners, to furnish the sheriff with a copy of the order of appointments, or to furnish the sheriff with a statement signed by him of the overseer on any road precinct within their election precincts, and a description of such road precincts, with the names and grades of the road assigned to such overseer, or to furnish the sheriff with a statement of the names of the apportioners of the election precinct or precincts through which any part of the road passes, as required by law, must, on conviction, be fined not less than twenty dollars.

4128. **Failing to keep in repair, and to keep closed gates erected across public roads.**—Any person, who, having erected a gate across a public road by authority of the court of county commissioners, or board of county revenue, or by authority of any act of the general assembly, or any person who succeeds such person in the ownership, control, or possession of such gate, or in the benefits to be derived therefrom, or whose duty it is to keep the same in repair, fails for three or more days to keep such gate in good repair, or any person who leaves open such a gate, must, on conviction, be fined not more than twenty dollars. *Dec. 16, 1878, p. 172.*

4129 (4810). **Indictment and proof against overseer or apportioner.**—In an indictment against an overseer or apportioner of a public road, it is sufficient to charge in general terms, that the defendant has failed to discharge his duties as such apportioner or overseer; and the acts or omissions constituting his neglect of duty may be proved on the trial, as well as the excuse therefor, in such cases as excuses are allowed.

See note to section 4125.

4130 (1645). **Refusal of overseer to act after resignation not accepted.**—If the judge of probate and county commissioners shall consider insufficient any excuse made by any person appointed overseer of public roads for not accepting the appointment, or shall refuse to accept his resignation of the appointment, and such person thereafter neglects or refuses to act under such appointment, he must, on conviction, be fined not less than twenty, nor more than fifty dollars.

4131 (4903). **Compensation of apportioner presenting overseer.**—Any apportioner appointed to attend court to prosecute an overseer, who attends for such purpose, is entitled to four cents a mile and two dollars a day, to be taxed in the bill of costs if the defendant is convicted; or on failure to find a bill, or to convict, or if the defendant proves insolvent, to be paid out of the county treasury on the certificate of the clerk.

4132 (4901). **Evidence on trial of overseer for neglect of duty.**—On the trial of any person for neglect of duty as overseer, the return of his appointment by the sheriff, or proof of such service in case of its loss, and the acts or admissions of such person to that effect are evidence of his being overseer; that the road is a public road may be proved by his acts and admissions, and by the use of it as such; and no proof is required, on the part of the state, except that such person was overseer of the road at the time of the default, and that such road was a public road, and proof of the default.

4133 (4902). **Order recognizing road is evidence.**—Any order of the court of county commissioners, by which a road is recognized as a public road, is presumptive evidence thereof.

4134 (4259). **Failure to keep principal office of turnpike in proper county.**—If the president and directors or managers of any plank, macadamized, or turnpike road company shall fail to hold meetings and keep the principal office for the transaction of the business of such company in the county in which the principal portion of such plank or turnpike road may lie, or at one of the other termini of such road, they shall each be liable to indictment for a misdemeanor, and, on conviction, shall be fined for every such offense fifty dollars; and all acts of the company in violation of the provisions of this section are null and void.

4135 (4255). **Obstructing streams used for floating timber to market.**—Any person, who, during the season of high waters, leaves, or causes to be left, in any of the streams of this state used for floating timber to market, saw logs, or hewn or square timber, which he has put, or caused to be put, into such stream, so massed or collected together as to obstruct such stream, and who does not use diligence to effect a removal of such obstructions, must, on conviction, be fined not less than twenty-five, nor more than two hundred and fifty dollars.

4136 (4254). **Obstructing navigable water-course.**—Any person obstructing a navigable water-course in this state must, on conviction, be fined not less than fifty dollars.*

Feb. 17, 1885,
p. 154, sec. 2.

4137. Mobile harbor; fastening rafts and obstructing ship channel in Mobile bay.—Any person, who makes any vessel, boat, or water-craft of any description, or any raft or collection of logs, lumber, or timber, fast to any beacon or light stake or piling which may be of any use or benefit in making use of the dredged channel in the bay of Mobile, is liable to indictment

---

* See act, entitled "An act to regulate the floating of logs, timber and lumber upon the rivers, or other streams in this state, and provide a penalty for obstructing such streams," approved February 28, 1887.—Pamph. Acts 1886-7, p. 132.

in the city court of Mobile, or circuit court of Mobile county,
or any other court of competent jurisdiction, and must, on conviction, be fined not more than five hundred dollars, and may
also be imprisoned in the county jail, or sentenced to hard labor
for the county, for not more than six months.

4138. Same; injuring ship channel, beacon-light, etc. Ib. sec. 3.
Any person, who knowingly or willfully causes, or is concerned
in causing, any damage or injury to any part of the dredged
channel, as it now exists, or may hereafter exist, at any point
or points between the upper or northern limits of the port of
Mobile and the lower part of the bay of Mobile, or to any beacon-
light, stake, piling, or other matter, or thing, which is or may be
used, or intended to be used, in connection with such dredged
channel for the better navigation of the same, is liable to indictment in the city court of Mobile, or the circuit court of
Mobile county, or any other court of competent jurisdiction,
and, on conviction, must be fined not more than ten thousand
dollars, and may also be imprisoned in the penitentiary for not
more than twenty years.

4139. Same; master of vessel drawing more than twelve Ib. sec. 5.
feet passing channel without permit, etc.—Any master or
person in charge of any vessel drawing more than twelve feet
of water, which may enter into the dredged channel between
the upper limits of the port of Mobile and the outer bar of the
bay or harbor of Mobile, without a permit from the harbor-
master, or in violation of the rules and regulations of the commissioners of pilotage of the port and harbor of Mobile, is liable
to indictment in the city court of Mobile, or circuit court of
Mobile county, or any other court of competent jurisdiction, and
must, on conviction, be fined not more than ten thousand dollars,
and may also be imprisoned in the penitentiary for not more
than ten years.

CHAPTER 9.

OFFENSES AGAINST PUBLIC TRADE, PUBLIC POLICY, PUBLIC POLICE AND
ECONOMY.

Article 1.—Usury.

2.—Trading at night in farm products.

3.—Free banking, and emitting and circulating change-bills.

4.—Illegal tolls and freights.

5.—Illegal and fraudulent dealings in fertilizers.

6.—Concerning co-operative associations.

7.—Illegal measures.

8.—Laws for preservation of oysters, fish, game and live stock.

9.—Marriage records and illegal ceremonies.

10.—Levying on county property.

11.—Wearing military insignia unlawfully.

Article I.

USURY.

4140 (4435). **Usury by individual banker.**—Any banker,
who discounts any note, bill of exchange, or draft at a higher
rate of interest than eight per cent. per annum, not including
the difference of exchange, is guilty of a misdemeanor.

Article II.

TRADING AT NIGHT IN FARM PRODUCTS.

As amended,
Feb. 12, 1879,
p. 63.

4141 (4369). **Trading in farm products between sunset and
sunrise; exception.** — Any person, who buys, sells, receives,
barters, or disposes of any cotton, corn, wheat, oats, peas, or po-
tatoes, after the hour of sunset, and before the hour of sunrise
of the next succeeding day, or any person, who in any manner
moves, carries, conveys, or transports, except within the limits
of the farm or plantation on which it is raised or grown, any
seed-cotton between the hours of sunset and sunrise of the next
succeeding day, must, on conviction, be fined not less than ten,
nor more than five hundred dollars, and may also be imprisoned
in the county jail, or sentenced to hard labor for the county, for
not more than twelve months; but this section shall not affect
the right of municipal corporations to establish and regulate,
under their charters, public markets within their limits, for the
sale of commodities for culinary purposes, nor the right of any
proprietor or owner of any plantation or premises to sell on
such plantation or premises the necessary grain and provisions
for the subsistence of man and beast for the night to traveling
or transient persons, or for the use of agricultural laborers in
his own employment on such plantation or premises; nor shall
the provisions of this section apply to any person carrying seed-
cotton to a gin for the purpose of having the same ginned.

Constitutionality of statute.—Davis' case, 68 Ala 58. Want of knowledge or
consent of owner of products not an element of this offense, and his knowledge of

the act or consent thereto, when done by another, is no defense.—Gilliam's case, 71 Ala. 10. Instructions by principal to agent to buy farm products, presumptions; act and declaration of agent as evidence against principal.—Russell's case, 71 Ala. 348. Sufficiency of indictment; may be in the alternative.—Russell's case, 71 Ala. 348. Necessary averments.—Ib. 348. See Grattan's case, Ib. 344; Davis' case, 68 Ala. 58.

4142. Failure to apply farm produce to payment of lien for rent or advances.—Any person, who knowingly takes or receives any cotton or other farm produce upon which there is a lien for rent or advances, or both, or the proceeds thereof, and who fails to apply the same to the payment of the rent, or the discharge of the lien, whether the same is in the hands of a third party or not, must, on conviction, be punished as if he had stolen the same.

ARTICLE III.

EMITTING AND CIRCULATING CHANGE-BILLS.

4143 (4433). **Emitting change-bills as money.**—Any officer or agent of any private corporation or association, or any other person, who makes, emits, signs, or countersigns, or causes or procures to be made, emitted, signed, or countersigned, without authority of law, any paper to answer the purposes of money, or for general circulation, must, on conviction, be fined not more than five hundred dollars, and may also be imprisoned in the county jail, or sentenced to hard labor for the county, for not more than one year.

Norvell's case, 50 Ala. 174; Durr's case, 59 Ala. 24.

4144 (4434). **Circulating such change-bills.**—Any person, who passes or circulates in this state any paper issued without authority of law, to answer the purposes of money, must, on conviction, be fined not less than twenty, nor more than one hundred dollars.

See citations to preceding section.

ARTICLE IV.

ILLEGAL TOLLS, FREIGHTS AND FERRIES.

4145. Unlawful pooling of freights.—Any officer, agent, or servant of a person or corporation operating a railroad, who aids in making or carrying out an agreement between railroads, commonly called a pool, for the division between themselves of the freight-carrying business of any place in this state, whereby trade is restrained by the establishment of extortionate rates and the prevention of free competition, unless such agreement has been approved by the railroad commissioners, must, on conviction, be fined not less than fifty, nor more than two hundred dollars. *Feb. 23, 1883, p. 152, sec. 2.*

4146. Extortion by railroad.—Any person or corporation operating a railroad, who commits extortion in transportation-charges, as defined by law, must, on conviction, be fined not less than ten, nor more than five hundred dollars. *Feb. 26, 1881, p. 86, sec. 4.*

4147. Reduction of regular rates by railroads.—Any person or corporation operating a railroad, who makes, and any *Ib. secs. 9, 10, 11.*

person who knowingly accepts, a lower transportation-rate for person or freight than the published tariff, must, on conviction, be fined not less than ten, nor more than five hundred dollars.

Ib. secs. 3, 9; as amended, Feb. 28, 1883, p. 190.

4148. Failure of railroad to publish freight-rates at depots. Any person or corporation operating a railroad, who fails to post and keep posted at all freight depots the tariff of rates for transporting freight, showing general and special rates for each class, must, on conviction, be fined not less than twenty, nor more than one hundred dollars.

As amended, Nov. 29, 1880, p. 40.

4149 (1680). Keeping toll-bridge or ferry without license. Any person, who keeps any ferry, toll-bridge, or causeway, for ferriage or toll, without license, must, on conviction, be fined not less than twenty, nor more than one hundred dollars, or imprisoned in the county jail, or sentenced to hard labor for the county, for not less than thirty days.

4150 (4400). Illegal toll by miller.—Any person, who, being the owner or keeper of any public mill, or the agent or servant of such owner or keeper, takes or receives for grinding corn, wheat, or any other kind of grain, either as toll, or by sale or exchange, more than one-eighth of the grain ground or brought to the mill to be ground, must, on conviction, be fined not less than ten, nor more than one hundred dollars.

4151 (4401). Illegal toll by bridge or turnpike companies. Any person, who, being or acting as an officer, agent, servant, or employe of any turnpike company, macadamized road company, or other incorporated road or bridge company, takes, receives, or demands any greater charge or toll for travel or passage over such road or bridge than is authorized by the charter of such company, or, if the charter does not specify the amount of toll to be charged or taken, fixes, prescribes, takes, receives, or demands any unreasonable charge or toll, to be determined by the jury, must, on conviction, be fined not more than one hundred dollars.

4152 (1689). Excessive tolls; penalty.—Any keeper of any public ferry, toll-bridge, or causeway, who demands or receives from any person a higher rate of toll than is prescribed by the court of county commissioners, is guilty of a misdemeanor.

Lewis' case, 41 Ala. 414.

— — - -

ARTICLE V.

ILLEGAL AND FRAUDULENT DEALINGS IN FERTILIZERS.

Feb. 23, 1883, p. 184, sec. 6; as amended, Feb. 17, 1885, p 172, sec. 8.

4153. Dealing in fertilizers without submitting statement to commissioner.—Any person, who manufactures or exchanges, sells, or offers for sale or exchange, any fertilizer, without first submitting the statement required by law to the commissioner of agriculture, must, on conviction, be fined not more than five hundred dollars for each offense.

Feb. 17, 1885, p. 172, sec. 10.

4154. Selling fertilizers without attaching proper tags. Any person, who sells, exchanges, or offers for sale or exchange, any bag, package, or barrel of fertilizer, which has not been tagged as provided by law, must, on conviction, be fined not less than fifty dollars for each offense.

4155. Using more than once, and counterfeiting tags, etc. Feb. 23, 1883, p. 195, sec. 16; as amended, Feb. 17, 1885, p. 174, sec. 20 Any person, who counterfeits the tag prepared by the commissioner of agriculture, or who knowingly uses a counterfeit of such tag, or who uses a second time a genuine tag, or who uses the tag of a former season, must, on conviction, be fined one hundred dollars.

4156. Making false certificate of analysis of fertilizer. Ib. sec. 25. Any chemist, who willfully makes a false certificate of the analysis, or of the ingredients of any fertilizer, intended or offered for sale or exchange, must, on conviction, be imprisoned in the penitentiary for not less than two, nor more than five years.

4157. Dealing in commercial fertilizers without license. Feb. 17, 1885, p. 176, sec. 28. Any person, who sells or exchanges fertilizers, without having obtained a license from the commissioner of agriculture, as provided by law, must, on conviction, be fined not less than one hundred dollars for each offense.

4158. Fraud in manufacture, sale, or exchange of fertilizer. Ib. sec. 16. Any person, who commits a fraud in the manufacture, sale, or exchange of any fertilizer, or of any of the ingredients of a fertilizer, must, on conviction, be fined not less than one hundred dollars for each offense.

ARTICLE VI.
CONCERNING MUTUAL AID ASSOCIATIONS.

4159. Reports of mutual aid associations.—Any officer or agent of a mutual aid association, as defined by law, whose duty it is to make the annual report to the auditor, or designate the principal place of business, or agent for service of process of such association, as required by law, and who fails so to do, or who makes a false report, must, on conviction, be fined not less than one hundred, nor more than five hundred dollars, or imprisoned in the county jail for not less than ten days, nor more than one year, one or both, at the discretion of the court. Feb. 23, 1883, p. 171, sec. 7.

4160. Agent of a mutual aid association.—Any person, who acts as solicitor, collector, or otherwise as agent of a mutual aid association, as defined by law, knowing the same not to have complied with the provisions of this Code relating specially to such associations, must, on conviction, be fined not less than one hundred, nor more than five hundred dollars, or imprisoned in the county jail for not less than ten days, nor more than one year, one or both, at the discretion of the court. Ib.

ARTICLE VII.
ILLEGAL MEASURES.

4161. Illegal measurement in buying and selling oysters. Dec. 11, 1882, p. 13. Any person, who, on buying or selling oysters in the shell by measure, uses any other than the stave measure of the shape and dimensions required by law, must, on conviction, be fined not less than ten, nor more than one hundred dollars.

ARTICLE VIII.

LAWS FOR PRESERVATION OF OYSTERS, FISH, GAME AND LIVE STOCK.

4162 (4438). **Catching oysters otherwise than with tongs.**
Any person, who takes or catches oysters by using any other
implement or instrument than the oyster tongs heretofore generally used for that purpose, is guilty of a misdemeanor.

4163 (4439). **Violating oyster regulations.** — Any person,
who violates the provisions of section 1385 or 1386, must, on
conviction, be imprisoned in the county jail for not more than
one year, and may be fined not more than five hundred dollars,
at the discretion of the court.

*Dec. 11, 1882,
p. 12.*
4164. Taking and catching oysters by non-residents.
Any person, not being a resident of this state, who takes or
catches oysters in any manner in the waters within the jurisdiction of this state, is guilty of a misdemeanor.

4165 (4441). **Resistance of sheriff arresting any person or
seizing boat violating oyster regulations.**—Any person, who
willfully opposes or resists the sheriff, or person aiding the
sheriff in the performance of his duty, under proceedings to
enforce the law for the preservation of oysters, in arresting, or
attempting to arrest, any person engaged in the unlawful taking of oysters in any of the waters of this state, or in seizing,
or attempting to seize, any boat or vessel, or the tackle or furniture of such boat or vessel, used in such unlawful taking,
must, on conviction, be fined not less than fifty, nor more than
one thousand dollars, and may also be imprisoned in the county
jail, or sentenced to hard labor for the county, for not more
than six months.*

4166 (4442). **Poisoning or taking fish by nets in Tennessee river or tributaries.**—Any person, who takes fish by net,
or poisons fish in the Tennessee river, or its tributaries, must,
on conviction, be fined not more than fifty dollars; one-half of
the fine shall go to the informer, and the balance to be paid
into the common school fund of the township in which the offense was committed, for the benefit of the common schools of
such township; but the word "net" in this section shall not include seine.

*Jan. 20, 18'9,
p. 174.*
**4167. Obstructing and preventing fish from running up
rivers or creeks.**—Any person, who, by means of dams, traps,
or other obstructions, prevents the passage of fish up the waters
of any river or creek in this state, must, on conviction, be fined
not more than one hundred dollars; but nothing in this section
shall be so construed as to prevent the introduction of traps or
other means of catching fish in such rivers or creeks, which will
permit fish to pass through or around the same.

*As amended,
Feb. 19, 1883,
p. 60.*
4168 (4241). **Poisoning stream, or using explosive substance, to catch fish.**—Any person, who takes, catches, kills,
or attempts to take, catch, or kill, fish in any waters of the state,
by poisoning the stream or body of water in which they are
found, or by the use of any poisonous substance put in the
water, or by the use of fish berries, lime, giant powder, dyna-

---

* See act entitled "An act for the protection of oyster culture in the State of
Alabama," approved February 28, 1887.—Pamph. Acts, 1886–7, p. 133.

mite, gunpowder, or any other explosive substance, must, on conviction, be fined not less than ten, nor more than one hundred dollars; one-half of which shall be paid to the informer.

4169 (4406). **Hunting wild hogs.**—Any person, who, without first giving notice to at least three freeholders in the neighborhood, hunts, catches, or kills wild hogs unmarked, with dog or gun, must, on conviction, be fined not less than ten, nor more than one hundred dollars.

4170 (4407). **Fire hunting.**—Any person, who, in the nighttime, hunts deer by fire, and with a gun, must, on conviction. be fined not less than ten, nor more than one hundred dollars.

4171 (4405). **Permitting sheep-killing dogs or hogs to run at large.**—Any person, who, owning or having in his possession, or under his control, any dog or hog known to worry or kill sheep, domestic fowls, or goats, who suffers such dog or hog to run at large, must, on conviction, be fined not less than five, nor more than fifty dollars. *As amended, Feb. 26, 1881, p. 49.*

ARTICLE IX.

MARRIAGE RECORDS AND ILLEGAL CEREMONIES.

4172 (4429). **Failure of probate judge to make record.** Any judge of probate, who fails for more than five days after any marriage license issued by him has been returned by the officer, minister, or other person solemnizing the marriage, to record the same, or to record the certificate of the celebration of the marriage, or to record any consent required by law to be given before issuing a marriage license, is guilty of a misdemeanor.

4173 (4430). **Marrying parties under age, or within prohibited degree.**—Any person, solemnizing the rites of matrimony, with the knowledge that either party is under the age of legal consent, or within the degrees prohibited by law, must, on conviction, be fined not less than one thousand dollars.

4174 (4431). **Certificate of marriage to be returned, etc.** Any judge, minister of the gospel, justice of the peace, or other person uniting together persons in matrimony, or any clerk or keeper of the minutes of a religious society, celebrating marriage by the consent of the parties, before the congregation, who fails to return a certificate thereof to the judge of probate, as required by law, is guilty of a misdemeanor.

4175 (2684). **Solicitors to be notified of offenses.**—It is the duty of the judge of probate to give notice to the solicitor of all offenses under this article.

ARTICLE X.

LEVYING ON COUNTY PROPERTY.

4176 (4421). **Levying on court-house or other county property.**—Any sheriff, or other officer, who levies upon any court-house, poor-house, or other property belonging to any county, must, on conviction, be fined not less than one thousand dollars, and imprisoned in the county jail for not less than twelve months.

ARTICLE XI.

WEARING MILITARY INSIGNIA UNLAWFULLY.

March 1, 1881, p. 108, sec. 1.   **4177. Wearing military insignia of rank without being commissioned.**—Any person, not being duly commissioned, who wears the insignia of rank of any officer of the Alabama State Troops, must, on conviction, be fined not less than fifty dollars.

CHAPTER 10.

OFFENSES AGAINST SUFFRAGE.

ARTICLE 1.—Neglect of duty by officers of election.
2.—Illegal voting, and other offenses by and concerning electors.

ARTICLE I.

NEGLECT OF DUTY BY OFFICERS OF ELECTION.

4178 (4279). **Failure of sheriff to give notice of special election.**—Any sheriff, who fails to give notice of a special election ordered by the governor, as required by law, is guilty of a misdemeanor.

4179 (4280). **Failure of officer to serve notices in contests of elections.**—Any sheriff or constable, who fails to give the notices necessary to be served in cases of contested elections, within the time and in the mode prescribed, if practicable for him to do so, must, on conviction, be fined not less than one hundred, nor more than five hundred dollars.

4180 (4281). **Failure of sheriff to notify judge of probate and clerk of special election.**—Any sheriff, who fails to notify the judge of probate and clerk of the circuit court that any special election is ordered by the governor, as required by law, must, on conviction, be fined not less than one hundred, nor more than five hundred dollars.

4181 (4282). **Failure of sheriff to be present and keep order on election day.**—Any sheriff or deputy, who willfully or corruptly fails to perform any duty imposed by section 377 (281) of the Code, must, on conviction, be fined not less than one thousand, nor more than five thousand dollars, and be imprisoned in the penitentiary for not less than two, nor more than five years, at the discretion of the jury; and, upon conviction, the office of such sheriff is thereby vacated.

4182 (4283). **Failure to deliver votes and poll-list to county returning officer.**—Any returning officer of the precinct, who fails to deliver the statement of votes and the poll-list to the returning officer of the county, within the time required by law, must, on conviction, be fined not less than one hundred, nor more than five hundred dollars, and must also be imprisoned in the county jail for not more than six months.

4183 (4284). **Failure of officers to perform duty under election law.**—If any inspector, clerk, or other officer, on whom any duty is imposed by the election laws, willfully neglects to perform such duty, or is guilty of any corrupt conduct in the execution of the same, and no other punishment is provided for such neglect or conduct, he must, on conviction, be fined not less than one hundred, nor more than one thousand dollars; but no person shall be deemed an inspector, clerk, or officer, within the meaning of this section, until he first shall have taken an oath well and truly to discharge the duties of such office, to the best of his ability, or until he shall have performed some of the duties pertaining to such office. The failure or refusal of any person to accept office, or his failure or refusal to discharge and perform the duties of such office at any time after his appointment thereto, and prior to his taking the oath of such office, and before he shall have discharged and performed any of the duties thereof, shall not, in either event, be deemed a violation of this section.

4184 (4290). **Special charge to grand jury as to violations of election laws.**—It is the duty of the judge of the circuit, city, or criminal court to specially charge the grand jury and direct them to especially inquire into all illegal voting, and also into any and all illegal acts committed by inspectors, returning officers, or other officers of election.

ARTICLE II.

ILLEGAL VOTING AND OTHER OFFENSES BY AND CONCERNING ELECTORS.

4185 (4289). **Illegal voting or attempting to vote.**—Any person, who votes more than once at any election held in this state, or deposits more than one ballot for the same office, as his vote at such election, or knowingly attempts to vote when he is not entitled to do so, or is guilty of any kind of illegal or fraudulent voting, must, on conviction, be imprisoned in the penitentiary for not less than two, nor more than five years, at the discretion of the jury.

Word " election " means act of casting and receiving ballots; the day and time of voting.—Harris v. Tucker, 54 Ala. 205. Elective franchise; nature of.—Washington's case, 75 Ala. 582. Disfranchisement by conviction of petit larceny.—Anderson's case, 72 Ala. 187; Washington's case, 75 Ala. 582. Sec. 3, art. 8, of constitution construed; not an ex post facto law, or bill of attainder.—Ib. 582. Domicil, once acquired, not lost until new one actually gained. *facto et animo*; mere intention to change, without actual removal with intention of remaining, does not cause loss of domicil.—Hallett's case, 8 Ala. 161. Must be knowledge on part of person voting, of facts which disqualify him.—Gordon's case, 52 Ala. 308; Carter's case, 55 Ala. 181. But if one votes recklessly or carelessly, when the facts are doubtful, his ignorance no excuse; and jury will determine whether he acted honestly or recklessly.—Gordon's case, 52 Ala. 308. Sufficiency of indictment.—Wilson's case, 52 Ala. 299; Gordon's case, Ib. 308; Carter's case, 55 Ala. 181. Poll-list best evidence of who voted.—Wilson's case, 52 Ala. 299; Hunter's case, 55 Ala. 767. But, unless certified by inspector, is not competent without proof of correctness.—Ib. 767.

4186 (4291). **Voting without registration and taking oath.** Any person voting at any county or state election, who has not registered and taken and subscribed to the registration oath, must, ou conviction, be fined not less than one hundred, nor more than one thousand dollars, or imprisoned in the county jail, or sentenced to hard labor for the county for not less than one, nor more than six months.

4187 (4292). **Bribing, or attempting to influence voter.** Any person, who, by bribery, or offering to bribe, or by any other corrupt means, attempts to influence any elector in giving his vote, or deter him from giving the same, or to disturb, or to hinder him in the free exercise of the right of suffrage, at any election, must, on conviction, be fined not less than one hundred, nor more than one thousand dollars, and sentenced to hard labor for the county, or imprisoned in the county jail, for not less than thirty days, nor more than six months, at the discretion of the jury.

4188 (4293). **Altering or changing vote of elector.**—Any person, who fraudulently alters or changes the vote of any elector, by which such elector is prevented from voting as he intended, must, on conviction, be fined not less than one hundred, nor more than one thousand dollars, and imprisoned in the county jail for not less than thirty days, nor more than six months.

4189 (4294). **Disturbing elector on election day.**—Any person, who, on election day, disturbs or prevents, or attempts to prevent, any elector from freely casting his ballot, must, on conviction, be fined not less than five hundred, nor more than one thousand dollars, and also sentenced to hard labor for the county, or imprisoned in the county jail, for not less than six months, nor more than one year.

4190 (283, 4285). **Becoming intoxicated about voting-place on election day.**—Any person found drunk or intoxicated at or about any polling-place during any election day, is guilty of a misdemeanor.

4191 (284, 4286). **Disposing of liquor on election day and day preceding.**—Any person, who sells or gives away any vinous, spirituous, or malt liquors during the day on which any election is held in this state, or on the day preceding, must, on conviction, be fined and imprisoned at the discretion of the court.

CHAPTER 11.

OFFENSES NOT SPECIALLY PROVIDED FOR.

4192 (4447). **Misdemeanor for which no special punishment has been provided.**—Any person, who commits a public offense, which is a misdemeanor at common law, or by statute, and the punishment of which is not particularly specified in this Code, must, on conviction, be fined not more than five hundred dollars, and may also be imprisoned in the county jail, or sentenced to hard labor for the county, for not more than six months.

See Redman's case, 33 Ala. 428.

TITLE III.

CRIMINAL COURTS AND PROCEDURE.

CHAPTER 1.

CRIMINAL COURTS.

ARTICLE I.

CRIMINAL COURTS IN GENERAL.

4193 (4626). **Criminal jurisdiction vested in what courts and officers.**—The criminal jurisdiction of this state is vested in the circuit courts, city courts, county courts, justices of the peace, and such other courts and officers as are by law clothed with criminal jurisdiction.

Inherent power of courts to adjourn after opening of term.—Williams' case, 67 Ala. 186.

4194 (571, 618, 657, 694, 746, 758). **Punishments by the respective courts for contempt.**—The courts of this state may punish for contempts by fine and imprisonment, one or both, as follows: The supreme court, by fine not exceeding one hundred dollars, and imprisonment not exceeding ten days; the chancery, circuit and city courts, by fine not exceeding fifty dollars, and imprisonment not exceeding five days; the courts of probate and county courts and registers in chancery, by fine not exceeding twenty dollars, and imprisonment not exceeding twenty-four hours; the courts of county commissioners, by fine not exceeding ten dollars, and imprisonment not exceeding six hours; and justices of the peace, by fine not exceeding six dollars, and imprisonment not exceeding six hours.

Courts of justice have inherent power to punish all persons for contempt of their rules and orders, for disobedience of their process, and for disturbing them in their proceedings.—Ex parte Hardy, 68 Ala. 303; Withers' case, 36 Ala. 252. Cannot be revised by appellate court, or by habeas corpus.—Ex parte Hardy, supra. When attachment for contempt a civil remedy.—Ib. Contempt by an attorney, and power of court to remove or suspend.—Withers' case, supra. Rufusal to pay over money under a chancery decree; jurisdiction, discretion. etc.—Ex parte Walker, 25 Ala. 81.

ARTICLE II.

THE CIRCUIT AND CITY COURTS.

4195. Jurisdiction of city courts.—The city courts have, in the counties in which they are respectively established, unless otherwise provided, the same criminal jurisdiction, both original and appellate, that the circuit courts have in other counties.

4196 (4627). **Jurisdiction of circuit courts.** — The circuit courts have original jurisdiction of all felonies and misdemeanors, committed in the several counties in which they may be held, under the regulations prescribed by law; and they have appellate jurisdiction of all criminal cases tried before the county courts, or before justices of the peace, under the rules hereinafter prescribed.

Incompetency of judge. *Nemo judex in causa propria.*—Castleberry's case, 23 Ala. 88. No objection that the presiding judge is connected by marriage with the owner of the building as to which the burglary was alleged to have been committed.—Newman's case, 49 Ala. 9. Objection to competency of presiding judge of county court no ground for reversal of judgment.—Sale's case, 68 Ala. 530. Relation of judge to person slain, though not within the letter of the statute, renders judge incompetent to preside at trial of slayer for murder.—Gill's case, 61 Ala. 169. Incompetency no ground for reversing the judgment.—Sale's case, 68 Ala. 530.

ARTICLE III.

COUNTY COURTS AND PROCEEDINGS THEREIN.

4197 (719). **Probate judge ex officio judge of county court; official oath.**—The judges of probate shall be, ex officio, the judges of the county courts of their respective counties; and each of the said judges shall, before he enters on the discharge of the duties of his office, take and subscribe the oaths prescribed by law for other judicial officers, and further swear that he will faithfully report to the court of county commissioners a just and true statement of the services performed by him for which he is entitled to fees; which oaths must be filed in the office of the clerk of the circuit court.

4198 (720). **Official bond of county court judge.** — The judges of the several county courts shall each enter into bond, payable to the State of Alabama, with two or more good and sufficient sureties, to be approved by the judge of the circuit court, in the penalty of five thousand dollars, conditioned that he will faithfully perform the duties of his office, and will pay into the county treasury, punctually, all the moneys, fines and forfeitures that come into his hands by virtue of his said office.

4199 (721). **Clerk of county court.**—The judges of the county courts are the clerks of their respective courts, but may, at their own expense, employ a clerk, who may do all acts not judicial in their character.

Clerk has no power to take affidavits for warrant of arrest, or to administer oaths. Lloyd's case, 70 Ala. 32. Mere issuance of alias warrant of arrest, not a judicial act, and may be done by clerk.—McLeod v. McLeod, 75 Ala. 483.

4200 (722). **Terms attended by sheriff, etc.; his fees.**—The terms of the county court shall be attended by the sheriff or deputy sheriff; and, in their absence, some suitable person shall be appointed by the court to act in their stead, whose compensation shall be two dollars a day, to be paid out of the county treasury.

4201 (718). **Jurisdiction of county courts.** — The county courts have original jurisdiction, concurrent with the circuit and city courts, of all misdemeanors committed in their respective counties.

No jurisdiction to impose upon sheriff fine for not executing writ of arrest; sheriff entitled to prohibition to restrain such action.—State v. McDuffie, 52 Ala. 4.

4202 (723). **Monthly terms held; notice published.**—A county court, for the trial of misdemeanors, shall be held once a month in each county in this state, at the court-house thereof; the day of the week and month in which the court is held to be fixed by the judge, and ten days' notice thereof to be given by him, prior to the first term, in a newspaper published in the county, or some adjoining county, or by posting the same at the door of the court-house, and three other public places in the county; but a failure to give such notice shall not affect the validity of his judgments or sentences.

4203 (724). **Courts always open for trial of certain cases.** The county courts in the several counties in this state shall be open, at the discretion of the judges, any day during the week, except Sunday, for the trial of offenses coming within their jurisdiction, in all cases where the party or parties charged cannot give bond and security for their appearance at the regular terms of said courts, or desire an immediate trial; and, in such cases, causes may be continued for good cause shown under the regulations governing the continuances of causes in justices' courts; but nothing herein contained shall be so construed as to prevent or interfere with the regular terms of county courts.

4204 (4702). **Warrant of arrest issued by judge or justice on affidavit.**—A party aggrieved, or desiring to bring a charge of misdemeanor before the county court, may apply to the judge thereof, or to some justice of the peace of the county, for a warrant of arrest; and, upon making affidavit in writing, that he has probable cause for believing, and does believe that an offense (designating the misdemeanor by name, or by some other phrase which, in common parlance, designates it), has been committed in said county by C. D. (naming the offender), on the person (or property, as the case may be) of A. B. (naming the person injured), then the judge of said court, or justice of the peace, shall issue his warrant of arrest.

Affidavit not confined to offenses against the person or property, as form indicates.—Sale's case, 68 Ala. 530. Same particularity as in describing offense by indictment, not required; sufficient to designate offense by name, or by some phrase which, in common parlance, describes it.—Brazelton's case, 66 Ala. 96. Time need not be alleged.—Bell's case, 75 Ala. 25.

4205 (4703). **Form of warrant.**—The warrant of arrest may be in the following form:

9—VOL. II.

" The State of Alabama, ⎱ To any lawful officer of the State of
—— county. ⎰ Alabama :

" You are hereby commanded to arrest C. D., and bring him before me on the —— day of ——, next, to answer the State of Alabama of a charge of (describe the offense as stated in the affidavit), preferred by A. B.

" Witness my hand, this —— day of ——, 18—.

" D. C., County Judge.

" Summon E. F. and G. H., witnesses for the state; J. K. and L. M., witnesses for the defendant.

" D. C., County Judge."

4206 (4704). **By whom warrant executed.**—The sheriff or any constable of the county may execute the warrant of arrest, and bring the defendant before the court; and may also summon the witnesses and serve all other process.

4207 (4705). **Speedy trial; continuance.**—Justice shall be speedily administered in such court. If the accused and prosecutor are present before the court, or if the accused is present and the prosecutor has notice by having sued out the warrant of arrest, or otherwise, then the case stands for trial, and may be disposed of; but, for good cause shown, the trial may be adjourned to the next succeeding term.

4208 (4706). **Bail; form of undertaking.**—If the court is not in session when the defendant is brought before the judge thereof, or if the case should be continued for trial at a subsequent term, the defendant may be admitted to bail, on his entering into bond with two good sureties, in such sum as the judge of the court may prescribe; which bond may be in the following or equivalent words :

" The State of Alabama, ⎱ We, C. D., and O. P. and Q. R., his
—— county. ⎰ sureties, acknowledge ourselves indebted to the State of Alabama, in the sum of —— dollars; to be void if I, C. D., appear at the next term of the county court of said county, and from term to term until discharged, and answer the charge of (describe the offense), preferred against me by A. B.

" Witness our hands, this —— day of ——, 18—.

" C. D.,
" O. P.,
" Q. R."

"Approved:
"D. C., County Judge."

4209 (4707). **Bail taken by arresting officer.**—In like manner, the judge of the county court must, when he issues his warrant of arrest, indorse on the same the amount for which the defendant may give bail; and in such case the officer arresting must admit the defendant to bail, on his entering into bond, in substance as given in the preceding section, with two good sureties, and approved by such officer.

4210 (4708). **Subpœnas; by whom issued and executed.** The judge of the county court, or any justice of the peace of the county, may issue subpœnas for witnesses, at the instance of the prosecutor or defendant; and it is the duty of the arresting officer, the sheriff, or any constable, to whom they are delivered, to execute and return them to court.

4211 (4709). **Form of subpœna.**—Subpœnas may be substantially in the following form:

"The State of Alabama, ⎱ To any lawful officer of said state:
——— county.   ⎰

"Summon E. F., witness for the state (or J. K., witness for the defendant, as the case may be), to appear before the county court of said county, on the ——— day of ———, and testify in a case in said court of the State vs. C. D. for (here describe the offense), and to appear from term to term until discharged.

"Witness my hand, this ——— day of ———, 18—.
                    "D. C., County Judge,
                    (or S. T., Justice of the Peace.)"

4212 (4710). **Judgment nisi on default of appearance.**—If the defendant fail to appear as required by his bond, the county court shall enter up a forfeiture against him and his sureties, which may be in the following form:

"The State   ⎱ In the county court of ———
   .vs.   ⎰ county, ——— day of ———,
C. D., defendant;   18—.
O. P. and Q. R., his sureties.

"In this case, C. D. failing to appear and answer the charge against him for (here describe the offense as in the affidavit), a judgment is entered against him and his said sureties for ——— dollars (the amount of the penalty of the bond), in favor of the state, for the use of the county of ———, unless they appear at the next term of this court and show cause to the contrary; and it is ordered that notice issue to them."

4213 (4711). **Scire facias thereon.**—The county judge shall thereupon issue a notice to said defendant, and cause it, together with a copy of the conditional judgment rendered, to be served on said defendant, or to be left at his last known place of residence or habitation in said county, three days before the next term of his court, which notice may be in the following form:

"The State of Alabama, ⎱ To any lawful officer of said state:
——— county.   ⎰

"Notify C. D. that a conditional judgment was rendered against him and his sureties, O. P. and Q. R., of which the inclosed is a copy.

"Witness my hand, this ——— day of ———, 18—.
                    "C. D., County Judge."

4214 (4712). **Judgment final on default.**—If the defendant, on being thus notified, fails to appear, or appears but fails to show a satisfactory excuse for his default, and no sufficient cause is shown for a continuance of the case, the court shall render judgment final, which may be in the following form:

"The State   ⎱ Proceedings for (here describe
   vs.   ⎰ the offense as in the affidavit).
C. D., defendant; O. P. and
Q. R., his sureties for arrest.

"In this case, the defendant being notified, and offering no sufficient excuse for his default, the judgment is made final against him and his sureties in favor of the State of Alabama, for the use of the county of ———."

4215 (4713). **Remission of forfeiture.**—If the defendant appears and submits to trial, the court may release him and his sureties from any part of the forfeiture which seems just; in which case the following should be added to the judgment-entry: "But the court releases the defendants from —— dollars of the said judgment."

4216 (4714). **Judgment against defaulting witness.** — If witnesses, after being summoned, fail to appear and testify, as commanded, a conditional judgment may be rendered against them; if state witnesses, in favor of the state, for the use of the county; if defendant's witnesses, in favor of such defendant; and, in such cases, the proceedings may, in all material respects, be made to conform to those given for forfeitures of bail-bonds. The penalty for non-attendance by a witness in the county court is fifty dollars, and the judgment must be entered for that amount.

4217 (4715). **Alias warrant of arrest or subpœna.**—When a forfeiture has been taken against a defendant and the sureties on his bail-bond, it shall be the duty of the court to issue another warrant of arrest against the defendant, upon which the same proceedings shall be had as upon the original warrant; and when a forfeiture has been entered against a witness for non-attendance, another subpœna may be issued for him, upon which the same proceedings may be had as upon the original subpœna.

4218 (4716). **Copy of accusation delivered to defendant on demand.**—When brought before the county court for trial, the accused, if he demands it, must be furnished with a copy of the accusation, as contained in the warrant of arrest.

4219 (4717). **Proceedings on demand of trial by jury.**—If he demands a trial by jury, it shall be the duty of the judge to require him to enter into bond, with good sureties, in such sum as such judge may deem sufficient, conditioned for his appearance at the next term of the circuit or city court of the county, to answer the charge; and to return such bond, if given, to the clerk of the court before which the accused is required by it to appear; and if the accused fails to give such bond, he must be committed to the county jail until the next term of the circuit or city court of the county having jurisdiction of the offense, unless he elects, in the meantime, to perform hard labor for the county as provided by law.

When jury trial demanded, the case is transferred, and goes before the grand jury, where indictment is necessary for trial in circuit or city court.—Clark's case. 46 Ala. 307.

4220 (4718). **Judge to decide law and fact without jury.** In trials before the county court, the judge shall determine both the law and the facts, without the intervention of a jury, and shall award the punishment which the character of the offense demands; and no statement of the offense need be made other than that contained in the affidavit and warrant of arrest.

4221 (4719). **Form of judgment of conviction.**—The judgment in case of conviction may be in the following form:

" The State ⎰ (Here state the offense by name, or as described
vs.   ⎱   in the affidavit.)
C. D.

" On hearing the evidence, the court is satisfied of the guilt of defendant, and awards the following punishment: (Here state the punishment imposed), and the costs of the proceedings.
                                "D. C., Judge of County Court."

4222 (4720). **Judgment discharging defendant.**—If the defendant is acquitted, the judgment-entry must be that the defendant is discharged.

4223 (4721). **When judgment for costs against prosecutor.** If the prosecution appears to the court to be malicious or frivolous, the court shall tax the prosecutor with the costs, in which case the judgment-entry may be as follows:

" The State ⎰ Prosecution for (here describe the offense by
vs.   ⎱   name, or some familiar description), instituted by
C. D.   A. B.

" In this case, the prosecution appearing to be malicious (or frivolous), the costs are taxed against A. B., the prosecutor."

4224 (4722). **Jeofails and amendments.**—It shall be no objection to the proceedings of the county court, either in that court or elsewhere, that they are imperfect or inaccurate; and when its proceedings are reviewed on appeal or certiorari, all amendable errors shall be regarded as amended, so as to present only the substantial inquiry of the guilt or innocence of the accused.

4225 (4723). **Issue and return of executions.**—Executions issued from the county court shall be made returnable to a term of such court six months after the rendition of the judgment upon which the same is issued, and six months shall intervene between the issue and return of any subsequent execution from such court.

4226 (4724). **Appeal to circuit or city court; appeal bond.** In all cases of conviction in the county court, the defendant shall have the right of appeal to the circuit or city court of the county, on entering into bond, with two or more sufficient sureties, to appear at the term of the court to which the appeal is taken, and from term to term until discharged; the bond to be in such penalty as the judge of the county court may prescribe, and to be approved by him.

Appeal from county court cannot be dismissed because county court had adjourned before appeal sued out.—Mobley's case, 53 Ala. 646.

4227 (4725). **Transcript, etc., returned to court.**—When an appeal is taken under the preceding section, the judge of the county court shall make out a copy of all the proceedings had in his court, except the subpœnas for witnesses and the appeal bond, certify the same as correct, and hand the transcript, together with the appeal bond, to the clerk of the circuit or city court, who shall place the same on his trial docket of criminal cases.

4228 (4726). **Subpœnas for witnesses on appeal.**—In cases of appeal from the county court, the judge of the court shall issue subpœnas for such witnesses as may be required, both for

the state and for the accused, returnable to the next term of the
court, to which the appeal is taken; which subpœnas shall be
executed by the sheriff, and returned to such circuit or city
court; and if witnesses so summoned fail to appear and testify
as required, they shall be liable to the same penalties, forfeitures and proceedings, as if the subpœnas had been issued out
of the circuit or city court.

4229 (4727). **Forfeiture of appeal bond; alias warrant of
arrest to issue.**—If the defendant fails to appear at the circuit
or city court as required by the appeal bond, he shall be liable
to the same penalties, forfeitures and proceedings, as on a forfeited bail-bond taken in that court; and a new warrant of
arrest may issue from that court, without any other authority
therefor.

4230 (4728). **Arrest on warrant as on capias.**—Such warrant of arrest must be directed to any sheriff of the State of
Alabama; and when the defendant is arrested, he must be dealt
with in all respects as if the arrest had been made on capias
from the circuit court.

4231 (4729). **Trial of appeal de novo; statement of cause
of complaint.**—The trial in the circuit or city court shall be de
novo, and without any indictment or presentment by the grand
jury; but the solicitor shall make a brief statement of the
cause of complaint, signed by him, which may be in the following form:

"The State of Alabama,   } In the circuit (or city court), ——
—— county.   } term, 18—.   On appeal from the
                         } county court.

"The State of Alabama, by its solicitor, complains of C. D.
that, within twelve months before the commencement of this
prosecution, he did (here describe the offense as in cases of indictment).   G. H., Solicitor."

Brief statement of the "complaint," signed by the solicitor, is essential to trial
on appeal; and proceeding without it, unless waived, is erroneous.—Moss' case.
42 Ala. 546. But parties may, by consent, dispense with filing of complaint by
solicitor and substitute for it affidavit on which warrant for arrest issued.—Carlisle's
case, 76 Ala. 75. This "statement of cause of complaint" is analogous to an information at common law, and may be amended by leave of court.—Tatum's case,
66 Ala. 465.

4232 (4730). **Practice, evidence, etc., same as in other
cases.**—On the trial of such appeals, the court shall be governed by the same rules, as to evidence, practice, finding of the
jury, and punishment, as if the case had originated in that court.

- -

ARTICLE IV.

JUSTICES OF THE PEACE AND PROCEEDINGS BEFORE THEM.

4233 (4628). **Jurisdiction of justices of the peace.**—Justices
of the peace have, in their respective counties, concurrently
with the county courts, jurisdiction of the following offenses:
Violations of Sunday, vagrancy, assaults, assaults and batteries,
and affrays, in which no stick or other weapon is used; and,
when the value of the commodity which is the subject of the
crime does not exceed ten dollars, of larceny, whether at com-

mon law, or by statute, obtaining money by false pretenses or token with intent to defraud another, embezzlement, and receiving stolen or embezzled goods, knowing them to be stolen or embezzled; and for failure to work on public road after legal notice, and of offenses for cruelty to animals, and of public drunkenness.

Have jurisdiction of petit larceny concurrent with circuit and city court, when value does not exceed ten dollars, and may sentence to hard labor not exceeding twelve months.—Ex parte Hixon, 41 Ala. 410. No jurisdiction of assaults and batteries with weapons; hence, judgment in such offense is void, and no bar to subsequent indictment.—Danzey's case, 68 Ala. 296. No jurisdiction to impose hard labor for non-payment of costs.—Ex parte McKivett, 55 Ala. 236. See Ex parte Sam, 51 Ala. 34.

4234 (759, 4698). **Required to keep docket and exhibit it to grand jury; other duties.**—It is the duty of every justice of the peace and notary public having and exercising the jurisdiction of justices of the peace,—

1. To keep a docket of all criminal cases tried, which docket shall set forth the nature of each case, the judgment rendered therein, an itemized copy of the bill of costs, by whom and of whom the fine and costs were collected, and the disposition made thereof; and such justice of the peace and notary public must attend in person, or make a report in writing of his docket to the grand jury of his county, for their inspection during each term of the circuit or city court.

2. To perform such other duties as are, or may be required of him by law.

4235 (4694). **Copy of accusation delivered to defendant on demand.**—When a person is arrested and brought before a justice of the peace, charged with a public offense, of which such justice has jurisdiction under the provisions of this Code, he must be furnished, if he demand it, with a copy of the accusation, as contained in the warrant of arrest.

4236 (4699). **Forms; same as in county court.**—The forms for proceedings before the county court, under the provisions of the preceding article, or others substantially the same, may be used by a justice of the peace in cases tried before him.

The initiatory step in criminal proceedings, by which the jurisdiction of a justice of the peace is called into exercise, is a complaint on oath, charging the person named with the commission of a specified offense.—Drake's case, 68 Ala. 510. And all such proceedings before justices in the exercise of enlarged jurisdiction must conform to these statutory provisions.—Ib. Insufficient affidavit as to wantonly killing an animal; when charges no offense, and effect on appeal.—Blankenshire's case, 70 Ala. 10. Affidavit "that he has reason for believing, and does believe," etc., sufficient.—Sale's ease, 68 Ala. 530.

4237 (4697.) **Justice to decide law and facts without jury.** In all trials before a justice of the peace of causes which are within his jurisdiction, he must determine both the law and the facts without the intervention of a jury, and award the punishment which the offense may demand.

May sentence to hard labor not exceeding twelve months.—Ex parte Sam, 51 Ala. 34. But not for costs.—Ex parte McKivett, 55 Ala. 236. Duty of justice under this section.—Ex parte Dunklin, 72 Ala. 241.

4238 (4695). **Proceedings when defendant demands trial by jury.**—If the defendant demands a trial by jury, he must be required to enter into bond, with good sureties, conditioned for his appearance at the next term of the circuit or city court of the county to answer the charge; and, failing to give such bond, must be committed to the county jail until the next term of the circuit or city court having jurisdiction of the offense, unless he elect, in the meantime, to perform hard labor for the county as provided by law.

Justice has no jurisdiction to try a party demanding a jury, but must bind him over or hold him to next term of circuit court.—Ex parte Dunklin, 72 Ala. 241.

4239 (4696). **Trial; continuances.**—If the accused and the prosecutor are both present, and also the witnesses for the prosecution and defense, and the accused does not demand a trial by jury, the trial must proceed before the justice, unless, for good cause shown, he continues it to some other day not more than ten days distant.

4240 (3611, 3614). **Subpœnas and attachments for witnesses.**—The justice, on the application of either party, must issue subpœnas for witnesses, stating therein the name of the party by whom the witness is summoned, and the time and place of trial, which must be executed in the same manner as subpœnas in civil cases; and if any witness duly summoned fails to attend, he may be compelled by attachment to appear and give evidence.

4241 (3613, 3614). **Proceedings against defaulting witness.** If any witness, duly summoned, fails to attend, a forfeiture may be taken against him and enforced as in civil cases before such justices.

As amended, Feb. 13, 1879, p. 54.

4242 (4700). **Appeal to circuit or county court; appeal bond.**—In cases tried before a justice of the peace, the defendant, if convicted, shall have the right to appeal to the next ensuing term of the circuit or city court of the county, on entering into bond, with sufficient sureties, in such sum as the justice may require, conditioned that he will appear at the court to which the appeal is taken, until discharged by due course of law.

4243 (4701). **Appeal; how tried.**—The trial in the circuit or city court, on appeal from a judgment rendered by a justice, shall be de novo, and shall be governed in all respects by the rules and regulations prescribed for the trial of appeals from the county court.

CHAPTER 2.

SOLICITORS.

4244 (769). **How solicitors elected.**—A solicitor for each judicial circuit in the state must be elected by joint vote of the general assembly, and his term of office shall be for six years.

4245 (770). **Vacancies; how filled.**—Vacancies in such office are filled by the governor.

4246 (771). **Must reside in circuit, or vacate office; notice of vacancy.**—Every solicitor must reside in his circuit at the time of his election and during his continuance in office, or he vacates his office; and it is the duty of the judge of the circuit to notify the governor of such failure, who must supply the vacancy.

4247 (772). **Their duties within their circuit.**—Their duties are, within their circuits,—

1. To attend on the grand juries, advise them in relation to matters of law, and examine and swear witnesses before them.

2. To draw up all indictments and to prosecute all indictable offenses.

3. To prosecute and defend any civil action in the circuit court, in the prosecution or defense of which the state is interested.

4. To inquire whether registers in chancery have performed the duty required of them in section 743 (646), and must, in every case of failure, move against such register as required by section 3131 (3392).

5. If a criminal prosecution is removed from a court of his circuit to a court of the United States, to appear in such court and represent the state; and if it be impracticable for him, consistently with his other duties, to attend such court, he may designate and appoint an attorney practicing therein to appear for, and represent the state. ^{Nov. 26, 1884, p. 72.}

6. On or before the first Monday in October in each year, to make report in writing to the attorney-general, stating the number and names of persons prosecuted during the year preceding the date of his report in the several counties within the territorial limits of his office, the character of the alleged offenses, the result of the trial, and the punishments imposed, and the amount of his fee collected in every case. For failure to perform this duty, he must, on conviction, be fined not less than one hundred dollars. ^{Feb. 5, 1883, p. 39.}

7. To attend each special term of the circuit court held for the trial of persons charged with felony; and on failure so to do, a conditional judgment must be rendered against him for fifty dollars, to be made absolute on notice to him at the next term thereafter, unless a good excuse is rendered.

8. To perform such other duties as are, or may be required by law.

4248 (773). **Duty to attend court; penalty for absence.** The solicitors must attend each regular term of the circuit court in their circuits, and remain until the business of the state is disposed of; if absent, a conditional judgment must be rendered against them for one hundred dollars, to be made absolute on notice to such solicitor at the next term thereafter, unless a good excuse is rendered.

4249 (774). **Must attend special terms; penalty on failure.**—The solicitor must also attend each special term of the circuit court, held for trial of persons charged with felony; and on failure so to do, a conditional judgment must be rendered against him for fifty dollars, to be made absolute as in the preceding section, unless a good excuse is rendered.

4250 (775). **When attorney appointed to act as solicitor; compensation.**—The presiding judge, when the solicitor is absent, or when he is connected with the party against whom it is his duty to appear, by consanguinity or affinity within the fourth degree, or when there is a vacancy in the office from any cause, or when the general assembly has failed to elect a solicitor, or when the solicitor refuses to act, must appoint a ^{As amended, Feb. 18, 1879, p. 42.}

competent attorney to act in the solicitor's place, who shall act
during the absence or disqualification of the solicitor, or until
the office is filled by the appointment of the governor, or by an
election by the general assembly, or while the solicitor refuses
to act; and in all such cases the attorney so appointed shall be
entitled to all the fees allowed to solicitors, which shall be taxed
against the defendant, on conviction, and collected in the same
manner that solicitor's fees are collected.

4251 (776). **Solicitor suspended when indicted.**—When it
shall be made known to any circuit or city court that an indictment is pending against the person who is acting as solicitor of
the county in which the court is held, the court must make an
order suspending such solicitor; and the solicitor so suspended
shall not act as solicitor until such order of suspension shall be
set aside.

Conviction of felony vacates office.—Ex parte Diggs, 50 Ala. 78. County
solicitor a "ministerial officer," indictable for receiving a bribe, although merely
acting solicitor de facto.—Diggs' case, 49 Ala. 311.

4252 (777). **Same; appointment pro tem.**—When any solicitor is suspended, the court shall appoint a solicitor pro tem.,
who shall perform the duties of the office of solicitor, and receive the fees and emoluments thereof, from such appointment
until the original order suspending the solicitor shall be set
aside.

See note to preceding section.

4253 (778). **When order of suspension set aside.**—When
it shall be known to the court that there is no indictment pending in the court in which such indictment was found, or in any
court to which a cause may have been removed by change of
venue, against a solicitor who has been suspended, the order
suspending such solicitor shall be set aside.

4254 (779). **Shall not commence prosecution on own affidavit; exceptions.**—It shall not be lawful for a solicitor to
commence a criminal prosecution by his own affidavit, except
for an offense against his person or his property, or the affidavit
be upon his personal knowledge of the commission of the
offense charged, except for violation of the revenue laws of the
state.

When prosecution will not be dismissed as being brought in violation of this
statute.—Sale's case, 68 Ala. 530. Statute construed.—Ib.

CHAPTER 3.

PRELIMINARY PROCEEDINGS; ARREST AND BAIL.

ARTICLE 1.--Complaint, depositions, and warrant of arrest.

    2.—By whom, how and where arrests may be made.

    3.—Discharge on bail before, or without preliminary examination.

    4.—Preliminary examination and its incidents.

ARTICLE I.

COMPLAINT, DEPOSITIONS AND WARRANT OF ARREST.

4255 (4647). **Definition of complaint.**—The complaint is an allegation, made before a proper magistrate, that a person has been guilty of a designated public offense.

This and three succeeding sections apply only to preliminary proceedings before committing magistrates, and not to criminal prosecutions before the county court, and justices of the peace —Sale's case, 68 Ala. 530. Technical accuracy not required in preliminary proceedings; what sufficient.—Brown's case, 63 Ala. 97; Rhodes v. King, 52 Ala 272.

4256 (4648). **Plaintiff examined on oath; depositions reduced to writing, and subscribed.**—Upon a complaint being made to any one of the magistrates specified in section 4680 (4026) that such offense has, in the opinion of the complainant, been committed, the magistrate must examine the complainant and such witnesses as he may propose, on oath, take their depositions in writing, and cause them to be subscribed by the persons making them.

4257 (4649). **What depositions must state.**—The depositions must set forth the facts stated by the complainant and his witnesses, tending to establish the commission of the offense and the guilt of the defendant.

Duty of committing magistrate under this section.—Harris' case, 73 Ala. 495. Statutes authorizing the taking of testimony by depositions in criminal cases have no application to preliminary examinations.—Couch's case, 63 Ala. 163.

4258 (4650). **Warrant of arrest to issue, if probable cause shown.**—If the magistrate is reasonably satisfied from such depositions that the offense complained of has been committed, and there is reasonable ground to believe that the defendant is guilty thereof, he must issue a warrant of arrest.

4259 (4651, 4652). **Form and contents of warrant; to whom directed and by whom executed.**—A warrant of arrest is an order in writing, issued and signed by a magistrate, stating the substance of the complaint, directed to a proper officer, and commanding him to arrest the defendant; and such warrant must designate the name of the defendant, if known, but if it state that the name is unknown to the magistrate, then no name need be inserted. It must also state the offense, either by name, or so that it can be clearly inferred; the county in which it was issued must appear from some part of the warrant; and the warrant must be signed by the magistrate, with his name and initials of office, or the same must in some way appear from the warrant. It must be directed "To any lawful officer of the state," but if executed by any lawful officer, having authority to execute it, it is valid, without regard to its direction. It may be, in substance, as follows:

"The State of Alabama, ⎱ To any lawful officer of the state:
—— county.   ⎰

"Complaint on oath having been made before me that the offense of (designating or describing it) has been committed, and accusing C. D. thereof; you are therefore commanded forthwith to arrest C. D., and bring him before me.

"Dated the —— day of ——, 18——.

"(Signed)   E. F. Justice of the Peace
(or other magistrate, as the case may be)."

Technical accuracy not required; sufficient to designate offense, either in complaint or warrant, by name only, or by words from which it may be inferred. Brown's case 63 Ala. 97; Rhodes v. King, 52 Ala. 272; Crosby v. Hawthorn, 25 Ala. 221. Mere clerical misprision (omitting the word "me") does not effect sufficiency of warrant.—Johnson's case, 73 Ala. 21.

ARTICLE II.

BY WHOM, HOW AND WHEN ARRESTS MAY BE MADE.

4260 (4653). **What officers may make arrests.**—An arrest may be made, under a warrant, or without a warrant, by any sheriff, or other officer acting as sheriff, or his deputy, or by any constable, acting within their respective counties, or by any marshal, deputy marshal, or policeman of any incorporated city or town, within the limits of the county.

Policeman may arrest anywhere in the county.—Williams' case, 44 Ala. 41. Power of marshal and constables to arrest without a warrant, and to imprison after arrest.—Hayes v. Mitchell, 69 Ala. 452. Right to resist illegal arrest; murder to kill one accused of misdemeanor, to prevent flight; rule different in felony.—Williams' case, supra.

4261 (4654). **Arrest by officer under warrant; when and how made.**—Any officer may execute a warrant of arrest on any day· and at any time; he must, in doing so, inform the defendant of his authority, and, if required, must show the warrant; and if he is refused admittance, after notice of his authority and purpose, he may break an outer or inner door or window of a dwelling-house, in order to make the arrest.

Warrant void on its face will not protect officer executing it.—Noles' case, 24 Ala. 672; Sassnett v. Weathers, 21 Ala. 673; Crumpton v. Newman, 12 Ala. 199; Duckworth v. Johnston, 7 Ala. 578. Warrant issued by notary as ex officio justice of the peace, after his term of office has expired, invalid, and does not authorize arrest by officer, unless shown that notary was officer de facto.—Cary's case, 76 Ala. 78. What constitutes officer de facto.—Ib.; Heath's case, 36 Ala. 273.

4262 (4664). **Arrest by officer without warrant; when and for what allowed.**—An officer may also arrest any person, without warrant, on any day and at any time, for any public offense committed, or a breach of the peace threatened in his presence; or when a felony has been committed, though not in his presence, by the person arrested, or when a felony has been committed, and he has reasonable cause to believe that the person arrested committed it; or when he has reasonable cause to believe that the person arrested has committed a felony, although it may afterwards appear that a felony had not in fact been committed; or on a charge made, upon reasonable cause, that the person arrested has committed a felony.

Arrests without warrant not forbidden by constitution; it is the issue of warrant without oath or affirmation which is prohibited.—Williams' case, 44 Ala. 41.

4263 (4665). **Duty and authority of officer in making arrest without warrant.**—When arresting a person without a warrant, the officer must inform him of his authority and the cause of arrest, except when he is arrested in the actual commission of a public offense, or on pursuit; and has authority to break open an outer or inner door or window of a dwelling-house, if, after notice of his office and purpose, he is refused admittance.

4264 (4666). **Private person must assist officer.**—It is the duty of every person, when required to do so by an officer, to assist him in making an arrest.

4265 (4667). **Arrest on order of magistrate without warrant; when made.**—When a public offense is committed in the presence of a magistrate, he may, by verbal or written order, command any person to arrest the offender; and, when arrested, may thereupon proceed as if such offender had been brought before him on a warrant of arrest.

4266 (4668, 4670). **When private person may arrest.**—A private person may arrest another for any public offense committed in his presence; or where a felony has been committed, though not in his presence, by the person arrested; or where a felony has been committed, and he has reasonable cause to believe that the person arrested committed it; and an arrest for felony may be made by a private person on any day, and at any time.

Private person acts by permission, not by command of the law.—Morrell v. Quarles, 35 Ala. 544.

4267 (4669). **His duty and authority in such case.**—He must, at the time of the arrest, inform the person to be arrested of the cause thereof, except when such person is in the actual commission of an offense, or arrested on pursuit; and if he is refused admittance, after notice of his intention, and the person to be arrested has committed a felony, he may break open an outer or inner door or window of a dwelling-house.

4268 (4671). **Must take person arrested before magistrate.** It is the duty of any private person, having arrested another for the commission of any public offense, to take him without unnecessary delay before a magistrate, or to deliver him to some one of the officers specified in section 4260 (4653), who must forthwith take him before a magistrate.

Cary's case, 76 Ala. 78.

4269 (4672). **Re-arrest after escape or rescue.**—If a person arrested escapes or is rescued, he may be immediately pursued by the officer or person in whose custody he was, and retaken at any time, and in any place in the state; and if such officer or person is refused admittance, after notice of his intention, he may break open an outer or inner door or window of a dwelling-house, in order to retake the person so escaping or rescued.

4270 (4655). **Warrant executed, where; when written indorsement required.**—A warrant of arrest, when issued by a judge of the supreme or circuit court, or by a chancellor, may be executed in any county in the state; but if issued by any other magistrate, it must be executed in the county in which it was issued, unless the defendant is in another county; and when the defendant is in another county, it may be executed therein, on a written indorsement on the warrant by a magistrate of that county, signed by him, to the following effect: "This warrant may be executed in —— county."

Justice of the peace no authority to issue warrant for arrest of person to answer charge in another county.—Woodall v. McMillan, 38 Ala. 622.

4271 (4656). **Authority of officer to pursue and arrest in another county.**—Any lawful officer, having a warrant of arrest to execute, may pursue the defendant into another county; and, on obtaining an indorsement on the warrant by a magistrate of that county, signed by such magistrate, to the following effect: "A. B. is authorized to execute this warrant in —— county," may summon persons to assist him in making the arrest, and exercise the same authority as in his own county.

Statute construed; does not mean that execution of warrant must be begun in the county of the arresting officer, while accused is there, and followed up in the event of his fleeing to another county.—Coleman's case, 63 Ala. 93.

4272 (4657). **Indorsement on warrant by magistrate.**—The indorsement of the magistrate, according to the provisions of the last two sections, must not be made unless he is satisfied from his own knowledge, or from the oral or written statement, on oath, of some credible persons, proving the handwriting of the magistrate issuing the warrant, in the one case, and in the other, that the person in pursuit is an officer authorized to make the arrest in the county in which the warrant issued.

4273 (4658). **Magistrate not liable on indorsement.**—No magistrate, having complied with the provisions of the last section, is liable to any indictment or action for making such indorsement, although it may afterwards appear that such warrant was illegally issued, or that the person was not authorized to execute the same.

4274 (4663). **When defendant must be carried before magistrate issuing warrant.**—When the warrant of arrest is executed in any other county than the one in which it is issued, and is for felony, or when for a misdemeanor, and the defendant is not bailed according to the provisions of sections 4275 (4659) and 4276 (4660), he must be brought before the magistrate issuing the warrant, or if such magistrate is unable to attend, or his office vacant, before some other magistrate of the county in which such warrant issued; and the warrant, with a proper return thereon, must be delivered to such magistrate.

ARTICLE III.

DISCHARGE ON BAIL, BEFORE OR WITHOUT PRELIMINARY EXAMINATION.

4275 (4659). **When officer arresting may discharge on bail.** When the offense described in the warrant is a misdemeanor, and it is executed by the sheriff or his deputy, such sheriff or deputy may, on the request of the defendant, discharge him, on sufficient bail for his appearance at the next term of the court having jurisdiction of the offense, to answer any indictment which may be found against him therefor; and, if such court is in session, for his appearance at such court.

Sheriff or deputy not required to certify recognizance; being found on file connects it with the return on the capias.—Shreeve's case, 11 Ala. 679. If justice issuing warrant has no jurisdiction to try the case, sheriff may take bail for defendant to appear at next term of court having jurisdiction, or at the present term, if court in session; but if conditioned to appear before the justice, it is void.—Jones' case, 63 Ala. 161.

4276 (4660). **Discharge on bail by magistrate.**—When the offense described in the warrant is a misdemeanor, and it is not executed by the sheriff or his deputy, at the defendant's request, he may be brought before a magistrate of the county in which the warrant was executed; and such magistrate may, without examination, discharge such defendant, upon sufficient bail for his appearance before the court having cognizance of the offense.

4277 (4661). **Same; presumption in fixing amount of bail.** When the bail is taken under the provisions of the last two sections, the officer or magistrate, in fixing the amount of bail, must act on the presumption that the offense is of an aggravated nature.

4278 (4662). **Undertaking and warrant returned to court.** The magistrate admitting the defendant to bail, under the provisions of section 4276 (4660), must certify the same upon the warrant, and deliver such warrant, with the undertaking, to the officer who executed the warrant; who must cause the same to be delivered, without unnecessary delay, to the clerk of the court in which the defendant is bound by his undertaking to appear.

ARTICLE IV.

PRELIMINARY EXAMINATION AND ITS INCIDENTS.

4279 (4693). **Magistrate may associate others with him.** Any magistrate to whom complaint is made, or before whom any defendant is brought charged with a public offense, may associate with himself one or more magistrates of equal grade; and the powers and duties in this chapter prescribed may be executed and performed by them.

4280 (4673). **Adjournment of examination; defendant bailed or committed ad interim; etc.**—When a defendant is brought before a magistrate, under a warrant of arrest, for examination, such magistrate may adjourn the examination from time to time, as may be necessary, not exceeding ten days at one time, without the consent of the defendant, and to the same, or a different place in the county; and, in such case, if the defendant is charged with a capital offense, he must be committed to jail in the meantime; but if the offense is not capital, he may give bail, in such sum as the magistrate directs, for his appearance for such further examination, and for the want thereof must be committed; and on the day to which the examination was adjourned, he may be brought before the magistrate by his verbal order to the officer who had charge of him, or by order in writing to a different person, if the custody has been changed.

When recognizance void for uncertainty.—Allen's case, 33 Ala. 422.

4281 (4674). **Default of defendant admitted to bail certified to court; proceedings thereon.**—If the defendant does not appear before the magistrate at the time to which the examination is adjourned, he must certify the default on the undertaking of bail, and return the same to the next circuit or city court of his county; and the like proceedings must be had thereon as upon the breach of an undertaking in that court, the certificate of the magistrate being presumptive evidence of the default of the defendant.

4282 (4675). **On failure of magistrate to attend, another may act in his stead.**—If the magistrate adjourning the examination fails to attend on the day to which such examination is adjourned, any other magistrate of the county may attend in his place and proceed with the examination, or, if the defendant fails to appear, enter his default, and certify the same, with the undertaking of bail, to the next circuit or city court of the county, according to the provisions of the preceding sections; and the like proceedings may be had thereon as if certified by the magistrate taking the same.

4283 (4676). **Alias warrant of arrest.**—On the failure of the defendant to appear, the magistrate certifying the default, or any other magistrate, may issue another warrant of arrest, upon which the same proceedings may be had against the defendant as on the original warrant.

4284 (4677). **Examination; how conducted.**—The magistrate before whom any person is brought, charged with a public offense, must, as soon as may be, examine the complainant and the witnesses for the prosecution, on oath, in the presence of the defendant; and after the testimony for the prosecution is heard, the witnesses for the defendant must be sworn and examined.

4285 (4678, 4679). **Right of defendant to appear by counsel; examination, how conducted.**—The defendant may appear by counsel, and the magistrate may, on application, direct the witnesses for the prosecution or defense, or both, to be kept separate, so that they cannot hear the evidence, or converse with each other until examined; such examination is under the control of the magistrate, and should be so conducted as to elicit the facts of the case.

4286 (4679). **Testimony of witnesses reduced to writing and subscribed.**—The evidence of the witnesses examined must be reduced to writing by the magistrate, or under his direction, and signed by the witnesses respectively.

4287 (4680). **When defendant must be discharged.**—Upon the whole evidence, if it appears to the magistrate that no offense has been committed, or that there is no probable cause for charging the defendant therewith, he must be discharged.

4288 (4681). **If probable cause shown, discharged on bail, or committed.**—If it appears that an offense has been committed, and there is probable cause to believe that the defendant is guilty thereof, he must be discharged, if the offense is bailable, upon giving sufficient bail; but if sufficient bail is not given, or if the offense is not bailable, he must be committed to jail by an order in writing.

4289 (4682). **Form of commitment after preliminary examination.**—The commitment may be, in substance, as follows:

"The State of Alabama, } To the jailer of —— county:
—— county.

"On the examination of A. B., charged with the offense of murder (or other offense, as the case may be, describing it by name, or so that it may be clearly inferred), it appearing that such offense has been committed, and that there is sufficient cause to believe that A. B. is guilty thereof, you are, therefore, commanded to receive him into your custody, and detain him until he is legally discharged.

"Dated this —— day of ——, 18—.

"C. D., Justice of the Peace.
(or other officer, as the case may be.)"

4290 (4683). **The defendant, if committed, may elect to perform hard labor for county; duties of officers.**—If the defendant is charged with a misdemeanor, and is ordered to be committed to the county jail, he may elect to perform hard labor for the county pending his trial. It shall be the duty of the magistrate committing him to inform him of his right to make such election, and of the advantages accruing to him thereby; and if he so elect, it shall be the duty of the magistrate to make an order allowing him to do so, and to certify that fact to the court at which he is required to appear. It shall be the duty of the sheriff to carry every person in his custody charged with a misdemeanor before the judge of probate, or, if he is absent, before the clerk of the circuit court, within twelve hours after receiving such person in custody; and it shall be the duty of such judge or clerk to inform such prisoner of his right to make such election, and of the advantage accruing to him thereby; and if he shall elect to perform such hard labor, such judge or clerk shall make an order allowing him to do so, and shall certify that fact to the court at which he is required to appear; and if he is convicted when tried, it shall be the duty of the court, in determining his punishment, to take into consideration the amount of labor performed by him. It shall be the duty of each justice of the peace and notary public to render to the grand jury of the county, on the first day of each term of the circuit or city court, a statement, in writing and under oath, of the name of each defendant charged with a misdemeanor committed by him, the date of such commitment, and whether or not he gave such defendant the information required by this section. It shall be the duty of the sheriff to render to the grand jury his county, on the first day of each term of the circuit court, a statement, in writing and under oath, setting forth the name of every person charged with a misdemeanor coming into his custody since his last preceding statement, when he received such defendant, and when he carried him before the judge of probate, or clerk of the circuit court, as provided by this section. It shall be the duty of the judge of probate and clerk of the circuit court to render

to the grand jury of the county, on the first day of each term of
the circuit court, a statement, in writing and under oath, of the
name of each defendant brought before them by the sheriff under this section, of the date when he was so brought before them,
and whether or not they gave him the information required by
this section.

Giles' case, 52 Ala. 29; Avery's case, Ib. 340.

4291 (4684). **Bail taken by sheriff on commitment for
bailable offense.**—Whenever a person is committed to jail for
a bailable offense, under the provisions of this chapter, the
magistrate must indorse on the commitment the amount of bail
required, and sign his name thereto; and the sheriff of the
county to which he is committed may discharge him on giving
sufficient bail in the amount so indorsed; and must, in such
case, return the undertaking to the court to which such person
is bound to appear, within five days thereafter. Any justice of
the peace who fails to fix the amount of bail and to indorse the
same on the mittimus, as required by this section, must, on conviction, be fined not more than fifty dollars.

Antonez' case, 26 Ala. 81; Evans' case, 63 Ala. 195.

4292 (4685). **Witness bound over to court.**—The magistrate must also require the witnesses for the prosecution to enter
into an undertaking, in the sum of one hundred dollars each,
to appear and testify at the court having cognizance of the offense; and, if requested by the defendant, may require his witnesses to enter into such undertaking.

4293 (4686, 4687). **Form of undertaking of witness when
bound over to court on preliminary examination.**—The undertaking of the witnesses for the prosecution or defense may
be, in substance, as follows:

"The State of Alabama, } We, A. B., C. D. and E. F., wit-
——— county. } nesses against (or for, as the case may
be) G. H., charged with a public offense, do each agree to appear at the next circuit (or city) court of ——— county, to give
evidence against (or for, as the case may be) him, and, failing so
to do, to pay to the State of Alabama (or to the said G. H., if
the undertaking is for the defendant's witnesses) one hundred
dollars. Dated this, ——— day of ———, 18—.

(Signed)   "A. B.,
                                     "C. D.,
                                     "E. F.

"Taken by L. M., Justice of the Peace (or as the case may be)."

4294 (4688). **When surety for appearance required of
witness.**—Whenever the magistrate has good reason to believe
that a witness for the prosecution will not appear to testify, he
may order such witness to enter into an undertaking to appear
and testify in a larger sum, and with sufficient sureties; but
such surety must not be required from any witness who does
not reside in this state, and within fifty miles of the place where
the examination takes place.

4295 (4689). **When surety required of minors and married women.**—Married women and minors, when material witnesses for the prosecution, may also be required, in the discre-

tion of the magistrate, to procure sureties, who will undertake for their appearance to testify.

4296 (4690). **Commitment of witness on default of undertaking.**—Any witness required to enter into an undertaking, with or without surety, must, on failure or refusal, be committed to jail.

4297 (4691). **Discharge by sheriff.**—In such case, the magistrate must state in the commitment the amount of the undertaking, and whether surety is required; and the witness must be discharged by the sheriff, on entering into the undertaking as required.

4298 (4692). **Examinations and undertakings returned to court; penalty on failure.**—All examinations and undertakings by parties or witnesses, taken under this chapter, must be returned by the magistrate to the court at which the defendant or witness is bound to appear, by the first day thereof; and any magistrate failing so to do may be compelled by rule of court, and, in case of disobedience, by attachment for contempt.

CHAPTER 4.

JURORS AND JURIES.

ARTICLE I.

QUALIFICATION, SELECTION AND EXEMPTION OF JURORS.

4299 (4732). **List of householders and freeholders procured by sheriff.**—It is the duty of the sheriff of each county to obtain biennially a list of all the householders and freeholders residing in his county, from which list must be selected, as hereinafter provided, the names of such persons as may be thought competent to discharge the duties of grand and petit jurors for the county. *

What a mere immaterial irregularity under this section.—Cross' case, 63 Ala. 40. Should be freeholder or householder; when name returned by clerk to sheriff. Middleton's case, 5 Port. 484. Meaning of term "householder."—Aaron's case, 37 Ala. 106; Sylvester's case, 72 Ala. 201. Who not a "freeholder."—Iverson's case, 52 Ala. 170. A man must be a citizen, not a foreigner or alien.—Judson v. Eslava, Minor, 2; Primrose's case, 3 Ala. 546; Boyington's case, 2 Port. 100. Citizen must not be left off jury because of race or color.—Green's case, 73 Ala. 26.

---

* By act, entitled "An act to more effectually secure competent and well-qualified jurors in the several counties of this state," etc., this section is expressly, and other sections of this chapter are, by implication, repealed. On account of its

4300 (4733). **Jurors selected from list; when and by whom; qualification.**—The sheriff, judge of probate, and clerk of the circuit or city court, or any two of them, must meet biennially, on the first Monday in May, or within thirty days thereafter, at the office of the clerk of the circuit or city court, and select from said list the names of such persons as, in their

importance in the administration of the law, civil and criminal, and of the changes made in this Code as adopted, the commissioner deemed it best to give the entire act in a note.   The act, omitting the caption, is as follows:

"SECTION 1. *Be it enacted by the General Assembly of Alabama,* That the county commissioners of the various counties of this state, or the members of boards of revenue in such counties as have such boards, not including probate judges, shall constitute a board of jury commissioners, who shall discharge and perform in their respective counties all the duties in relation to the selection and drawing of grand and petit juries now required by law to be performed by the judges of probate, sheriffs and clerks of the circuit, criminal, or city courts of said county.   Such commissioners shall, in addition to the oath now required by law, take an oath faithfully to discharge the duties required of them by this act, and to keep secret the counsel of themselves and their associates, and not to disclose the name of any juror drawn until the venire shall have been issued for such juror, which oath shall be in writing and subscribed by the commissioners as a part of their official oath.   Each commissioner shall receive, in full of all compensation, the same pay he is entitled to receive as a county commissioner or member of the board of revenue, which shall be paid by the county treasurer upon the certified statement of the president of the board of jury commissioners, provided for by this act, of the amount due each commissioner.

"SEC. 2. *Be it further enacted,* That said commissioners shall hold their first meeting the next day after the adjournment of the commissioners' court, or the first session of the board of revenue, to be held after the first Monday in April, 1887, and shall at such meeting elect one of their number president of the board, perform all the duties required by this act, and draw all the jurors, grand and petit, for the circuit and city courts, to be held in the respective counties, whose term shall begin after the first day of July, 1887, and before the first day of January, 1888.   The next meeting of the board of jury commissioners herein provided for, and each subsequent meeting thereafter, shall be held on the next day after adjournment of the last regular term of the court of county commissioners, or session of the board of revenue held in each year.   After the first meeting, if for any reason a meeting of the board of jury commissioners is not held at the time appointed for such meeting, a meeting shall be held on a call of the president of the board, as soon after the time appointed for such meeting as practicable.   Such board of jury commissioners shall meet at the court-house of the county, or other place provided by law for the sitting of the court of county commissioners or board of revenue; and no other person than said jury commissioners shall be present at such meeting.

"SEC. 3. *Be it further enacted,* That said commissioners, at such meeting, shall select from the male residents of the county, over twenty-one, and under sixty years of age, who are householders or freeholders, the names of all such persons, not exempt from jury duty, as, in their opinion, are fit and competent to discharge the duties of grand and petit jurors, with honesty, impartiality, and intelligence.   Said commissioners shall prepare a list of the names so selected, stating thereon the place of residence, and occupation of each person, if known to them, and shall file a certified copy of such list, in a sealed envelope, in the office of the judge of probate, within five days after making said selection.   It shall be the duty of the judge of probate to keep such list securely, and not to allow the seal of the envelope to be broken, or such list to be inspected by any one, save said commission, unless under an order of the judge of the circuit or city court of his county.

"SEC. 4. *Be it further enacted,* That when said list is completed, said commissioners must write the name of each person therein contained, with his place of residence and occupation, if it appears from the list, on a separate piece of paper, and must fold or roll up such piece of paper, as nearly as may be, in the same manner, so that the name may not be visible, and deposit the same in a box, which must be secured by sufficient locks and seal.   Said commissioners shall, at their session hereinbefore provided, proceed to draw from said box a grand jury for each regular term of any court to be held during the next ensuing year in the county for which a grand jury is required by law, not less than fifteen, nor more than twenty-one persons for each of said grand juries, to be composed of such persons as are duly qualified to serve as grand jurors, and next the names of the requisite number of persons to serve as petit jurors for each of said courts, allowing not more thirty-six, nor less than thirty persons for each week of the term prescribed by law, or, if the term is unlimited, for each week during which, in the opinion of the clerk of

opinion, are competent to discharge the duties of grand and petit jurors with honesty, impartiality and intelligence, and are esteemed in the community for their integrity, fair character and sound judgment; but no person must be selected who is under twenty-one, or over sixty years of age, or who is a habitual drunkard, or who is afflicted with a permanent disease.

4301 (4784). **Persons exempt from jury duty.**—The following persons are exempt from jury duty, unless by their own consent: Professors and students of universities and colleges; As amended, Feb. 7, 1879, p. 117, sec. 44; March 1, 1881, p. 114, sec. 80.

---

that court, a jury will be required; and the juries for each week shall be drawn separately and successively, and every piece of paper, on which is written the name of the person so drawn, must be destroyed.

"SEC. 5. *Be it further enacted*, That said commission shall prepare a list of the names of the persons drawn as grand jurors, and also of the persons drawn as petit jurors for each week of each term separately, and envelope and seal the same, with an indorsement on the outside of the package, to the clerk of such court; and said clerk shall retain said package in his possession, without breaking the seal or opening the same, until thirty days before the term of court for which such jurors are drawn, and he shall, at least twenty days before the term of court, open such package, and issue an order in writing to the sheriff of the county, commanding him to summon the persons drawn as grand jurors to appear and serve in that capacity, and a similar order for the persons drawn as petit jurors, specifying in the orders the full name, place of residence, and occupation of each person, when known, and the particular week for which each petit juror is to serve; and the manner in which said order shall be executed and returned, and all proceedings had thereon shall be the same as now prescribed by law; *Provided*, That if any sheriff shall negligently fail to summon any person whom he is so commanded to summon, he shall be held guilty of a contempt of court, and it shall be the duty of the court to fine him not more than one hundred dollars for each person not summoned, and he may also be imprisoned for not more than ten days; the return of any such person as not found shall be prima facie evidence of such negligence on the part of the sheriff, and he shall be so punished by the court, unless he shows good cause to the contrary.

"SEC. 6. *Be it further enacted*, That the commissioners shall deposit in the box from which the names are drawn, copies of all lists furnished to the clerk of any court, as provided in the preceding section, and he shall deposit said box, securely locked and sealed, in the office of the judge of probate. The president of said board shall keep the key to said box, but the judge of the circuit court, criminal court, or city court, shall have access to said box in order to compare the venire issued by the clerk with the copy of the list furnished to the clerk. If a special or an adjourned term of any court in which a jury is required is called, the clerk of such court shall forthwith notify the commissioners, who shall meet and draw the grand and petit juries, one or both, required for such term, and shall furnish a list of the same to the clerk of the court, at least twenty days before the term, in the same manner as for a regular term, and the clerk shall issue to the sheriff the proper order for summoning such grand and petit jurors as for a regular term; and the sheriff shall be subject to the same penalty for failing to summon jurors to a special term as for failing to summon them to a regular term.

"SEC. 7. *Be it further enacted*, That a majority of said commissioners shall constitute a quorum. Said commissioners shall at each meeting select one of their number president of their board, to preside at such meeting, and he shall continue in such office until the next meeting.

SEC. 8. *Be it further enacted*, That if any person, summoned to attend as a grand or petit juror, shall fail to obey such summons, without good excuse, to be determined by the court, he shall be deemed guilty of a contempt of court; and if no sufficient excuse be rendered for him at the time of his default, a rule shall issue to him to show cause why he shall not be adjudged guilty of such contempt and fined accordingly; if he shall fail at the next term after such notice to render such excuse, he shall be fined by the judge not more than one hundred dollars, and may be imprisoned in the county jail for not more than ten days.

"SEC. 9. *Be it further enacted*, That out of the grand jurors so summoned and attending, the court shall organize a grand jury, as now provided by law; and if, by reason of sickness, or non-attendance, or any cause, a sufficient number shall not appear, or if the number shall be reduced below fifteen, the court shall order the sheriff to summon from the qualified citizens of the county twice the number necessary to complete the grand jury, and from such number shall be drawn, in the manner required by law, a sufficient number to complete the grand jury; and out of the persons summoned as petit jurors, and attending, the court shall organize two petit juries of twelve men each, and if any are over, they, shall be held, unless, in the opinion of the court, they may be excused for the term. If a sufficient num-

teachers and pupils of academies and common schools; ministers in charge of churches; judges of the several courts; attorneys at law during the time they practice their profession; practicing physicians; county commissioners; officers of the United States; officers of the executive department of the state government; sheriffs and their deputies; clerks of courts and coroners; justices of the peace and constables, during their continuance in office; keepers of public mills, ferries, toll-bridges and toll-gates; the officers of any railroad or other road constructed under the authority of this state, whose duties would materially interfere with serving on juries; the officers and crew of any steamboat navigating the rivers of this state; members of incorporated

---

ber of those summoned as petit jurors do not attend, or are incompetent, or are excused by the court, to constitute two juries, then the court shall order the sheriff to summon from the qualified citizens of the county a sufficient number to complete the two juries.

"SEC. 10. *Be it further enacted,* That when any capital case or cases stand for trial, the court shall, at least one entire day before the same are set for trial, cause the box containing the names of jurors to be brought into the court-room, and, after having the same well shaken, the presiding judge shall then and there publicly draw therefrom not less than twenty-five, nor more than fifty, of said names for each capital case, a list of which shall be immediately made out by the clerk of said court, and an order issued to the sheriff to summon the same to appear upon the day set for trial, in like manner and under like penalties as provided for summoning grand and petit jurors in section five of this act, and the names of the jurors so drawn, together with the panel of petit jurors organized for the week, shall constitute the venire from which the juries, to try said capital case or cases, shall be selected; *Provided,* That if, at the time appointed for the trial of the capital case, a jury should not be made of those summoned and who appear, or if said venire should be exhausted by reason of challenges, or otherwise, then the court shall order the sheriff to summon twice the number necessary to complete the jury, from the qualified citizens of the county; and from the persons thus summoned who appear, there shall be drawn in the manner required by law a sufficient number to complete the jury to try said case, and the court shall continue to repeat the order until the jury is completed.

"SEC. 11. *Be it further enacted,* That when the term of the court continues two or more weeks, and by law the criminal docket is not taken up until the second or third week of the same, the court, in its discretion, may, on any day of the term, fix the trial of a capital case for any day of a subsequent week of the term, during which such case may be tried, and if the sheriff shall serve a copy of the special jury drawn to try said case, together with a copy of the jurors drawn and summoned for such week, together with a copy of the indictment, one entire day before the day set for the trial, that shall be held a compliance with the law requiring a copy of the jury and indictment to be served on the defendant, as hereinbefore provided.

"SEC. 12. *Be it further enacted,* That if at any time, when said jury commission meets to draw the juries, as provided in sections four and six of this act, there should be an insufficient number of jurors' names in the jury-box from which to draw the necessary juries therein required, then it is made the duty of said jury commission to proceed, as required in sections three and four of this act, to provide the necessary list of jurors, and place the same in said jury-box, and proceed to complete the drawing of said juries; and if in drawing a special jury for the trial of a capital case, as provided in section ten of this act, said jury-box should become exhausted, said trial should not be delayed, but the court shall direct the sheriff to summon from the qualified citizens of the county the specified number of jurors necessary to complete said venire, and to proceed with said trial.

"SEC. 13. *Be it further enacted,* That upon the trial of any felony not capital, the defendant shall be entitled to eight peremptory challenges, and the state four; and upon the trial of any misdemeanor, the defendant shall be entitled to five peremptory challenges, and the state three. When two or more defendants are tried jointly for a capital offense, or other felony, each defendant shall be entitled to one-half the peremptory challenges allowed by this act; and on the trial of two or more defendants for any misdemeanor, each defendant shall be entitled to three peremptory challenges. In civil cases it shall be a ground of peremptory challenge, that a juror is plaintiff or defendant in any case which stands for trial during the week of the term at which he is challenged. It shall also be a ground of challenge in any cause, that a juror is related to any party or attorney, who was his attorney of record in the cause to be tried before the case was called for trial, by consan-

fire companies; officers of the penitentiary; the superintendent and physician of the insane hospital, and his assistants; all mail contractors, mail agents and public stage-drivers; one druggist in a town or village having but one drug-store; every commissioned officer, non-commissioned officer, musician and private, during the time he is a member of the Alabama State Troops; and all township superintendents of public schools.*

Exemption from jury service subject to legislative regulation or repeal.—Dunlap's case, 76 Ala. 460.   Exemption (in this case of over age) is a personal privilege, which juror may waive, and not a disqualification.—Spigener's case, 62 Ala. 383; Williams' case, 67 Ala. 183.   Coroner is competent juror, though may claim privilege not to serve.—Jackson's case, 74 Ala. 26.   Court not authorized to discharge person regularly summoned on his simple statement that he "is a fireman," without other proof of his right to claim benefit of statutory exemption of "members of incorporated fire companies."—Phillips' case, 68 Ala. 469.—Party claiming exemption must prove it.—Ib.

4302 (4735). **Exemptions on account of age made known by affidavit.**—Any person selected as a grand or petit juror, who is exempt on account of age, may make known his exemption by affidavit, setting forth the facts constituting such exemption, which he may forward to the sheriff, who shall file it in the court.

4303 (4741). **Incompetency of jurors to serve more than one week in each year; exceptions.**—No person shall be competent to serve on a petit jury in any county in this state for more than one week in any year, unless actually engaged in the trial of a case submitted to them before the expiration of their week of service, in which case it shall be lawful for them to continue its consideration until they render a verdict, or are discharged by the court; but in those counties in which there is a city court, persons may serve one week in each year in the city court, in addition to the week in the circuit court; nor shall any person serve as a grand juror for more than one term consecutively in any county in this state during any one year,

---

guinity within the ninth degree, or affinity within the fifth degree, or is a partner in business of such party; *Provided*, That nothing contained herein shall repeal any common-law right of challenge.

"SEC. 14. *Be it further enacted*, That any commissioner, who willfully or negligently fails to discharge any of the duties required of him by this act, or shall engage in drawing a jury or juror in any other manner or order than that herein required, shall be guilty of a misdemeanor, and, upon conviction, shall be fined not less than fifty, nor more than one thousand dollars.

"SEC. 15. *Be it further enacted*, That any person, who shall attempt to corruptly influence any of said commissioners, or any other officer charged with the execution of any duty under this act, in the performance of any of his duties, shall, on conviction, be fined not less than one thousand dollars, and shall also be imprisoned in the state penitentiary for not less than two, nor more than twenty years, and shall forever be disqualified from holding any office of honor, trust, or profit under the laws of this State.

"SEC. 16. *Be it further enacted*, That said commissioners shall, as far as possible, guard against selecting any persons, exempt by law from jury duty, and, to this end, may avail themselves of any source of information within their reach.

"SEC. 17. *Be it further enacted*, That section 4732 of the Code of Alabama, and all other laws and parts of laws, general and special, conflicting with the provisions of this act, be, and the same are hereby repealed; but all laws now in force in relation to jurors, their drawing, selecting, or qualification, not in conflict with this act, are hereby continued in full force and effect. But the provisions of this act shall not apply to the counties of Henry, Mobile, Dallas, Talladega, Clay, Marengo, Cherokee, Etowah, St. Clair, Coffee, Dale, Geneva, Marshall, and Montgomery.

* By act approved February 26, 1887 (Pamph. Acts, 1886-7, p. 67), consular agents of foreign governments, who are residents of this state, are exempt from performing jury duty.

whether in the city, circuit, or criminal court of such county; and it is hereby made the duty of the court to see, before any person is sworn as a juror, that he is not incompetent under the provisions of this section; but this section shall not apply to such persons as may be specially summoned to serve as jurors in a capital case, or to jurors summoned to attend the coroner on his inquest, but shall be held to apply to all talesmen in civil and criminal cases, as well as to the regular panel of jurors, and to all juries which may be summoned to pass upon issues of fact in proceedings in the courts of probate and courts of chancery, and of justices of the peace.

ARTICLE II.

DRAWING AND SUMMONING JURORS IN GENERAL.

4304 (4736). **List of selected persons filed in probate court.** A list of the persons selected as jurors must be written in a fair hand, setting forth the christian name and surname of each, with his place of residence and occupation, if known, which list must be filed in the office of the judge of probate, within ten days after the selection is made.

4305 (4737). **Names separated, folded up, and put in box.** The judge of probate, on receiving such list, must write the name of each person therein contained, with his place of residence and occupation, if it appears from the list, on a separate piece of paper, must fold or roll up such pieces of paper as nearly as may be in the same manner, so that the name may not be visible, and deposit the same in a box, which must be secured by sufficient locks, and kept by him.

4306 (4738). **Jurors for regular terms; when drawn; how many, etc.**—At least twenty days before the day fixed by law for holding each regular term of the circuit or city court of the county, the judge of probate, sheriff and clerk of the circuit or city court, or a majority of them, must draw from the box the names of eighteen persons to serve as grand jurors at such court; and also the names of the requisite number of other persons to serve as petit jurors, allowing thirty persons for each week of the term prescribed by law, or, if the term is unlimited, for each week during which, in the opinion of the clerk, a jury will be required.

4307 (4740). **Manner of drawing jurors.**—The drawing of jurors must be conducted as follows: One of the officers present must shake the box containing the names, so as to mix the slips of paper as much as possible. One of them must then publicly draw out of the box, in the presence of the others, eighteen names for the grand jury, if the drawing is for a regular term, or for a special term at which a grand jury is required, and the requisite number for petit jurors; and if for a special term at which a grand jury is not required, the requisite number of petit jurors only. A minute of the drawing must be kept by one of the officers, and each name, as it is drawn, must be entered before another is drawn. If after the required number of names has been drawn, it appears that any one of the persons so drawn is dead, or has become insane, or has permanently removed from the county, or is otherwise disqualified, an entry of such death or disqualification must be made on the minutes, the slip containing the name must be destroyed, and another name must be drawn as before; and the same proceedings must be had, as often as may be necessary, until the whole number of jurors is completed. The minutes of the drawing must then be signed by the officers present, and filed in the office of the judge of probate.

Jury not drawn in strict accordance with statute, must be quashed on motion of accused—Brazier's case, 44 Ala. 387. But provisions now directory.—See section 4314. As to duties of officers and power of courts over the selecting and drawing of grand and petit jurors, see Green's case, 73 Ala. 26. Legislature has power to establish mode of drawing jurors.—Williams' case, 61 Ala. 33.

4308 (4742). **Names drawn deposited in separate box; when drawn again.**—The slips of paper drawn from the box under the provisions of the preceding section must be deposited in another box, which must be secured by sufficient locks, and safely kept by the judge of probate; and said slips must not be again placed in the first box, nor must the persons whose names are written thereon be required to serve as grand or petit jurors, until all the names contained in the first box have been drawn, or until a new list of the householders and freeholders of the county has been provided by the sheriff, as required by section 4299 (4732), unless the names of such persons are returned to the first box under the provisions of section 4313 (4752).

4309 (4743). **List of jurors drawn delivered to clerk.**—A list of the jurors so drawn to serve as grand jurors, with the place of residence and occupation of each, if known, must be made out by the judge of probate, signed by him, and delivered to the clerk of the circuit or city court, as the case may be; and a similar list of the persons drawn as petit jurors, specifying the week for which each was drawn.

4310 (4744). **Venire for grand and petit jurors issued by clerk.**—On the receipt of such lists, the clerk must issue an order, in writing, to the sheriff of the county, commanding him to summon the persons drawn as grand jurors to appear and serve in that capacity, and a similar order for the summons of the persons drawn to serve as petit jurors, specifying in the orders the full name, place of residence and occupation of each person, and the particular week for which each petit juror is to serve.

Venire not void for want of seal of clerk who issues it.—Maher's case, 1 Port. 265.   What sufficient order summoning jurors.—Battle's case, 54 Ala. 93.

4311 (4745). **Executed and returned; when and how.**—The orders for the summons of jurors, provided for in the preceding section, must be executed by the sheriff, or other person acting in his place, by giving personal notice to each person, or by leaving a written notice at the place of his residence with some member of his family, or some person residing in the same house, three days before the day appointed for the commencement of the court; and must be returned to the clerk of the court from which it issued, with the proper return thereon, by the day appointed for the meeting of the court.

It is not material whether the writ of venire facias be directed to "any sheriff of the State of Alabama" or to the sheriff of the particular county, the writ being executed and returned by the proper officer.—Stedman's case, 7 Port. 495; Phillips' case, 2 Ala. 297. What is and what is not ground for quashing the venire. Fields' case, 52 Ala. 348; Aiken's case, 35 Ala. 399; Bill's case, 29 Ala. 38; Stedman's case, 7 Port. 495. Presumptions after plea and verdict that law was complied with, etc.—Williams' case, 3 Stew. 454.

4312 (4746). **Substitutes prohibited.**—No sheriff, deputy sheriff, bailiff, or other officer, charged with the summoning of any jury, must accept or receive any substitute for any person who may be drawn to serve, or whom he may be directed to summon as a juror, but he must serve the person drawn or directed.

4313 (4752). **Names of jurors not attending or excused returned to jury-box; exception.**—Immediately after the adjournment of the court, the clerk must furnish the judge of probate with a list of the names of all persons drawn as jurors who failed to attend, or were excused or discharged by the court for the term, or whose services were entirely dispensed with on account of the adjournment or failure of the court; the slips of paper containing the names of those who were excused or discharged on account of any disqualification, or other cause of a permanent nature, must be destroyed, and the names of all the others must again be deposited by the judge of probate in the box containing the undrawn ballots.

4314 (4759). **What provisions directory merely.**—The provisions of this chapter in relation to the selection, drawing and summoning of jurors are merely directory; and juries selected, drawn and summoned, whether at an earlier or later day, must be deemed legal, and possess the power to perform all the duties belonging to grand and petit juries respectively.

Statute construed; any departure from provisions regulating drawings, etc., of grand jurors, which works no injury to accused, is no ground of objection to the whole array.—Bales' case, 63 Ala. 30.

4315 (4762). **Fine against officer for neglect in drawing and summoning jury.**—When, by any neglect of the duties imposed by this article on the judge of probate, sheriff and clerk of the circuit or city court, a grand or petit jury is not duly drawn and summoned at any term of the court, a conditional fine of five hundred dollars may be imposed by the court on the officers in default, to be entered and made absolute as against defaulting jurors.

ARTICLE III.

SPECIAL JURIES, AND REGULAR JURIES AT SPECIAL TERMS.

4316 (4761). **Special juries organized in default of regular.** If, in consequence of any neglect on the part of the judge of probate, sheriff, or clerk of the circuit or city court, or from any other cause, no grand or petit jury is returned to serve at any term of the court, or no petit jury summoned for any week thereof, the court may, by an order entered on the minutes, direct the sheriff forthwith to summons eighteen persons qualified to serve as grand jurors, and the requisite number to serve as petit jurors; and the persons so summoned, failing to attend, are subject to the same penalties as if they had been regularly drawn and summoned, to be recovered in the same manner; the court may supply any deficiency, as in other cases, and a jury thus organized is in all respects legal.

4317 (4757). **Special grand jury at regular term.**—When any indictable offense is committed during the session of the court, and after the grand jury has been discharged, the court may, in its discretion, cause an order to be entered on the minutes commanding the sheriff forthwith to summon eighteen persons possessing the requisite qualifications of grand jurors; which order the sheriff must immediately execute, and the persons summoned by him must attend, and, if required, serve as grand jurors under the same penalties as are by law prescribed for persons regularly drawn and summoned as grand jurors; and from the persons so attending, with such others as may be necessary to supply any deficiency (to be summoned and drawn as in other cases), a special grand jury must be organized, sworn and charged, as in other cases; and it is the duty of such special grand jury to investigate the offense, and to proceed thereon as a regular grand jury.

Court having quashed the venire drawn and summoned as grand jurors for the term, has no power to organize another in their stead; and the acts of such unauthorized grand jury are void.—O'Byrnes' case, 51 Ala. 25.

4318 (4758). **Grand jury at special term.**—A grand jury may be organized at any special term of the circuit or city court, whenever, in the opinion of the presiding judge, the public good requires it; such grand jury to be organized in the same manner, and its proceedings to be governed in all respects by the same rules as by law provided for a grand jury organized at a regular term of the court.

Power to organize grand jury at special term.—Floyd's case, 55 Ala. 61. See, also, as to how jurors for special term (of city court) may be drawn.—Levy's case, 48 Ala. 171; Taylor's case, Ib. 180. And when motion to quash venire properly overruled in such case.—Levy's case, supra. Indictment found at special term and proceedings.—Harrington's case, 36 Ala. 236; Aaron's case, 39 Ala. 684.

4319 (4739). **Petit jurors for special terms.**—When a special term of the court is to be held for the trial of unfinished business, the names of thirty persons must be drawn from the box to serve as petit jurors for each week of the term, and such drawing must take place twenty days before the commencement of the term; when for the trial of a person charged with a felony, fifty names must be drawn, if the offense may be punished capitally, and if not, twenty-four, to serve as petit jurors; and such drawing must take place ten days before the commencement of the term.

ARTICLE IV.

SPECIAL PETIT JURIES IN CAPITAL CASES.

4320 (4874). **Order for jurors in capital case.**—For the trial of a person charged with a capital offense, or of two or more such persons tried together, the court must make an order commanding the sheriff to summon not less than fifty, nor more than one hundred persons, including those summoned on the regular juries for the week, or term, when the term does not exceed one week.

This section construed in Bland's case, 75 Ala. 574 (re-affirming Floyd's case, 55 Ala. 61; Shelton's case, 73 Ala. 5; and Posey's case, 73 Ala. 490). Proper practice under this section.—Posey's case, 73 Ala. 490. The "regular jurors for the week" in said section means the regular jurors "*in attendance*," not those excused.—Lee's case, 55 Ala. 259; Floyd's case, Ib. 61. Provisions of this section mandatory.—Posey's case, 73 Ala. 490. Mandatory requirements in capital cases must affirmatively appear in record.—Spicer's case, 69 Ala. 159. Record need not show that return was made by proper officer.—Brown's case, 74 Ala. 478. When error as to in judgment of conviction not ground of reversal.—Bland's case, 75 Ala. 574. Province of court to determine the number of jurors.—Blevins' case, 68 Ala. 92; Hubbard's case, 72 Ala. 164. Practice of excusing jurors in capital case before their names are called.—Sylvester's case, 71 Ala. 17. Power of court to discharge or excuse juror.—Phillips' case, 68 Ala. 469.

4321 (4875). **Penalty on defaulting juror.**—Any person summoned as a juror under the provisions of the last section, who fails to attend, or refuses to serve, must be fined not less than fifty dollars, which may be reduced by the court, if the circumstances justify reduction; such fine to be collected and applied in the same manner as fines imposed on jurors in other cases.

4322 (4876). **Mistake in juror's name no cause to quash or continue.**—A mistake in the name of any person summoned as a juror for the trial of a capital offense, either in the venire or in the list of jurors delivered to the defendant, is not sufficient cause to quash the venire, or to delay or continue the trial, unless the court, in its discretion, is of opinion that the ends of justice so require; but the court must in such case direct the names of such persons to be discarded, and others to be forthwith summoned to supply their places; and the persons so summoned shall be disposed of in the same manner as if they had been summoned in the first instance.

No objection to venire on account of disqualification of jurors summoned. Roberts' case, 68 Ala. 515; Fields' case, 52 Ala. 348. Summoning less number than named in venire; effect of duplicating name in the list.—Roberts' case, 68 Ala. 515. Mistake in names of jurors not sufficient ground to quash venire.—Roberts' case, 68 Ala. 156; Floyd's case, 55 Ala. 61; Rash's case, 61 Ala. 89; Fields' case, 52 Ala. 348; Hall's case, 51 Ala. 9; Johnson's case, 47 Ala. 10; Hubbard's case. 72 Ala. 164; Jackson's case, 76 Ala. 26.

4323 (4877). **Talesmen peremptorily challenged, but no list served.**—The defendant is not entitled to a list of the persons summoned under the provisions of the last section, but may peremptorily challenge any of them, if drawn on the jury for his trial, in addition to the other peremptory challenges allowed him by law.

4324 (4878). **Manner of drawing jury.**—On the trial of a person charged with a capital offense, the names of the jurors summoned for his trial, as well as the names of the regular jurors in attendance, must be written on slips of paper, folded or rolled up, placed in a box, or some substitute therefor, and shaken together; and such officer as may be designated by the court must, in his presence, draw out such slips, one by one, until the jury is completed; if all such slips are drawn, and the jury is not made up, the court must direct the sheriff to summon at least twice the number of jurors required to complete the jury, whose names are also to be written on slips of paper, deposited and drawn as herein prescribed; and if such number is exhausted, the same proceedings must be had until the jury is complete.

Discretionary with court to have names of jurors called from clerk's desk or outside.—Hall's case, 51 Ala. 9; Waller's case, 40 Ala. 325. Court not obliged to send for absent juror at defendant's request; but otherwise, if such juror in jail. Johnson's case, 47 Ala. 10. What not error, where four of jurors in the venire, were engaged as jurors in the trial of another cause at the time copy was served on prisoner.—Redd's case, 69 Ala. 255.

ARTICLE V.

DUTY OF COURT TO ASCERTAIN QUALIFICATIONS BEFORE SWEARING JURORS.

4325 (4760). **Duty prescribed.**—It is the duty of the court, before administering the oath prescribed by law to any grand, petit, or tales juror, to ascertain that such juror possesses the qualifications required by law; and the duty required of the court by this section shall be considered imperative.

When objection that court failed to ascertain qualifications of jurors comes too late.—James' case, 53 Ala. 381. See Finley's case, 61 Ala. 201. Not essential that record should show a compliance with this section; presumption that court did its duty, and its judgment upon them a discretion not revisable.—James' case, supra.

ARTICLE VI.

PETIT JURY AND TALESMEN; ARRANGING, SWEARING, CHALLENGING.

4326 (4763). **Petit juries arranged for business.**—To dispose of the petit jurors for the transaction of business, the clerk must, on the day on which they are summoned to attend, prepare by lot a list of their names; the first twelve must be sworn and called the first jury; the next twelve must then be sworn and called the second jury; and if there are any more petit jurors in attendance, they may be placed on a third jury, or put on either of the other juries, as occasion may require; and the jurors may be transferred from one jury to another, as the convenience of the court, or the dispatch of business requires.

4327 (4764). **Talesmen.**—When, by reason of challenges, or any other cause, it is rendered necessary, the court may cause petit jurors to be summoned, either from the by-standers or from the county at large, to supply any deficiency on a regular jury, or to form one or more entire juries, as the occasion may require; such jurors are called talesmen, and must not be compelled to serve longer than the day for which they were respectively summoned, unless detained longer in the trial of an issue, or the execution of a writ of inquiry, submitted to the jury of which they are respectively members, or unless they are re-summoned; and any such jurors, failing to attend, or withdrawing without leave of the court before the expiration of his term of service, may be fined twenty dollars by the court, for which a conditional judgment may be entered, to be made absolute as in the case of regular jurors.

When defendant requests court to order more than necessary number of talesmen, he cannot afterward object to such order.—Allen's case, 74 Ala. 557.

4328 (4765). **Oath of petit juror.**—The following oath must be administered by the clerk, in the presence of the court, to each of the petit jurors: "You do solemnly swear (or affirm, as the case may be) that you will well and truly try all issues, and execute all writs of inquiry, which may be submitted to you during the present term (or week, as the case may be), and true verdicts render according to the evidence; so help you

God;" and the same oath must be administered to the talesmen, substituting the word "day" for "term."

The presumption is that the correct oath was administered, when it appears from the recital in the judgment-entry that the jury were "duly sworn," or sworn "according to law," unless it also appears that a substantially different or defective oath was administered.—See Allen's case, 71 Ala. 6; Storey's case, Ib. 335, and the cases therein cited. It is the safer practice for the judgment-entry to recite simply that the jury "was sworn according to law," not setting out the oath.—Roberts' case, 68 Ala. 515; Allen's case, 71 Ala. 6; Storey's case, Ib. 335. See, also, Cary's case, 76 Ala. 78; Peterson's case, 74 Ala. 34; Johnson's case, Ib. 537. (But the succeeding section relieves it of error, unless record shows objection was made.) Where special jury is impaneled, better practice to swear juror separately, as he is selected.—Allen's case, 60 Ala. 19.

Feb. 17, 1885, p. 138. **4329. When defective oath no ground for reversal of criminal case by supreme court.**—No criminal cause taken by appeal to the supreme court shall be reversed because of any defect in the administration of the oath to any grand or petit jury, unless the record in the cause discloses the fact, that some objection was taken in the court below, during the progress of the trial, based on such defect; but this rule shall not apply to cases where it appears affirmatively from the record that the appellant did not have the benefit of counsel on his trial in the court from which the appeal was taken.

As amended, Feb. 17, 1885, p. 187. **4330** (4879, 4880). **Peremptory challenges; number allowed state and defendant.**—The state is entitled to fourteen peremptory challenges on the trial of a capital offense, to ten, on the trial of any felony not capital, to four, on the trial of any misdemeanor, and to four, on the trial of bastardy proceedings; the defendant is entitled to twenty-one peremptory challenges, when on trial for a capital offense, to fifteen, on trial for any felony not capital, to six, when on trial for a misdemeanor, and to six, when on trial in bastardy proceedings.

On joint trial of two or more defendants, each has right to full number of challenges.—Brister's case, 26 Ala. 107. State must pass on jurors before defense. Spigener's case, 62 Ala. 383. After state challenges, court may require defendant to pass on remaining jurors before filling up jury.—Wilson's case, 31 Ala. 371. Juror, if inadvertently taken, may be peremptorily challenged by defendant at any time before he is sworn.—Murray's case, 48 Ala. 675. Unless waived, defendant's right of challenge not lost until the oath is tendered to juror.—Ib.; Drake's case, 51 Ala. 30; Spigener's case, 62 Ala. 383. But too late after juror is sworn. Rash's case, 61 Ala. 89. Or after solicitor and defendant have expressed satisfaction with jury as organized.—Sparks' case, 59 Ala. 82; Spigener's case, 62 Ala. 383. Law increasing number of challenges for state and defense; trial had under new law.—Lore's case, 4 Ala. 173.

4331 (4881, 4884). **Challenges for cause.**—It is a good ground for challenge by either party,—

1. That the person has not been a resident householder or freeholder of the county, for the last preceding year.

2. That he is not a citizen of Alabama.

3. That he has been indicted within the last twelve months for an offense of the same character as that with which the defendant is charged.

4. That he is connected by consanguinity within the ninth degree, or by affinity within the fifth degree (computing according to the rules of the civil law), either with the defendant, or with the prosecutor, or the person alleged to be injured.

5. That he has been convicted of a felony.

6. That he has an interest in the conviction or acquittal of the defendant, or has made any promise, or given any assurance, that he will convict or acquit the defendant.

7. That he has a fixed opinion as to the guilt or innocence of the defendant, which would bias his verdict.

8. That he is under twenty-one, or over seventy years of age.

9. That he is of unsound mind; and

10. That he is a witness for the other party.

This statute not repealed or affected by section 4300.—Iverson's case, 52 Ala. 170. Non-residence in county cause for challenge.—Hall's case, 51 Ala. 9; Gray's case, 55 Ala. 86; Hall's case, 40 Ala. 698. Term "householder" implies more than mere occupant of room or house.—Aaron's case, 37 Ala. 106. One who has merely "rented lands for last twelve months," is not a "freeholder" or "householder."—Iverson's case, 52 Ala. 170. Yearly tenant not a freeholder.—Aaron's case, 37 Ala. 106. "Householders" and "freeholders" include man living with his family in wife's house belonging to separate estate.—Sylvester's case, 72 Ala. 201. "Assault with intent to murder" is offense of "same character" as murder under this statute.—Crockett's case, 38 Ala. 387. That juror is on appearance bond of defendant is cause for challenge by state.—Brazelton's case, 66 Ala. 96. As to relations of lawyer and client, master and servant, etc., as causes of challenge, see Ib. 98. That juror is first cousin to prosecuting attorney, is not cause for challenge.—Washington's case, 58 Ala. 355. An opinion founded merely on rumor, or formed on the hypothesis of the truth of facts which he has heard, and without the hearing of other facts which may contradict them or lessen their weight, is not cause for challenge.—Bales' case, 63 Ala. 30. Nor is a juror subject to challenge merely because he has formed an opinion as to the guilt or innocence of the accused, which may be changed by the evidence.—Beason's case, 72 Ala. 191. See, also, Carson's case, 50 Ala. 134; Williams' case, 3 Stew. 454; Morea's case, 2 Ala. 275; Hall's case, 51 Ala. 9. When held good cause of challenge. Crockett's case, 38 Ala. 387; Ned's case, 7 Port. 187; Quesenberry's case, 3 Stew. & Port. 308. Age does not disqualify, and not cause for challenge, unless juror is under twenty-one, or over seventy years of age; but may be claimed as exemption. Williams' case, 67 Ala. 183; Spigener's case, 62 Ala. 383. Challenges for cause not confined to causes enumerated in Code.—Smith's case, 55 Ala. 1 (overruling, on this point, Leyman's case, 45 Ala. 72; Boggs' case, Ib. 30). Held cause for challenge, that juror served on trial of another person charged with selling liquor to same intemperate person.—Smith's case, 55 Ala. 1. Also that juror served on previous trial of same case, or has been summoned as a witness for state.—Commander's case, 60 Ala. 1; Atkin's case, Ib. 45. Also that juror was on the grand jury which found the indictment.—Birdsong's case, 47 Ala. 68. But challenge comes too late, if prisoner has accepted him.—Battle's case, 54 Ala. 93. Also, in capital case, where juror on regular jury for the week had previously convicted prisoner's co-defendant, as to whom there had been a severance.—Wesley's case, 61 Ala. 282. Juror is not incompetent because he is a witness in the case.—Bell's case, 44 Ala. 393. (Although, under the statute, he may be challenged for cause.) Challenge for cause may be permitted after solicitor and defendant expressed satisfaction with jury, if cause existed and was not sooner discovered.—Sparks' case, 59 Ala. 82; Roberts' case, 68 Ala. 515. But too late after juror sworn.—Ib. See Drake's case, 51 Ala. 30; Stalls' case, 28 Ala. 25; Williams' case, 3 Stew. 454. To knowingly accept disqualified juror, estops right to complain.—Brown's case, 52 Ala. 345. Presumption that party knew, unless contrary appears.—Ib. Also presumed that juror was qualified, if record is silent on the subject.—Rash's case, 61 Ala. 89. Error in disallowing challenge for cause; when not cured by allowing extra number of peremptory challenges.—Iverson's case, 52 Ala. 170. Not error for court, after examining juror, to disallow examination by prisoner's counsel for purpose of ascertaining cause of challenge.—Bales' case, 63 Ala. 30.

4332 (4882, 4884). **Same; how proved.**—Of the causes of challenge specified in the last preceding section, the first four may be proved by the oath of the person summoned, or by other evidence; the fifth and sixth, by other testimony only; the seventh, by the oath of the person alone; and the eighth, ninth and tenth, as the court may direct.

4333 (4883). **Additional ground of challenge in certain cases in favor of state.**—On the trial for any offense which may be punished capitally, or by imprisonment in the penitentiary, it is a good cause of challenge by the state that the person has a fixed opinion against capital or penitentiary punishments, or thinks that a conviction should not be had on circumstantial evidence; which cause of challenge may be proved by the oath of the person, or by other evidence.

State may challenge for fixed opinion against capital or penitentiary punishment, or waive or forbear to exercise such right.—Murphy's case, 37 Ala. 142; Lyman's case, 45 Ala. 78. But it is not ground for challenge by defense, nor can defendant complain of state for waiving such cause of challenge.—Wesley's case, 61 Ala. 282. It is a good cause of challenge by the state, in felonies or misdemeanors, that a juror will not convict on circumstantial evidence alone.—Smith's case, 55 Ala. 1. And also, when indictment charges capital offense, to a juror who says that he is not opposed to conviction on circumstantial evidence, but is opposed to punishing capitally on such evidence.—Jackson's case, 74 Ala. 26; Garrett's case, 76 Ala. 18. When error for court to exclude juror, after being accepted by both sides, because of juror's contradictory statements, under oath, as to his qualifications.—Lyman's case, 45 Ala. 78.

4334 (4885). **Court may excuse unfit person.**—Any person, who appears to the court to be unfit to serve on the jury, may be excused on his own motion, or at the instance of either party.

This statute not intended to add to number of causes of challenge, but to allow juror to be excused, when physically unable or unfit to sit on jury until trial is ended.—Lyman's case, 45 Ala. 72; Marshall's case, 8 Ala. 302. Power of court to excuse jurors, who, for reasons personal to themselves, should be exempt from serving; also may reject juror who admits cause of challenge.—Marshall's case, supra.

4335 (4751). **Other excuses allowed by court.**—The court may excuse from service any person summoned as a juror, if he is disqualified or exempt, or for any other reasonable or proper cause, to be determined by the court.

4336 (4886). **Alien not entitled to jury of aliens.**—An alien is not entitled to a jury composed, in part or wholly, of aliens or strangers.

ARTICLE VII.

THE GRAND JURY; ITS FORMATION, OATH, POWERS, DUTIES AND BUSINESS.

4337 (4753). **Grand jury; number; foreman.**—At least fifteen persons must be sworn on the grand jury, one of whom must be appointed as foreman by the court; and if he is discharged or excused for any cause after the jury is sworn or charged, the court may appoint another in his place.

Challenge of grand jurors by party about to be indicted, not allowed.—Hughes' case, 1 Ala. 655. Instruction of court to grand jury can neither be excepted to nor assigned as error.—Perkins' case, 66 Ala. 457.

4338 (4754). **If fifteen do not appear, or number reduced, how supplied.**—If fifteen persons, duly qualified to serve as grand jurors, do not appear, or if the number of those who appear is reduced below fifteen by reason of discharges, or excuses allowed by the court, or by any other cause, the court must cause an order to be entered on the minutes, commanding the sheriff to summon from the qualified citizens of the county twice the number of persons required to complete the grand jury, which order the sheriff must forthwith execute; and the persons summoned by him are bound to appear presently, and, if necessary, to serve as grand jurors, under the same penalties as if they had been regularly drawn and summoned on the original list of grand jurors for the term; and of the persons so summoned, if a greater number appear than is necessary to complete the grand jury, the names must be written on separate slips of paper, which must be folded or rolled up, so that the name may not be visible, placed in a box, or some substitute therefor, and from them must be drawn, under the direction of the court, a sufficient number of names to complete the grand jury.

If fifteen appear, court has no power to add any more; and if more are added, their acts are invalid.—Cross' case, 63 Ala. 40; Berry's case, Ib. 126. Court may order twice as many to be summoned as needed to complete number to eighteen or fifteen or any intermediate number.—Kilgore's case, 74 Ala. 1. See Yancy's case, 63 Ala. 141; Couch's case, Ib. 163; Scott's case, Ib. 59. Grand jury ordered to be completed "from the by-standers" is invalid.—Couch's case, Ib. 163; Finley's case, 61 Ala. 201; Benson's case, 68 Ala. 513; Couch's case, 63 Ala. 163. The exact words "qualified citizens of the county" need not be used, if words used have same meaning.—Yancy's case, 63 Ala. 141.

4339 (4755). **Oath of foreman.**—The following oath must be administered to the foreman of the grand jury: "You, as foreman of the grand jury of ——— county, do solemnly swear (or affirm, as the case may be) that you will diligently inquire, and true presentment make, of all indictable offenses given you in charge, as well as those brought to your knowledge, committed or triable within the county; the state's counsel, your fellows', and your own, you shall keep secret; you shall present no person from envy, hatred, or malice, nor leave any one unpresented from fear, affection, reward, or the hope thereof; but you shall present all things truly, as they come to your knowledge, to the best of your understanding; so help you God."

Sufficient recital in record that jury were legally sworn.—Lumpkin's case, 68 Ala. 56; Battle's case, 54 Ala. 93. Presumption that jury were properly sworn. Battle's case, supra.

4340 (4756). **Oath of other grand jurors.**—After the oath above prescribed has been administered to the foreman, the following oath must be administered to the other grand jurors: "The same oath which your foreman has taken, on his part, you and and each of you, on your respective parts, shall well and truly observe and keep; so help you God."

4341 (825, 4767). **Duty of grand jury as to county jail.**—It is the duty of the grand jury to make a personal inspection of the condition of the county jail, in regard to its sufficiency for the safe-keeping of prisoners, their accommodation and health, and to inquire into the manner in which the same has been kept since the last term of the court; and if it be found that such jail is not constructed in the manner prescribed by law, and so strongly and securely built as to prevent the escape of prisoners confined therein, and properly ventilated, they must, as often as may be necessary, cause the persons composing the court of county commissioners, at the time such jail was insufficient, to be indicted.

4342 (4767). **To examine condition of treasury, and official bonds; to inquire of indictable offenses, etc.**—It is the duty of the grand jury to examine into the condition of the county treasury, and the bonds of all county officers with regard to their correctness and sufficiency, and to report upon the same; to inquire into all indictable offenses committed or triable within the county, which, as they may be advised by the court, are not barred by lapse of time, or some other cause; and to perform such other duties as are, or may be by law required of them.

Feb. 22. 1881,
p. 11, sec. 4;
Dec. 11. 1882,
p. 14, sec. 2.

4343. To inquire into sheriff's accounts with state for feeding prisoners.—It is the duty of the sheriff to deliver the book in which he enters his accounts with the state for feeding prisoners to the foreman of the grand jury of the circuit or city court of such county, upon the first day of each term thereof; and it shall be the duty of the grand jury to inquire into the correctness of such accounts as may have been so made out since the preceding term.

4344 (5022). To examine fee-book of probate judge.—It is the duty of the solicitor and grand jury, at every term of the circuit or city court, to examine the fee-book of the probate judge, and ascertain if illegal fees have been corruptly received.

Feb. 7, 1879,
p. 140, sec. 66.

4345. To examine books and papers of county superintendent of education.—It is the duty of the solicitor and the grand jury, at every term of the circuit or city court, to examine the books and papers of the county superintendent of education.

4346 (4768). Entitled to free access to jail and county offices.—They are entitled to free access, at all proper hours, to the county jail, and to the office of the county treasury, and to the examination, without charge, of all records and other papers in any of the county offices connected in any way with their duties.

4347 (4774). Witnesses and evidence; issue of subpœnas; proceedings against defaulters.—The solicitor, or the clerk of the court, on the application of the grand jury, must issue subpœnas for any witnesses whom they may require to give evidence before them; and if witnesses so summoned fail to attend, the subpœnas must be returned to court, with the default thereon indorsed, signed by the foreman; and the same proceedings may thereupon be had against them as against other defaulting witnesses, the indorsement of the foreman being presumptive evidence of the default.

Sufficiency of scire facias against such witness; what will not support final judgment.—Durden's case, 32 Ala. 579.

As amended,
March 1, 1881,
p. 36.

4348 (4215). Solicitor authorized to summon witnesses.
Solicitors have authority, and it is their duty, in term time or in vacation, to issue a subpœna for any person whom they may desire to appear before the grand jury, to give evidence of any violation of the law.

As amended,
Feb. 23, 1883,
p. 158.

4349 (4773). Witnesses; by whom sworn; certificates of attendance; list and book kept and returned.—Witnesses before the grand jury may be sworn by the solicitor or foreman, and a list of all witnesses summoned, and in attendance before such jury during each term, must be kept by the foreman; and he shall give to each of such witnesses a certificate, stating the number of the case in which such witness attended, the number of days of his actual attendance, the number of miles traveled by him and the amount due him; and each of such items the foreman shall enter in a book kept for that purpose; and such book and list, certified by the foreman to be correct, must be by him returned into court, and by the clerk filed and kept as a part of the records of such court.

4350 (4776). **Legal evidence only received before grand jury.**—In the investigation of a charge for any indictable offense, the grand jury can receive no other evidence than is given by witnesses before them, or furnished by legal documentary evidence; and any witness may be examined and compelled to testify as to any offense within his knowledge.

Objection to indictment found without proper evidence, and returned by less than twelve jurors, available by motion to quash or strike from files, not by plea. Sparrenberger's case, 53 Ala. 481; Perkins' case, 66 Ala. 457.   See Washington's case, 63 Ala. 189.   What not legal documentary evidence; no inquiry allowed as to sufficiency of legal evidence—Sparrenberger's case, supra.   If competent witness examined before grand jury, such motion cannot be entertained.—Washington's case, 63 Ala. 189.

4351 (4780). **When juror may be required to disclose testimony.**—A grand juror may be required by any court to disclose the testimony of any witness examined before the grand jury, for the purpose of ascertaining whether it is consistent with the testimony given by the witness before the court, or on a charge of perjury against him.

4352 (4769). **Indictment discretionary in misdemeanors, etc.**—The grand jury are not bound to find an indictment for any misdemeanor, where no prosecutor appears, unless twelve of their number think it necessary for the public good.

4353 (4777). **Indictment; concurrence of twelve jurors necessary; how indorsed.**—The concurrence of at least twelve grand jurors is necessary to find an indictment; and when so found, it must be indorsed "a true bill," and the indorsement signed by the foreman.

Immaterial variance between name (Hutcheson) of foreman, and name (Hutchinson) indorsed.—Steadman's case, 7 Port. 496.   Variance immaterial, if idem sonans.—Jackson's case, 74 Ala. 26.   Also where it is J. H. Karter on indictment, and John H. Carter in minute entry.—McDaniel's case 76 Ala. 1.   Indorsement "true bill" essential.—Mose's case, 35 Ala. 421.   Name of foreman signed by clerk of jury to indorsement "true bill" in presence, and by direction of foreman, reprehensible, but does not invalidate indictment.—Benson's case, 68 Ala. 544. Indorsement by foreman and filing by clerk sufficient evidence of validity of indictment.—Hubbard's case, 72 Ala. 164.   Court takes judicial notice of term at which indictment returned and filed.—Overton's case, 60 Ala. 73.   What shown to be sufficient compliance with statute as to indorsement, presentation, and filing of indictment.—Wesley's case, 52 Ala. 182; McCuller's case, 49 Ala. 39.   Examination and refusal to find bill cannot affect power and action of succeeding grand jury.—Nicholson's case, 72 Ala. 178.

4354 (4778). **Indorsement of prosecutor's name, etc.**—If a prosecutor appears, his name must be indorsed by the foreman on the indictment; and if no prosecutor appears, the words "no prosecutor" must be indorsed thereon.

These indorsements merely directory, and their omission will not invalidate the indictment.—Hughes' case, 1 Ala. 655.   See Ashwood's case, 63 Ala. 120.

4355 (4779). **Liability of prosecutor and foreman for costs.** When the indictment is for a misdemeanor, and the court is of opinion that the prosecution is frivolous or malicious, the prosecutor is liable for the costs; and if the foreman of the grand jury fails to make the indorsement required of him by the last preceding section, he is liable for the costs as if he were the prosecutor.

Prosecutor can be taxed for costs only in misdemeanors; and record must show that prosecution appeared frivolous or malicious.—Burns' case, 5 Ala. 227; Tuck's case, 8 Ala. 664.

4356 (4770). **Juror must disclose offenses known to him.** If any grand juror knows, or has reason to believe, that a public offense has been committed, which may be indicted and tried in that county, it is his duty to disclose the same to his fellow jurors, who must thereupon investigate it.

4357 (4771). **Juror must withdraw when interested.**—A grand juror must not be present at, or take any part in the deliberations of his fellow jurors respecting any public offense with which he is charged, or which was committed against his person or property, or when he is a prosecutor, or when he is connected by blood or marriage with the person charged.

Grand jury cannot be called, and required to expurgate themselves of any supposed interest or bias, at the instance of one in jail, and expecting an indictment to be preferred against him.—Clarissa's case, 11 Ala. 57. Objection made by plea. Ib 57.

4358 (4772). **Deficiency in such case; how supplied.**—If, by reason of the provisions of the preceding section, the number of grand jurors is reduced below thirteen in the investigation of any matter, the court must supply the deficiency from the by-standers; and the persons so placed on the grand jury must serve only during such investigation.

4359 (4775). **Attendance of solicitor.**—The solicitor must attend before the grand jury when required by them, and he may do so whenever he sees fit, for the purpose of examining witnesses in their presence, or giving them legal advice as to any matter connected with their duties, and he may appear before them at any time to give information as to any matter cognizable by them; but he must not be present at the expression of opinions, or the giving of their votes on any matter before them.

An attorney is not authorized to go before the grand jury at request of the solicitor and perform his duties; yet indictment, so found, should not be quashed because of such unauthorized appearance of the attorney.—Blevins' case, 68 Ala. 92.

ARTICLE VIII.

PROCEEDINGS AGAINST DEFAULTING JUROR.

4360 (4747). **Judgment against defaulting juror.**—Any person, duly summoned as a grand or petit juror, who fails to attend as commanded, must be fined by the court not less than fifty, nor more than one hundred dollars, for which a conditional judgment must be rendered against him in favor of the state, for the use of the particular county, to be made absolute unless he appears and renders a good excuse for his non-attendance.

Judgment final cannot be set aside and avoided by the court at a subsequent term; and if it is so done, the supreme court will reverse second ruling on appeal by state.—Gardner's case, 45 Ala. 51.

4361 (4748). **Excuse for default made at same or subsequent term.**—A juror may render his excuse for non-attendance at the same term at which such conditional judgment was rendered against him, or at any subsequent term before the judgment is made absolute; and if the excuse is deemed sufficient by the court, he must be discharged from the fine and costs; and the judgment must in no case be made absolute, unless he appears, or is personally served with notice, as hereinafter provided.

4362 (4749). **Sci. fa. on judgment nisi.**—If a defaulting juror fails to appear, and render his excuse to the court, at the term at which a conditional judgment is rendered against him, the clerk must issue a notice to him of the rendition of such conditional judgment, and that the same will be made absolute at the next term, unless he appears and shows a good excuse for his default; which notice must be executed by the sheriff, or other officer acting in his place, by serving the defaulter with a copy thereof; and if not executed by the next term of the court, it may be renewed to the next succeeding term, and so on until the same is executed.

4363 (4750). **Judgment final.**—On such notice being returned executed by the proper officer, if the defaulter fails to appear, or fails to render a good excuse for his default, the judgment must be made absolute against him.

As to proceedings on scire facias, see Pomeroy's case, 40 Ala. 63; Grund's case, Ib. 709; Hatch's case, Ib. 718; Hall's case, 15 Ala. 431; Craig's case, 12 Ala. 363; Ellison's case, 8 Ala. 273; Hinson's case, 4 Ala. 671; Hayter's case, 7 Port. 156; Lloyd's case, Minor, 34.

CHAPTER 5.

INDICTMENTS.

ARTICLE I.

DEFINITION, FORM AND CONTENTS.

4364 (4782, 4783). **Definition; not distinguished from presentment.**—An indictment is an accusation in writing presented by the grand jury of the county, charging a person with an indictable offense; the distinction between indictments and presentments is abolished.

Mose's case, 35 Ala. 425.

4365 (4784). **Caption and conclusion.**—An indictment must contain, in the caption or body thereof, the name of the state, county, court and term, in and at which it is preferred, and must conclude "against the peace and dignity of the State of Alabama."

The nature, office and materiality of the caption.—Goodloe's case, 60 Ala. 93; Overton's case, Ib. 73; Harrington's case, 36 Ala. 236; Reeves' case, 20 Ala. 33; Murphy's case, 9 Port. 487; Rose's case, Minor, 28. Must be sufficiently shown by the record.—Goodloe's case, supra. Looked to in aid of indictment as part of record.—Morgan's case, 19 Ala. 556; Lawson's case, 20 Ala. 65; Noles' case, 24 Ala. 672; Perkins' case, 50 Ala. 154. Applies to each count, and is not struck out. though first count quashed.—Pairo's case, 49 Ala. 24. Immaterial if words "city court," instead of "city court of Selma," are used.—Harrison's case, 55 Ala. 239; Bonner's case, Ib. 242. If it states the name of the county, omission of word county from body of indictment is not material defect.—Caldwell's case, 49 Ala. 34. Nor the substitution of the word court for county.—Perkins' case, 50 Ala. 154. And the same as to the term at which the indictment was found.—Quinn's case, 49 Ala. 353. Not necessary that each count should conclude "against the peace and dignity of the State of Alabama," if the indictment so concludes.—McGuire's case, 37 Ala. 161. And it is not demurrable for concluding "against the peace and dignity of the State of Alabama" (as in the statute), instead of "against the peace and dignity of the state" (as in the constitution, art. 6, sec. 28).—Washington's case, 53 Ala. 29. But if the "State of Alabama" is mentioned in the caption, the conclusion may be against, etc., of "the state," without adding "of Alabama." Atwell's case, 63 Ala. 61.

4366 (4824). **Forms in Code sufficient.**—The manner of stating the act constituting the offense, as set forth in the forms given in title six, part five of this Code, is sufficient in all cases in which the forms there given are applicable; in other cases, forms may be used as near similar as the nature of the case and the rules prescribed in this chapter will permit.

4367 (4815). **Formal defects not fatal.**—An indictment must not be held insufficient, nor can the trial, judgment, or other proceedings thereon, be affected by reason of any defect or imperfection in any matter of form which does not prejudice the substantial rights of the defendant on the trial.

4368 (4785). **Statement of offense.**—The indictment must state the facts constituting the offense in ordinary and concise language, without prolixity or repetition, in such a manner as to enable a person of common understanding to know what is intended, and with that degree of certainty which will enable the court, on conviction, to pronounce the proper judgment; and in no case are the words "force and arms" or "contrary to the form of the statute" necessary.

Applies only to statutory offenses.—Goree's case, 71 Ala. 9. In common-law misdemeanors, made felonies by statute, not necessary to allege that the act was feloniously done.—Beasley's case, 18 Ala. 535; Butler's case, 22 Ala. 43. Where offense consists of repetition or continuation of acts, they need not be set out. Sterne's case, 20 Ala. 43; Lawson's case, Ib. 65. Exceptions created by a *proviso* to an act need not be negatived.—Carson's case, 69 Ala. 235. See, also, Grattan's case, 71 Ala. 344; Clark's case, 19 Ala. 552. Must charge acts, not specially defined, in plain, unambiguous, not slang or technical language.—Daniel's case, 61 Ala. 4. Every fact and circumstance, not necessary ingredient of offense, may be rejected as surplusage.—Stedman's case, 7 Port. 495; McGehee's case, 52 Ala. 224. Or words uselessly repeated or superadded.—Lodano's case, 25 Ala. 64; McGehee's case, supra.

4369 (4801). **Construction of words used.**—The words used in an indictment must be construed in their usual acceptation in common language, except words and phrases defined by law, which must be construed according to their legal meaning.

Bad punctuation does not vitiate an indictment.—Ward's case, 50 Ala. 120. Nor use of character *&* instead of word "*and*."—Pickens' case, 58 Ala. 364. Nor use of word *was* instead of "*were*."—Pond's case, 55 Ala. 196. Use of figures instead of letters permissible sometimes, but a bad practice.—Raiford's case, 7 Port. 101; Diggs' case, 49 Ala. 311. The omission of the last letter of the word "*gold*," making it "*gol*," in describing money stolen, is mere misprision.—Grant's case, 35 Ala. 201. Use of word "*charged*" instead of "*charge*," when not fatal.—Brazier's case, 44 Ala. 387. Use of words "*maice* aforethought," instead of "*malice* aforethought," vitiates as to intended charge.—Wood's case, 50 Ala. 144. Averment of "*Buter*" for "*Butler*," in describing the county, corrected by caption.—Reeves' case, 20 Ala. 33.

4370 (4792). **Statute words not necessary; what words sufficient.**—Words used in a statute to define an offense need not be strictly pursued in the indictment; it is sufficient to use other words conveying the same meaning.

Indictment for offense created by statute must conform substantially to description in statute.—Bryan's case, 45 Ala. 86; Skains' case, 21 Ala. 218; Pettibone's case, 19 Ala. 586; Eubanks' case, 17 Ala. 181. Hence, Code form of indictment insufficient, if it fails to describe offense, etc.—Danner's case, 54 Ala. 127; Smith's case, 63 Ala. 55; and cases above cited in this note. Held sufficient generally to follow language of statute.—Mason's case, 42 Ala. 543; Johnson's case, 32 Ala. 583; Bush's case, 18 Ala. 415; Rayford's case, 7 Port. 101; Plunket's case, 2 Stew. 101; Lodano's case, 25 Ala. 64; Smith's case, 22 Ala. 54; Stedman's case, 7 Port. 495; Clark's case, 19 Ala. 552; Beasley's case, 18 Ala. 535; Batre's case, Ib. 119; Eubanks' case, 17 Ala. 181; Mahan's case, 2 Ala. 340; Click's case, Ib. 26; Duncan's case, 9 Port. 260; Briley's case, 8 Port. 472; Smith's case, 63 Ala. 55. If statute words are not employed, the words used must have as full signification.—Sparrenberger's case, 53 Ala. 481; Ben's case, 22 Ala. 9; Ward's case, Ib. 16; Bullock's case, 13 Ala. 413; Worrell's case, 12 Ala. 732. Charging words in addition to those in statute, thereby taking the offense out of statute, vitiates indictment.—Mahan's case, 2 Ala. 340. Insufficient to pursue words of statute which merely designates without describing offense.—Anthony's case, 29 Ala. 27; Beasley's case, 18 Ala. 535; Turnipseed's case, 6 Ala. 664. See also Williams' case, 15 Ala. 259. When indictment in language of statute insufficient.—Grattan's case, 71 Ala. 344; Danner's case, 54 Ala. 127. When must conform to letter or substance of statute creating particular local offense.—Camp's case, 27 Ala. 54. Where statute prescribes different punishment for different individuals indictment must specify the class within which defendant is amenable.—Hirschfelder's case, 18 Ala. 112.

4371 (4793). **Offense described as at common law; punishment.**—In an indictment for an offense which was indictable at common law, the offense may be charged or described as at common law, and the defendant, if convicted, must receive the punishment prescribed by the statute.

Indictment good at common law sufficient under the statute.—Sparks' case, 59 Ala. 82; Diggs' case. 49 Ala. 311. Formerly indictment under the statute merely punishing common-law offense, required to be found as at common law.—Absence's case, 4 Port. 397; Stedman's case, 7 Port. 495.

4372 (4794). **Special and general terms in statutory definition.**—When a statute creating or defining an offense uses special or particular terms, an indictment on it may use the general term which, in common language, embraces the special term.

For act done by acts or means other than those particularized, such acts or means must be specified more particularly than by general description in statute. Danner's case, 54 Ala. 127. They must be described in plain and proper language, not by slang or technical words.—Daniel's case, 61 Ala. 4. When indictment charging general term insufficient.—Horton's case, 53 Ala. 488; Johnson's case, 32 Ala. 583; Bush's case, 18 Ala. 415; Raiford's case, 7 Port. 101; Plunket's case, 2 Stew. 101.

4373 (4788). **Statement of time.**—It is not necessary to state the precise time at which the offense was committed; but it may be alleged to have been committed on any day before the finding of the indictment, or generally before the finding of the indictment, unless time is a material ingredient of the offense.

Specific time need not be averred, unless a material ingredient of the offense. Molett's case, 33 Ala. 408; Doyle's case, 49 Ala. 28   Sufficient to charge that offense was committed "before the finding of the indictment."—Thompson's case, 25 Ala. 41. And must be proved that the offense was committed before indictment found; of which a reasonable doubt authorizes acquittal.—Armistead's case, 43 Ala. 340. See McGuire's case, 37 Ala. 161. If alleged under videlicet, need not be proved as laid.—McDade's case, 20 Ala. 81. Need not allege that offense was committed after passage of a recent act alleged to be violated.—Harris' case, 60 Ala. 50. See, also, Adams' case, Ib. 52. As to allegation and variance in limit of time allowed in taking out license.—Henback's case, 53 Ala. 523. Time of offense as a necessary averment at common law.—Beckwith's case. 1 Stew. 318; Lassley's case, 7 Port. 526; Shelton's case, 1 Stew. & Port. 208; Roberts' case, 19 Ala. 526.

4374 (4787). **Statement and proof of venue.**—It is not necessary to allege where the offense was committed; but it must be proved, on the trial, to have been committed within the jurisdiction of the county in which the indictment is preferred.

Legislature has the power to dispense with necessity of averring venue.—Noles' case, 24 Ala. 672. Averment of county in margin.— Reeves' case, 20 Ala. 33. Venue must always be proved.—Tidwell's case, 70 Ala. 33; Salomon's case, 27 Ala. 27; Brown's case, Ib. 47; Huffman's case, 28 Ala. 48; Speight's case, 29 Ala. 32; Farrall's case, 32 Ala. 557; Green's case, 41 Ala. 419; Frank's case, 40 Ala. 9; Clark's case, 46 Ala. 309; Sparks' case, 59 Ala 82; Cawthorn's case, 63 Ala. 157. May be proved after argument begun.—Pond's case, 55 Ala. 196. Proof of county boundaries; when a question of fact and when of law.—Tidwell's case, 70 Ala. 33. Failure to prove venue, taken advantage of by general charge to acquit.—Childs' case, 55 Ala. 28; Williams' case, 54 Ala. 131; Clark s case, 46 Ala. 307. Or demurrer to evidence sustained, if no proof of venue.—Martin's case, 62 Ala. 240. Such proof must appear by bill of exceptions, if purporting to set out all the evidence, on appeal.—Riddle's case, 49 Ala. 389; Walker's case, 52 Ala. 192; Williams' case, 54 Ala. 132; Sampson's case, Ib. 241; Ellsberry's case, 52 Ala. 8. Charges ignoring proof of venue erroneous.—Henry's case, 36 Ala. 268; David's case, 40 Ala. 69; Clark's case, 46 Ala. 307; Gooden's case, 55 Ala. 178; Bain's case, 61 Ala. 75. But see Cunningham's case, 73 Ala. 51. But supreme court will not interfere in the absence of instructions given or refused, and when no exception was reserved.—Hubbard's case, 72 Ala. 169; Huggin's case, 41 Ala. 393; Elsberry's case, 52 Ala. 8; West's case, 76 Ala. 98.

4375 (4795). **Description of public place.**—When, to constitute the offense, an act must be done in a public place, and such public place is not more particularly defined in the statute, it is sufficient to allege that the act was done "in a public place" generally.

4376 (4786). **Name or description of defendant when unknown.**—The indictment must be certain as to the person charged; but when his name is unknown to the grand jury, it may be so alleged without further identification.

Identity of persons presumed from identity of names, in absence of evidence that same name is borne by another in the community.—Garrett's case, 76 Ala. 18. Evidence of identity.—Ib. Statute is mere affirmation of common law.—Washington's case, 68 Ala. 85. Either christian or surname may be alleged under alias. Lee's case, 55 Ala. 259; Haley's case, 63 Ala, 89. And may be identified by either name.—Evans' case, 62 Ala. 6. Insertion or omission of middle name immaterial. Edmundson's case. 17 Ala. 179. See, also, Diggs' case, 49 Ala. 311. And so of a mistake in the middle name, if alleged.—Pace's case, 69 Ala. 231. Not sufficient to allege defendant's name by initials, without additional averments.—Gerrish's case, 53 Ala. 476. Need not allege whether defendant was slave or freeman.—Jeffries' case, 39 Ala. 655. Such averments rejected as surplusage.—McGehee's case. 52 Ala. 224. Where offense alleged to have been committed by freedman, presumed, in absence of other proof, to have been committed since slavery was abolished.—Tempe's case, 40 Ala. 350. When not uncertain, as to whether defeudants charged individually, or as private corporation.—Barnett's case, 54 Ala. 579. Mistake in spelling, if pronunciation unchanged, is immaterial variance under doctrine of idem sonans.—Page's case, 61 Ala. 17. The following held **idem sonans**: "*Booth*" and "*Boothe*" (Jackson's case, 74 Ala. 26); "*Louis*" and "*Lewis*" (Block's case, 66 Ala. 493); "*Edmundson*" and "*Edmindson*" (Edmundson's case, 17 Ala. 179); "*Burdet*" and "*Boudet*," "*Boredet*" or "*Bouredet*" (Aaron's case, 37 Ala. 106). The following held **not idem sonans**: "*Mincher*" and "*Minchen*" (Adams' case, 67 Ala. 87); "*Zachary*" and "*Zacharia*" (Lawrence's case, 59 Ala. 61). When idem sonans a question for the jury.—Underwood's case, 72 Ala. 220; Lawrence's case, 59 Ala. 61. The christian names of third persons, or persons only collaterally concerned, may be alleged by initials, if it appears on the trial to be the person meant.—Franklin's case, 52 Ala.414; Gerrish's case, 53 Ala. 476; Haley's case, 63 Ala. 83; Thompson's case, 48 Ala. 165. But the policy of this statute should be extended to description of third persons with same certainty as defendants.—Morningstar's case, 52 Ala. 405. Cases showing material and immaterial variance in names or description of third persons.—Jacobs' case, 61 Ala. •448; Hinds' case, 55 Ala. 145; Brown's case, 47 Ala. 47; Owen's case, 48 Ala. 328. Grand juries and solicitors in all cases should try and ascertain true names, and, if unknown, may be so alleged without further description.—Morningstar's case, 52 Ala. 405; Gerrish's case, 53 Ala. 470; Cheek's case, 38 Ala. 227. Also may allege christian name, or surname, as unknown.—Bryant's case, 36 Ala. 270; Skinner's case, 30 Ala. 524. Yet proof that name was known by grand jury, or could have been ascertained by due diligence, authorizes acquittal as to persons so alleged, but not if name known since indictment or trial.—Cheek's case, supra. But see as to unknown facts, Duvall's case, 63 Ala. 12. But indictment must not pretend to give a name and also aver (in same count) name to be unknown.—Jones' case, 63 Ala. 27. Yet this rule held not to apply when no name is alleged, but initials only are averred.—Gerrish's case, 53 Ala. 470.

4377 (4789). **Facts unknown to jury; so alleged.**—Any fact which is unknown to the grand jury, and which is not a material ingredient of the offense, may be so charged in the indictment.

Such averment is sufficient if the fact was actually unknown, even if it could have been ascertained by reasonable diligence.—Duvall's case, 63 Ala. 12.

4378 (4790). **Means unknown; so alleged.**—When the means by which the offense was committed are unknown to the grand jury, and do not enter into the essence of the offense, the indictment may allege that they are unknown to the jury.

4379 (4791). **Legal presumptions, and matters judicially known.**—Presumptions of law and matters of which judicial notice is taken, need not be stated.

Refers only to presumptions of law which forbid all dispute; not to disputable presumptions which may be overcome by proof.—Henry's case, 33 Ala. 389. See McDaniel's case, 76 Ala. 1; Cary's case, Ib. 78. Courts take judicial notice of public officers, and their official acts.—Beggs' case, 55 Ala. 108. Charters of municipal corporations and special statutes conferring on them special powers.—Mayor v. Wetumpka Wharf Co., 63 Ala. 611; City Council v. Hughes, 65 Ala. 201. But not of the ordinances of municipal corporations.—Furham v. Mayor, 54 Ala. 263. Of a statute which, though local in its nature, extends to all persons who may come within territory described, and is therefore public statute.—Carson's case, 69 Ala. 235. But not of a private act (as turnpike charter).—Moore's case, 26 Ala. 88. Of notaries with powers of justice and other commissioned officers.—Coleman's case, 63 Ala. 93. That "lager beer" is a "malt liquor."—Watson's case, 55 Ala. 158. Of the meaning of "malt liquor" as used in statutes.—Adler's case, 55 Ala. 16. Of the value of U. S. currency and treasury notes.—Grant's case, 55 Ala. 201; Duvall's case, 63 Ala. 12. Of journals of two houses of general assembly. Moody's case, 48 Ala. 115. Of grand jury and terms of filing indictments.—Overton's case, 60 Ala. 74. Of the names of counties of this state.—Ib.; Reeves' case, 20 Ala. 33. Of things generally known.—S. & N. R. R. Co. v. Pilgreen, 62 Ala. 305. Also of Webster's Unabridged Dictionary as standard authority for meaning of English words.—Adler's case, 55 Ala. 16. But not of laws of a sister state. Forsythe v. Preer, 62 Ala. 443. As to other matters of which courts take judicial notice, see Sprowl v. Lawrence, 33 Ala. 674; Allman v. Owen, 31 Ala. 167; McDaniel's case, 76 Ala. 1; Cary's case, Ib. 78.

4380 (4799). **Averment of intent to injure or defraud.**—When an intent to injure or defraud is necessary to constitute the offense, it is sufficient to allege an intent to injure or defraud generally, without naming the particular person, corporation, or government intended to be injured or defrauded.

Williams' case, 61 Ala. 33.

4381 (4800). **Averment of ownership of property.**—When any property, upon or in relation to which the offense was committed, belongs to several partners or owners, it is sufficient to allege the ownership to be in any one or more of such partners or owners. As amended, Dec. 4, 1878, p. 46.

Williams' case, 67 Ala. 183; Whites's case, 72 Ala. 195; Bass' case, 63 Ala. 108.

4382 (4812). **Description of animal in offense committed concerning same.**—In an indictment for the larceny of any animal, or for any other public offense committed in reference to any animal, it is sufficient to describe the animal by such name as, in the common understanding, embraces it, without designating its sex.

See note to section 3789.

ARTICLE II.

ALTERNATIVE AVERMENTS, AND JOINDER OF OFFENSES.

4383 (4796). **Statements of means or intents in alternative.**—When the offense may be committed by different means, or with different intents, such means or intents may be alleged in the same count in the alternative.

Indictment charging the appropriation of specified sums, "or other large sums of money," is not within either of the three sections of this article, as showing different means, intents and results, or offenses.—Noble's case, 59 Ala. 78. These statutes change the common-law rule, and intended to prevent a multiplicity of counts.—Sparrenberger's case, 53 Ala. 481; Noble's case, supra; Horton's case, 53 Ala. 488.

4384 (4797). **Same as to different results.**—When an act is criminal, if producing different results, such results may be charged in the same count in the alternative.

These statutes not applicable where particular acts or means are followed by more comprehensive generic term, which is immediately preceded by words "or other." Johnson's case, 32 Ala. 583; and other cases cited in note to section 3786. An averment as "justice of peace or notary public," allowable.—Murphy's case, 55 Ala. 252. Also "did remove or conceal one bale of cotton," etc.—Nixon's case, 55 Ala. 120; Atwell's case, 63 Ala. 61. Also did steal "national bank-notes, or gold or silver coin," etc.—Wesley's case, 61 Ala. 282. "Did sell vinous or malt liquors" to a minor.—Adler's case, 55 Ala. 16. Also that defendants were "members or partners of a corporation or co-partnership."—Barnett's case, 54 Ala. 579. Also that one maliciously injured a "mare or an ox."—Burgess' case, 44 Ala. 190. Also to allege that assault was committed by pouring, or attempting to pour, a mixture of spirits of turpentine and pepper."—Murdock's case, 65 Ala. 520. Also "did carnally know or abuse," etc.—Johnson's case, 50 Ala. 456. But insufficient to allege house burned as a "barn or stable," "a barn-house or building."—Horton's case, 60 Ala. 72. Also defective to aver that defendant "sold, bartered, or otherwise disposed of, or permitted to be taken, spirituous, vinous, or malt liquors in less than, etc." Raisler's case, 55 Ala. 64.

4385 (4798). **Joinder of offenses in same count.** — When offenses are of the same character, and subject to the same punishment, the defendant may be charged with the commission of either in the same count in the alternative.

This statute merely permits to be charged in one count, what the common law permitted in different counts, and is not unconstitutional.—Burdine's case, 25 Ala. 60; Sherrod's case, Ib. 78; Horton's case, 53 Ala. 488; Sparrenberger's case, Ib. 481; Noble's case, 59 Ala. 78. But each alternative averment must present an indictable offense.—Pickett's case, 60 Ala. 77; Horton's case and Noble's case, supra. Two grades of same offense, whether misdemeanor or felony, visited with same kind of penalty, may be joined in same count.—Ward's case, 22 Ala. 16; Swallow's case, Ib. 20; Ben's case, Ib. 9; Mooney's case, 8 Ala. 328; Barber's case, 34 Ala. 213. See further, as to the doctrine of joinder of offenses in same or different counts, Wooster's case, 55 Ala. 217 (overruling Norvell's case, 50 Ala. 174); Quinn s case, 49 Ala. 353; Johnson's case, 35 Ala. 370. As to the right to make the prosecutor elect, see Mayo's case, 30 Ala. 32; Hugh's case, 35 Ala. 351; Elam's case, 26 Ala. 48; Smith's case, 52 Ala. 384; Johnson's case, 29 Ala. 62; Bonham's case, 65 Ala. 456; Oxford's case, 33 Ala. 416; Seibert's case, 40 Ala. 60; Beason's case, 72 Ala. 191; Beasley's case, 59 Ala. 20; Bass' case, 63 Ala. 108; Peacher's case, 61 Ala. 22; Ex parte Tompkins, 58 Ala. 71. Election on joinder of several misdemeanors not required, and prosecution may seek a conviction on all of them, and they may be tried at same time.—Wooster's case, 55 Ala. 217.

ARTICLE III.

PRESENTING, FILING, WITHDRAWING, CERTIFYING AND RECORDING INDICTMENTS.

4386 (4821). **Indictments filed, but not entered on minutes; inspection of.** — All indictments must be presented to the court by the foreman of the grand jury, in the presence of at least eleven other jurors; must be indorsed "filed," and the indorsement dated and signed by the clerk; but no entry of an indictment found must be made on the minutes, nor must any indictment be inspected by any other person than the solicitor, the presiding judge and the clerk of the court, until the defendant has been arrested, or has given bail for his appearance.

Court has control over these matters and may cause clerk to indorse, etc., as of date of, filing, etc., at any time during term.—Franklin's case, 28 Ala. 9.   Returning and filing need not appear on minutes.—Mose's case, 35 Ala. 421; Russell's case, 33 Ala. 366.   When cannot arrest judgment on account of informality, in finding, returning, or filing.—Russell's case, 33 Ala. 366. What entry shows sufficient return and presentation.—McCuller's case, 49 Ala. 39; Wesley's case, 52 Ala. 182. When date of filing indorsed is evidence.—Sellers' case, 52 Ala. 368.

4387 (4822). **Withdrawal and filing of indictment.**—In all criminal cases in the circuit court, in which a capias has issued for two terms, and has been returned "not found," the solicitor may, by leave of the court, withdraw and file the indictment, with leave to reinstate the same when the ends of justice require such reinstatement.

When operates a discontinuance and how available to defendant.—Drinkard's case, 20 Ala. 9.

4388. Secret records of indictments made and kept by clerk; uses of.—The clerk of the court in which indictments are returned shall, within twenty days after the filing thereof, and without allowing them to be taken out of his custody or control, record the same, with the indorsement thereon, in a well-bound book, which shall be properly indexed and kept secret, as indictments are required to be kept secret, before the arrest of the defendant; and if the office of the clerk is furnished with an iron safe or vault, it shall be kept therein; but the court may require the production of such book, on the trial of a defendant, for comparison of the indictment against such defendant with the record thereof, only in cases where the trial is had on a certified copy of the indictment as provided by law.

Jan. 23, 1885,
p. 98, secs. 1, 3.

ARTICLE IV.

AMENDMENTS; NOLLE PROSEQUI; NEW INDICTMENT.

4389 (4816). **Amendment allowed by consent on account of variance.**—An indictment may be amended, with the consent of the defendant, when the name of the defendant is incorrectly stated, or when any person, property, or matter therein stated is incorrectly described.

See note to succeeding section.

4390 (4817). **When nol. pros. entered, and new indictment ordered to be preferred.**—If the defendant will not consent to such amendment, the prosecution may be dismissed at any time before the jury retires, as to the count in the indictment to which the variance applies; and the court may order another indictment to be preferred at the same, or at a subsequent term, in which case an entry of record must be made to the effect following:

"The State ⎫   In this case, it appeared from the evidence that
   vs.   ⎬ there was a variance between the allegations of
  A. B.   ⎭ the indictment and the proof in this (setting out the variance); or it appeared from the evidence that the de-

fendant's name was —— —— (stating it); and the defendant refusing to allow the indictment to be amended, the prosecution was dismissed before the jury retired, and another indictment was ordered to be preferred.

Unsafe practice and reversible error to permit amendment without consent of accused.—Gregory's case, 46 Ala. 151; Johnson's case, Ib. 212.   Allowed by consent of accused.—Ross' case, 55 Ala. 177.   On variance between allegations and proof, nol. pros. may be had, and accused tried under new indictment; also where indictment fatally defective; accused not in jeopardy.—Martha's case, 26 Ala. 72; White's case, 49 Ala. 344; Weston's case, 63 Ala. 155.   Statute not unconstitutional.—Kreps' case, 8 Ala. 951.   Suspends running of statute of limitation; what judgment entry must show to suspend limitations; when defendant entitled to acquittal.—Coleman's case, 71 Ala. 312.   When error to enter nol. pros. as to one of two defendants.—McGehee's case, 58 Ala. 360.

Article V.

INDICTMENT LOST OR DESTROYED; SUBSTITUTE.

4391 (4818). **Indictment lost or destroyed, another preferred.**—When an indictment is lost, mislaid, or destroyed, the court may, on satisfactory proof thereof, order another indictment to be preferred at the term at which such proof is made, or at a subsequent term; in which case an entry of record must be made to the effect following:

"The State⎫   In this case, it appearing to the court that an
   vs.   ⎬ indictment was preferred against the defendant at
A. B.   ⎭ the —— term, 18— (stating the time), and that said indictment is lost, mislaid, or destroyed; it is, therefore, ordered that a new indictment be preferred against the defendant for the same offense."

At common law, if indictment was lost or destroyed, it could not be substituted. Ganaway's case, 22 Ala. 772.   Inherent power in court to substitute indictment lost during trial.—Bradford's case, 54 Ala. 230.

Jan. 22, 1885,
p. 98, sec. 2.

4392. If recorded, a certified copy of record produced. When it is shown to the court that an original indictment, recorded as required by law, has been lost, destroyed, or so mutilated as to be illegible, the court shall direct the clerk to make and certify a copy thereof from such record, upon which the defendant may be arraigned and tried as upon the original indictment.

Article VI.

INDICTMENT QUASHED, OR JUDGMENT ARRESTED, AND NEW INDICTMENT.

4393 (4823). **Not quashed, etc., without leave of court.** An indictment must not be quashed, dismissed, discontinued, or abandoned, without, the permission of the court; and such permission must be entered of record.

When nolle prosequi entered as to an acquitted defendant, after verdict and reversal by supreme court of one convicted, to cure objection of a misjoinder of two defendants.—Cox' case, 76 Ala. 68, citing Berry's case, 65 Ala. 117.   Permission to nol. pros. not final judgment from which writ of error will lie.—Willingham's case, 14 Ala. 539.   Court may allow a nol. pros. where demurrer interposed, without passing on demurrer.—Lacey's case, 58 Ala. 385; Wooster's case, Ib. 217. Also to one of several counts after close of evidence, which is acquittal as to such count.—Barnett's case, 54 Ala. 579.   But see Grogan's case, 44 Ala. 9.   Operates an acquittal after jeopardy begins.—Grogan's case, 44 Ala. 9.   No bar to subsequent indictment.—Martha's case, 26 Ala. 72.   Nol. pros. as to one count, before jeopardy, merely destroys, but does not acquit of that count.—Walker's case, 61 Ala. 30.   Nol. pros. as to one count, in absence of some of the defendants, destroys such count as to them, as well as to those present —Ib.   When error to enter nol. pros. as to one of two defendants.—McGehee's case, 58 Ala. 360.   Indictment found at unauthorized special term should be quashed.—Davis' case, 46 Ala. 80. Motion to quash or strike from files, and other objections to indictment as a court record, come before pleading on merits.—Jackson's case, 74 Ala. 26.   Court not bound to quash defective indictment on motion, but may put defendant to demurrer. Jones' case, 5 Ala. 666; Boulo's case 49 Ala. 22.   Motion to quash in sound discretion of court; what not an exception.—White's case, 74 Ala. 31.   Must be made first in court below, not on appeal.—Jackson's case, 74 Ala. 26.   Held that if one count quashed on motion, all vitiated.—Rose's case, Minor, 28.   But not so on demurrer.—Turner's case, 40 Ala. 21.   Improper, in support of motion, to show that twelve of first grand jury did not concur in the finding.—Spigener's case, 62 Ala. 383.

4394 (4819). **If quashed or judgment arrested, another indictment preferred.**—When the judgment is arrested, or the indictment quashed, on account of any defects therein, or because it was not found by a grand jury regularly organized, or because it charged no offense, or for any other cause, the court may order another indictment to be preferred for the offense charged, or intended to be charged; and in such case an entry of record must be made setting forth the facts.

If record shows reversible irregularity in organization of grand jury, indictment should be quashed, and case ordered before another grand jury.—Weston's case, 63 Ala. 155.   Sufficiency of a new indictment must be tested as if it were found at time former was found.—McIntyre's case, 55 Ala. 167.   Court has inherent power without the statute to hold accused to answer new indictment, without hearing testimony to show guilt.—Ex parte Graves, 61 Ala. 381.   Indictment quashed on demurrer while grand jury in session, no error to hold prisoner until they find new indictment.—Crumpton's case, 43 Ala. 31.   The better and more usual practice is, to defer the nol. pros., or quashing of the defective indictment, until the second indictment is found.—Perkins' case, 66 Ala. 457.   Suspends statute of limitations. See note to section 3715.   **Motion in arrest of judgment** must be disposed of before sentence.—Hood's case, 44 Ala. 81.   Can only be predicated on matter of record, without aid of bill of exceptions.—Sparks' case, 59 Ala. 82; Morgan's case, 48 Ala. 65; Brown's case, 52 Ala. 345; Blount's case, 49 Ala. 381.   Any objection sustaining a demurrer will sustain such motion.—Francois' case, 20 Ala. 83; Nicholson's case, 18 Ala. 529; Beasley's case, Ib. 535; Martin's case, 28 Ala. 71; s. c., 29 Ala. 30; Beckwith's case, 1 Stew. 318.   Will be sustained when jury fail to ascertain degree of murder.—Johnson's case, 17 Ala. 618.   Also, if trial had on pleas of not guilty and former acquittal at same time in felony.—Faulk's case, 52 Ala. 416.   Also if indictment found by grand jury organized by court without authority.—O'Byrnes' case, 51 Ala. 25.   Separation or misconduct of jury no ground for this motion, but may be for a new trial.—Williams' case, 48 Ala. 85; Morgan's case, Ib. 65; Crocker's case, 47 Ala. 53; Franklin's case, 29 Ala. 14; Brister's case, 26 Ala. 107.   Also when verdict against evidence or charge of court. Blount's case, 49 Ala. 381.   This motion not available, on the ground that a juror had been a member of the indicting grand jury.—Battle's case, 54 Ala. 93.   Nor that a christian name of a third person was alleged by initials only.—Lyon's case, 61 Ala. 224.   Nor because record fails to show whether conviction was for act committed before or after passage of statute making felony out of what had been misdemeanor.—McDowell's case, 61 Ala. 172.

CHAPTER 6.

ARREST AND COMMITMENT AFTER INDICTMENT.

ARTICLE I.

ARREST WITHOUT WRIT.

4395 (4825). **Defendant, if present, arrested without process.**—After an indictment has been returned by the grand jury, the court may order any defendant who is present, and who has not been arrested, to be taken into custody without process.

ARTICLE II.

ISSUE AND EXECUTION OF WRIT.

4396 (4826). **Writ of arrest issued by the clerk, solicitor, or judge.**—A writ of arrest must be issued by the clerk forthwith after the finding of the indictment against each defendant who is not in actual custody, or who has not been bailed, or whose undertaking of bail has been declared forfeited; or it may be issued without an order of court, either in term time or vacation, by the solicitor of the circuit, or by any circuit judge.

4397 (4827). **Form of writ of arrest for felony.**—When the indictment is for a felony, the writ of arrest may be in the following form:

"State of Alabama, } To any sheriff of the state:
—— county.

"An indictment having been found against A. B., at the —— term —— 18—, of the —— court of —— county, for the offense of —— (describing the offense so as to show that it is a felony), you, are, therefore, commanded forthwith to arrest the said defendant and commit him to jail; and that you return this writ according to law. Dated this, —— day of ——, 18—.

"(Signed)   C. D.,

"Clerk of the Circuit Court of —— County."

4398 (4828). **Form of same for misdemeanor.**—When the indictment is for a misdemeanor, the writ of arrest may be in the same form, except that after the words "commit him to jail," must be added the words, "unless he give bail to answer said indictment."

4399 (4839). **Alias and pluries writs.**—As many writs of arrest may be issued as necessary; and after any forfeiture is taken, another writ of arrest may be issued without an order.

4400 (4829). **Writ of arrest executed by sheriff, etc.**—A writ of arrest may be executed by the sheriff of any county in the state, or by his deputy; and such officers have the same powers and authority, in relation to arrest under a writ of arrest, as are by law conferred upon them in executing a warrant of arrest.*

ARTICLE III.
DISPOSITION OF PRISONER; COPY AND RETURN OF THE WRIT.

4401 (4833). **On commitment, copy of writ delivered to jailer.**—When any defendant is committed to jail under a writ of arrest, the sheriff must return or deliver to the jailer a copy of the writ; which copy is as good authority for the detention of the defendant as the original writ.

4402 (4834). **Return of writ executed with undertaking of bail; when and how made.**—All writs of arrest, with the undertaking of bail when given, must be returned by the sheriff to the clerk of the court from which they were issued, with the proper return thereon indorsed; if the writ is executed, the return must be made within five days after service; but if executed out of the county in which the indictment was found, the return may be made by depositing the writ in the post-office, within five days after service, in a sealed envelope, directed to the clerk of the court, at the court-house of his county, with the title of the case, and the character of the process indorsed on the envelope.

4403 (4835). **Return of writ not executed; when and how made.**—When any writ of arrest is not executed, it must be returned by the sheriff to the clerk of the court from which it was issued by the third day of such court, or before the case is called in order; and when the return is made by the sheriff of any other county than that in which the indictment was found, it may be made by mail, as prescribed by the preceding section.

4404 (4836). **Sheriff attached and fined for failure to make return; certificate of postmaster as evidence.**—Any sheriff, who fails to comply with the provisions of the last two sections, may be compelled to make the return by attachment, and also forfeits to the state, for the use of the county, fifty dollars, which may be recovered with costs against him and his sureties, or any of them, having three days' notice thereof, by motion in the court in which the indictment was found; and on the trial of such motion, the certificate of the postmaster is presumptive evidence of the deposit of the writ of arrest, the superscription, and indorsement on the envelope.

4405 (4837). **Returns by mail taken from office by clerk, etc.; expense paid by county.**—The clerk of the court must take from the post-office all packages addressed to him, which are indorsed according to the provisions of section 4402 (4834), and the expense of the same must be paid by the county.

---

* On February 28, 1887, an act was approved, prescribing process on indictments against corporations, and prescribing the manner of trying said indictments. See Pamph. Acts 1886–7, p. 116.

CHAPTER 7.

ADMISSION TO AND TAKING OF BAIL, AND PROCEEDINGS ON FORFEITURE.

ARTICLE I.

MEANING OF ADMISSION TO, AND TAKING OF BAIL.

4406 (4840). **Admission to bail defined.** —Admission to bail is the order of a competent court, magistrate, or officer, that the defendant be discharged from actual custody on bail.

4407 (4841). **Taking of bail defined.**—The taking of bail consists in the acceptance by a competent court, magistrate, or officer, of sufficient bail for the appearance of the defendant according to the legal effect of his undertaking, or for the payment to the state of a certain specified sum if he does not appear.

In absence of statute authorizing it, an officer cannot delegate his power to admit to bail.—Butler v. Foster, 14 Ala. 323; Antonez' case, 26 Ala. 81. Nor can he receive or authorize a sum of money as substitute for bail.—Butler v. Foster, 14 Ala. 323.

ARTICLE II.

WHO MAY ADMIT TO, AND TAKE BAIL; PROCEEDINGS ON APPLICATION, AND REVISION BY SUPREME COURT.

4408 (4830). **Discharge on bail by sheriff or deputy for misdemeanor; minimum bail fifty dollars.** —If the offense charged in the indictment is a misdemeanor, the defendant must be discharged by the sheriff, or his deputy, on giving sufficient bail; but the amount of bail must in no case be less than fifty dollars.

See note to section 4410.

4409 (4831). **How and by whom bail for felony taken in vacation.**—If the indictment charges a felony, and the defendant fails to give bail in open court, the court must make an order, and cause the same to be entered of record, fixing the amount of bail required; and the sheriff has authority, and it is his duty, to discharge such defendant in vacation, on his giving bail as required by such order.

4410 (4832). **When sheriff may discharge on bail for misdemeanor.**—If the indictment charges a misdemeanor, and the defendant is committed to jail for want of bail, the sheriff may, at any time, discharge him on his giving bail in the amount required.

Bail under this section a matter of right, and sheriff's duty is unconditional. Hammons' case, 59 Ala. 164; Callahan's case, 60 Ala. 65.

4411 (4849). **Bail for felonies; how fixed; taken by sheriff in vacation.**—Circuit and city judges may, during term time, by order entered on the minutes, fix the amount of bail required in all cases of bailable felonies pending in the court, and direct the sheriff to take bail accordingly in vacation; and, in like manner, when an application for bail is made to any judge or chancellor in vacation, such judge or chancellor may fix the amount of bail required, and authorize the sheriff to take bail accordingly.*

Judges cannot authorize sheriff to take bail in term time and sheriff has no power to do so; recognizance so taken is void.—Gray's case, 43 Ala. 41; Governor v. Jackson, 15 Ala. 703; Antonez' case, 26 Ala. 81. Judge, in term time, fixes amount of bail to be taken in vacation.—Callahan's case, 60 Ala. 65. Recognizance taken by sheriff pursuant to order of court, by consent of solicitor indorsed on application for habeas corpus, held valid, although case not heard, and prisoner not present, and judge holding court in another county of the circuit.—Ib. 65.

4412 (4848). **When probate judge may take bail.**—A judge of probate, within his county, has the same authority to admit to bail that is by law conferred on a chancellor or circuit judge to admit to bail in vacation.

Ex parte Keeling, 50 Ala. 474; Ex parte Ray, 45 Ala. 15; Hale's case, 24 Ala. 80.

4413 (4850). **Only one application allowed; exceptions reserved and taken to supreme court.**—When an application for bail is made to a chancellor, or to any circuit or city court in term time, or to any circuit judge, city judge, or judge of probate in vacation, and is refused, no subsequent application can be made; but the evidence in such case may be set out on exceptions, and application made thereon to the supreme court.

If case heard before lower court on evidence, etc., defendant cannot claim another such hearing; only remedy, to set out evidence on exceptions, and apply to supreme court.—Ex parte Carroll, 36 Ala. 300; Ex parte Campbell, 20 Ala. 89. If bail refused, he may petition supreme court for a revision.—Ex parte Croom, 19 Ala. 561. But unless lower court clearly erred, its decision permitted to stand. Ex parte McAnally, 53 Ala. 496; Ex parte McCrary, 22 Ala. 65; Ex parte Weaver, 55 Ala. 250; Ex parte Allen, Ib. 258; Ex parte Nettles, 58 Ala. 268. The way to get the case heard before the supreme court.—Ex parte Croom, 19 Ala. 561. Not a matter of right to withdraw application for bail; state has an interest in the hearing, if begun, and court may proceed to determine it.—Ex parte Campbell, 20 Ala. 89.

4414 (4851). **How bail fixed and taken in such case; duty of sheriff.**—When an order is made by the supreme court admitting a defendant to bail, the order must fix the amount of bail required, and direct the same to be taken by the chancellor or judge to whom the primary application was made, or by the sheriff of the county in which the defendant is confined; and

---

* On February 28, 1887 (Pamph. Acts 1886-7, p. 117), an act was passed, providing as follows: (1) "That whenever any bill of indictment is filed in any court in this state, charging the defendant with a bailable felony, and the defendant is not on trial for the offense so charged in the indictment, the judge of the court must forthwith indorse on said bill the amount of bail required of the defendant. But this act shall not be construed, or have the effect to prevent the defendant from applying for bail in any other manner provided by law, nor for the reduction of 'bail." (2) "Whenever a writ of arrest is issued upon said indictment, the clerk issuing said writ must indorse thereon an order to the sheriff to take bail of the defendant in the amount fixed by the judge, and indorse on said bill of indictment."

when such bail is ordered to be taken by a chancellor or judge, the sheriff having the custody of the defendant must carry him before such chancellor or judge for that purpose.

ARTICLE III.

WHEN BAIL ALLOWED BY LAW.

4415 (4842). **When bail not allowed.**—A defendant cannot be admitted to bail when he is charged with an offense which may be punished by death, if the court or magistrate is of the opinion, on the evidence adduced, that he is guilty of the offense in the degree punished capitally; nor when he is charged with a personal injury on another which is likely to produce death, and which was committed under such circumstances as would constitute murder in the first degree if death should ensue.

The common-law rule of admitting to bail, and the constitution and statutes construed in connection therewith.—Ex parte Croom, 19 Ala. 561; Ex parte Bryant, 34 Ala. 270; Ex parte McAnally, 53 Ala. 496; Ex parte Mahone, 30 Ala. 49; Hammons' case, 59 Ala. 164.   Rules in determining whether case bailable: (1) *May* the offense be punished capitally, not that it *must* be.—Ex parte McCrary, 22 Ala. 65; Ex parte McAnally, 53 Ala. 496.   (2) If it may, and the proof is evident, or the presumption great, of the defendant's guilt, bail should be denied —Ib. 65; Ib. 495; Ex parte Mahone, 30 Ala. 49; Ex parte Banks. 28 Ala. 89; Ex parte Howard, 30 Ala. 43; Ex parte Bryant, 34 Ala. 270.   (3) If a well-founded doubt exists as to defendant's guilt, the proof cannot be said to be evident, or the presumption great; and the accused is then entitled to bail as a matter of right.—Ex parte Bryant, 34 Ala. 270; Ex parte Banks, 28 Ala. 89; Ex parte Acree, 63 Ala 234. (4) Accused must be presumed to be guilty in the highest degree, which presumption must be overcome by proof.—Ex parte Vaughan, 44 Ala. 417.   (5) Bail may be denied whenever the judge would sustain a capital conviction by a jury on the same evidence.—Ex parte McAnally, 53 Ala. 496; Ex parte Nettles, 58 Ala. 268; Ex parte Brown, 65 Ala. 446.   (6) Bail should be denied in assault with intent to murder, when wounded party in danger of dying within a year and a day.—Ex parte Andrews, 19 Ala. 582.   Pecuniary condition of defendant taken into account. Ex parte Banks, 28 Ala. 89.

4416 (4843). **When matter of right.**—In all other cases than those above specified, the defendant is, before conviction, entitled to bail as a matter of right.

In case of misdemeanor.—Hammons' case, 59 Ala. 164; Callahan's case, 60 Ala. 65.   In capital felonies "unless proof evident or presumption great."—Ex parte McAnally, 53 Ala. 496; Hammons' case, 59 Ala. 164.   See, also, note to preceding section.

4417 (4844). **When allowed in capital cases on two continuances by state.**—In cases punished capitally, the defendant is entitled to bail, as a matter of right, when the state, after the finding of the indictment, has continued the case twice, without his consent, for the testimony of absent witnesses.

Under this section, the right to bail is confined to continuances "for the testimony of absent witnesses;" does not extend to continuances for other causes.—Ex parte Carroll, 36 Ala. 300.

4418 (4845). **When dismissal of indictment taken as a continuance.**—In such case, if the indictment is dismissed, the defendant, on application for bail, is entitled to the benefit of any continuance had upon such indictment by the state for absent witnesses; and if another indictment is not found at the same court at which the former is dismissed, the order of dismissal is to be taken as a continuance by the state for absent witnesses.

ARTICLE IV.

FORM, QUALIFICATIONS, AND RETURN OF BAIL.

4419 (4846). **Bail in open court; form of entry.**—When bail is taken in open court, it must be entered on the minutes, and may be as follows:

"The State ⎫   Came into court the said A. B., and also C. D.,
   vs.   ⎬ and E. F., and agreed to pay the State of Alabama
A. B.   ⎭ —— dollars (specifying the sum prescribed by the court), unless the said A. B. appears at the present term of this court, and from term to term thereafter until discharged by law, to answer a criminal prosecution for an assault and battery (or other offense, as the case may be)."

4420 (4847). **Bail not in open court; form and requisites of.**—When not taken in open court, the undertaking of bail must be in writing, signed by the defendant and at least two sufficient sureties, and approved by the magistrate or officer taking the same; and may be substantially in the following form:

"The State of Alabama, ⎫   We, A. B., C. D. and E. F., agree
—— county.   ⎬ to pay to the State of Alabama ——
dollars (the sum prescribed by the magistrate or officer), unless the said A. B. appears at the next term of the —— court of —— county, and from term to term thereafter until discharged by law, to answer a criminal prosecution for the offense of —— (specifying the particular offense with which he is charged).

                  (Signed)   "A. B.
                                    "C. D.
                                    "E. F."

"Approved, G. H., Judge, etc."

Undertaking of bail, taken on Sunday, during vacation, valid and sanctioned by law.—Hammons' case, 59 Ala. 164. So, an undertaking is not void because of certain irregularities on habeas corpus.—Merrill's case, 46 Ala. 82. Parties may sign by initial, or mark, or other designation.—Hammons' case, supra. Not void because officer fails to indorse thereon "approved," and sign such indorsement. Ozeley's case, 59 Ala. 94. Its acceptance, etc., may be otherwise proved.—Ib. An agreement to become bail, on deposit of amount of money with surety, is void as against public policy; and money so paid cannot be recovered back.—Dunkin v. Hodge, 46 Ala. 523. A recognizance held valid, though not sealed.—Hall's case, 9 Ala. 827. So of a recognizance certified by justice of peace under his signature. Howie's case, 1 Ala. 113; Badger's case, 5 Ala. 21. Omission of names from body of undertaking does not impair it, if regularly acknowledged.—Badger's case, supra. Bond with condition not required by law, not invalid, but only inoperative as to such condition.—Whitted v. Governor, 6 Port. 335; Howie's case, 1 Ala. 113. Not affected by change of time of holding court from that expressed.—Walker's case, 6 Ala. 350. When recognizance joint and several.—Ellison's case, 8 Ala. 273. The following held sufficient designation or description of the offense: Of selling lottery tickets, etc.—Keipp's case, 49 Ala. 337. Of conspiracy.—Hall's case, 15 Ala. 431. Of carrying concealed weapons.—Hall's case, 9 Ala. 827. Of retailing without license.—Shreeve's case, 11 Ala. 676. Of resisting process.—Browder's case, 9 Ala. 58. Of malicious mischief; the indictment being for "intentionally injuring telegraph wires."—Welch's case, 36 Ala. 277. So of manslaughter, the indictment being for murder.—Gresham's case, 48 Ala. 625. Variance in defendant's name immaterial.—Tolison's case, 39 Ala. 103.

4421 (4855). **Qualifications of bail.**—The qualifications of bail are, that each must be a resident of this state, and a householder and freeholder therein, and that each must be worth, exclusive of property exempt from execution, the amount expressed in the undertaking; but the court, magistrate, or officer, in taking bail, may allow more than two persons to justify severally as bail in amounts less than that expressed in the undertaking, provided the whole be equivalent to two sufficient bail.

4422 (4854). **How bail given by lunatics, married women and infants.**—It is not necessary that lunatics, married women, or infants should themselves execute or acknowledge the undertaking of bail; but any other person may enter into an undertaking for their appearance.

4423 (4856). **Certain officers forbidden to become bail in certain cases.**—It shall not be lawful for any judicial or ministerial officer of this state to go bail for any prisoner or other person tried before him, or put in his charge under any criminal accusation, or to sign any bond or other obligation for the release or appearance of such person, either before himself or any other officer or officers.

4424 (4857). **Bail required to qualify when doubtful.** When there is a reasonable doubt as to the sufficiency of the bail, they may be required by the court, magistrate, or officer, to answer fully on oath as to their qualifications.

4425 (4861). **Undertakings returned to court.**—All undertakings of bail must be returned by the magistrate or officer by whom taken to the clerk of the court before which the defendant is bound to appear, within the same time, and in the same manner as is provided by section 4402 (4834), for the return of writs of arrest.

4426 (4862). **When new undertaking may be required by court.**—The court, before which any defendant is bound to appear, may require him to enter into a new undertaking, when it appears to said court that the original undertaking was insufficient when entered into, or has since become insufficient from any cause whatever.

ARTICLE V.

EFFECT OF UNDERTAKING AND DISCHARGE OF BAIL.

4427 (4852). **Effect of undertaking; to what extent binds parties thereto.**—The undertaking of bail binds the parties thereto, jointly and severally, for the appearance of the defendant on the first day of the court, from day to day of such term, and from day to day of each term thereafter, until he is discharged by law; and, if the trial is removed to another county, for the appearance of the defendant from day to day of each term of the court to which it is removed until discharged by law.

When bail not discharged.—Ingram's case, 27 Ala. 17.   Death of principal, before forfeiture taken, discharges bail.—Pynes' case, 45 Ala. 52.

4428 (4858). **Bail not discharged by irregularities or by want of qualification.**—No bail are discharged by reason of the want of any of the qualifications required in this chapter, or by reason of there not being the requisite number of bail, or by reason of any other agreement than is expressed in the undertaking, or by reason of the infancy, coverture, lunacy, or any other incapacity of any of the other parties thereto, or because the defendant has not joined in the same.

4429 (4859). **Bail discharged by surrender of principal; may arrest, or authorize arrest of principal.**—Bail may, at any time before they are finally discharged, exonerate themselves by surrendering the defendant; and for that purpose, they may arrest the defendant, on a certified copy of the undertaking, at any place in the state, or may authorize another person to arrest him, by an indorsement in writing on such copy.

This section construed.—Kilgrow's case, 76 Ala. 101. Legal effect of undertaking, when judgment of conviction suspended on appeal, and bail given to appear at next term, etc.—Williams' case, 55 Ala. 71.

4430 (4860). **Surrender of defendant to sheriff necessary to exonerate bail; when new bail allowed.**—To exonerate the bail, the surrender of the defendant must be made to the sheriff of the county in which the court is held to which the defendant is bound to appear, or to which the trial has been removed; and if the charge is for a misdemeanor, the sheriff may discharge him on his giving new bail; otherwise, must keep him in jail until discharged by law.

ARTICLE VI.

FORFEITURE OF UNDERTAKING, AND PROCEEDINGS THEREON.

4431 (4853). **Undertaking of bail; essence of, and when forfeited.**—The essence of all undertakings of bail, whether upon a warrant, writ of arrest, suspension of judgment, writ of error, or in any other case, is the appearance of the defendant at court; and the undertaking is forfeited by the failure of the defendant to appear, although the offense, judgment, or other matter is incorrectly described in such undertaking, the particular case or matter to which the undertaking is applicable being made to appear to the court.

There must be some designation or description, although its correctness is of slight importance; and though undertaking shows the indictment is not for any punishable offense, it is no defense to forfeiture and proceedings.—Eldred's case, 31 Ala. 393; Vasser's case, 32 Ala. 586; Toleson's case, 39 Ala. 103; Keipp's case, 49 Ala. 337. Technical accuracy in describing the offense was never required; a substantial description sufficient.—Hall's case, 9 Ala. 827; Weaver's case, 18 Ala. 293. But if no offense, case, or prosecution is mentioned, the undertaking is deficient, and the statute has no application.—Whitley's case, 40 Ala. 728. And its deficiencies cannot be supplied by parol evidence.—Ib.; Dover's case, 45 Ala. 244. When parol proof may aid.—Vasser's case, 32 Ala. 586. Nor does this statute apply where there is a description of a different offense; for instance, a bond designating or describing offense as *perjury* cannot hold under charge of *burglary*. Gray's case, 43 Ala. 41.

4432 (4863). **Proceedings on forfeiture of undertaking; judgment nisi.**—Whenever an undertaking of bail is forfeited by the failure of the defendant to appear as required, a conditional judgment must be rendered by the court in favor of the state, for the use of the proper county, against the parties to the undertaking for the sum therein expressed; which judgment may be substantially as follows:

"The State   } Indictment for assault and battery (or other of-
  vs.   } fense, as the case may be).
A. B.   }

"It appearing to the court that the said A. B., together with C. D. and E. F., agreed to pay the State of Alabama ———

dollars (the sum specified in the undertaking), unless the said A. B. appeared at this term of the court to answer in this case; and the said A. B. having failed to appear, it is therefore ordered that the State of Alabama, for the use of —— county, recover of the said A. B., C. D. and E. F. on said undertaking the sum of —— dollars (the sum specified in the undertaking), unless they appear at the next term of this court, and show cause why this judgment should not be made absolute."

Judgment nisi in the form prescribed by the Code is sufficient.—Cantaline's case, 33 Ala. 439. It should state the offense, or designate it (as in the form), to sustain judgment final.—Gresham's case, 48 Ala. 625; Faulk's case, 9 Ala. 919; Lindsay's case, 15 Ala. 44; Hall's case. Ib. 431. And must not recite charge variant from that in recognizance.—Howie's case, 1 Ala. 113; Farr's case, 6 Ala. 795; Faulk's case, 9 Ala. 919; Badger's case, 5 Ala. 21; Gray's case, 43 Ala. 41. But need not set out the recognizance.—Howie's case, 1 Ala. 113. Nor literally describe it; for, if stated according to its legal effect, neither plea of nul tiel record nor demurrer will be sustained.—Williams' case, 55 Ala. 71. Judgment nisi need not show that sureties were called to produce the principal.—Hinson's case, 4 Ala. 671; Richardson's case, 31 Ala. 347.

4433 (4864). **Same; scire facias or notice of judgment nisi.** A notice of the rendition of such judgment must be issued by the clerk to each defendant, which notice may be in the following form:

"The State of Alabama, ⎫ To A. B., C. D. and E. F.: You are —— county.   ⎬ hereby notified that, at the —— term 18—, of the —— court of said county, a judgment was rendered against you, of which the following is a copy: (Setting out the conditional judgment); and the said judgment will be made absolute against you at the next term of said court, unless you then appear and show cause against the same."

Proceedings by scire facias, a civil action in which state is plaintiff and recognizors defendants.—See Peck's case, 63 Ala. 201; Hunt's case, Ib. 196; Dover's case, 45 Ala. 255; Hall's case, 15 Ala. 431; Lloyd's case, Minor, 34. The county is the beneficiary in the suit.—Dover's case, 45 Ala. 255. Only the statutory form of undertaking of bail can be enforced by the statutory remedy.—Ib. Power of the court, in excusing default, or in discharging or fixing liability of bail, is not absolute.—Hammons' case, 59 Ala. 164. The notice should set out the judgment, or recite it substantially.—Gresham's case, 48 Ala. 625. Should be so framed that each party may show cause why judgment should not be made absolute against him.—Hunt's case, 63 Ala. 196. Good plea that recognizance extorted from principal by duress of illegal and forcible imprisonment.—Brantley's case, 27 Ala. 44. When estopped from pleading that it was extorted.—Whitted v. Governor, 6 Port. 335. Death of accused before forfeiture good defense.—Pynes' case, 45 Ala. 52. Also, if undertaking be for appearance "at this term," if case reversed and forfeiture at a subsequent term set up by plea of nul tiel record, craving oyer, etc.—Williams' case, 55 Ala. 72. Bail bond prima facie sufficient: proof of its execution, if denied, must be set up in defense by proper proof; too late on appeal.—Gresham's case, 48 Ala. 625. When sureties cannot raise objection to manner of arrest, or sufficiency of indictment.—Peck's case, 63 Ala. 201. Legal sufficiency of indictment cannot be tested by demurrer to scire facias.—Ib.; Eldred's case, 31 Ala. 393; Williams' case, 20 Ala. 63; Weaver's case, 18 Ala. 293. Not good plea, that defendant, at time of judgment nisi, was confined in penitentiary of another state.—Cain's case, 55 Ala. 170. When plea demurrable.—Merrill's case, 46 Ala. 82.

4434 (4865). **Notice or scire facias executed; return.**—The notice may be executed by the sheriff of any county in the state, and must be returned by the officer executing it, with his proper return thereon indorsed, by the first day of the next term of the court from which it issued.

4435 (4866). **Alias notice; two returns "not found" equivalent to personal service.**—If the notice is not served on any of the parties to the undertaking, such other notices as are necessary may from time to time be issued; but two returns of "not found" by the proper officer are equivalent to personal service.

Keipp's case, 49 Ala. 337; Hunt's case, 63 Ala. 196.

4436 (4867). **Conditional judgment set aside, reduced, or made absolute.**—If the defendants appear and show sufficient cause for the default, to be determined by the court, the conditional judgment must be set aside; but if the excuse is not sufficient, or if they fail to appear, the judgment must be made absolute for the entire sum expressed in the undertaking, or any portion thereof, according to the circumstances.

Judgment final against all should show that all failed to appear, or, appearing, failed to show sufficient excuse.—Hunt's case, 63 Ala. 196. Cannot render judgment final against sureties, and set aside judgment nisi against principal, in same entry; works discontinuance as to surety.—Hatch's case, 40 Ala. 718. Court may impose full amount, or any part of penalty.—Cain's case, 55 Ala. 170. Confinement of defendant under conviction in another state, though not an excuse, may mitigate the penalty.—Ib. To support judgment final, record must show return of scire facias "executed," or two returns "not found."—Hunt's case, 63 Ala. 196. When supreme court will amend, and discontinue as to one surety not served or returned "not found."—Ib. When sureties cannot complain on appeal of refusal of court to require clerk to enter certain matters on record.—Hendon's case, 49 Ala. 380. When judgment sustained though alias scire facias not set out in record.—Cantaline's case, 33 Ala. 439. Undertaking no part of record, unless made so by plea or bill of exceptions.—Hendon's case, 49 Ala. 380; Richardson's case, 31 Ala. 347; Shreeve's case, 11 Ala. 676; Robinson's case, 5 Ala. 706. Final judgment on an undertaking of bail cannot be compromised with solicitor.—Dunkin v. Hodge, 46 Ala. 523.

4437 (4868). **Excuses for default heard at any time, and allowed without cost.**—Excuses for defaults must be heard by the court, on application, at any time when not engaged in other business; and when a conditional judgment is set aside, no cost must be imposed on the defendants.

CHAPTER 8.

ARRAIGNMENT AND PLEA.

ARTICLE I.

PLEA ON ARRAIGNMENT.

4438 (4870). **When prisoner stands mute, or refuses to plead.**—If a defendant, when arraigned, refuses or neglects to plead, or stands mute, the court must cause the plea of not guilty to be entered for him.

Final arraignment; when not indispensable in felony.—Fernandez' case, 7 Ala. 511; Pario's case, 36 Ala. 232. Unnecessary for rearraignment after reversal.—Levy's case, 49 Ala. 390. The same on second trial.—Mose's case, 36 Ala. 211. Joinder by the state in issue tendered by plea of not guilty, is merely formal, and failure of record to recite an amendable defect.—Brown's case, 74 Ala. 478.

4439 (4871). **When prisoner pleads guilty.**—If he pleads guilty, the court must cause the punishment to be determined by a jury, except where the punishment is by law required to be fixed by the court, and may, in all cases in which a plea of guilty is entered, cause witnesses to be examined, to ascertain the character of the offense.

ARTICLE II.

FORMAL PLEAS.

4440 (4888). **Plea in abatement must be verified.**—No plea in abatement, or other dilatory plea to an indictment, must be received, unless it is verified by oath, or unless its truth appears by some matter of record, or other written evidence accompanying it.

Subscribed, sworn to and attested by clerk sufficient **verification** without formal affidavit.—Middleton's case, 5 Port. 484. The rule of practice as to **filing** pleas in time allowed does not apply to criminal cases.—Nixon's case, 68 Ala. 535. In time, if filed at first term at which defendant appears.—Lawrence's case, 59 Ala. 61. Several pleas of abatement allowed.—Greenwood's case, 5 Port. 474. Discretionary with court to grant or refuse withdrawal of plea of not guilty, to file plea in abatement.—Williams' case. 3 Stew. 454; Hubbard's case, 72 Ala. 164. Need not be signed by counsel; proper conclusion.—Middleton's case, 5 Port. 484. Defects in plea cured by state joining issue thereon.—Ligon's case, 7 Port. 167. A substantial **misnomer** in either the christian or surname may be pleaded in abatement.—Lynes' case, 5 Port. 236; Washington's case, 68 Ala. 85. Mere misspelling immaterial misnomer, unless it affects pronunciation.—Ib.; Underwood's case, 72 Ala. 220. What plea of misnomer must state.—Bright's case. 76 Ala. 96. Must set out defendant's true name, and deny that he is known by name in indictment; else demurrable.—Wren's case, 70 Ala. 1. Misnomer must be taken advantage of before arraignment and plea to merits; else too late. Miller's case, 54 Ala. 155; Daniels' case, 60 Ala. 56. When not stricken out on motion as frivolous.—Diggs' case, 49 Ala. 311. When replication "that defendant is as well known by the name laid in the indictment as by any other," not demurrable. Gerrish's case, 53 Ala. 476. Such replication is full answer to the plea.—Washington's case, 68 Ala. 85. Defendant's admission before mayor's court, from silence when name called, admissible to prove name.—White's case, 72 Ala. 195. Relevancy of evidence as to custom or usage.—Ib.

4441 (4803). **Judgment pleaded without averring jurisdictional facts.** — In pleading a judgment, or other judicial proceeding or determination of any court, or officer, such judgment, proceeding, or determination may be alleged to have been duly made or rendered, without stating the facts conferring jurisdiction; but the facts necessary to show jurisdiction must be proved on the trial.

4442 (4891). **How character of plea determined.**—In criminal proceedings, a plea is to be determined according to its substance, and not by its commencement or conclusion.

4443 (4629). **Prosecution of misdemeanor when first commenced in county court or before justice; abatement of.** The original jurisdiction of the circuit and city courts over felonies and misdemeanors is, in all things, unchanged, except that when a prosecution for a misdemeanor has been first commenced, and is still pending in the county court, or before a justice of the peace having final jurisdiction, the prosecution in the circuit or city court shall be abated on plea.

Moore's case, 71 Ala. 307.

4444 (4630). **Requisites of plea; when jury instructed to find issue for state.**—The plea provided for in the preceding section must state that the prosecution in the county court, or before the justice, was commenced without the agency, request, participation, connivance, or authority of the defendant, and must be sworn to. Each and every averment of the plea may be traversed and denied; and if on the trial of the issue it appears that such prosecution was commenced by the agency, request, participation, connivance, or authority of the defendant, then the jury must be instructed, if they find either of these facts to exist, to find the issue in favor of the state; and the case must proceed to trial in the circuit or city court, as the case may be.

Moore's case, 71 Ala. 307.

4445 (4889). **Objections to indictment for defect in grand jury; when not available; exception.**—No objection can be taken to an indictment, by plea in abatement, or otherwise, on the ground that any member of the grand jury was not legally qualified, or that the grand jurors were not legally drawn or summoned, or on any other ground going to the formation of the grand jury, except that the jurors were not drawn in the presence of the officers designated by law; and neither this objection nor any other can be taken to the formation of a special grand jury summoned by the direction of the court.

Objection going to formation of jury only allowed in two classes of cases: (1) When not drawn in presence of officers designated by law; (2) when there is some order of court or action of the judge appearing on record relating to organization of grand jury which is contrary to, or unauthorized by the statute.—Billingslea's case, 68 Ala. 486. See, also, Finley's case, 61 Ala. 201; Cross' case, 63 Ala. 40 (and cases cited); Boulo's case, 51 Ala. 18; Preston's case, 63 Ala. 127. False personation of a grand juror good ground for plea to indictment.—Nixon's case, 68 Ala. 535. Objection to indictment on account of incompetency of grand jurors. Oliver's case, 66 Ala. 8. That one of grand jurors was over age, is no ground for quashing or abating indictment.—Spigener's case, 62 Ala. 383. This section not repealed by special jury law for Montgomery and other counties.—Oliver's case, supra. See, also, James' case, 53 Ala. 383. When plea in abatement no answer to indictment.—James' case, 53 Ala. 380. See Mose's case, 58 Ala. 117. When, and when not, objections can be made first time on error.—Sander's case, 55 Ala. 183. Objection that grand jurors were not sworn, cannot be made first time on appeal.—Floyd's case, 30 Ala. 511. Objection to grand jury too late after pleading to merits.—Nixon's case, 68 Ala. 535; Horton's case, 47 Ala. 58; Battle's case, 54 Ala. 93. Statute requiring objections to be made at first term cannot apply to impossible cases, as when parties not arrested, or detained in jail in another county. Nixon's case, supra; Horton's case, supra; Russell's case, 33 Ala. 366. Statute changed to conform to these decisions.

4446 (4890). **When such plea filed; if sustained, new indictment preferred; limitation of prosecution.**—A plea to an indictment, on the ground that the grand jurors by whom it was found were not drawn in the presence of the officers designated by law, must, if accused has been arrested, be filed at the term at which the indictment is found, and if accused has not been arrested, it must be filed at the first term at which it is practicable after the defendant's arrest, and in either case before a plea to the merits; if sustained, the defendant must not be discharged, but must be held in custody, or bailed, as the case may be, to answer another indictment at the same or the next term of the court; and the time elapsing between the first and second indictments, in such case, must not be computed as a part of the period limited by law for the prosecution of the offense.

See note to preceding section.

CHAPTER 9.

TRIAL AND ITS INCIDENTS.

ARTICLE 1.—Setting cases for trial.

2.—Appointing counsel to defend, and serving copy of venire and in-dictment.

3.—Trial; joint or several.

4.—Keeping together and discharging the jury.

5.—Witnesses; modes of procuring their attendance and testimony.

6.—Witnesses; depositions taken, when and how.

7.—Proceedings against defaulting witnesses.

8.—Witnesses; their competency and sufficiency; accomplices and de-fendants.

9.—Examination of witnesses, and matters of proof in general.

10.—Verdict and polling of the jury.

11.—Change of venue, or removal of trial to another county.

Constitutional right of "a speedy public trial" by "jury," construed.—Ex parte State, 76 Ala. 482; Noles' case, 24 Ala. 672; Tim's case, 26 Ala. 165. Extends only to prosecutions by "indictment or information."—Tim's case, supra; Con-nelly's case, 60 Ala. 89. Statute authorizing a waiver of trial by jury, by trans-ferring case to inferior court, not unconstitutional.—Ib. Waiver of trial by jury; revision of judgment on facts.—Wren's case, 70 Ala. 1; Summers' case, 70 Ala. 16. Waiver of trial by jury; right questionable.—Sanders' case, 55 Ala. 43. Trial with less than twelve jurors, not permitted, even with the defendant's consent. Bell's case, 44 Ala. 393. Impeachment law providing for trial without jury, not unconstitutional.—Buckley's case, 54 Ala. 599. Defendant entitled to disposition of his case during term then being held if possible, etc.—Lee's case, 52 Ala. 321. Right of accused to be present during trial, etc.—Ex parte Bryan, 44 Ala. 402; Hughes' case, 2 Ala. 102; Slocovitch's case, 46 Ala. 227; Henry's case, 33 Ala. 389; Hall's case, 40 Ala. 698; Sylvester's case, 71 Ala. 17; Cook's case, 60 Ala. 39; Hughes' case, 2 Ala. 102; Eliza's case, 39 Ala. 694; Gibson's case, Ib. 693; Waller's case, 40 Ala. 325. What entry sufficiently shows presence of prisoner throughout the trial.—Snow's case, 58 Ala. 372. Shackling or manacling prisoner during trial, in discretion of court, but resorted to only in extreme cases.—Faire's case, 58 Ala. 74. When put upon trial, sheriff has custody of prisoner, by opera-tion of law, without an order.—Hodges' case, 8 Ala. 55.

ARTICLE I.

SETTING CASES FOR TRIAL.

4447 (4869). **Cases set for particular days; exceptions.** It is the duty of the clerk of the circuit or city court to set for trial all criminal cases in his court, except capital cases, and cases of parties in custody, for particular days; and no case so set shall be called for trial before such day.

Practice in setting capital cases for trial; record must affirmatively show order appointing a day.—Spicer's case, 69 Ala. 162. Also, personal presence of prisoner at such time.—Sylvester's case, 71 Ala. 17; Hall's case, 40 Ala. 698; Henry's case, 33 Ala. 389.

ARTICLE II.

APPOINTING COUNSEL TO DEFEND, AND SERVING COPY OF VENIRE AND INDICTMENT.

4448 (4872). **When counsel appointed for defendant in capital case.**—If the defendant is indicted for a capital offense, and is unable to employ counsel, the court must appoint counsel for him, not exceeding two, who must be allowed access to him, if confined, at all reasonable hours.

4449 (4872). **Service of copy of indictment and list of jurors on defendant in capital case.**—If the defendant is indicted for a capital offense, a copy of the indictment and a list of the jurors summoned for his trial, including the regular jury summoned for the week in which his case is set for trial, must be served on him, or on counsel appearing for him, at least one entire day before the day set for his trial.

Accused has constitutional right in every criminal case, whatever the charge, to have copy of indictment before trial, if demanded (Const., art. 1, sec. 7); but not of venire.—Driskill's case, 45 Ala. 21. Such right waived if not asserted at proper time.—Ib. But no right to have copies *delivered* to him, unless charged with capital felony.—Ib. When waived in capital case, defendant cannot object on appeal. Miller's case, 45 Ala. 24. When order to sheriff to serve list, etc., free from error. Shelton's case, 73 Ala. 8 (limiting Floyd's case, 55 Ala. 61). Record must affirmatively show copy and list were served, if in actual confinement, at least one entire day before trial.—Robertson's case, 43 Ala. 325; Lacy's case, 45 Ala. 80; Flanagan's case, 46 Ala. 703; Bugg's case, 47 Ala. 50; Crocker's case, Ib. 53. "One entire day" in law is twenty-four hours, beginning and ending at twelve at night; Sunday not counted.—Robertson's case, 43 Ala. 325. Day of delivery and of trial excluded.—McLendon's case, 1 Stew. 195. If prisoner in actual confinement, delivery to counsel not sufficient.—Brister's case, 26 Ala. 107. If not in confinement, he or his counsel of record entitled to copies on application.—Bill's case, 29 Ala. 34; Bain's case, 70 Ala. 4. Words "served," "serving," when equivalent to word "delivered" in the statute.—Walker's case, 52 Ala. 192. See Stephens' case, 47 Ala. 696. When objection to service of imperfect copy not available.—Wade's case, 50 Ala. 164. Refusal to summon talesmen.—Levy's case, 49 Ala. 390. Copy of a copy sufficient on change of venue.—Brister's case, 26 Ala. 107. Validity of service not affected by nolle prosequi of one count.—Scott's case, 37 Ala. 117. When substantial compliance with statute shown by record.—Rodger's case 50 Ala. 102. Non-compliance with order under statute cannot be first made on error. Lewis' case, 51 Ala. 1. Record need not affirmatively show compliance with statute.—Shelton's case, 73 Ala. 5. Such compliance presumed from silence of record.—Phillips' case, 68 Ala. 469; Mitchell's case, 58 Ala. 417; Spicer's case, 69 Ala. 159; Shelton's case, 73 Ala. 5. Service of list containing one less than ordered.—Williams' case, 48 Ala. 85. Effect of material variance between original indictment and copy served.—Tidwell's case, 70 Ala. 33. Sufficiency of copy. Hubbard's case, 72 Ala. 164; McDaniel's case, 76 Ala. 1. Variance fatal on objection if slightest change in meaning.—Ezell's case, 54 Ala. 165. Or if material variance in name.—Nutt's case, 63 Ala. 180. When objection to defective service comes too late.—Evans' case, 62 Ala. 6. Acknowledgment, in open court, of service, precludes dispute of service or further inquiry.—Wesley's case, 52 Ala. 182. No objection to venire if prisoner not misled.—Aiken's case, 35 Ala. 399. Error to discharge juror after list served on prisoner.—Parsons' case, 22 Ala. 50. Not necessary to read copies to prisoner in jail, nor to serve copy also on his counsel. Aaron's case, 39 Ala. 75. Court may determine spelling of name of juror as written in the list.—Taylor's case, 48 Ala. 180. Making and serving list of jurors are ministerial duties, and amendable.—Kenan's case, 73 Ala. 15. Mistakes in names of jurors no ground for quashing the venire.—Hubbard's case, 72 Ala. 164. Counsel appointed to defend not entitled to fees from county.—Posey v. Mobile, 50 Ala. 6.

4450 (4873). **List of talesmen not served.**—If the persons summoned as jurors fail to appear, or if the panel is exhausted by challenges, neither the defendant nor his counsel is entitled to a list of the persons summoned to supply their places.

ARTICLE III.

TRIAL; JOINT OR SEVERAL.

4451 (4892). **Trial, joint or several, at the election of either defendant.**—When two or more defendants are jointly indicted, they may be tried, either jointly or separately, as either may elect.

Separate trial or severance not a matter of right, but of discretion of court. Wade's case, 40 Ala. 74; Hawkins' case, 9 Ala. 137; Parmer's case, 41 Ala. 416; Thompson's case, 25 Ala. 41 (Statute now different). Insanity of one defendant and separate arraignment of other, works a severance.—Marler's case, 67 Ala. 65.

ARTICLE IV.

KEEPING TOGETHER AND DISCHARGING THE JURY.

4452 (4887). **When kept together, jury provided with lodging and refreshments.**—Whenever a jury is, by order of the court, kept together without separation during any night, or for an unusual length of time, it is the duty of the sheriff, with the approval of the court, at the expense of the county, to provide for the jurors suitable lodging and refreshments.

4453 (4906). **Discharge of sick juror before retirement.** If, before the jury retires, one of them becomes so sick as to incapacitate him for the performance of his duty, or any other cause renders it necessary, in the opinion of the court, to discharge a juror, such juror may be discharged, another summoned in his place, and the trial commenced anew.

Discharge of jury on account of sickness of one does not authorize acquittal, even if court refuses to summon another jury and commence anew; defendant not in jeopardy.—Mixon's case, 55 Ala. 129. What the record should show.—Robinson's case, 52 Ala. 587. Sudden illness of juror or prisoner may authorize discharge.—Ned's case, 7 Port. 187. Also sickness of juror's family.—Parsons' case, 22 Ala. 50. Court should be cautious about discharging jury. Barrett's case, 35 Ala. 406. Judge may exercise a discretion, if necessities arise and reasonable time allowed jury for deliberation.—Ib. 406; Powell's case, 19 Ala. 577. Unauthorized discharge of a jury is equivalent to an acquittal, and is available on plea of former acquittal; what amounts to illegal discharge —McCauley's case, 26 Ala. 135; Bell's case, 44 Ala. 393; Ex parte Clements, 50 Ala. 459; Bell's case, 48 Ala. 684; Cook's case, 60 Ala. 39. Court has no discretionary power in a capital case to discharge a jury for not agreeing.—Ned's case, 7 Port. 187; Parsons' case, 22 Ala. 50. Where a juror discharged himself, after being declared competent, and court supplied his place, held error.—Powell's case, 48 Ala. 154 Separation and misconduct of jury; effect of as ground for new trial.—Williams' case, 48 Ala. 85; s. c., 45 Ala. 58; Crocker's case, 47 Ala. 53; Robbins' case, 49 Ala. 394; Butler's case, 72 Ala. 179. Court recommends that separation of jury in all, as in capital felonies. be forbidden —Williams' case, 45 Ala. 58.

4454 (4907). **Discharge of sick juror, etc., after retirement.**—If, after the jury retire, one of them becomes so sick as to prevent the discharge of his duty, or any other cause or accident occurs to prevent their being kept together for deliberation, they may be discharged.

See note to preceding section.

4455 (4908). **Discharge by adjournment.**—A final adjourn- of the court discharges the jury.

See note to section 4453.

ARTICLE V.

WITNESSES; MODES OF PROCURING THEIR ATTENDANCE AND TESTIMONY.

4456 (4918). **Subpœna not issued before arrest or bail.**—No subpœna must be issued in a criminal case, unless the defendant is in custody, or has given bail to answer the charge.

4457 (4919). **Subpœnas for defendant's witnesses.**—If the defendant is in custody, or has given bail to answer the charge, it is the duty of the clerk of the court in which the prosecution is pending, on his application, to issue subpœnas for such witnesses as he requires, as well during the sitting of the court as in vacation.

4458 (4920). **Subpœnas for state witnesses.**—The clerk must also issue subpœnas for all witnesses on the part of the state, whose names are so marked on the indictment, if any, and for such other witnesses as the solicitor may direct him to summon.

4459 (4921). **Solicitor may issue subpœnas.**—The solicitor also has authority to issue subpœnas for witnesses on the part of the state, to appear either before the grand jury, or before any court in his circuit.

4460 (4923). **Summoning and attendance of witnesses.** It is the duty of clerks of the city and circuit courts to subpœna witnesses in causes set for trial to the day fixed for such trial, at the first term that such causes are placed upon the docket; and it shall not be necessary to re-subpœna such witnesses to subsequent terms, but they shall be required to attend at such subsequent terms, upon the day fixed for the trial of such causes, and from day to day of such terms as required by the court until such causes are disposed of.

4461 (4924). **Witnesses to attend on Wednesday, or second Monday.**—Where the term of the court is by law limited to one week, witnesses must be subpœnaed to attend on Wednesday of that week; and where the term is longer than one week, they must be subpœnaed to attend on Monday of the second week; and the criminal docket must, in each case, be taken up on the day on which the witnesses are subpœnaed to attend.

4462 (4925). **Subpœnaed but once, except on reversal of judgment.**—Witnesses subpœnaed are bound to attend from term to term until the case is disposed of; but if a judgment is rendered in the case, which is reversed by the supreme court, new subpœnas must be issued for the state witnesses, and also for the defendant's witnesses on his application.

4463 (4926). **Witnesses at special terms.**—When a special term is directed for the trial of a person charged with a felony, all witnesses must be subpœnaed, or recognized to attend such special term.

4464 (4922). **Subpœnas; how executed.**—Subpœnas in criminal cases must be executed as in civil cases.

Article VI.

WITNESSES; DEPOSITIONS TAKEN, WHEN AND HOW.

4465 (4932). **Depositions in criminal cases; when taken by defendant.**—The defendant may take the deposition of any witness, who, from age, infirmity, or sickness, is unable to attend court; or who resides out of the state, or more than one hundred miles from the place of trial, computing by the route usually traveled; or who is absent from the state; or where the defense, or a material part thereof, depends exclusively on the testimony of the witness.

The provisions of this article apply to cases pending in court; not to preliminary examinations.—Couch's case. 63 Ala. 163.

4466 (4933). **Affidavit, interrogatories, etc.**—When the defendant desires to take the deposition of any witness under the provisions of the preceding section, he must make affidavit before some officer authorized to administer oaths, setting forth some one or more of the above causes for taking the deposition, and that the testimony of the witness is material, and must file with the clerk interrogatories to be propounded to the witness; a copy of which interrogatories must be served on the prosecutor, or on the solicitor, if either of them is in the county;.and such prosecutor or solicitor may, within ten days thereafter, file cross interrogatories, to which the defendant may, within a like period of ten days, file rebutting interrogatories; at the expiration of which time, or, if no cross interrogatories are filed, at the expiration of ten days from the filing of the interrogatories in chief, the clerk must issue a commission, accompanied with a copy of all the interrogatories filed; and the deposition must be taken at such time and place as the commissioner may appoint. If neither the solicitor nor prosecutor is in the county, service of the interrogatories may be had by filing the interrogatories in the office of the clerk for ten days.

4467 (4934). **When taken by state.**—The deposition of any witness on the part of the state may be taken in like manner, and for similar causes, when the defendant files his written consent thereto.

4468 (4935). **Taken as in civil cases; when not read.** Depositions taken under the provisions of the three preceding sections are governed by the same rules which are applicable to depositions taken in civil cases at law; and no such deposition can be read in evidence on the trial, if it appear that the witness is alive, and able to attend court, and within its jurisdiction.

4469 (4614). **Deposition of convict for defendant; notice served on solicitor.**—The defendant in any criminal prosecution may take the testimony of any convict in the penitentiary, on interrogatories and notice, as in other cases of taking testimony by interrogatories, the convict's answer being taken on oath and returned with the commission, as in other cases; but the notice, in such case, with a copy of the interrogatories, must be served on the solicitor of the circuit in which the prosecution is pending.

This provision has no reference to the competency of witness, but leaves that to general law; cross-interrogatories without objection is waiver of incompetency, otherwise objection allowed at any time before trial.—P. & M. Ins. Co. v. Tunstall, 72 Ala. 142.

ARTICLE VII.

PROCEEDINGS AGAINST DEFAULTING WITNESSES.

4470 (4929). **Penalty against defaulting witness; judgment nisi.**—Any witness, who is duly summoned in a criminal case, and who fails to appear as commanded, forfeits one hundred dollars to the party at whose instance he was summoned, for which a conditional judgment must be rendered against him.

4471 (4930). **Judgment absolute.**—When a conditional judgment has been rendered against a defaulting witness in a criminal case, if he does not appear at the same term and show a sufficient excuse for his default, a notice must be issued by the clerk of the court, notifying him of the rendition of such conditional judgment, and that the same will be made absolute at the next term of the court, unless he appears and shows sufficient excuse for his default; which notice must be served by the sheriff and returned three days before the next term of the court; and if he fails to appear as required, or fails to show a sufficient excuse for his default, to be determined by the court, the judgment must be made absolute against him.

When two judgments rendered against defaulting witness, his proper remedy is to move to vacate last judgment.—Ryan's case, 13 Ala. 514.

4472 (4931). **Two returns "not found" equivalent to personal service.**—If two notices of the rendition of such conditional judgment are returned "not found" by the proper officer, such returns are equivalent to personal service, and the judgment may be made absolute thereon.

ARTICLE VIII.

WITNESSES; THEIR COMPETENCY AND SUFFICIENCY; ACCOMPLICES AND DEFENDANTS.

Competency of children as witnesses.—Carter's case, 63 Ala. 52; Wade's case, 50 Ala. 164; Bain's case, 61 Ala. 76; Morea's case, 2 Ala. 275; Beason's case, 72 Ala. 191. A child once declared incompetent may outgrow such incompetency, and be allowed to testify at a second trial of same case.—Kelly's case, 75 Ala. 21. **Of husband and wife,** for and against each other.—See Tucker's case, 71 Ala. 343; Johnson's case, 47 Ala. 10; Miller's case, 45 Ala. 24; Williams' case, 44 Ala. 24; Hampton's case, 45 Ala. 82; Jackson's case, 53 Ala. 472; Powell's case, 58 Ala. 362; Fincher's case, Ib. 215; Childs' case, 55 Ala. 25; Cotton's case, 62 Ala. 12; Robertson's case, 42 Ala. 509; Woods' case, 76 Ala. 35. Wherever husband and wife admissible **against,** they are competent for each other.—Tucker's case, 71 Ala. 343; Neill's case, 6 Ala. 685, 686. But see Johnson's case. 47 Ala. 10. Adulterous connection on promise of marriage does not disqualify.—Robertson's case, 42 Ala. 509. **Witnesses having direct interest,** when not incompetent.—Hall's case, 53 Ala. 634 (qualifying Truss' case. 9 Port. 126); Gassenheimer's case, 52 Ala. 313; Bohannan's case, 73 Ala. 47; Daniels' case, 60 Ala. 56 (overruling Northcott's case, 43 Ala. 330); Sandy's case, 60 Ala. 58. **Experts;** medical and surgical opinions, etc.—Rash's case, 61 Ala. 89; Page's case, Ib. 10; Mitchell's case, 58 Ala. 417; Ex parte Dement, 53 Ala. 389; DePhues' case, 44 Ala. 32; McLean's case, 16 Ala. 672; Hubbard's case, 72 Ala. 164. In forgery.—Johnson's case, 35 Ala. 370. Identity of wheat.—Walker's case, 58 Ala. 393. Whether liquor is intoxicating.—Carson's case, 69 Ala. 235. Of value of a mill.—Hudson's case, 61 Ala. 334.

4473. The defendant in criminal cases a competent witness for himself.—On the trial of all indictments, complaints, or other criminal proceedings, the person on trial shall, at his own request, but not otherwise, be a competent witness; and his failure to make such request shall not create any presumption against him, nor be the subject of comment by counsel. Feb. 17, 1885, p. 189.

Before the amendment of this section, it permitted defendant to make an unsworn statement; as to nature of which see Blackburn's case, 71 Ala. 319; Chappell's case, Ib. 322; Beasley's case, Ib. 328. Weight of, and how considered by the jury.—Ib. Act construed.—Chappell's case, 71 Ala. 322. Defendant could not then be examined or impeached, as he was not a witness.—Ib.; Whizenant's case,

Ib. 383.   Could be commented on by counsel.—Ib.   The defendant could not state his motive or belief. — Ib. 377; Burke's case, Ib.   As to defendant's statement under such previous law, see, also, Williams' case, 74 Ala. 18.

4474. Interest of witness.—There shall be no exclusion of a witness in a criminal case because, on conviction of the defendant, he may be entitled to a reward, or to a restoration of property, or to the whole or any part of the fine or penalty inflicted; such objection is addressed to the credibility, not to the competency of the witness.

4475 (4905). **Competency of juror; must reveal fact known to him; how sworn and examined.**—If a juror has personal knowledge respecting any fact in controversy, he must declare it in open court during the trial; and if during the retirement of the jury, a juror declares a fact as of his own knowledge, which could be evidence in the cause, the jury must forthwith return into court, and such juror must, in either case, be sworn and examined as a witness in the presence of the parties.

Being witness does not make one incompetent as juror, yet is ground for challenge for cause.—Bell's case, 44 Ala. 393; Commander's case, 60 Ala. 1; Atkins' case, Ib. 45.

4476 (4895). **Testimony of accomplices; must be corroborated to authorize conviction of felony.**—A conviction of felony cannot be had on the testimony of an accomplice, unless corroborated by other evidence tending to connect the defendant with the commission of the offense; and such corroborative evidence, if it merely shows the commission of the offense, or the circumstances thereof, is not sufficient.

Accomplice defined; includes all *particeps criminis.*—Davidson's case, 33 Ala. 350.   Statute construed.—Lumpkin's case, 68 Ala. 56; Marler's case, Ib. 580. What corroboration necessary.—Ib. 56; Ib. 580; Marler's case, 67 Ala. 55.   Need not be corroborated in every material part.—Lockett's case. 63 Ala. 5; Smith's case, 59 Ala. 104; Montgomery's case, 40 Ala. 684.   Flight and proximity to crime as corroborative evidence.—Ross' case, 74 Ala. 532.   Test of complicity is, could the witness be indicted for the offense, either as principal or accessory; if not, he is competent.—Bass' case, 37 Ala. 469.   Corroborative evidence required when complicity is shown; not if jury in doubt as to witness' complicity —Ross' case. 74 Ala. 532.   When confession as to part of offense, sufficient corroboration. Snoddy's case, 75 Ala. 23.   Caution by court as to testimony of accomplice. Lumpkin's case, 68 Ala. 56.   Competency of wife against husband's accomplice. Woods' case, 76 Ala. 35.   Sufficiency of her testimony as corroborating accomplice.—Ib.   Essential requisites to constitute complicity; must be a community of purpose.—See Harrington's case, 36 Ala. 236; Frank's case, 27 Ala. 37; Thompson's case, 25 Ala. 41; Davidson's case, 33 Ala. 350; English's case, 35 Ala. 428; Bird's case, 36 Ala. 279; Smith's case, 37 Ala. 472.   Admissibility of threats made against deceased, by accomplice who is a witness, to show malice in witness to impeach him.—Marler's case, 67 Ala. 55.   In misdemeanors, but not in felonies, a conviction may be had on uncorroborated testimony of accomplice alone.—Mose's case, 58 Ala. 117; Lockett's case, 63 Ala. 5.   How weighed in misdemeanors. Mose's case, supra.   When cannot refuse to answer questions tending to criminate himself.—Lockett's case, supra.   When changing rule of evidence will be ex post facto.—Hart's case, 40 Ala. 32.

4477 (4893). **Discharge and acquittal of defendant to be witness for state.**—When two or more defendants are jointly indicted, the court may, at any time before the evidence for the defense has commenced, order any defendant to be discharged from the indictment, in order that he may be a witness for the prosecution; and such order operates as an acquittal of such defendant, provided he does testify.

4478 (4894). **Competency of co-defendant as witness; when verdict of acquittal directed.**—When two or more defendants are jointly indicted, the court may direct a verdict of acquittal to be entered in favor of any one of them, against whom there is not, in the opinion of the court, evidence sufficient to put him on his defense; and being acquitted, he may be a witness.

Statute imposes delicate and responsible duties in discretion of court; when its action not reviewed.—Gassenheimer's case, 52 Ala. 313.   When court may disallow a co-defendant to be discharged and testify, although no evidence against him.—Brister's case, 26 Ala. 107.   When court may refuse to pass on evidence and discharge a co-defendant.—Washington's case, 58 Ala. 355.   If case against co-defendant nol. prosed, or if there is a severance, he may be a witness.—Henderson's case, 70 Ala. 23.   Defendants as witnesses for and against each other; when allowed. · See Henderson's case, 70 Ala. 23; Marler's case, 67 Ala. 65; Morgan's case, 45 Ala. 65.

ARTICLE IX.

EXAMINATION OF WITNESSES; AND MATTERS OF PROOF IN GENERAL.

4479 (4897). **Proof of intent to injure or defraud.**—When an intent to injure, defraud, or cheat, is necessary to be shown in order to constitute the offense, it is sufficient if such intent be to injure, defraud, or cheat the United States, this state, or any other state, or any public officer thereof, or any county, city, town, corporation, body politic, or private individual.

4480 (4898). **Proof of intent, mode, means, etc.; duty of jury.**—When the intent with which, the mode in, or the means by which, an act is done, is essential to the commission of the offense, and such offense may be committed with different intents, in different modes, or by different means, if the jury are satisfied that the act was committed with one of the intents, in one of the modes, or by either of the means charged, it is sufficient; and they must convict, although uncertain as to which of the intents charged existed, or in which mode, or by which of the means charged, such act was committed.

When criminal intent depends on knowledge of particular facts, honest ignorance or mistake of such facts may absolve from criminality.—See Dotson's case, 62 Ala. 141.   Criminal intent presumed from an unlawful act.—Bain's case, 61 Ala. 76.   Criminality necessarily follows from an act intentionally done.—Hoover's case, 59 Ala. 57.   The law presumes that every person intends to do what he does; and that the natural, necessary, and probable consequences of his acts were intended.—McElroy's case, 75 Ala. 9; Stein's case, 37 Ala. 123.   Intention or motive, how proved; is an inferential fact for jury.—Burke's case, 71 Ala. 377; Whizenant's case, Ib. 383.   Cannot be testified to by a witness or defendant.—Ib. 383.   What a variance in proof from allegation of mode or means.—See Phillips' case, 68 Ala. 469; Rodgers' case, 50 Ala. 102.

4481 (4899). **Proof as to results of acts, etc.; when duty of jury to convict.**—When an act done may be attended by more results than one, either of which is sufficient to constitute the offense, the jury must convict, if satisfied that any one of the results charged was produced by the act, although uncertain as to which.

ARTICLE X.

VERDICT AND POLLING OF THE JURY.

4482 (4904). **Verdict may be of less offense than charged, etc.**—When the indictment charges an offense of which there are different degrees, the jury may find the defendant not guilty of the degree charged, and guilty of any degree inferior thereto, or of an attempt to commit the offense charged; and the de-

fendant may also be found guilty of any offense which is necessarily included in that with which he is charged, whether it be
a felony or a misdemeanor.

Conviction allowed of assault, or assault and battery, under indictment for assault
to murder.—Turbeville's case. 40 Ala. 715; Mooney's case, 33 Ala. 419.   Of assault
to rape, or of an assault and battery, under indictment for rape.—Richardson's
case, 54 Ala. 158; Lewis' case, 30 Ala. 54.   Of petit larceny under indictment for
grand larceny.—Cohen's case, 50 Ala. 109.   Of assault and battery under indictment for affray.—McLellan's case, 53 Ala. 640.   Same under indictment for maltreatment of convict.—Sander's case, 55 Ala. 43.   Of larceny under indictment for
robbery.—Allen's case, 58 Ala. 98.   Of attempt to commit larceny under indictment for larceny.—Wolf's case, 41 Ala. 412; Edmond's case, 70 Ala. 8.   See
Burke's case, 74 Ala. 399.   Under indictment for murder of white person by slave,
conviction could be had for manslaughter.—Henry's case, 33 Ala. 389; Hudson's
case 34 Ala. 253.

4483 (4909). **Verdict and judgment as to several of joint
defendants.**—When several persons are indicted and tried jointly, if the jury cannot agree upon a verdict as to all, they may
render a verdict as to those in regard to whom they agree, on
which a judgment must be entered accordingly; and the case,
as to the other defendants, may be tried by another jury.

Where two jointly indicted and proof shows offense committed severally, can be
no conviction of either or both.—Johnson's case, 44 Ala. 414   Nor if each committed offense at different times.—McGehee's case, 58 Ala. 360.   Nor conviction of
one on proof of 'other's guilt.—Rowland's case, 55 Ala. 210.

4484 (4910). **Polling jury.**—When a verdict is rendered, and
before it is recorded, the jury may be polled, on the requirement
of either party; in which case, they must be severally asked if
it is their verdict; and if any answer in the negative, the jury
must be sent out for further deliberation.

State or defendant has right to poll jury; accused should be present.—Hughes'
case, 2 Ala. 102; Brister's case, 26 Ala. 107.   Cannot be exercised until verdict
read aloud in court.—Brister's case, supra.   Inquiry cannot be made into reasons
or motives for assenting to verdict.—Winslow's case, 76 Ala. 42.   Right waived or
lost by prisoner failing to assert it at proper time, or by consenting for clerk to receive verdict, etc.—Brown's case, 63 Ala. 97.

ARTICLE XI.

CHANGE OF VENUE, OR REMOVAL OF TRIAL TO ANOTHER COUNTY.

As amended,
Feb. 17, 1885,
p. 140.

4485 (4911). **Change of venue; trial removed on defendant's application, etc.**—Any person charged with an indictable
offense may have his trial removed to another county, on making application to the court, setting forth specifically the reason
why he cannot have a fair and impartial trial in the county in
which the indictment is found; which application must be sworn
to by him, and must be made as early as practicable before the
trial, or may be made after conviction, on a new trial being
granted, and the refusal of such application may, after final
judgment, be reviewed and revised on appeal.

What application must state.—Taylor's case, 48 Ala. 181.   Practice; both parties may be heard.—Ib.; Ex parte Chase, 43 Ala. 303.   When counter affidavit insufficient.—Birdsong's case, 47 Ala. 68.   What not sufficient objection to affidavits.
Taylor's case, 48 Ala. 180.   Court not bound to hear oral testimony.—Ib.   When
application too long delayed.—Wolf's case, 49 Ala. 359.   Agreement of counsel is
no legal reason to remand case back to county from which removed, nor for mandamus to compel such action.—Ex parte Dennis, 48 Ala. 305.   But if case is so
transferred back, accused estopped from questioning validity of order of such tran-
fer.—Paris' case, 36 Ala. 232.   City court has jurisdiction to try case from another
county.—Lewis' case, 49 Ala. 1.   Order of removal must be made in presence of
accused.—Ex parte Bryan, 44 Ala. 402.   Change of venue sets aside continuance.

Ex parte Johnson, 18 Ala. 414.   Prior to amendatory statute noted, the granting or refusing of change of venue was held discretionary with the trial court, and not revisable, in Evans' case, 62 Ala. 6; Bryan's case, 43 Ala. 321; Wesley's case, 61 Ala. 282; Kelly's case. 52 Ala. 361 (overruling the contrary doctrine in Ex parte Chase. 43 Ala. 303; Edwards' case, 49 Ala. 334; Lewis' case, Ib. 1; Birdsong's case, 47 Ala. 68; Taylor's case, 48 Ala. 180; Murphy's case, 45 Ala. 32). See Posey's case, 73 Ala. 490; Ex parte Banks, 28 Ala. 28; Ware's case, 10 Ala. 814; Brookshire's case, 2 Ala. 303.

4486 (4912). **Removal to nearest county, and but once.** The trial must be removed to the nearest county free from exception, and can be removed but once.

Can be removed but once.—Ex parte Dennis, 48 Ala. 304; Aiken's case, 35 Ala. 399.   Must be to nearest unobjectionable county, regardless of convenience of witnesses, time of court. etc.—Ex parte Reeves, 51 Ala. 55.   Court must choose the county.—Ex parte Hodges, 59 Ala. 305.   Presumption in favor of correctness of order of removal.—Lewis' case, 49 Ala. 1.

4487 (4913). **Consent to depositions, and payment of mileage to clerk.**—When the defendant is charged with a misdemeanor, an order for the removal of his trial must not be made, unless he consents of record that the witnesses for the prosecution may be examined on interrogatories, on such terms as the court may prescribe; and he must also, at the time the order is made, pay the clerk five cents for each mile to and from the court-house of the county to which the trial is removed.

4488 (4914). **Transcript certified by clerk, and subpœnas forwarded.**—When an order for the removal of the trial is made, the clerk must make out a transcript of all the entries, orders and proceedings in the case, including the organization of the grand jury, the indictment, the indorsements thereon, all the entries relating thereto, the undertakings or recognizances of the defendant, all the orders and judgments thereon, and the order for the removal of the trial; must attach his certificate thereto, and forward the package under seal, by a special messenger, or by express, or by registered mail, or deliver it in person, to the clerk of the court to which the trial is ordered to be removed; and he must also inclose in the package, and forward or deliver in the same manner, the original subpœnas in the case.

Transcript need not be under seal; may be amended or certified in new county. Childs' case, 55 Ala. 25; Boddie's case, 52 Ala. 395; Hall's case, 51 Ala. 9 (overruling Williams' case, 48 Ala. 85).   When objection to certificate shall be made. Boddie's case, supra.   How certified transcript supplied if lost or destroyed. Dunn's case, 60 Ala. 35.   Clerk must not transmit original papers.—Harrall's case, 26 Ala. 52.

4489 (4915). **Subpœnas issued; by whom.**—At any time before the delivery of the transcript to the clerk of the court to which the trial is removed, subpœnas for witnesses must be issued, on the application of either the defendant or the solicitor, by the clerk of the court in which the indictment was found, commanding such witnesses to appear at the court to which the trial is removed, which subpœnas must be executed by the sheriff, and returned to the clerk of the latter court; and the clerk must, after the delivery of the transcript to him, issue the subpœnas for witnesses.

4490 (4916). **Trial had on transcript; certiorari ordered when necessary.**—The defendant must be tried in the court to which the case is removed, on the copy of the indictment thus certified; and such court may, if necessary, on a proper showing, order the clerk of the court in which the indictment was found to correct any mistake in the transcript, or to certify any portion of the record which he may have omitted.

Court may issue certiorari for certified copies of papers, etc., if originals have been sent; will not operate discontinuance.—Harrall's case, 26 Ala. 52. Sufficiency of transcript.--Scott's case, 37 Ala. 117; Brister's case, 26 Ala. 107. Defective certificate may be supplied by testimony of clerk.—Hall's case, 51 Ala. 9; Bishop's case, 30 Ala. 34. What record of conviction on change of venue must show; when agreement of counsel insufficient.—Goodloe's case, 60 Ala. 93. See, also, note to Section 4488

4491 (4917). **Fines and forfeitures, fees of jurors and witnesses not affected by removal.**—All fines and forfeitures in such cases go to the county in which the indictment was found, and judgment must be rendered accordingly; and the fees of all jurors and witnesses, on being properly certified by the clerk of the court to which the trial is removed, are a charge on the county in which the indictment was found, in like manner as if the trial had not been removed.

Greene County v. Hale County, 61 Ala. 72.

CHAPTER 10.

JUDGMENT, SENTENCE, PUNISHMENT.

ARTICLE I.

LEGAL PUNISHMENTS SPECIFIED.

4492 (4450). **Legal punishments specified; when court may sentence to hard labor.**—The only legal punishments, besides removal from office and disqualification to hold office, are fines, hard labor for the county, imprisonment in the county jail, imprisonment in the penitentiary, which includes hard labor for the state, and death by hanging. And in all cases in which the period of imprisonment in the penitentiary, or hard labor for the county, is more than two years, the judge must sentence the party to imprisonment in the penitentiary; and in all cases of conviction for felonies, in which such imprisonment or hard labor is for more than twelve months, and not more than two years, the judge may sentence the party to imprisonment in the penitentiary, or confinement in the county jail, or to hard labor for the county, at his discretion, any other section of this Code to the contrary notwithstanding; and in all cases in which the imprisonment or sentence to hard labor is twelve months, or less, the party must be sentenced to imprisonment in the county jail, or to hard labor for the county.

Origin of this statute; effected a repeal of inconsistent laws existing at time of its passage, where hard labor for more than two years was allowed.—Steele's case, 61 Ala. 213. Sentence for longer or shorter term than allowed, erroneous and void.

Brown's case, 47 Ala. 47.   Yet sentence will be corrected by supreme court for being vague and indefinite.—Bradley's case, 69 Ala. 318; Burch's case, 55 Ala. 136. Sentence to hard labor in penitentiary, same as sentence to penitentiary, and does not vitiate sentence.—Brown's case, 74 Ala. 478.   Term of two years being fixed upon, court may elect to sentence to hard labor or penitentiary.—Hobbs' case, 75 Ala. 1.   In felonies, record must affirmatively show presence of prisoner when sentence imposed.—Gibson's case, 39 Ala. 693; Eliza's case, Ib. 694.

4493 (4451). **Benefit of clergy.**—There is no benefit of clergy in this state.

ARTICLE II.
PUNISHMENT FIXED BY THE COURT.

4494 (4484, 4506). **Punishment; when fixed by the court.** When an offense is punishable by imprisonment in the penitentiary, or hard labor for the county, the court must impose the term of punishment, unless the power is expressly conferred on the jury.

When law requires court to fix punishment, error to leave it to jury.—Leoni's case, 44 Ala. 110.   Verdict of guilty merely does not authorize court to fix a fine. Melton's case, 45 Ala. 56.   Verdict of guilty where the fine is fixed by statute. McPherson's case, 54 Ala. 221.   Does not authorize court to impose fine.—Melton's case, 45 Ala. 56.   When court imposes punishment on plea of guilty of misdemeanor.—Drake's case 60 Ala. 42.

4495 (4507). **Imprisonment; may be for life, if no limit prescribed.**—When no maximum limit to the duration of the imprisonment is prescribed by law, the court may, in its discretion, sentence the offender to imprisonment for the term of his natural life.

4496 (4509, 4510). **Sentence on second conviction for same offense.**—On a second conviction of the same offense committed after the convict has served out his term of punishment on the former conviction, or has been pardoned, he must be sentenced to a longer term than before, by at least one-fourth of the former term, unless that exceeds the longest term prescribed by law ; and the provisions of this section apply where the first conviction was in another state.

4497 (4483). **Shortest term of labor ten days.**—Punishment by hard labor for the county shall never be for a less period than ten days.

4498 (4485). **Imprisonment in county jail; by whom imposed.**—When an offense is punishable by imprisonment in the county jail, such imprisonment must be imposed by the court, unless the discretion is expressly conferred on the jury.

Power to imprison in petit larceny vested in judge, not in jury.—Moss' case, 42 Ala. 546.   Also, in case of libel, may add imprisonment to fine—Reid's case, 53 Ala. 402.   Court may fix measure of punishment where a fine is imposed by jury in petit larceny.—Lacey's case, 58 Ala. 385.

ARTICLE III.
PUNISHMENTS DETERMINED BY THE JURY.

4499 (4452). **Fines assessed by jury; how remitted or reduced.**—In prosecution by indictment the jury shall fix and determine the amount of the fine; and no judge shall remit or

reduce the fine so fixed, unless he spreads his reasons for so
doing in full on the minutes of his court.

Fine must be imposed by jury, on plea of guilty of assault with pistol, under
indictment for assault to murder.—Nelson's case, 46 Ala. 186.   Also for retailing
without license.—McPherson's case, 54 Ala. 221.

4500 (4453). **When jury need not impose fine, but leave
punishment to court.**—When an offense may be punished, in
addition to a fine, by imprisonment or hard labor for the county,
the jury shall not be required to impose a fine, if, in their judgment, the defendant should only be punished in some other
mode, but may, in such case, only find him guilty, and leave
the imposition of the punishment to the court.

Verdict of guilty, where a fine is fixed by law, as in revenue cases, will authorize sentence of imprisonment.—McPherson's case, 54 Ala. 221.   But a verdict of
guilty merely will not authorize court to impose a fine.—Melton's case, 45 Ala. 56.

ARTICLE IV.

CONFESSION OF JUDGMENT, AND IMPRISONMENT OR HARD LABOR FOR FAILURE TO
PAY FINE AND COSTS.

4501 (4457). **Prosecutor taxed with costs may confess
judgment; else imprisoned ten days.**—When the costs are
imposed on the prosecutor, he may confess judgment for the
same, with good and sufficient sureties; and, failing to do so,
or to pay the same presently, must be imprisoned in the county
jail, or sentenced to hard labor for the county, for ten days.

4502 (4454). **Confession of judgment by defendant for fine
and costs.**—When a fine is assessed, the court may allow the
defendant to confess judgment, with good and sufficient sureties, for the fine and costs.

Confession of judgment release of error, when.— Hearn's case, 62 Ala. 218.
Where several are jointly indicted and convicted, separate judgments rendered
against each.—McLeod's case, 35 Ala. 395.   For fine and forfeiture against wife,
husband must be party to judgment and equally amenable, etc. — Rather's case,
1 Port. 137, 138.   On appeal in misdemeanors, prisoner released on confessing
judgment; vacated by reversal.—Burke's case, 71 Ala. 377.   As to sureties, confession of judgment a civil liability.—State v. Allen, 71 Ala. 543; Hearn's case. 62
Ala. 218.   But as to the principal, property not exempt from execution, etc.— State
v. Allen, supra.   Presumption of waiver of exemption as to sureties, etc.—Hearn's
case, supra.

4503 (4455). **On default in payment of fine and costs,
imprisonment or hard labor imposed.**—If the fine and costs
are not paid, or a judgment confessed according to the provisions of the preceding section, the defendant must either be imprisoned in the county jail, or, at the discretion of the court,
sentenced to hard labor for the county as follows: If the fine
does not exceed twenty dollars, ten days; if it exceeds twenty,
and does not exceed fifty dollars, twenty days; if it exceeds
fifty, and does not exceed one hundred dollars, thirty days; if it
exceeds one hundred, and does not exceed one hundred and
fifty dollars, fifty days; if it exceeds one hundred and fifty, and
does not exceed two hundred dollars, seventy days; if it exceeds
two hundred, and does not exceed three hundred dollars, ninety
days; and for every additional one hundred dollars, or fractional
part thereof, twenty-five days.

This statute not unconstitutional; costs do not constitute a debt within its
meaning.—Morgan's case, 47 Ala. 34; Caldwell's case, 55 Ala. 133; McDowell's

case, 61 Ala. 176   See Nelson's case, 46 Ala. 186.   And imprisonment imposed
for costs, although fine is paid.—Nelson's case, 46 Ala. 186.   This statute provides
for fixing term of hard labor according to fine, while the next section regulates the
term for the unpaid costs.—Williams' case, 55 Ala. 166.   When fine of fifty dollars
only punishment imposed, statutory limit of hard labor is twenty days.—Burch's
case. 55 Ala. 136.   See Burke's case, 71 Ala. 379; s. c., 74 Ala. 399; Gidden's
v. Cremshaw Co., 74 Ala. 471.

4504 (4731). **When additional hard labor imposed for costs;**   As amended,
Feb. 26, 1881,
rules in reference to.—If, on conviction, judgment is rendered   p. 37.
against the accused that he perform hard labor for the county,
and if the costs are not presently paid, or judgment confessed
therefor, as provided by law, then the court may impose additional hard labor for the county for such period, not to exceed
eight months in cases of misdemeanor, and fifteen months in
cases of felony, as may be sufficient to pay the costs, at a rate
not less than thirty cents per diem for each day; and such convict must be discharged from the sentence against him for costs
on the payment thereof, or any balance due thereon, by the hire
of such convict, or otherwise; and the certificate of the judge
or clerk of the court in which the conviction was had, that the
costs, or the residue thereof, after deducting the amount realized from the hire of the convict, have been paid, or that the
hire or labor of the convict, as the case may be, amounts to
a sum sufficient to pay the costs, shall be sufficient evidence to
authorize such discharge.

This section regulates term for unpaid costs.—Williams' case, 55 Ala. 166.   Justice of the peace no jurisdiction to impose hard labor or imprisonment for non-
payment of costs.—Ex parte McKivett, 55 Ala. 236.   When two convicted jointly,
additional hard labor imposed on each to satisfy one half the costs.—Coleman's
case, 55 Ala. 173.   When sentence to hard labor is inconsistent, uncertain, and er-
rone us in part, and corrected by supreme court.—Bradley's case, 69 Ala. 318.
When sentence to hard labor for costs is sufficient; what must specify.—Croom's
case, 71 Ala. 14; Walker's case, 58 Ala. 393; Walton's case, 62 Ala. 197; McDaniel's case, 53 Ala. 522   See, also, Hall's case, Ib. 463; McIntosh's case, 52 Ala. 355;
Coleman's case, 55 Ala. 173.

ARTICLE V.

EFFECT OF SENTENCE.

4505 (4511). **Sentence to penitentiary terminates right of
executor, administrator, or guardian.**—A sentence of imprisonment in the penitentiary, imprisonment in the county jail, or
hard labor for the county, for a term of twelve months, or more,
terminates the right of the convict to execute the office of executor, administrator, or guardian, in the same manner as if
he had been removed from office, and extinguishes all private
trusts not susceptible of delegation by him.

4506 (4512). **Effect of sentence of imprisonment for life.**
A convict sentenced to imprisonment for life is regarded as civilly dead, but may, nevertheless, at any time within six months
after his sentence, make and publish his last will and testa-
ment.

4507 (151). **Sentence of officer to penitentiary vacates
office; restored on reversal, but not if pardoned.**—When any
person, holding any office or place under the authority of this
state, is sentenced by any court of the United States, of this
state, or any other state, to imprisonment in the penitentiary,

his office or place is vacated from the time of the sentence; and if the judgment is reversed, he must be restored; but if pardoned, he must not.

Ex parte Diggs, 50 Ala. 78.

CHAPTER 11.

APPEAL AND WRIT OF ERROR.

ARTICLE 1.—Bill of exceptions and assignments of error.

2.—Appeal.

3.—Writ of error.

4.—Judgment on error and appeal.

ARTICLE I.

BILL OF EXCEPTIONS AND ASSIGNMENTS OF ERROR.

4508 (4978). **Questions of law reserved by defendant, by bill of exceptions.**—Any question of law arising in any of the proceedings in a criminal case, tried in the circuit or city court, may be reserved by the defendant, but not by the state, for the consideration of the supreme court; and if the question does not distinctly appear on the record, it must be reserved by bill of exceptions, duly taken and signed by the presiding judge, as in civil cases.

Under laws now in force, two methods are available to defendant for a revision of judgment of conviction, each having different field of operations, namely, **appeal and writ of error**; when one or the other available.—Ex parte Knight, 61 Ala. 483. **Exceptions must not be general**; specific objections must be pointed out.—Cohen's case, 50 Ala. 108; Irvin's case, Ib. 181; Gray's case, 63 Ala. 69; Hardin's case, Ib. 39; McGehee's case, 52 Ala. 224; Farley's case, 72 Ala. 170; Woods' case, 76 Ala. 35; Dickey's case, 68 Ala. 508; Williams' case, 68 Ala. 551. And point of objection must appear to have been subject of exception when made.—Reynolds' case, 68 Ala. 502. **Exception to charge of court** must be taken before jury leave the bar.—Reynolds' case, supra. **Certainty requisite in setting out matter of exception.**—Boswell's case, 63 Ala. 307; Strawbridge's case, 48 Ala. 308; Ex parte Mayfield, 63 Ala. 203; Burns' case, 49 Ala. 370. **Exception induced by party excepting**, not allowed.—Leonard's case, 66 Ala. 461; Shelton's case, 73 Ala. 5. **Bill of exceptions not necessary**, when error affirmatively appears of record. — Foster's case, 39 Ala. 229; Ex parte Knight, 61 Ala. 483. **Error without injury**, no ground of exception or complaint.—Taylor's case, 48 Ala. 157; Blevins' case, 68 Ala. 92; Edwards' case, 49 Ala. 334; Childs' case, 52 Ala. 14. When rule of "error without injury" does not apply.—Williams' case, 47 Ala. 659; Carson's case, 50 Ala. 135. When not applied in murder.—Mitchell's case, 60 Ala. 26. **Contents of bill of exceptions**; what sufficient recitals; should not be too voluminous; only material matters to be stated.—Smith's case, 68 Ala. 429. **Bill construed most strongly against exceptor.**—Powell's case, 25 Ala. 21. See Leyman's case, 47 Ala. 686. **When there is conflict between judgment entry and bill of exceptions**, latter will control.—Reynolds' case, 68 Ala. 502. **Judge not bound to sign bill**, unless matter wherein court is supposed to err is made intelligible.—Strawbridge's case, 48 Ala. 308; Ex parte Mayfield, 63 Ala. 203. **Motion to establish** bill of exceptions. Judge's case, 58 Ala. 402. See Ex parte Mayfield, 63 Ala. 203. **Solicitor alone can consent to signing** after adjournment of court.—Ex parte Mayfield, 63 Ala. 203. Bill of exceptions taken on 20th July, 1871, and signed 18th following December in vacation, under agreement, etc., is valid.—Stephens' case, 47 Ala. 696. Must affirmatively appear to have been signed in time prescribed.—Ib. Where court adjourned at midnight Saturday, bill signed next morning not considered part of record; when taken and signed as required by law, becomes part of the record.—Williams' case, 47 Ala. 659; Bryant's case, 36 Ala. 270. **Mandamus to compel signing.**—Etheridge v. Hall, 7 Port. 47; Ex parte Huckabee, 71 Ala. 427. **General charge of the court.** Power of court to state evidence.—Tidwell's case, 70 Ala. 33. How should present the case.—Ib. Requisites of general charge.—Martin's case, 47 Ala. 564; Judge's case, 58 Ala. 407; Evans' case, 62 Ala. 6; Woodbury's case, 69 Ala. 242; Jackson's case, Ib. 250. May read extracts from reported decisions.—Holley's case, 75 Ala. 14. If separable into two disconnected propositions, when erroneous.—Martin's case, 47 Ala. 564. Should charge on different aspects of the case.—Smith's case, 68 Ala. 424. Should not need explanation.—Wicks' case, 44 Ala. 398. Nor be upon irrelevant evidence.—DePhue's case, Ib. 32. May state a conflict in evidence.—Charles' case, 49 Ala. 332. May charge as to the evil consequences of the offense.—Weed's case, 55 Ala. 13; Shorter's case, 63 Ala. 130. **Charge on the effect of the evidence**, to convict or acquit; cannot be given ex mero motu.—Edgar's case, 43 Ala. 312; Beaseley's case, 50 Ala. 149; Foster's case, 47 Ala. 643. See Davidson's case, 63 Ala. 432. Nor if there is any material conflict in the evidence.—Allman v. Gann, 29 Ala. 240; Williams' case, 47 Ala. 659; Sanders' case, 58 Ala. 371. Nor when the evidence is circumstantial, or any material fact is to be inferred, and not a legal presumption from it.—Perkins' case, 50 Ala. 154; Sims' case, 43 Ala. 33; Sultzner's case, Ib. 24; Ward's case, 37 Ala. 158; Morgan's chse, 33 Ala. 413; Easterling's case, 30 Ala. 46; Oliver's case, 17 Ala. 587; Weil's case, 52 Ala. 19. Nor where the evidence only tends to prove the case.—Carter's case, 44 Ala. 29. When should give such charge for defendant.—Green's case, 68 Ala. 539. When for the state.—McInnis' case, 51 Ala. 23. **Charges asked by parties.** If the charge states correct law, and is not abstract, it must be given.—Carson's case, 50 Ala. 135; Williams' case, 47 Ala. 659; Eiland's case, 52 Ala. 322; Edgar's case, 43 Ala. 45. Must be given or refused without qualification.—Edgar's case, 43 Ala. 45; Eiland's case, 52 Ala. 322; Clifton's case, 73 Ala. 473; Rice's case, 47 Ala. 38. If it requires explanation to prevent misleading, may be refused.—Dotson's case, 62 Ala. 141; Farrish's case, 63 Ala. 164; Duvall's case, Ib. 12. But the statute does not deprive the court of the right to simplify or explain charges tending to mislead the jury. Morris' case, 25 Ala. 57; Eiland's case, 52 Ala. 322; Turbeville's case, 40 Ala. 715; Hogg's case, 52 Ala. 2. If charge merely tends to mislead, party objecting should ask explanatory charges.—Evans' case, 62 Ala. 6; Eiland's case, 52 Ala. 322; Diggs' case, 49 Ala. 311; Scully's case, 39 Ala. 240; Wills' case, 74 Ala. 21; Williams' case, Ib. 18. Charges to be construed in connection with the general charge and other charges given.—Cunningham's case, 73 Ala. 51; Scott's case, 37 Ala. 117. Statute applies only to written charges.—Warren's case, 46 Ala. 549; Jacobson's case, 55 Ala. 151; Richardson's case, 54 Ala. 158. Record need not show charges indorsed "given" or "refused;" when presumed.—Allen's case, 74 Ala. 557. When charge presumed to have been in writing; when made part of record. When not.—Little's case, 58 Ala. 265.

4509 (4990). **Assignment or joinder of error unnecessary; duty of court.**—In cases taken to the supreme court under the provisions of this chapter, no assignment of errors, or joinder in errors is necessary; but the court must render such judgment on the record as the law demands.

Though not required, yet a brief would aid the court.—Robinson's case, 46 Ala. 10; Williams' case, 47 Ala. 659. See Hunter's case, 48 Ala. 272. Court must look to whole record.—Ex parte Whitaker, 43 Ala. 323; Williams' case, 47 Ala. 659; Foster's case, 39 Ala. 229. See Brazier's case, 44 Ala. 387. In any case, if errors apparent on the record are injurious to accused, cause will be reversed. Williams' case, 47 Ala. 659; Ex parte Knight, 61 Ala 483.

Article II.

APPEAL.

Does not lie until after final judgment on verdict; dismissed if prematurely taken.—Gore's case, 58 Ala. 391; Lee's case, 52 Ala. 321; Thomason's case, 70 Ala. 20. See Reece's case, Minor, 266; Harkins' case, 6 Ala. 57. Nor will appeal lie while motion for new trial pending.—Overton's case, 60 Ala. 73. Nor from order holding accused to answer an indictment.—May's case, 55 Ala. 164. Nor when defendant escaped; proceedings in such case.—Warwick's case, 73 Ala. 486 (overruling Parsons' case, 22 Ala. 50). All legitimate presumptions indulged in favor of primary court.—Childs' case, 58 Ala. 349; Mack's case, 63 Ala. 138; Green's case, 73 Ala. 26. When case stricken from docket of supreme court for want of jurisdiction.—Brigman's case, 46 Ala. 72. When decisions of United States supreme court binding.—Green's case, 73 Ala. 26.

4510 (4979). **Transcript; when made out and forwarded.** When any question of law is reserved for the consideration of the supreme court, it is the duty of the clerk of the court in which the case was tried to make out a full and accurate transcript of the record, attach his certificate thereto, and transmit it to the clerk of the supreme court, within twenty days after the adjournment of the court from which the appeal is taken.

4511 (4980). **In case of felony, judgment rendered and execution suspended.**—When such question is reserved in case of a felony, judgment must be rendered against the defendant, but the execution thereof must be suspended until the cause is decided by the supreme court.

4512 (4981). **In case of misdemeanor, judgment suspended, and defendant bailed.**—When such question is reserved in case of a misdemeanor, judgment must be rendered on the conviction, but the execution thereof must be suspended until the decision of the cause by the supreme court; and the defendant may give bail, with sufficient sureties, conditioned that he will appear and abide the judgment rendered.

Effect of bail bond; practice in such cases; extension of suspension, etc., Lowry's case, 29 Ala. 45. Defendant may confess judgment in misdemeanor, to avoid imprisonment, and if case reversed, such judgment vacated.—Burke's case, 71 Ala. 377. Legal effect of such undertaking —Williams' case, 55 Ala. 71. When no variance in description of undertaking in judgment nisi.—Ib What will discharge bail, and how pleaded.--Ib.

4513 (4982). **On forfeiture of undertaking, writ of arrest to issue, etc.**—If the defendant fails to appear according to the undertaking, a writ of arrest must be issued; if not taken on such writ, another must be issued, and so on until the judgment has been executed; and if taken on any writ of arrest, he must be committed to jail, or may be admitted to bail by the sheriff on giving sufficient bail for his appearance at the next term of the court to abide by the judgment rendered; but such bail must be at least in the same amount as the first undertaking. which amount must be indorsed by the clerk on the writ of arrest.

4514 (4983). **Proceedings on a forfeited undertaking.** When any undertaking of bail under the provisions of the preceding section is forfeited by the failure of the defendant to appear according to its terms, the same proceedings must be had thereon as on the forfeiture of other undertakings of bail in the circuit or city court.

<small>Dec. 8, 1880, p. 65.</small>

4515. Appeal allowed state when statute declared unconstitutional; duty of clerk.—In all criminal cases, when the act of the legislature under which the indictment is found, is held to be unconstitutional, the solicitor may take an appeal, on behalf of the state, to the supreme court, which appeal shall be certified as other appeals in criminal cases; and the clerk must transmit without delay a transcript of the record and certificate of appeal to the supreme court.

What record must show to maintain the appeal.--Bauerman's case, 72 Ala. 252.

ARTICLE III.

WRIT OF ERROR.

4516 (4984). **By whom and when granted.**—A writ of error on any judgment rendered in a criminal case may issue on an order to that effect by any one of the judges of the supreme court in vacation, or by the supreme court in term time, addressed to the clerk of the court in which the judgment was rendered; but such writ must only be granted on some error of law apparent on the transcript of the record.

When no question of law has been reserved by bill of exceptions, defendant may obtain revision of judgment by common-law writ of error; how grantable, when, and for what.—Ex parte Knight, 61 Ala. 483.

4517 (4985). **Transcript, etc., made out and delivered to defendant.**—On the filing of such order with the clerk of the court in which the judgment was rendered, such clerk must give the party filing it a certificate of the filing thereof; must make out a writ of error, and a transcript of the record and proceedings had in the cause; attach his certificate, and the writ of error, to such transcript, and deliver the same, on demand, to the party suing out the writ, or to his attorney.

4518 (4986). **Order granting writ entered on minutes; writ prosecuted to return term, else dismissed.**—When a writ of error is awarded by a judge of the supreme court in vacation, such judge must cause an entry of such order to be made on the minutes of the court at its next term; and if any writ of error is not prosecuted to the term to which it is returnable, it must be dismissed, and no writ of error afterwards allowed.

4519 (4987). **Execution of sentence suspended, etc.**—If the defendant is in the custody of the sheriff, and the order allowing the writ directs a stay of proceedings on the judgment, the sheriff must, on being served with the clerk's certificate that the order has been filed, and with a copy of the order, keep and detain the defendant in his custody, without executing the sentence which may have been passed on his conviction, to abide the judgment that may be rendered on the writ of error.

4520 (4988). **In case of misdemeanor, defendant bailed.** If the conviction is for an offense which is punishable by a fine, or by imprisonment in the county jail, or by hard labor for the county, the judge or court awarding the writ must also direct the clerk of the court in which the conviction was had to admit the defendant to bail in a sum to be prescribed by such judge or court, with sufficient sureties, conditioned for his appearance at the next term of the court in which the conviction was had, to abide such judgment as may be rendered on the writ of error.

4521 (4989). **Proceedings on forfeiture of undertaking; writ of arrest.**—If the defendant fails to appear according to the undertaking, a writ of arrest must be issued, and the same proceedings be thereon had as are prescribed by section 4513 (4982); and the same proceedings must be had on the forfeited undertaking as on the forfeiture of other undertakings of bail in said court.

ARTICLE IV.

JUDGMENT ON ERROR AND APPEAL.

4522 (4991). **Affirmance of judgment.**—If the judgment is affirmed, the supreme court must direct the sentence to be executed, and, if the day appointed for the execution of the sentence has passed, must specify a day for the execution of the sentence; and the judgment and sentence must be executed accordingly.

4523 (4992). **Reversal of judgment.** —If the judgment is reversed, the supreme court may order a new trial, or that the defendant be discharged, or that he be held in custody until discharged by due course of law, or make such other order as the case may require; and if the defendant is ordered to be discharged, no forfeiture can be taken on his undertaking of bail.

Settled law of this state, that on reversal of judgment, or new trial granted, defendant may be tried again.—Turner's case, 40 Ala. 21; Jeffries' case, Ib. 381; Waller's case, Ib. 325; Cobia's case, 16 Ala. 781; Slack's case, 6 Ala. 676; Hughes' case, 2 Ala. 102.

CHAPTER 12.

REPRIEVES, COMMUTATIONS AND PARDONS.

ARTICLE 1.—Statement of presiding judge.

2.—Stay of execution.

3.—Power to remit, commute, or pardon, and proceedings thereon.

ARTICLE I.

STATEMENT OF PRESIDING JUDGE.

4524 (5004). **Statement filed by judge in executive office; when required.**—When any defendant, on conviction, is sentenced to imprisonment in the penitentiary, for the term of five years or more, it is the duty of the presiding judge to make a statement in writing, setting forth the name of the defendant, the term of the court at which he was tried, the offense of which he was convicted, the character of the evidence against him, the circumstances of aggravation or mitigation developed on the trial, and the proof in reference to his previous character; which statement must be signed by the judge, and must, within thirty days thereafter, be transmitted by the clerk to the governor, to be filed in the executive office.

ARTICLE II.

STAY OF EXECUTION.

4525 (5003). **Execution of sentence postponed to make application for pardon.**—When any defendant is convicted and sentenced to death, or to imprisonment in the penitentiary, the presiding judge, if he is of the opinion that such defendant should be pardoned, may postpone the execution of the sentence for such time as may appear necessary to obtain the action of the governor on an application for pardon.

ARTICLE III.

POWER TO REMIT, COMMUTE, OR PARDON, AND PROCEEDINGS THEREON.

4526 (4994, 4995). **Power of governor to pardon; entry and attestation of pardons.**—In all cases, except treason and impeachment, the governor has power, after conviction, and not otherwise, to grant reprieves, commutations and pardons, and to remit fines and forfeitures; and he must cause to be entered, in a book kept for that purpose, his reasons therefor, and must preserve on file all documents on which he acted; and it is the duty of the secretary of state to attest the reprieve, commutation, or pardon, when granted.

The governor may remit the entire fine, which destroys validity of judgment, except as to the costs.—Chisholm's case, 42 Ala. 528. Release of imprisonment alone is not release of the fine.—Richardson's case, 18 Ala. 109. Legislature cannot, directly or indirectly, remit fines and forfeitures, or grant pardons, except for treason or impeachment.—Haley v. Clark, 26 Ala. 439. Delivery and acceptance necessary to complete pardon; what operates as delivery and acceptance; when acceptance presumed.—Ex parte Powell, 73 Ala. 517.

4527 (4993). **Notice of application for pardon; copy and proof of notice must accompany application.**—In all cases in which any application is made to the governor to pardon any person convicted of crime, or to remit any fine or forfeiture, the person making such application must first give two weeks' notice, by publication to that effect in a weekly newspaper, if any weekly newspaper is published in the county in which the offender was convicted, or in which one or more of the persons reside for whose benefit the remission of such fine, or forfeiture, or pardon, is sought; and if there is no weekly newspaper published in such county, then by notice in writing, posted at the court-house door of such county, and at three other public places in the county; and in every instance where any such application is made to the governor, a copy of the notice and proof of the fact that such publication has been made, must accompany the application.

4528 (4997). **Commutation when punishment by death imposed.**—When punishment of death is imposed, he may, with the consent of the defendant, commute such punishment by substituting for it imprisonment in the penitentiary, or sentence to hard labor for the county, for not less than two years.

4529 (4998). **Same; for offenses hereafter committed.** When punishment of death is imposed for an offense hereafter committed, except murder, rape, robbery, burglary, or arson, he may, with the consent of the defendant, commute such punishment by substituting for it imprisonment in the penitentiary, or sentence to hard labor for the county, for not less than two years.

4530 (4999). **Commutation of imprisonment to hard labor.** When sentence of imprisonment in the penitentiary is imposed, he may commute such punishment by substituting for it sentence to hard labor for the county, for a term equal to the unexpired portion of the defendant's sentence.

4531 (5000). **Commuted sentence certified to clerk of court and recorded and enforced.**—When any sentence is commuted under the provisions of the two preceding sections, the governor must cause a statement of such commutation to be certified to the clerk of the court in which the conviction was had, who must enter the same of record at the next ensuing term, under the direction of the presiding judge; and such commuted sentence must be executed as if it had been rendered by said court.

4532 (5001). **Remission of imprisonment on recommendation of inspectors.**—The governor may, in his discretion, remit a part of the imprisonment of a convict in the penitentiary, on the written recommendation of the board of inspectors, to the effect that such convict has conducted himself in an unexceptionable manner during his imprisonment, and that the remission of the remainder thereof would not, in their opinion, be inconsistent with the public good; but no such remission must be granted on the recommendations of the inspectors alone, unless the convict has been imprisoned one-third of the term for which he was sentenced, or, when sentenced for life, or for more than twenty years, has served at least seven years.

Feb. 13, 1879,
p. 47, sec. 4;
Feb. 23, 1883,
p. 147.

4533 (5002). **Deduction from term of punishment by governor on report by inspectors of good conduct.**—Whenever the inspectors of convicts shall report to the governor that the conduct of any convict sentenced to the penitentiary, or to hard labor for the county, has been unexceptionable during any one year or years of the time of his imprisonment, the governor may, in his discretion, order two months to be deducted from such convict's sentence for each year or years of good conduct, for the first four years of his sentence, and three months from each year or years of good conduct during the next four years of his sentence, and four months from each year or years of good conduct during all the rest of his sentence over eight years; and this time shall be deducted from the time of imprisonment for which such convict was sentenced.

CHAPTER 13.

EXECUTION OF JUDGMENT AND SENTENCE, AND THE LAW CONCERNING THE CONVICT SYSTEM.

ARTICLE 1.—Execution for fine and costs.

2.—Imprisonment in the county jail.

3.—The convict system; organization, officers, and their duties in general.

4.—The convict system; hiring and hard labor of convicts for the county.

5.—The convict system; imprisonment in the penitentiary; hiring and hard labor of state convicts.

6.—Execution of sentence of death.

ARTICLE I.

EXECUTION FOR FINE AND COSTS.

4534 (4456). **Execution issues as in civil cases.**—Execution may issue for the fine and costs, or any portion thereof, remaining unpaid, as in civil cases.

ARTICLE II.

IMPRISONMENT IN THE COUNTY JAIL.

4535 (4486). **Legal custody and charge of jail.**—The sheriff has the legal custody and charge of the jail in his county, and of all prisoners committed thereto (except in cases otherwise provided by law), and may appoint a jailer, for whose acts he is civilly responsible.

4536 (4487). **Who may be confined in jail.**—In addition to convicts sentenced to imprisonment in the county jail, the jail is used as a prison for the safe-keeping or confinement of the following persons: (1) Persons committed for trial for public offenses; (2) convicts sentenced to imprisonment in the penitentiary, until their removal thereto; (3) persons committed for contempt, or on civil process; (4) persons committed on failure to give security for their appearance as witnesses in any criminal case; (5) persons charged with, or convicted of a criminal offense against the United States; and (6) all other persons committed thereto by authority of law.

4537 (4495). **Commencement of subsequent imprisonment on two or more convictions.**—When a convict is sentenced to confinement in the county jail on two or more convictions, the imprisonment on the second, and on each subsequent conviction, must commence at the termination of the imprisonment on the preceding sentence.

4538 (4488). **Commitments and discharges filed and preserved.**—It is the duty of the sheriff, or of the jailer under his direction, to file in regular order, and safely preserve the process or order by which any prisoner is committed to jail, or discharged therefrom, or an attested copy of such process or order.

4539 (4489). **Jail, prisoners, etc., delivered to successor.** On the death, resignation, removal from office, or expiration of term of office, of any sheriff, or of any coroner acting as sheriff, the jail must be delivered over to his successor, or to the person authorized by law to take charge of it, together with the prisoners therein, the files of commitments and discharges, and every thing belonging or appertaining to the jail.

4540 (4491). **What prisoners kept separate.**—Men and women, except husband and wife, must not be kept in the same room; and white and colored prisoners, before conviction, must also be kept separate and apart, if there be a sufficient number of apartments for that purpose.*

4541 (4492). **Support of prisoner furnished by himself or jailer.**—Any person committed to jail may furnish his own support, under such precautions as may be adopted by the jailer to prevent escapes; and the jailer must furnish a support to those prisoners who do not provide it for themselves.

4542 (4493). **Necessary clothing, medicines, etc., to insolvent prisoners.**—Necessary clothing and bedding must be furnished by the sheriff or jailer, at the expense of the county, to those prisoners who are unable to provide them for them-

---

* "Men" and "women" substituted by joint committee for "male and female prisoners."

selves; and also necessary medicines and medical attention to those who are sick, when they are unable to provide them for themselves.

4543 (4494). **Prisoners not allowed to receive spirituous liquors.**—No person confined in jail must, on any pretext whatever, be furnished with, or allowed to receive, any spirituous or vinous liquors, except on the written order of a physician, stating that such liquor is necessary for his health.

4544 (4496). **Removal of prisoners on account of fire.** When the county jail, or any building contiguous thereto, is on fire, and there is reason to apprehend that the prisoners may be thereby injured or endangered, the sheriff or jailer may remove them to a safe and convenient place, and confine them there so long as may be necessary to avoid the danger.

4545 (4497). **Removal of prisoners in ill health.**—When the life or health of any prisoner, who is not confined under process from any court of the United States, may be seriously endangered by longer confinement in jail, and that fact is made to appear clearly to any circuit judge, or to the judge of the city, or county court of the county, such judge must, by an order in writing, direct the sheriff or jailer to remove him to some suitable place, as near as may be to the jail, and there safely keep him until his health is sufficiently restored to authorize his recommitment to jail.

4546 (4498). **Same; guards summoned.**—When any prisoner or prisoners is or are removed from the jail under the provisions of either of the two preceding sections, the sheriff or jailer has authority, and it is his duty, to summon such guards as may be necessary to insure their safe-keeping.

4547 (4499). **When jail unsafe, guards summoned to prevent escapes.**—When the county jail is insufficient, and there is reason to apprehend an escape, the sheriff has authority, and it is his duty, to summon as many guards as may be necessary to prevent an escape.

4548 (4500). **Same; commitment to nearest sufficient jail.** In all criminal cases, either before or after conviction, and in cases of contempt, if it is shown to the court, judge, or committing magistrate, that the jail of the proper county is insufficient for the safe-keeping of the prisoner, or that there is no jail in the county, the commitment must be to the nearest sufficient jail; and the reason of such change must be entered on the minutes of the court, or stated in the warrant, or indorsed thereon, and signed by the magistrate; and the jailer of the county to which the commitment is made must receive and confine the prisoner on such commitment, or a certified copy of such order.

March 1, 1881, p. 11.   **4549. Notice of confinement of prisoner in another county.** When any person charged with the commission of any crime is arrested and confined in any county other than that in which he is triable, the sheriff having such person in custody shall at once notify the sheriff of the county in which such person is triable of the fact of such arrest and confinement; and, upon the receipt of such notice, the sheriff of the county last named shall apply to the proper authority for an order for the removal of such person to the jail of such county.

4550 (4501). **Removal of prisoners from one jail to another.**
If the jail of any county is destroyed, or becomes insufficient
or unsafe, or any epidemic dangerous to life is prevalent in the
vicinity, or there be danger of rescue or lawless violence to any
prisoner, any circuit judge, or the judge of the city or county
court of the county, may, on the application of the sheriff, and
proof of the fact, direct the removal of any prisoner or prisoners to the nearest sufficient jail in any other county; and it
is the duty of such judge, in such case, to make an indorsement on the order or process of commitment, stating the reason
why such removal is ordered, and to date and sign such indorsement.

4551 (4502). **Guards summoned; escape of such prisoners.**
When it becomes necessary to remove any prisoner from the
jail of one county to another, in any case by law provided, the
sheriff, or other officer having charge of such prisoner, has authority, and it is his duty, to summon such guards as may be
necessary to prevent an escape.

4552 (4503). **List of prisoners certified by sheriff to circuit judge.**—It is the duty of the sheriff, on the first day of
each term of the circuit or city court of his county, to make
out and deliver to the presiding judge a certified list of the
names of all the prisoners confined in the jail, and of the offenses with which they are charged, or of which they have
been convicted.

4553 (4504). **United States prisoners.**—The sheriff or jailer
must, if the jail of the county is sufficient, receive into his
custody any person committed under any criminal charge or
offense against the United States, and safely keep such prisoner, according to the order or process of commitment, until
duly discharged by law; and he is liable to the same penalties
for the escape of such prisoner as for the escape of a prisoner
committed under the authority of this state.

4554 (4505). **Same; marshal liable for fees.**—The United
States marshal must become individually responsible to the
jailer for all the jail fees of any prisoner committed under the
authority of the United States, as well as the fifty cents per
month for the use of the jail for each prisoner, according to the
provisions of the resolution of the congress of the United
States, adopted on the 22d day of September, A. D. 1789.

4555. Sheriff to report prisoners committed and discharged. Feb. 22, 1881,
When a prisoner is committed to the county jail, it is the duty p 9.
of the sheriff of such county, in person or by deputy, to report
in writing to the clerk of the city or circuit court of such county,
within ten days next succeeding the commitment, the name of
such prisoner, the day of his entering such jail, and by what
authority, and upon what charge committed; and when a prisoner is discharged from, or otherwise leaves such jail, the
sheriff shall report to such clerk, within two days next succeeding, the name of such prisoner and by what authority, and
when he so left or was discharged.

14—VOL. II.

ARTICLE III.

THE CONVICT SYSTEM; ORGANIZATION; OFFICERS, AND THEIR DUTIES IN GENERAL

Feb. 17, 1885.
p. 187, sec. 1.

4556. Board of inspectors, and term of office.—There shall be appointed by the governor, by and with the advice and consent of the senate, a president of the board of inspectors, and two other inspectors of convicts; who, together, shall constitute the board of inspectors of convicts, and shall have general supervision and control of the state and county convicts; the term of office of the inspectors shall ·be for six years, but the term of the first appointees shall expire, one at the end of two years, one at the end of four years, and the other at the end of six years.

Feb. 22, 1883,
p. 157, ser. 11.

4557. Duty of president; subordinate officers, how appointed.—The president of the board of inspectors shall superintend the management and working of the convicts, and, when practicable, give to the same his daily supervision, and shall make monthly statements to the governor of the health and treatment of the convicts; and all subordinate officers, persons, or guards, except the physician, having the control, direction, or guarding of such convicts, shall be appointed and paid by the contractor, but may be removed or discharged by the president of the board of inspectors. It shall be the duty of the president of the board of inspectors of convicts to see that the laws in relation to convicts, and the rules of the board of inspectors, are enforced; and his orders shall be obeyed by all contractors, officers, guards and convicts.

Feb. 17, 1885,
p. 187, sec. 7.

4558. Appointment and duty of clerk.—There shall be appointed by the president of the board of inspectors a clerk, who, under his direction, shall keep the books and records pertaining to state and county convicts, and shall perform such other duties as may be required by the board.

Ib. sec 30

4559. President and clerk reside at the capital.—The president of the board of inspectors and the clerk shall reside at the capital of the state, and the president of the board must be provided with an office in the capitol.

4560 (4542). **Meetings of the inspectors.**—The board of inspectors shall hold regular meetings at the office of the president of the board on the first Wednesday of January, April, July and October of each year, and the president may call special meetings of the board at such time and place as he may think proper; and he shall, if present, preside at all such meetings.

4561 (4543). **Minutes of proceedings.**—The board of inspectors must keep, or cause to be kept, regular minutes of all their meetings and proceedings, which must be signed by them, and kept in the office of the president.

4562 (4544). **Inspectors must adopt rules for direction of penitentiary officers.**—The board of inspectors must, from time to time, establish rules and regulations for the direction of the officers having control of state or county convicts in the discharge of their duties, for the government and discipline of the convicts, and the custody and preservation of the public property; which rules and regulations must be submitted to the governor for approval, and may be modified or annulled by him.

4563. Must adopt rules to prevent inhuman treatment. The board of inspectors shall adopt such rules, to be approved by the governor, as are necessary to prevent inhuman treatment, or cruel or excessive punishment of convicts, and also to regulate the time and amount of work to be performed by them, and the manner of working them.

Feb. 22, 1883, p. 184, sec. 14.

46, '9.9

4564. Duty as to visiting places of confinement, etc.; monthly statements filed.—One of the inspectors shall visit once in two weeks, and oftener if required by the governor, the several places of confinement of all convicts; and the visiting inspectors shall examine the food, clothes, quarters, bedding, provisions made for the sick, and general treatment, and if he finds anything wrong, he shall point out the same to the warden of the prison, and immediately notify the president of the board; and the president of the board, and each inspector, shall file monthly in the office a statement of the work done by him, and the condition of the convicts at the places visited during the preceding month; but the inspectors shall not be required to visit county convicts hired in the county where convicted, except when worked in mines or on railroads.

Ib.

4565. Card stating date of conviction, etc., to be furnished each convict.—The president of the board of inspectors shall furnish each convict, within a month after his confinement, a card, on which shall be written or printed, or partly written and partly printed, the date of such convict's conviction, and the term and expiration of his sentence.

Feb. 17, 1885, p. 187, sec. 39.

4566. Date of expiration of sentence furnished each hirer.—Upon application, the date of the expiration of the sentence of each convict must be furnished in writing to the hirer by the probate judge, or president of the board of inspectors, or other person or body having charge of convicts by special regulations.

Feb. 22, 1883, p. 184, sec. 22.

4567 (4555). **Correspondence and documents relating to convict system to be preserved.**—The president of the board of inspectors shall cause to be preserved certified copies of all his official correspondence with the governor, inspectors, and other public officers, which, together with all books, accounts, vouchers and documents relating to the office of the president and board of inspectors, shall be considered as public documents, and kept on file in the office of the board of inspectors.

4568. Books of convicts, contractor's accounts, etc., to be kept in office.—In the office of the board of inspectors of convicts shall be kept a book, or books, in which there shall be kept a record of all state and county convicts, showing the date of conviction, crime, sentence, county and court in which convicted, place and person to whom hired, and terms and amount of hire, and such other information as the board may prescribe; and there shall be kept also in a well-bound book, or books, an account with each contractor for convicts, showing at all times fully and correctly the state of the account of each contractor; and there shall also be kept such other books as the board may deem proper.

Feb. 17, 1885, p. 187, sec. 8.

4569. Accounts with contractors made out monthly; settlement with auditor, etc.—On the first day of each month the president of the board shall cause to be made out by the clerk

Ib. sec. 9.

an account against each contractor, showing the number of convicts and the amount of hire due from each contractor for the past month, copies of which shall be furnished respectively to the contractors and to the auditor. Within ten days after receiving such account, such contractors respectively shall settle and pay such accounts to the auditor; and the amount due by each shall be certified into the state treasury, and an account thereof shall be kept by the auditor in a book or books, separate and distinct from other state accounts (as other accounts of public moneys are kept); but when the contract prescribes other than monthly payments, then the account thereof shall be made out under the direction of the president of the board, and settled by the contractor with the auditor, and certified into the treasury of the state, within ten days after the same is due, in all respects as herein provided; and if the contractor fails to settle within thirty days after receiving his account, the auditor shall notify the attorney-general, who shall at once bring suit for the amount due; and on such settlement with the auditor, the contractor shall be entitled to credit for the amount of costs paid by him since his last settlement, and shall file with the auditor an itemized bill of costs in each case, with the receipt of the clerk of the court for the amount paid.

Ib. sec. 23.

4570. Inspectors report violation of law to solicitor; where tried. —It shall be the duty of the president and of the inspectors to report to the solicitor of the circuit all violations of the law in regard to convicts that may come to their knowledge; and all indictments for the same shall be tried in the circuit court of the county where the offense was committed.

As amended,
Feb. 13, 1879,
p. 42.

4571 (4546). Report of inspectors to governor.—The board of inspectors must, at least thirty days before the commencement of each session of the general assembly, transmit to the governor a report of the transactions of the convict system during the past twenty-four months, showing the number of convicts confined, the offenses for which they were convicted, the counties from which they came, the terms of imprisonment for which they were respectively sentenced, their ages, former occupation, and conduct during each year; also, the number and names of all who have been pardoned or discharged, or who have died during each year, with the corresponding dates, and the particular disease supposed to have caused each death; also. the names of all convicts hired out, the name and residence of the person hiring such convicts, the time for which they were hired, and what religious instructions they are receiving; with such other information and suggestions as they think proper.

Feb. 7, 1879,
p. 170, sec. 4.

4572. Seal of office.—The governor shall prescribe the form and specifications of, and furnish the president of the board of inspectors with a seal of office, and pay for the same out of any moneys not otherwise appropriated.

Feb. 17, 1885,
p. 187, sec. 26.

4573. Governor general supervisor over inspectors; reports to him by them.—The governor shall have general superintendence and control of the inspectors, and see that they perform their duties; and there shall be made quarterly to him, by the president, and as often as he may require, a report of the condition of the convicts, and of the work done by each officer; and the governor shall, from time to time, require the office of the president of the board to be examined, and its condition reported to him by the officer appointed by him to examine public offices.

4574. Governor transmits reports to general assembly. Ib. sec. 27. It shall be the duty of the governor to transmit to the general assembly, immediately upon its assembling, full and complete printed reports made to him by the board of inspectors, and such other and further information as he may deem proper, payable out of the convict fund.

4575. Physician appointed by governor must report to Ib. sec. 8. **president of inspectors.**—The governor shall appoint a reputable and duly licensed physician for the state and county convicts, who shall reside at such place as the largest number of convicts are located and worked. He shall report monthly, and oftener if required, to the president of the board of inspectors the condition, health, and sanitary arrangement of the convicts, together with any recommendations as to any change necessary for the more humane treatment of state and county convicts; and it shall be the duty of such physician to devote his whole time and services exclusively to the supervision and care of, and practice upon the state and county convicts; and such physician shall visit any camp where state or county convicts are worked, when requested to do so by the president of the board of inspectors; and he shall hold office for the term of two years, and shall not accept any employment or compensation from any hirer of any state or county convicts; and said physician may be removed by the governor whenever he thinks it right to do so.

4576. Duties of physician; post mortem examination, etc. Ib. sec. 33. Such physician shall make a post mortem examination of every convict that dies while working out his term of service, and make a full statement to the inspectors of the facts ascertained by said examination; but no post mortem examination shall be made if, on an examination of the body of the convict, there is no reason to believe that such convict came to his death by cruel treatment, or unless the cause of death is uncertain or doubtful.

4577. Chaplain; appointment, duties and term of office. Ib. sec. 40. A chaplain shall be appointed by the inspectors, who shall devote his whole time to the moral improvement and religious instruction of convicts; his term of office shall be for two years.

4578 (4551). **Guards at penitentiary; appointment and removal.**—The guard at the penitentiary consists of one turnkey, and as many men as the president of the board of inspectors may deem necessary, who are appointed by him, and are under his direction and control, and may be removed by him at pleasure.

4579. Guards, warden and other officers; license required. Each prison or camp shall be under the control of a warden and such other persons as may be necessary, who shall be employed and paid by the contractor, and may be discharged at any time by the president of the board; but no person shall be employed to guard or control convicts without a license from the president of the board to act in such capacity.

4580. Power to pursue and arrest without a warrant.
Every officer and guard, regularly licensed and sworn, shall
have power to pursue and arrest any escaped convict in any
county of this state without a warrant; and he shall have the
same authority as a sheriff to summon persons to assist in
making such arrest, or to protect such convict from any violence
after arrest.

4581. Exempt from road and jury duty.—All guards, and
other persons having control of convicts shall be exempt from
working on the public roads, and from serving on juries.

4582. Oath of office.—Every officer and guard shall, before
entering on the duties of his office, take and subscribe before
some officer authorized to administer oaths the following oath:

"I, ———, do solemnly swear (or affirm, as the case may be)
that I will support the constitution of the United States and
the constitution of the State of Alabama, so long as I remain
a citizen thereof; that I will faithfully execute and discharge
all the duties required of me as ——— (designating the office),
and observe all the rules and regulations prescribed for the
government of convicts, so far as concerns my office; and will, in
no case, ill-treat or abuse any convict under my charge or control, nor inflict upon him any other or greater punishment than
may be prescribed by said rules and regulations; so help me
God."

Feb. 17, 1885.
p. 187, secs. 29,
31, 40.

4583. Salaries of officers.—The salary of the president of
the board of inspectors shall be eighteen hundred dollars per
annum, and the other inspectors fifteen hundred dollars each
per annum, and their traveling expenses while absent from their
place of residence on official duty; the salary of the clerk of
the board of inspectors shall be one thousand dollars per annum;
the salary of the physician shall be fifteen hundred dollars per
annum; of the chaplain one thousand dollars per annum; of
the turnkey at the walls three hundred dollars per annum
and his board; and of each guard at the walls two hundred
and fifty dollars per annum and his board; and each of said
officers shall be reimbursed his traveling expenses, when absent
from his residence, incurred in the actual discharge of his
official duty; and all accounts for expenses shall be verified
by oath.*

Ib. sec. 29.

4584. How salaries paid.—The salaries and expenses authorized by this article, and article five of this chapter, shall be paid
out of the receipts from the hire of state convicts in the state
treasury, on the approval of the governor, and out of no other
moneys; and so much of said receipts as may be necessary, each
year, is appropriated for such purpose.

— — —

ARTICLE IV.

THE CONVICT SYSTEM; HIRING AND HARD LABOR OF CONVICTS FOR THE COUNTY.†

**4585. Laws concerning state convicts applicable to county
convicts.**—All laws of the state and rules of the board of in-

---

* See act approved February 14, 1887.—Pamph. Acts 1886–7, p. 54.

† See act requiring "all judicial officers to report to the probate judge of the
respective counties, all sentences to hard labor for such counties," approved February 22, 1877.—Pamph. Acts 1886–7, p. 62.

spectors in regard to state convicts shall also apply to county convicts, except as otherwise provided by law.

4586 (4465). **Under control of the county commissioners.** Hard labor for the county shall be under the superintendence and control of the court of county commissioners, who shall determine in what manner and on what particular works the labor shall be performed; and all convicts sentenced to hard labor for the county shall be under the direction and control of the court of county commissioners, when worked or hired in the county where convicted, but otherwise they are to be under the superintendence and control of the board of inspectors of convicts.

As amended, Feb. 13, 1879. p. 46, sec. 1.

4587 (4480). **When supplies, etc., furnished by county; labor on county works.**—It shall be the duty of the court of county commissioners to make provision out of the county treasury for suitable food, clothing, lodging, medicine and medical attention, for such of the convicts sentenced to hard labor for the county as are not let to hire under the provisions of this article, and from time to time to give directions, general or special, for the employment of such convicts, sentenced to hard labor for the county, as are ordered to labor on the public works of the county.

4588 (4482). **Commencement of hard labor on conviction of two or more offenses.**—When a convict is sentenced to hard labor for the county on two or more convictions, the punishment of the second, or each subsequent conviction, must commence on the termination of the punishment for the preceding conviction; but no person shall be sentenced to hard labor for the county so that the aggregate of the sentences shall exceed two years for the crime, and the aggregate of sentences for costs shall exceed fifteen months.

4589. **Record kept of convicts sentenced to hard labor; report of probate judge, or agent.**—A record shall also be kept in the office of the board of inspectors, similar to that provided to be kept for state convicts, of all persons who are sentenced to hard labor for the county, and who, under the provisions of this article, may be confided to their supervision; and the probate judge, or agent of hard labor for the county, shall report to the board, at such times as the board may prescribe, the name, age, sex and race of each person sentenced to hard labor, date of conviction, crime, term of sentence, additional term for costs, date of expiration of sentence, and amount of costs; any probate judge failing or neglecting to make, or to have made by the agent of hard labor for his county, the reports required by law, may be impeached as in other cases; and he and the sureties on his official bond shall be liable to any person for all damages sustained by reason of such failure.

Feb. 17, 1885, p. 187, sec. 16

4590. Record of convicts.—The court of county commissioners shall provide a well-bound book, to be kept in the office of the judge of probate, subject, during office hours, to the inspection of the public, in which he shall enter the name of each convict sentenced to hard labor for the county, the date of hire, the name of the hirer, the place where the convict is to labor, the length of sentence, and the sum for which the convict was

Feb. 22, 1883, p. 134, sec. 18.

hired; and he shall also keep a record of the convicts sentenced to the penitentiary, showing the name, the offense of which he was convicted, and the date and termination of his sentence.

1b. sec. 19. **4591. Inspection of county convicts; stipulation in contract of hire; removal of convicts.**—When convicts are sentenced to hard labor for the county, and hired out by the court of county commissioners, it shall be the duty of the inspectors of state convicts to visit such convicts whenever they shall deem it necessary; and they shall rigidly scrutinize and inquire into the treatment and management of such convicts, and shall report to the judge of probate, in writing, the condition and treatment of such convicts. No contract shall be made by such court for hiring county convicts, without a stipulation therein that the contract shall end if the bond, in the opinion of the judge of probate, becomes insufficient, or if any convict is treated cruelly or inhumanly by the hirer or his employe. Whenever the board of inspectors shall notify the governor that convicts, who have been sentenced to hard labor for the county, should be removed from the place where they are at labor, or from the control of the person who has them hired, it shall be his duty to order the probate judge of the county, where said convicts were convicted, to remove them from such place, or to annul such contract, as the case may be; and any probate judge, neglecting or refusing to obey such order, shall be liable to impeachment and removal from office, as provided for in other cases.

4592. Appointment of county inspector.—The board of inspectors of convicts shall appoint in each county, the convicts of which are worked within its limits, a suitable person as county inspector, who shall visit and inspect such convicts in the same manner as the state inspectors do those worked outside of the county in which convicted. He shall report to the president of the board of inspectors, once a month, the treatment, condition and general management of such convicts. He shall receive for his services three dollars per day while actually engaged in the discharge of his duties, to be paid out of the county treasury.

Feb. 17, 1885,
p. 187, sec. 20. **4593. To whom not to be hired; when convicts not to be guarded.**—No person sentenced to hard labor shall be hired to any person related to him by consanguinity or affinity, or who is unfriendly to him, or who has not a proper prison, or immediately will prepare one for the confinement of such convicts at night, or when not at work, wherein he must be kept confined at such time. But in case of a convict convicted of misdemeanor, and hired in the county where convicted, the hirer shall not be required to keep such convict confined or attended by a guard, unless so required by an order of the court of county commissioners, incorporated in the contract of hiring.

4594 (4468). **Character of labor determined by county commissioners, when.**—The court of county commissioners shall, at their first term held in each year, or as soon thereafter as practicable, determine whether the convicts sentenced to hard labor shall be employed in laboring on the public works of the county, or shall be let to hire, and their decision shall be duly entered on the records of such court; but may be changed by the court at any subsequent term.

4595 (4466). **Hard labor; what included.**—Hard labor for the county includes labor on the public roads, public bridges, and other public works in the county; and authorizes the letting of such convicts to hire to labor anywhere within the state, as may be determined by the court of county commissioners.

4596 (4467). **Females not to labor on public highways.** No woman convicted of a public offense shall be required to work as a laborer on any public highway in this state. *

4597. Place and kind of labor expressed in contract; when changed.—Every contract for the hire of county convicts must express the kind of labor, and the place at which it is to be performed; and such convict must be restricted to such place and labor, which must not be changed except upon the recommendation of the court of county commissioners; and county convicts can only be sublet or re-hired in the same manner. Feb. 17, 1885, p. 187, sec. 21.

4598 (4469). **Hiring of convicts; how made.**—Should the court of county commissioners determine to let convicts, or any part of them, to hire, they may do so by themselves, or by some member of their body, or other person to be appointed by them.

4599 (4470, 4471). **Bond of hirer; how conditioned; when required clothing specified.**—The contract of hiring shall be secured by bond in writing, in a penalty of double the amount agreed on for hire, payable to the county, with two good and sufficient sureties, and conditioned to pay the amount of hire agreed on, and also to furnish the convict with a sufficiency of good and wholesome food, and with medicine and medical attention when necessary, and to treat the convicts humanely; and said contract may be for one or more years; and if the hiring be for a longer term than two months, or if the condition and comfort of the convict requires it, the hirer may also be required to furnish to the convict specified clothing, which shall also be expressed in the bond. The attorney-general shall prepare a form of contract and bond, which shall be furnished to the probate judge of each county by the president of the board of inspectors, which shall be used in all cases of the hiring of county convicts.

4600 (4472). **Actions on hirer's bond.**—Such bond may be put in suit in any court of the county for which the convicts were sentenced to hard labor having jurisdiction of the same; and the suit shall be governed by the rules governing other suits on penal bonds; and the recovery, if any, shall be paid into the county treasury for the use of the party for whose benefit the recovery is had.

4601 (4473). **If employed on public works, superintendent appointed; term of office and compensation.**—Should the court of county commissioners determine to employ persons sentenced to hard labor for the county, or any part of them, in work on the public roads, public bridges, or other public works of the county, then they are authorized to appoint a superintendent of public works, whose term of office shall expire when his successor is qualified; and who shall receive for his services such compensation as shall be fixed by the court of county commissioners.

---

* "Woman" substituted for "female" by joint committee.

4602 (4474). **Appointment of superintendent made at first term.**—Such appointment shall be made at the first term of the court of county commissioners in each and every year, or as soon thereafter as practicable.

As amended,
Feb. 18, 1879,
p. 46, sec. 2.

4603 (4475). **Form of official oath required; filed in probate office.**—The superintendent of public works, and each person employed as a guard over convicts sentenced to hard labor for the county, before he enters upon the discharge of his duties, shall take and subscribe the following oath before some officer authorized to administer the same: "I do solemnly swear that I will support the constitution of the United States, and the constitution of the State of Alabama, so long as I remain a citizen of said state, and that I will faithfully execute and discharge all duties required of me (as superintendent or guard of convicts, as the case may be), and that I will observe all rules and regulations prescribed for the government of convicts, so far as I am thereby directed, and will in no case ill-treat or abuse any convict under my charge or control, or inflict any other or greater punishment than may be prescribed by said rules and regulations;" and such oath shall be filed by the party taking the same in the office of the judge of probate of the county in which the convict is sentenced to hard labor.

4604 (4476). **Bond of superintendent.**—The superintendent of public works shall also enter into bond, payable to the county, and approved by the judge of probate, with two good and sufficient sureties, in the penalty of one thousand dollars, conditioned that he will faithfully perform the duties of his office, obey the orders of the court of county commissioners, and will not voluntarily permit the escape of any of the convicts committed to him.

4605 (4477). **Action on superintendent's bond.**—The bond of the superintendent may be put in suit and prosecuted in all respects as is provided in this article for suits on bonds given by hirers of convicts.

4606 (4478). **Duties of superintendent.**—The duties of the superintendent of public works are: Faithfully to obey and carry out the orders and directions of the court of county commissioners; to see that the convicts committed to him labor faithfully; not to overwork or maltreat the convicts; to see that the food and clothing delivered to him for the convicts are given to them at the proper time; to see that they are properly housed in inclement weather; to have proper medicine and medical attention bestowed on them when necessary; and not voluntarily or negligently to permit them to escape.

4607 (4479). **Vacancy in office of superintendent; how filled.**—Until there shall be an election of a superintendent of public works, and in cases of vacancy in the office, the judge of probate may appoint such officer; and such appointee shall hold office until his successor is elected and qualified.

ARTICLE V.

THE CONVICT SYSTEM; IMPRISONMENT IN THE PENITENTIARY; HIRING AND HARD
LABOR OF STATE CONVICTS.

4608 (4536). **President of board has charge of penitentiary; convicts therein and property thereof.**—The president of the board of inspectors has the charge and custody of the penitentiary, and of the convicts therein, with all the lands, buildings, furniture, tools, implements, stock, provisions, and other property thereunto belonging, and is hereby authorized and empowered to sell and dispose of all the machinery and appurtenances thereunto belonging, and all other property now at the penitentiary, and not in use, under such rules and regulations as may be adopted by the board of inspectors and approved by the governor.

4609. Temporary confinement, removal and allotment of state convicts; grounds of removal of inspectors. — When any convict is sentenced to the penitentiary, the judge of the court in which the sentence is had shall order such convict to be confined in the nearest secure jail; and the clerk of the court shall at once notify the president of the board of inspectors of the jail where such convict is confined, and forward to him a copy of the judgment-entry and sentence in the case, and a statement of the amount of the fees of the state's witnesses, officers' fees, and solicitor's fees incurred in the conviction, including the costs in the supreme court, if any, and inform him if any special care be necessary to guard such convict; and thereupon the president of the board, or a majority of the inspectors, shall assign such convict to the contractor who, by fair and equal allotment, is entitled to him, and shall notify said contractor of the amount of the costs, and said contractor shall pay to the clerk of the court in which such convict was convicted the costs in said case when the convict is delivered to him by the sheriff; provided that he shall not pay in any case more than one hundred and fifty dollars. No preference shall be given to one contractor over another; but each shall have his fair proportion of the convicts then subject to hire. And contractors shall have the right to inspect the records showing distribution and allotment of convicts, and may make complaint to the board of inspectors of any injustice or inequality, and from the decision of the board an appeal may be made to the governor, who shall have the power to examine, and be required to have exact justice done; and the failure or refusal of the president of the board, or the other inspectors, when the duty devolves on them, to comply with the provisions of this section, or to discharge their duties in other respects, shall be cause for removal by the governor. *

Feb. 17, 1885 p. 187, sec. 10.

4610. Delivery of such convicts to contractor.—The sheriff, having in his custody any person sentenced to the penitentiary, shall deliver such convict to the contractor who presents the written order of the president of the board of inspectors and a receipt of the clerk for the costs required to be paid by law for him, and shall take from such contractor duplicate receipts, upon blanks to be furnished by the board of inspectors, containing a

Ib. sec. 11.

---

* See act approved February 28, 1887.—Pamph. Acts 1886-7, p. 86.

descriptive list of such convict, one of which he shall retain, and the other he shall forward to the board of inspectors.

4611. Removal of convict not assigned to hard labor. When a person is convicted and sentenced to the penitentiary, who, by reason of sex or physical condition, is unfit to be assigned to any contractor, or to perform hard labor, or whose services may be needed for the state at the penitentiary, the president of the board of inspectors may remove such person from the jail to the penitentiary, and keep him there until such disability is removed, or until such person's services cease to be needed for the state.

4612 (4567). **Convicts confined in jail en route to penitentiary.**—It is the duty of all jailers, on the demand of the officer in charge of any convict being conveyed to the penitentiary, to receive and safely keep him, for the legal charge of feeding prisoners, whenever such officer may deem it necessary to have them secured for the night, or for any longer time they may be necessarily detained.

4613 (4574). **Description of convicts to be recorded; person searched.**—It is the duty of the president of the board of inspectors, upon the reception of any convict into the penitentiary, to take his height, and cause the same to be entered in a book, with the time when such convict was received, his name, age and complexion, color of his hair and eyes, the county in which convicted, the nature of the crime, period of imprisonment and place of nativity; and the baggage and person of every convict must be carefully searched, and every instrument taken therefrom by which he may effect his escape.

4614 (4575). **Warden to take charge of money, etc.**—The warden of each prison or camp must take in charge any property or money, or other thing of value, in the possession of any convict at the time of his delivery to him, and pay or deliver the same to such person as the convict may in writing direct, or to the convict on his discharge, or to his personal representatives in case of his death previous thereto; and should no personal representative be appointed within six months after his death, then into the state treasury.

4615 (4579). **Uniform.**—All convicts must be clothed, during the term of their imprisonment, in a comfortable manner in coarse and cheap clothing, made in a uniform and peculiar style, so as to distinguish them from other persons; the number of suits, material and style to be determined by the board of inspectors.

4616. Bibles.—The president of the board of inspectors, with the approval of the governor, may procure a sufficient number of bibles and other religious reading matter for the convicts, as may be necessary, not to exceed in cost more than two hundred dollars in any one year, and it shall be the duty of the chaplain to distribute the same among the convicts.

4617 (4581). **Diet and meals.**—The diet of the prisoners, in quantity and quality, must be such as is directed by the board of inspectors; the provisions sound and wholesome, and the regular hours of meals announced by the ringing of a bell, at the sound of which the convicts must assemble at their respective tables, except the sick, who must be furnished according to the directions of the physician.

4618 (4583). **Spirituous liquors.**—No spirituous or intoxicating liquors must, under any pretense, be introduced into the penitentiary, or into any convict prison or camp, except such as may be necessary for the hospital department.

4619. Convicts not worked on Christmas or fourth of July.—Convicts sentenced to the penitentiary or to hard labor for the county shall not be required to work on Christmas-day or the fourth day of July.

4620 (4508). **Commencement of subsequent imprisonment on two or more convictions.**—When a convict is sentenced to imprisonment in the penitentiary on two or more convictions, the imprisonment on the second, and on each subsequent conviction, must commence at the expiration of the imprisonment on the preceding conviction.

4621 (4571). **Removal of convict on reversal of judgment.** If any judgment of conviction is reversed, and the cause remanded, after the convict has been conveyed to the penitentiary, he may be removed to the county in which he was tried, by the sheriff of that county, or his deputy, in the same manner in which he was removed to the penitentiary; and all the provisions of this Code in regard to the authority, duties and compensation of officers and escapes, or attempts to escape, by convicts, are applicable to such removal.

4622 (4572). **Convicts imprisoned on commuted sentence.** The president of the board of inspectors must also receive into the penitentiary, on the written order of the governor, any convict whose sentence has been commuted, according to law, to imprisonment in the penitentiary, and must confine such person according to the terms of the commutation, and the rules and regulations established by law.

4623 (4573). **United States prisoners; account to auditor.** The president of the board of inspectors must receive into the penitentiary all convicts sentenced to imprisonment therein by any court of the United States held in this state, and must safely keep and employ them according to the rules and regulations of the institution, until the expiration of the term for which they were sentenced, or until they are otherwise discharged by law, and he must account to the auditor for all amounts received for the support of such prisoners.

4624 (4589). **Conversation between officers and convicts.** No officer or person holding any appointment, the duties of which are to be discharged in connection with the convict system, must say any thing in relation to the management of any prison in the presence of a convict, except it be to direct him in his duty, or to admonish him for a delinquency.

4625. Prison to be approved.—Each contractor shall keep his convicts in a prison which has been approved by the physician and the board of inspectors of convicts.

4626. Solitary confinement.—If any convict neglects or refuses to perform the labor assigned him, or willfully injures any of the materials, implements, or tools, or engages in conversation with any other convict, or in any other manner violates any of the regulations of the penitentiary, he may be punished by solitary confinement for a period not exceeding thirty days for each offense, at the discretion of the president of the board of inspectors, or person acting in his place.

4627 (4591). **Diet during such confinement.**—Every convict punished by solitary confinement, must be confined in a solitary cell, and fed with bread and water only during such confinement, unless the physician certify to the person in charge that the health of such convict requires other diet.

4628 (4609). **Service of process.**—When any suit is brought against any convict who is imprisoned in the penitentiary, the summons or subpœna must be delivered to the president of the board of inspectors, who must hand a copy to the convict, and return the original by mail, or by private conveyance, to the proper court, indorsing on the envelope the title of the suit and the character of the process; and any mesne process, which it may be necessary to issue in the progress of any suit, may be served in like manner; and if no appearance is entered for the convict, the court must require the plaintiff to prove his demand or cause of action.

4629 (4610). **Answer in chancery.**—When any convict in the penitentiary is made a defendant to any suit in chancery, and his answer to the bill is required, a commission must be issued by the register of the court in which the suit is pending, directed to the inspectors of the penitentiary, and authorizing and commanding some one of them to take the convict's answer. If the convict will voluntarily answer the bill, he may be allowed the aid of counsel to prepare his answer, at such convenient times as may be directed by the inspector executing the commission; and the answer must be sworn to before the inspector taking the same, and be returned by him, with the commission, to the proper court. But if the convict refuses or neglects to answer, for thirty days after he is required by the inspector to answer, the inspector must return the commission, and certify thereon such failure or neglect to answer; after which a decree pro confesso may be entered against the convict, unless the chancellor, for good cause shown, allows him further time to answer.

4630 (4613). **Testimony in civil suits.**—The testimony of convicts may be taken in civil suits on interrogatories and notice, as in other cases of taking testimony by interrogatories; the convict's answer being taken on oath, and returned with the commission, as in other cases.

4631 (4611). **Testimony for state in criminal cases.**—The presiding judge of any circuit or city court, having reason to believe that the testimony of any convict serving a sentence in the penitentiary, or to hard labor for the county, is necessary in any criminal prosecution by the state, and that other evidence cannot be obtained on behalf of the state, may order a writ to be issued by the clerk, commanding the president of the board of inspectors to have the convict before the court, on a specified day, to give testimony in the particular case for the state; and the president must have the convict before the court on a specified day, according to the mandate of the writ, employing a trustworthy deputy, with a sufficient guard, to convey such convict to the court; and after he has testified, the convict must be forthwith returned to the custody from whence he was brought.

4632 (4612). **Fees, guards, escapes, etc., on such removal; receipt of prisoner by sheriff.**—For conveying any convict under the provisions of the preceding section, the president of the board of inspectors is entitled to the actual expenses incurred in such removal, including the hire of necessary guards and their expenses; the guards and the convict are subject to the same liabilities and penalties for an escape, or attempt to escape; the sheriff or jailer of the county must, on the demand of the officer having charge of the convict, receive and safely keep such convict in the county jail during his attendance on the court, or while delayed in passing through the county, and is entitled to the usual legal charge for feeding prisoners.

4633 (4592). **Punishments.**—No convict must be punished in any other way than is herein provided, except by the authority of the board of inspectors, or as otherwise provided by law.

4634 (4595). **Insane convicts.**—The names of all convicts who, in the opinion of the physician, have become insane, must be forthwith reported by him to the president of the board of inspectors, who shall immediately cause such convicts to be removed to the hospital, and must also report their names to the governor, in order that proper steps may at once be taken for their removal.

4635 (4597). **Discharge.**—Each convict must, at the expiration of his term of confinement, be discharged from the penitentiary, and must be furnished by the president of the board of inspectors with a decent suit of clothes and with money sufficient to enable him to reach his destination, not exceeding ten dollars; but no convict must be discharged except at his own request, if he is sick at the time his term expires. *

4636 (4601). **Convicts committing offense, in penitentiary, confined until trial.**—Any convict who commits any one of the offenses prohibited by sections 3730 (4598), 3752 (4599) and 3998 (4600), or any other public offense, during his confinement in the penitentiary, must be confined therein like other convicts, until his trial takes place, but, after the expiration of his former term of confinement, if the subsequent offense is bailable, he may be discharged from confinement, on giving sufficient bail for his appearance.

4637 (4605). **Proceedings for recapture of escaped convicts.** Whenever any convict escapes, it is the duty of the president of the board of inspectors to take all proper measures for his apprehension, and for that purpose he will forthwith communicate to the governor the fact of such escape, the time when, and the circumstances under which it was committed, together with a particular description of the convict, his age, size, complexion, color of hair and eyes, from what county convicted, and for what offense and when; and the president of the board of inspectors shall, with the approval of the governor, offer a reward, not exceeding four hundred dollars, for the apprehension of such state convict, to be paid out of the proceeds of convict labor in the state treasury. But no warrant shall be issued for the payment of any such reward, unless there is filed in the office of the auditor the certificate of the president of the board of inspectors,

---

* See act approved February 28, 1887.—Pamph. Acts 1886-7, p. 90.

that such convict has been recaptured and restored to custody, with an indorsement thereon by the governor, ordering the reward to be paid.

4638 (4607). **Proof of conviction on trial of offenses by or concerning convicts, etc.**—On the trial of any penitentiary convict, or other person, for any offense committed within the penitentiary, the fact of confinement in the penitentiary is presumptive evidence of a legal conviction and sentence of imprisonment, and a copy of the transcript of the conviction and sentence, filed with the president of the board of inspectors, and certified by him to be correct, shall be received as evidence of such sentence.

4639 (4608). **Rules printed, explained to convicts, etc.** Such of the foregoing regulations, with all others that may hereafter be adopted by the legislature, or inspectors with the approbation of the governor, which it is necessary that the convicts should know, together with all the sections of this Code in relation to escapes by convicts from the penitentiary, must be printed so as to be conveniently read, and set up in each workshop and cell in a conspicuous place.

4640 (4556). **Officers exempt from road and jury duty.** All the officers of the penitentiary are, during their continuance in their respective offices, exempt from working on the public roads, and from serving as jurors.

4641. Hiring of state convicts; notice, sealed proposals, qualifications of bidders, etc.—All of the convicts may be hired to be worked outside of the walls; and when they are to be so hired, the president of the board of inspectors shall give notice thereof, by publication in one or more newspapers in each of the cities of Mobile, Montgomery, Birmingham and Huntsville, for at least thirty days previous to a day designated in said notice, that sealed proposals will be received at his office for the hire of convicts. The notice shall state the terms and conditions upon which the convicts shall be hired. The proposal for hire must be printed or written, and shall state the number and class of convicts wanted, and the price to be paid for each per month; and the kind and locality of labor to be performed, and shall be inclosed in an envelope and securely sealed, and there shall be nothing on the outside of said envelope except the name and address of the president of the board of inspectors, and across the left end of the envelope the words "Proposal for Convicts." The president of the board shall keep the proposals safely, and, on the day designated in the advertisement of hiring, the proposals shall be opened by him, in the presence of the governor and of the members of the board of inspectors, and the bids shall be rejected or accepted by the president of the board of inspectors, subject to the approval of the governor; and, in the acceptance or rejection of the bids, regard must be had to the character and reputation of the bidder, and his experience in managing convicts, the occupation, the healthfulness and accessibility of the place where they are to be worked, and regard must be had to locating the convicts as nearly together as possible for the convenience of frequent inspection, and the price bid; each proposal, accepted or rejected, must be so indorsed, with the date, and signed by the president of the board of inspectors and the governor, and must be kept by the president in his office, subject to examination by any citizen of the state.

4642 (4537). **To whom convicts not to be hired.** — No convict must be hired to a person related to such convict, either by consanguinity or affinity within the fifth degree, nor any person hostile to such convict, nor of known inhuman disposition.

4643. Inspectors or other officers must not be interested, or receive gift, etc. — No inspector, warden, physician of convicts, or state, county, or municipal officer, must be, in any manner whatever, interested in the work or profit of convict labor, and shall not receive any gift, gratuity, or favor of a valuable character, from any person or persons interested in such labor. Feb. 22, 1883 p. 137, sec. 13.

4644. Contracts prepared by attorney-general; how executed. — All contracts for the hire of convicts shall be prepared by, or under the direction of the attorney-general, and be executed in triplicate, each contractor signing each of the triplicates, as also the president of the board of inspectors, and each of said parts must bear the approval of the governor; one of said parts shall be retained by the contracting hirer, one shall be kept in the office of the president of the board of inspectors, and the other filed in the office of the auditor of the state; and each contract must contain a provision that the president of the board of inspectors may terminate the same at any time, with the approval of the governor; and the governor may terminate the same at any time, without assigning any reason. Ib sec. 2.

4645. Governor to transmit contracts and bonds to legislature. — It is the duty of the governor to transmit to the general assembly immediately, if in session, or so soon thereafter as it may convene, printed copies of all contracts for hiring out convicts, together with copies of the bonds for the faithful performance of such contracts. Ib. sec. 8.

4646. Convicts to be worked as expressed in the bid; re-hiring restricted. — No convict must be worked at a different place or occupation than expressed in the bid and contract, except upon the recommendation of the board of inspectors, stating the reason therefor, and approved by the governor; nor shall any convict be re-hired or placed in the keeping and control of any other person than the contractor, except upon the recommendation of the board of inspectors, and approved by the governor. Feb. 17, 1885. p. 187, sec. 14.

4647. Classification of convicts. — When convicts are hired, the contract may or may not provide for classification, at the discretion of the governor, but the advertisement must state whether or not they will be classified; but this section does not apply to classifications under present contracts; but no convict shall be classed, unless worked at an occupation at which the task can be apportioned to the class; in all other cases, the hiring shall be per capita. Ib. sec. 15.

4648. Not less than one hundred hired to one person; how governed; misdemeanor. — Not less than one hundred state or county convicts shall be hired to one person, or kept at one prison, and none of those hired to any person must be related Feb. 13, 1879, p. 174.

15—VOL. II.

to him by consanguinity or affinity; and they shall be governed, worked and guarded as prescribed by the rules and regulations prescribed for working penitentiary convicts outside the walls. The violation of this section is a misdemeanor, punishable, on conviction, by a fine not exceeding one thousand dollars, and hard labor not less than twelve months; but less than one hundred may be hired to one person, when worked within the county where convicted.

4649. Limitation of contracts.—Contracts for the hiring of state convicts shall be for not less than five years, nor more than ten years; and every contract may be terminated for cause by the president of the board of inspectors, with the approval of the governor, and may be terminated by the governor, at any time, without assigning any reason therefor.

Feb. 17, 1885, p. 187, sec. 2.

4650. Suits upon contracts; how and where brought. Suits upon contracts for the hire of state convicts shall be prosecuted in the name of the state; and such suits may be brought in the circuit court of Montgomery county, or city court of Montgomery.

Ib. sec. 12.

4651. Convict disabled without fault, supported by inspectors; provision in contract; suit by convict.—When a convict, without fault on his part, and while working out his sentence, receives personal injuries permanently disabling him from earning a living, the board of inspectors shall have power to make provision for his support until the expiration of his sentence, at a cost not to exceed eight dollars per month. And it is hereby made the duty of the president of the board of inspectors to insert a clause in every contract of hiring, fixing a liability upon such contractor to the state for any amount thus expended for the support until the termination of the contract: but nothing herein contained shall bar the right of such convict to bring his action against the contractor, or other person who may be legally responsible to him, for damages on account of such injuries.

Ib sec. 24.

4652. State officers prohibited from employment, etc., by person interested in convict labor.—No officer of the state shall accept from any person or corporation interested in convict labor any employment, or receive any compensation for services rendered such person or corporation.

4653 (4586). **Convicts permitted to work for themselves.** Convicts may be allowed to work for themselves after the performance of their daily tasks, in such manner as may be prescribed by the rules of the board of inspectors, and the proceeds of such labor shall be disposed of as the board shall provide by rule.

Feb. 22, 1883, p. 134, sec. 12.

4654. Punishment of convicts.—No cruel or excessive punishment shall be inflicted on any convict, and no corporal punishment of any kind shall be inflicted, except as shall have been previously prescribed by the rules of the board of inspectors, and of which such convict shall have been notified, and that only by the party authorized by the president of the board of inspectors to inflict punishment. And the party authorized by the president of the board of inspectors to inflict punishment shall keep a well-bound book, to be known as the record of punishments, in which he shall record all punishments, of what-

ever character, inflicted on convicts, giving name of convict
punished, offense, date, character and exact extent or quantity
of punishment; and any false entry in such record, or any failure to make entry therein, as required by this section, shall
be a misdemeanor. It shall be the duty of the president of the
board of inspectors to carefully examine this record at least
once in each month.

4655. Unfit labor and compartments prohibited.—No con- Ib. sec. 16.
vict must be required to perform any labor or task for which
he has been declared unfit or incapable by the physician; nor
must he be confined in barracks, or cells, or compartments, pro-
nounced by the physician to be unhealthy or unfit for his accommodation.

4656. When convict may be shackled.—Shackles and Feb. 17, 1885,
p. 187, sec. 32.
chains shall be placed on, and worn by convicts only by consent
of an inspector.

4657. When unlawful to work in mines or on railroads; Ib. secs. 35, 38.
when convict removed.—It is unlawful to work upon railroads any convicts; and it is unlawful for the inspectors, or any
person or officers, having charge of the hiring of either state or
county convicts, to hire any convict who is not physically ca-
pable of performing such service, to be worked in mines; and
whenever a convict is hired to be worked in the mines, and, subsequent to such hiring, it is made to appear that such work is
injurious to the health of the convict, such convict, on the
recommendation of the physician, or by order of the inspectors,
may be removed from such mine, and put to some other kind of
hard labor.

4658. When convicts not to be confined together.—It is Ib. sec. 19.
unlawful to work together, or to confine in the same room or
apartment, any convict or convicts who have been sentenced to
hard labor for the commission of a misdemeanor, not involving
moral turpitude, with any convict or convicts sentenced for the
commission of a felony; and it is unlawful for white and colored
convicts to be chained together, or to be allowed to sleep together, or to be confined in the same room or apartment, when
not at work; and it is unlawful to chain together, or confine
together in the same room or apartment, men and women convicts. Whenever, in the judgment of the governor and the
board of inspectors, it is practicable to do so, arrangements shall
be made for keeping white and colored convicts at separate pris-
ons, and they shall not be allowed to be kept at the same place.

4659. Convict discharged when term expires, and fur- Feb. 22, 1883,
p. 134, sec. 17.
nished with clothes and transportation.—It shall be the duty
of any person who has in his possession, or under his control,
any state convict, or county convict, to discharge said convict
at the expiration of his term of penal servitude, and to furnish
him with transportation to the county-seat wherein such convict
was sentenced to imprisonment. And he shall also furnish to
such convict one good suit of clothes, and fifty cents per day
for each estimated day's travel from the place where he is discharged to his destination, and one hat and pair of shoes.

4660. Hirer to deliver convict when contract terminated Ib. sec. 20.
by governor, or by its violation.—It shall be the duty of each

and every hirer of state or county convicts, when he shall be notified that his contract has been terminated, to deliver forthwith such convict or convicts in his possession or control, under such contract, to the president of the board of inspectors, or to the court of county commissioners, or to their agent, as the case may be.

Ib. sec. 23.

4661. Convicts not to go at large; exception.—Hirers and lessees of convicts shall not suffer or permit any person convicted and sentenced to a term of imprisonment, or penal servitude, under their control to go at large at any time during the term for which said person was sentenced, but shall keep such convicts safely confined or attended by a sufficient guard. Any person violating the provisions of this section shall be guilty of an escape, and punished accordingly; *Provided*, That the board of inspectors may, as a reward for good conduct, permit a convict to go about the premises of the person hiring him without a guard.

4662. Hirer to pay two hundred dollars for an escape; when refunded.—The contractor or hirer of convicts shall pay two hundred dollars to the state for each convict who escapes, whether such escape is owing to negligence or not; such amount to be refunded without interest upon the recapture of such convict, less the amount paid as a reward by the state.

4663 (4547). **Removal of convicts in case of epidemic, or other necessity.**—The inspectors may, with the approval of the governor, cause the convicts to be removed to such place of security within the state as they may deem expedient, whenever the prevalence of any epidemic, infectious, or contagious disease, or any other urgent necessity, may render such removal proper; taking all necessary precautions to insure the safe-keeping of the convicts, and to prevent their escape when removed.

Feb. 17, 1885,
p. 187, sec. 25

4664. Inspectors may summon and swear witnesses concerning treatment of convicts.—The inspectors shall have authority to summon, swear and examine witnesses as to any matter concerning the management and treatment of convicts.

ARTICLE VI.

EXECUTION OF SENTENCE OF DEATH.

4665 (4615). **When sentence of death executed.**—Whenever any person is sentenced to the punishment of death, the court must direct that he be hanged by the neck until he is dead; and such sentence must be executed by the proper executive officer of the law, on such day as the court may appoint, not less than four, nor more than eight weeks from the time of the sentence, unless such court suspends the execution, on account of the reference of some matter of law arising on the trial for the determination of the supreme court.

4666 (4616). **By whom executed.**—The sentence of courts, directing the execution of a person according to the provisions of the preceding section, must be executed by the sheriff or his deputy, or by the officer acting in his place.

4667 (4617). **Where executed.**—The punishment of death must be inflicted either in the prison where the convict is confined, or in some other building or inclosure, which must be closed from public view; and no person shall be permitted to be present or witness such punishment, except those who are specially permitted to do so by law. As amended, Dec. 3, 1878, p. 45.

4668 (4618). **Notice; officers and physicians may be present.**—Such officer must give at least three days' previous notice to the judge of the probate court, the clerk of the circuit or city court, at least three justices of the peace, if there be so many in the county, and the physicians in the neighborhood, who may be present and witness the execution; and the persons thus attending must make out and sign a certificate in writing, declaring that they witnessed the execution of the convict pursuant to his sentence.

4669 (4619). **Who else allowed to be present.**—Such officer must also permit the counsel of the convict, and such ministers of the gospel as he may desire, and his relations, to be present; and also such officers of the prison, deputies, constables, military guard, and other assistants, as he may think proper.

4670 (4620). **Pregnancy of female convict; jury summoned.**—If there is reason to believe that a female convict is pregnant, the sheriff must, with the concurrence of a judge of the circuit or city court, summon a jury of six disinterested persons, as many of whom must be physicians as practicable.

4671 (4621). **Same; fact determined by jury; notice to solicitor.**—The sheriff must also give notice to the solicitor, or, in his absence, to any attorney who may be appointed by a circuit or city judge to represent the state, and who has authority to issue subpœnas for witnesses; and the jury, under the direction of the sheriff, or officer acting in his place, must proceed to ascertain the fact of pregnancy; and must state their conclusion in writing, signed by them and the sheriff.

4672 (4622). **Same; if with child, sentence suspended and finding transmitted to governor.**—If such jury are of opinion, and so find, that the convict is with child, the sheriff, or officer acting in his place, must suspend the execution of the sentence, and transmit the finding of the jury to the governor.

4673 (4623). **Same; when not with child, governor issues warrant, and sentence executed.**—Whenever the governor is satisfied that such convict is no longer with child, he must issue his warrant to the sheriff appointing a day for her to be executed according to her sentence; and the sheriff, or other officer, must execute the sentence of the law on the day so appointed.

4674 (4624). **When convict sentenced, but not executed on day fixed.**—When, from any cause, any convict sentenced to death has not been executed pursuant to such sentence, the same stands in full force, and the circuit or city court of the county in which such convict was tried, on the application of the solicitor of the circuit, must direct the convict to be brought before it, or, if necessary, must issue an order in writing to that effect; and, upon such convict being brought before such court, it must inquire into the circumstances, and, if no legal reason exists against the execution of such sentence, must sentence the convict to execution on a day to be by such court appointed.

4675 (4625). Same; apprehension and commitment of.—If such convict is at large, any magistrate may issue a warrant for his apprehension; and, if no good reason is shown for his discharge, must commit him, that he be forthcoming to abide the order and sentence of the court in which he was tried.

Feb. 17, 1885, p. 143, sec. 1.

4676. When sheriff may order out troops at execution of criminal.—No sheriff shall order out, or put on duty, at the execution of any criminal, any company, or portion of state troops, except when a riot, attempt at rescue, or other outbreak, has actually occurred, which the posse comitatus is powerless to subdue, or unless there is reasonable cause to apprehend a riot, attempt at rescue, or other outbreak, which the posse comitatus cannot subdue or control.

Ib. sec. 2.

4677. When sheriff guilty of misdemeanor in ordering out troops.—Any sheriff, calling out, or putting on duty any company, or portion of state troops, in violation of the last preceding section, or who calls out, or puts on duty any portion of the state troops, although there be proper cause therefor, without first applying to the governor and obtaining his instructions in the premises, if there is time and opportunity beforehand to make such application and receive the governor's instructions, must, on conviction, be fined not less than five hundred, nor more than one thousand dollars.

Ib. sec. 3.

4678. Failure of sheriff to report to governor in such case, a misdemeanor.—In every case when state troops are ordered out, or put on duty by the sheriff on the occasion of the execution of any criminal, without first obtaining the instructions of the governor, it shall be the duty of the sheriff forthwith to notify the governor of the reasons for his action, and, within ten days thereafter, to make a written report, under oath, to the governor, setting forth the facts and circumstances necessitating the ordering out of such troops; and any sheriff, who fails to make such written report to the governor, must, on conviction, be fined not less than one hundred, nor more than two hundred dollars.

TITLE IV.

SPECIAL PROCEEDINGS.

CHAPTER 1.

PROCEEDINGS TO KEEP THE PEACE, AND THE EMPLOYMENT THEREFOR OF THE POSSE COMITATUS AND MILITARY FORCES OF THIS STATE.

ARTICLE I.

CONSERVATORS OF THE PEACE AND MAGISTRATES.

4679 (4025). **Sheriff chief conservator of peace; duty, and how executed.**—The sheriff is the principal conservator of the peace in his county, and it is his duty to suppress all riots, unlawful assemblies and affrays; in the execution of which duty, he may summon to his aid as many of the men of his county as he thinks proper, and any military company, or companies, as provided in article three of this chapter.

4680 (4026). **Who are magistrates; authority to bind over to keep the peace.**—The judges of the supreme and circuit courts, and the chancellors, throughout the state; the judges of the city courts, the judges of probate, the judges of the county courts, and justices of the peace, in their respective counties; and the mayor or chief officer of any incorporated town or city, within the limits of their respective corporations, are magistrates within the meaning of this chapter, and authorized to require persons to give security to keep the peace in the manner provided in the next article.

ARTICLE II.

PROCEEDINGS BEFORE MAGISTRATES TO KEEP THE PEACE.

4681 (4027). **Complaint before magistrate; testimony taken and subscribed by party.**—Whenever complaint is made to a magistrate, that any person has threatened, or is about to commit, an offense on the person or property of another, he must examine the complainant, and any witness he may produce, on oath, reduce such examination to writing, and cause it to be subscribed by the party so examined.

Noles' case, 24 Ala. 672.

4682 (4028). **When warrant of arrest to issue; contents.** If, on such examination, it appears that there is reason to fear the commission of any such offense by the person complained of, the magistrate must issue a warrant, directed to any lawful officer of the state, containing the substance of the complaint, and commanding such officer forthwith to arrest the person complained of, and bring him before him, or some other magistrate having jurisdiction of the matter.

Noles' case, 24 Ala. 672; Duckworth v. Johnston, 7 Ala. 578; Crumpton v. Newman, 12 Ala. 199.

4683 (4029). **Executed by whom.**—Such warrant may be executed by the sheriff, or other officer acting as sheriff, or his deputy, or by any constable of the county, or by any marshal or policeman of any incorporated city or town in the county.

4684 (4030). **Hearing; discharge of defendant.**—When the person complained of is brought before the magistrate, he and his witnesses must be heard in his defense; and if, on hearing the witnesses on both sides, it appears that there is no just reason to fear the commission of the offense, the defendant must be discharged.

4685 (4031). **Defendant competent witness in his own behalf.**—In all proceedings to keep the peace, the defendant shall be a competent witness to give evidence in his own behalf.

4686 (4032). **Costs on plaintiff, if complaint unfounded.** If the magistrate regard the complaint as unfounded, or frivolous, he may order the complainant to pay the costs of prosecution; and, upon making such order, an execution may issue to coerce the payment thereof.

4687 (4033). **Security to keep peace; when required.**—If, however, there is just reason to fear the commission of such offense, the defendant must be required to give security to keep the peace, in such sum as the magistrate may direct, towards all the people of this state, and particularly towards the person against whom, or whose property, there is reason to fear the offense may be committed, for such time as the magistrate may direct, not more than twelve, nor less than six months; but the defendant must not be required to appear at the next term of the circuit or city court, unless he has actually committed an offense cognizable in such court.

Goodwin v. Governor, 1 Stew. & Port. 465.

4688 (4034). **Form of undertaking to keep the peace.** The undertaking to keep the peace may be, in substance, as follows:

"The State of Alabama, ⎱   We, (here insert the names of the
———— county.   ⎰ defendant and his sureties), agree to
pay to the State of Alabama one thousand dollars (or such sum
as the magistrate directs), if the said (here insert the name of
the defendant) does not keep the peace for twelve months (or
as the case may be), from this undertaking, towards all the citizens of this state, and particularly towards (here insert the
name of the person against whom, or whose property, there is
reason to fear the commission of the offense).   Dated —— day
of ————, 18—.   (Signed)   "A. B.
                                                        "C. D.
                                                        "E. F.
"Approved, L. M., Justice of the Peace (or other magistrate,
as the case may be)."

4689 (4035). **Defendant discharged on giving, and committed on failure to give bond; commitment.**—Upon such
undertaking, with sufficient sureties, being given, the defendant
must be discharged; and if not given, the magistrate must
commit him to jail until he gives the same; specifying in the
warrant of commitment the cause thereof, the time he is required to keep the peace, and towards whom particularly, and
also the sum in which security is required.

4690 (4036). **Discharge by sheriff on giving undertaking.**
Any person, committed under the provisions of the preceding
section, may be discharged by the sheriff of the county in which
he is detained, upon entering into an undertaking to keep the
peace, with sufficient sureties, in the sum, and for the term required by the magistrate.

4691 (4037). **Costs on defendant and execution.**—In all
cases where a person is required to keep the peace, the magistrate may order the costs of the prosecution, or any part thereof, to be paid by such person; and an execution may issue for
the collection of the same.

4692 (4038). **Appeal to circuit or city court.**—Any person
required to keep the peace under the provisions of the preceding sections of this article, by any other magistrate than a
judge of the supreme or circuit court, or chancellor, on entering
into an undertaking, with sufficient sureties, in a sum equal to
that required of him to keep the peace, for the prosecution of
his appeal, and in the meantime to keep the peace, is entitled
to an appeal to the next circuit or city court of the county; and
the magistrate from whose order the appeal is taken may, in
such case, require such witnesses as he thinks necessary to enter
into an undertaking, in the sum of one hundred dollars each,
to appear at such court. Any person committed to jail by a
magistrate for failing to give security to keep the peace may
appeal to the circuit or city court, if in session, and if not in
session, to its next term, and may thereupon be discharged
from custody on giving bond with surety, in such penalty as
the judge of any court of record may prescribe, conditioned for
his appearance at such term of the court, and to keep the peace
towards all the people of the state, for the period of twelve
months, unless sooner discharged by law; and any person, who
has been required to give bond to keep the peace, and has given

such bond, may appeal, in like manner, upon giving security for the costs of such appeal; but such appeal shall not supersede the obligation of such peace bond, unless the court which tries such appeal shall discharge the defendant.*

Tomlin's case, 19 Ala. 9; Ex parte Coburn, 38 Ala. 237.

4693 (4039). **Form of undertaking on appeal.**—The undertaking on the appeal, under the provisions of the preceding section, may be, in substance, as follows:

"The State of Alabama, } An order having been made by A.
———— county. } B., a justice of the peace for said county (or other magistrate, as the case may be), requiring (here insert the name of the defendant) to keep the peace towards all the people of this state, and particularly towards (here insert the name of the person against whom, or whose property, there is reason to fear the offense may be committed), from which order the said defendant has taken an appeal to the next circuit court (or city court, as the case may be) of said county; now, therefore, we (here insert the names of the defendant and his sureties), agree to pay the State of Alabama (here insert the amount required by the magistrate) —— dollars, if the said defendant fail to prosecute his appeal to effect, and in the meantime to keep the peace towards (here insert the name of the person against whom, or whose property, there is reason to fear the offense may be committed). Dated this —— day of ——, 18—.   (Signed)   "A. B.
"C. D.
"E. F.
"Approved, L. M., Justice of the Peace (or other magistrate, as the case may be)."

4694 (4040). **Undertaking returned to court; failure subjects magistrate to attachment for contempt.**—Any undertaking given under any provision of this article must be returned by the magistrate taking the same to the clerk of the circuit or city court of the proper county, by the first day of the next court; and failing so to do, he may be attached for contempt.

4695 (4041). **Trial on appeal de novo; court may require new bond; costs and execution.**—The court to which an appeal, under the provisions of this article, is prosecuted, must examine the case anew, and may confirm the order of the magistrate, or discharge the appellant; or require him to enter into a new undertaking, with sufficient sureties, to keep the peace, in such sum and for such term as the court thinks proper; and may make such order in relation to the costs of the prosecution as seems just, which order may be enforced by execution.

4696 (4042). **Effect of undertaking when appeal not sustained.**—If the appellant fails to sustain his appeal, his undertaking remains in full force and effect as to any breach thereof, and also stands as security for any costs which are ordered by the court to be paid by the appellant; and execution may issue therefor against all parties to the same.

—————————
*Rewritten by joint committee.

4697 (4043). **When offense threatened in presence of court or magistrate.**—Any person, who, in the presence of a court or magistrate, commits or threatens to commit an offense against the person or property of another, or contends with another with angry words, may be ordered, without process, to enter into an undertaking to keep the peace for a term not exceeding twelve months, and, in case of refusal, be committed as in other cases.

4698 (4044). **Courts may require peace bonds of persons convicted.**—The circuit courts, the city courts and the county courts may, also, on the conviction of any person for an offense against the person or property of another, when necessary for the public good, require the defendant to enter into an undertaking, with sureties, to keep the peace for not exceeding twelve months, and, on his failure, may commit him.

4699 (4045). **Forfeiture of peace bond; how ascertained.** An undertaking to keep the peace is forfeited by the commission by the defendant of any offense upon the person or property of another; which may be ascertained by a jury, without the conviction of the defendant therefor, in the circuit or city court, on ten days' notice to the parties against whom the forfeiture is sought.

4700 (4046). **Court may remit penalty.**—The court, on a forfeiture of an undertaking to keep the peace, may remit any portion of the amount specified therein, according to the circumstances of the case.

ARTICLE III.

EMPLOYMENT OF MILITARY FORCES TO PRESERVE THE PEACE AND ENFORCE THE LAWS.

4701. When governor may call out military.—The governor may call out all or such portion of the militia and volunteer forces of the state, as he may deem advisable, to execute the laws, suppress insurrection, and repel invasion. [Feb. 18, 1879, p. 180, sec. 1.]

4702. Use of military prohibited, except as hereinafter provided.—No portion of the Alabama State Troops shall be called into service, or be used in the enforcement of the laws of this state, without the authority of the governor, except in cases hereinafter provided in this article. [Ib. sec. 2.]

4703. Civil officers may call on governor for troops when posse comitatus insufficient.—Whenever any circuit judge, chancellor, city court judge, sheriff, mayor, or intendant of any incorporated city, town, or village, shall have reasonable cause to apprehend the outbreak of any riot, rout, tumult, insurrection, mob, or combination to oppose the enforcement of the laws by force or violence, within the jurisdiction in which such officer is by law a conservator of the peace, which cannot be speedily suppressed or effectually prevented by the ordinary posse comitatus and peace officers, it shall forthwith become the duty of such judge, chancellor, sheriff, mayor, or intendant, to report the facts and circumstances in writing to the governor, and request him to order out such portion of the militia or volunteer forces of this state as may be necessary to enforce the [Ib. sec. 3.]

laws and preserve the peace; and it shall thereupon be the duty of the governor, if he deems such apprehension well founded, to order out, or direct to be held in readiness, such portion of the militia or volunteer forces of the state as he may deem advisable for the proper enforcement of the law; and he may direct the officer in command of the troops to report to the officer making such application, or to any other officer named in this section, to obey the orders of such civil officer; or, if the governor deem it advisable, may specially instruct the officer in command of such troops as to the duties required of them, and direct their execution under the immediate control of the governor.

Ib. sec. 4.

4704. When civil officers may direct officer in command to call out troops before applying to governor.—Whenever any riot, outbreak, tumult, mob, or rout, shall occur or be imminent. or there shall be an assemblage of persons over ten in number, with the intent to commit a felony, or to offer violence to person or property, or with the intent to oppose or resist, by force or violence, the execution of any law of this state, or any lawful process of any court or officer thereof, or the due execution, according to law, of any legal ordinance, or by-law of any municipal corporation, or any lawful process duly issued by any officer thereof, under such circumstances that timely application cannot be made to the governor, and action had thereon by him, as provided in the last preceding section, any of the civil officers mentioned in the last preceding section, if he ascertains, or has good reason to believe, that the ordinary posse comitatus, or civil power of the county, city, town, or village, where such violation of the laws and peace of this state occurs, or appears imminent, are, or would be unable to promptly suppress or prevent the same, may, without first making application to the governor, direct the highest commissioned officer of the Alabama State Troops, in the county where such lawlessness exists, or is threatened, to call out and report with his command to such civil officer, to enforce the laws, and to preserve the peace; and it shall be the duty of such commander, and all persons composing such command, to obey such order.

Ib. sec. 5.

4705. Dispersing riot, mob, or unlawful assembly; what must be done before using military force; exceptions.—Before using any military force in the dispersion of any riot, rout, tumult, mob, or other lawless or unlawful assembly, or combination mentioned in this article, it shall be the duty of the civil officer calling out such military force, or some other conservator of the peace, or if none be present, then of the officer in command of the troops, or some person by him deputed, to command the persons composing such riotous, tumultuous, or unlawful assemblage or mob, to disperse and retire peaceably to their respective abodes and business; but, in no case, shall it be necessary to use any set or particular form of words in ordering the dispersion of any riotous, tumultuous, or unlawful assembly; nor shall any such command be necessary, where the officer or person, in order to give it, would necessarily be put in imminent danger of loss of life, or great bodily harm, or where such unlawful assemblage or mob is engaged in the commission or perpetration of any forcible and atrocious felony, or in assault-

ing or attacking any civil officer, or person lawfully called to
aid in the preservation of the peace, or is otherwise engaged in
actual violence to persons or property.

4706. Failure to disperse a felony.—Any person or persons, *Ib. sec. 6.*
composing or taking part in any riot, rout, tumult, mob, or
lawless combination or assembly, mentioned in this article, who,
after being duly commanded to disperse, as hereinbefore provided in the last section, willfully and intentionally fails to do
so as soon as practicable, is guilty of a felony, and must, on
conviction, be imprisoned in the penitentiary for not less than
one, nor more than two years.

4707. Duty of officer on failure of persons to disperse; *Ib. sec. 7.*
when injury to person or property excusable.—After any
person or persons, composing or taking part, or about to take
part in any riot, mob, rout, tumult, or unlawful combination or
assembly, mentioned in this article, shall have been duly commanded to disperse, or where the circumstances are such that
no such command is requisite under the provisions of this article,
the civil officer to whom such military force is ordered to report,
or if there be no civil officer present, then such military officer
(or if such command is acting under the direct order of the
governor, then such officer within the limits provided in his instructions), shall take such steps and make such disposition for
the arrest, dispersion, or quelling of the persons composing or
taking part in any such mob, riot, tumult, outbreak, or unlawful
combination or assembly, mentioned in this article, as may be
deemed requisite to that end; and if, in doing so, any person is
killed, wounded, or otherwise injured, or any property injured
or destroyed, by the civil officer, or officer or member of the
militia or state troops, or other person lawfully aiding them,
such civil officer, military officer, or member of the militia or
state troops, or person lawfully aiding them, shall be held guilt-
less in all cases, unless it be made to appear that such killing,
wounding, or injury to person, or injury or destruction to property, was wanton or malicious, and without any seeming necessity or excuse.

4708. Throwing missiles at state troops or civil officer a *Ib. sec. 8.*
felony.—Any person, who unlawfully assaults, or fires at, or
throws any missile at, against, or upon any member, or body of
the militia or state troops, or civil officer, or other person lawfully aiding them, when assembling or assembled for the purpose of performing any duty under the provisions of this article, must, on conviction, be imprisoned in the penitentiary for
not less than two years, nor more than five years.

4709. When commanding officer may order troops to *Ib. sec. 9.*
quell riot.—If any portion of the militia or state troops, or
person lawfully aiding them in the performance of any duty
under the provisions of this article, are assaulted, attacked, or
are in imminent danger thereof, the commanding officer of such
militia or state troops need not await any orders from any civil
magistrate, but may at once proceed to quell such attack, and
take all other needful steps for the safety of his command.

4710. Persons must disperse when hostile act committed *Ib. sec. 10.*
by mob on military; penalty.—Whenever any shot is fired,

or missile thrown at, against, or upon any body of state troops or militia, or upon any officer or member thereof, assembling or assembled for the performance of any duty under the provisions of this article, it shall forthwith be the duty of every person in the assemblage from which such shot is fired, or missile thrown, to immediately disperse and retire therefrom, without awaiting any order to do so; and any person knowing or having reason to believe, that a shot has been so fired, or missile thrown from any assemblage of which such person forms a part, or with which he is present, and failing, without lawful excuse, to retire immediately from such assemblage, is guilty of a misdemeanor, and must, on conviction, be imprisoned in the county jail for not less than one month, nor more than one year; and any person so remaining in such assemblage, after being duly commanded to disperse, is guilty of a felony, and must, on conviction, be imprisoned in the penitentiary for not less than one, nor more than two years.

Ib. sec. 11.   **4711. Power of civil or military officer to clear streets, etc.** Whenever any rout, riot, or mob, has occurred, or is progressing, or is so imminent that any portion of the militia or state troops is, or has been called out for the performance of any duty under the provisions of this article, it shall be lawful for the civil officer under whose orders the militia or state forces are acting, or the commanding officer of such militia or state troops, if it be deemed advisable in subduing or preventing such mob or riot, or the outbreak thereof, to prohibit all persons from occupying or passing on any street, road, or place in the vicinity of the rout, mob, or riot, or place where the same is threatened, or where the militia or state troops may be for the time being, and otherwise to regulate passage and occupancy of such streets and places; any person, after being duly informed of such prohibition or regulation, who willfully and intentionally, without any lawful excuse, attempts to go or remain on such street, road, or place, and fails to depart after being warned to do so, is guilty of a misdemeanor, and must, on conviction, be fined not more than one thousand dollars, and may also be imprisoned in the county jail, or sentenced to hard labor, for not more than one hundred days; and, in such case, the officer in command of the troops or militia may forthwith arrest persons so offending, and turn them over to some civil magistrate.

Ib. se'. 12.   **4712. Troops guarding jail or prisoner may prevent persons coming near; penalty against intruders.**—The commanding officer of any body of militia or state troops, guarding any jail, public building, or other place, or escorting any prisoner, may, if he deem it advisable, prescribe a reasonable distance in the vicinity of such jail, public building, or other place, or escort of such prisoner, within which persons shall not come; and any person, knowingly and willfully, without lawful excuse, coming within such limits without the permission of such officer, and refusing to depart after being ordered to do so, shall be deemed guilty of a misdemeanor, and must, on conviction, be imprisoned in the county jail, or sentenced to hard labor for the county, for not more than three hundred days; and any person, so coming and remaining in such limits in the night-time, is guilty of a felony, and must, on conviction, be imprisoned in the penitentiary for not less than one, nor more than two years; and, in either case, it shall be the duty of the officer commanding such troops or militia forthwith to arrest persons thus offending, and turn them over to some civil magistrate.

4713. Report to governor, who may direct troops in all cases.—Whenever any militia or state troops are ordered out by a civil magistrate, under the provisions of this article, without first obtaining an order from the governor, it shall be the duty of the civil magistrate, and also of the commander of such militia or state troops, to report the facts as soon as practicable to the governor; and in all cases the governor may direct such militia or state troops to perform their duties under his immediate orders. Ib. sec. 13.

4714. Authority of governor to order out military forces in aid of civil authorities; regulations.—Whenever there is any insurrection or outbreak of a formidable character, which has overawed, or threatens to overawe, the ordinary civil authorities, and the authorities in such county, town, or city have attempted and failed to quell the same by the use of the posse comitatus, or it is apparent that such attempt would be useless, the governor, on a certificate of such facts from any four conservators of the peace in such county, city, or town, or from any circuit judge, chancellor, probate judge, sheriff, or justice of the supreme court, shall immediately order out such portion of the state troops or militia as he may deem necessary to enforce the laws and preserve the peace; and the governor may, when the urgency is great, order out such troops without any certificate from either of the officers mentioned in this section; but in no case shall the governor keep in service, in any county, city, or town of the state, for more than ten days, any troops or militia, other than those raised in such county, except in time of invasion or actual insurrection, unless some justice of the supreme court, or circuit judge, or chancellor of the circuit or division of which such county forms a part, or four justices of the peace in such county, or the sheriff thereof, shall certify to him that the longer presence of such militia or troops is requisite to the proper enforcement of the law, or the preservation of the peace therein. Ib. sec. 14.

4715. Change of venue allowed when person aiding to suppress riot indicted.—Any civil or military officer, or member of the state troops or militia, or any person lawfully aiding them in the performance of any duty required under the provisions of this article, indicted or sued for any injury to person or property in endeavoring to perform such duty, shall have the right, and it is hereby made the duty of the court in which such indictment or suit is pending, upon the application of any person so indicted or sued, to remove the trial of the indictment or suit to some county free from exception, other than that in which the indictment was found or injury done. Ib. sec. 15.

4716. Military officer may require written instructions; discretion as to manner of executing orders.—Any officer, whose command is called out under the provisions of this article, and reporting to any civil magistrate, may require such magistrate to make such order in writing, and prescribe therein Ib. sec. 16.

the outline of the duties required of him and his command, and
may decline to obey such orders until put in writing; and while
such commanding officer must obey all lawful commands of
such magistrate, such military officer may use his discretion as
to the manner of carrying out such orders, so long as he com-
plies with their spirit.

CHAPTER 2.

PROCEEDINGS TO ENFORCE THE LAW FOR THE PRESERVATION OF
OYSTERS.

Dec. 11, 1882
p. 12, sec. 1.

**4717. Non-residents prohibited from taking and catching
oysters; forfeiture of boat, etc.**—It is unlawful for any person, not a resident of this state, to take or catch oysters, in any
manner, in the waters within the jurisdiction of this state; and
any person violating the provisions of this section shall forfeit
not less than fifty, nor more than one hundred dollars, to be
recovered in the mode hereinafter prescribed; and the boat,
vessel, or craft employed in such unlawful business, with her
tackle, apparel, furniture and appurtenances, shall be forfeited
to the state.

Ib. sec. 2.

4718. Who considered non-resident; burden of proof.
No person shall be considered a resident of this state, within
the meaning of the term used in this chapter, who does not at
the time reside in, and who shall not have resided in this state
for twelve months next preceding the time when any offense
with which he is charged may have been committed; and, in
all questions arising as to residence under this chapter, the onus
probandi shall rest on the defendant.

4719 (1609, 1611). **Taking oysters with certain implements
prohibited; presumptive evidence of guilt.**—It is not lawful
to take or catch oysters in any of the waters of this state with
or by a scoop, rake, drag, or dredge, or by the use of any other
instrument than the oyster-tongs heretofore in general use for
taking oysters; and all persons violating the provisions of this
section shall forfeit fifty dollars, to be recovered in the mode
hereinafter prescribed, and also forfeit to the state the boat or
vessel employed in such unlawful business, her tackle, apparel
and furniture; and the finding on board the boat or vessel a
scoop, rake, or other instrument forbidden by this section, is
presumptive evidence of guilt.

As amended,
Dec. 11, 1882,
p. 12, sec. 3.

4720 (1610). **Proceedings for violation of this chapter.**
The sheriffs of the several counties bordering on the waters of
this state are specially charged with the execution of this law;
and it is their duty, if they know, or are credibly informed of
the violation of the provisions of this chapter, to take with them
such power as may be necessary, and to seize the boat, vessel,
or craft, her tackle, apparel, furniture and appurtenances, and
arrest all persons on board the same so unlawfully engaged, and
carry them before a justice of the peace of his county.

4721 (1616). **When sheriff may summon posse comitatus;** Ib. sec. 6.
same penalty as for resisting process.—If resistance be apprehended by the sheriff in the execution of this law, he may
summon to his aid the posse comitatus of his county, armed and
equipped as the occasion may require; and may press into his
service any steamboat or other vessel, not actually engaged in
carrying the public mail, at the risk and expense of the state;
and if resistance is made by the boatmen of the boat or vessel
attempted to be seized, such resistance is punishable in the
same manner as is now provided by law for resistance to process.

4722 (1611). **Justice to try cause and summon witnesses.** Ib. sec. 4.
Upon information given to the justice of the peace of the violation of the first or third section of this chapter, he may take
jurisdiction of the complaint, and cause such witnesses to be
summoned as the accused or the sheriff may require.

4723 (1612). **Justice to impose fine and to condemn boat,** Ib. sec. 5.
vessel, etc.—If upon the hearing the offense is established, the
justice must fine each of the offenders as is provided for in the
section of this chapter which is violated, and, if the fine is not
paid, must commit him or them to jail; and must also condemn
the boat, vessel, or craft, together with her tackle, apparel, furniture and appurtenances, forfeited to the state, and direct that
it be sold; and adjudge the cost of the proceeding before him
to be paid by the accused. If he is not satisfied from the proof
that the accusation is established, he must discharge the accused, and release the boat, vessel, or craft, and other property
seized.

4724 (1613). **Proceedings conducted in name of state; ap-** Ib. se . 6.
peal.—The proceedings before the justice must be carried on
in the name of the State of Alabama, and the parties con-.
demned, or either of them, may appeal from the sentence of
condemnation and fine, at any time within ten days from the
rendition thereof, to the circuit court of the county in which
the proceeding is had, or, if within the county of Mobile, to
the city court of Mobile, where the cause must be tried de
novo and prosecuted by the solicitor; and if the judgment is
affirmed, costs must be adjudged on behalf of the state, and
the solicitor be allowed a tax fee of fifty dollars.

4725 (1614). **When sale of boat stayed on appeal; judg-** Ib. sec. 6.
ment if case affirmed.—The sale of the boat or vessel is not
stayed by an appeal, unless the appellant enters into a bond, in
a penalty of twice the value of the boat or vessel, her tackle,
etc., the value to be determined by the justice, with sufficient
surety, payable to the State of Alabama, with condition to
prosecute the appeal to effect. The bond must be returned,
with the other papers in the cause, to the appellate court; and,
if the judgment of the justice is affirmed, judgment shall be
rendered against all the obligors therein for the amount of the
fines not paid, and for the value of the boat, her tackle, etc., to
be ascertained by proof, as well as the costs of the appellate
court.

4726 (1615). **Sale made as under execution; proceeds,** Ib sec. 6.
how disposed of.—If the judgment is not stayed by the execu-

tion of bond as aforesaid, the sheriff must, after the expiration of ten days, advertise and sell the boat or vessel, her tackle, etc., in the same manner as sales under execution ; and, after deducting all necessary expenses of the seizure and costs of sale, of which he shall render an account on oath, pay the residue to the county treasurer of the county in which the seizure is made, who may allow him ten per centum thereon for his trouble. The money thus received by the treasurer must be held for the same purposes as those arising from fines and forfeitures.

CHAPTER 3.

SEARCH WARRANTS.

4727 (4005). **Definition of warrant.**—A search warrant is an order in writing, in the name of the state, signed by a magistrate, directed to the sheriff, or to any constable of the county, commanding him to search for personal property, and bring it before the magistrate.

4728 (4006). **On what ground issued.**—It may be issued on any one of the following grounds :

1. Where the property was stolen or embezzled.

2. Where it was used as the means of committing a felony.

3. Where it is in the possession of any person with the intent to use it as a means of committing a public offense, or in the possession of another to whom he may have delivered it, for the purpose of concealing it, or preventing its discovery.

4729 (4007). **Probable cause and affidavit required.**—It can only be issued on probable cause, supported by affidavit, naming or describing the person, and particularly describing the property, and the place to be searched.

4730 (4008, 4009). **Complainant and witnesses examined on oath; contents of depositions.**—The magistrate, before issuing the warrant, must examine on oath the complainant and any witness he may produce, and take their depositions in writing, and cause them to be subscribed by the persons making them ; and the depositions must set forth the facts tending to establish the grounds of the application, or probable cause for believing that they exist.

4731 (4010). **Warrant to issue, if cause shown.**—If the magistrate is satisfied of the existence of the grounds of the application, or that there is probable ground to believe their existence, he must issue a search warrant signed by him, directed to the sheriff, or to any constable of the county, commanding him forthwith to search the person or place named for the property specified, and to bring it before the magistrate.

4732 (4011). **Search warrant; form of.**—The warrant may be substantially in the following form :

"The State of Alabama, } To the sheriff, or any constable of
——— county.   } ——— county :

"Proof by affidavit having this day been made before me by A. B. that (stating the particular ground on which the warrant is sued out; or, if the affidavits are not positive, that there is probable ground for believing that, etc.); you are, therefore, commanded, in the day-time (or at any time of the day or night, as the case may be), to make immediate search on the person of C. D. (or in the house of C. D., as the case may be), for the following property: (Particularly describing it), and if you find the same, or any part thereof, to bring it forthwith before me, at, etc. (stating place).   Dated the —— day of ——, 18—.

" (Signed)   E. F.,
" Justice of the Peace of said county,
(or other magistrate, as the case may be)."

4733 (4012). **Warrant executed by whom.**—The warrant may be executed by any one of the officers to whom it is directed, but by no other person, except in aid of such officer, at his request, he being present, and acting in its execution.

4734 (4013). **When executed; magistrate must state time in warrant.**—It must be executed in the day-time, unless the affidavits state positively that the property is on the person or in the place to be searched, in which case it may be executed at any time of the day or night; and the magistrate issuing it must state in the warrant, according to the character of the affidavits, whether it is to be executed by day, or at any time of the day or night.

4735 (4014). **Authority of officer in executing warrant.** To execute the warrant, the officer may break open any door or window of a house, or any part of a house, or any thing therein, if, after notice of his authority and purpose, he is refused admittance.

4736 (4015). **Property taken, where and from whom.** When the warrant is sued out on the first ground specified in the second section of this chapter, the property may be taken under the warrant from any house or other place in which it is concealed, or from the possession of any person by whom it was stolen or embezzled, or from any other person in whose possession it may be; when sued out on the second ground specified in such section, it may be·taken under the warrant from any house, or other place in which it is concealed, or from the possession of the person by whom it was so used, or from any other person in whose possession it may be; and when sued out on the third ground specified in such section, the property may be taken under the warrant from the possession of such person, or from any house, or other place occupied by him, or under his control, or from the possession of the person to whom he may so have delivered it.

4737 (4016). **Receipt given for property.**—When an officer takes property under the warrant, he must, if required, give a receipt to the person from whom it was taken, or in whose possession it was found.

4738 (4017). **Warrant returned in ten days, else void.** The warrant must be executed and returned to the magistrate by whom it was issued, within ten days after its date; and after that time, if not executed, it is void.

4739 (4018). **Contents of return of warrant; copies to parties.**—The officer, in his return of the warrant to the magistrate, must specify with particularity the property taken; and the applicant for the warrant, and the person from whose possession the property was taken are entitled to a copy of the return, signed by the magistrate.

4740 (4019). **Disposal of property by magistrate.**—When the property is taken under the warrant and delivered to the magistrate, he must, if it was stolen or embezzled, cause it to be delivered to the owner, on satisfactory proof of his title, and the payment by him of all fees; but if the warrant was issued on the second or third ground specified in the second section of this chapter, he must retain the property in his possession, subject to the order of the court to which he is required to return the proceedings, or of the court in which the offense is triable, in respect to which the property was taken.

Sullivan v. Robinson, 39 Ala. 613.

4741 (4020). **Contest of facts before magistrate.**—If the grounds on which the warrant was issued be controverted, the magistrate must proceed to hear the testimony, which must be reduced to writing, and authenticated in the manner prescribed in section 4730 (4008).

Henderson v. Felts, 58 Ala. 590.

4742 (4021). **When property restored to defendant.**—If it appear that the property is not the same as that described in the warrant, or that there is no probable cause for believing the existence of the ground on which the warrant issued, the magistrate must direct it to be restored to the person from whom it was taken.

4743 (4022). **Proceedings returned to court, unless property restored to defendant.**—The magistrate must, if the property is not directed to be restored under the provisions of the preceding section, annex together the search warrant, the return and depositions, and return them to the circuit court having power to inquire into the offense, in respect to which the search warrant was issued.

4744 (4023). **When costs taxed against plaintiff.** — The complainant must pay the fees of the warrant before he is entitled to the same, and must also pay the officer his fees for the the execution, before the same is executed; and if, on the hearing, it appear that there was no probable cause for believing the existence of the grounds on which the warrant was issued, the whole costs may be taxed against the complainant, and an execution issued therefor, returnable on any day the magistrate may direct.

4745 (4024). **Persons charged with a felony searched for weapons or evidence.**—When a person charged with a felony is supposed by the magistrate before whom he is brought, to have upon his person a dangerous weapon, or any thing which may be used as evidence of the commission of the offense, the magistrate may direct him to be searched in his presence, and such weapon or other thing to be retained, subject to the order of the court in which the defendant may be tried.

CHAPTER 4.

ABSCONDING FELONS AND FUGITIVES FROM JUSTICE; REWARDS AND
REQUISITIONS.

4746 (3976). **Governor authorized to offer reward for ab-** As amended
sconding felons.—Whenever.a felony has been committed, and Jan. 27, 1883
the perpetrator thereof is unknown, or when, being known, he p. 34.
absconds before being arrested, or escapes from custody, either
before or after conviction, the governor is authorized, in his discretion, to offer by proclamation a reward, not exceeding four
hundred dollars, for the apprehension or re-arrest of such person, within five years from the date of such proclamation; and
to draw his warrant on the state treasurer for the amount of
such reward, when necessary to be paid.

4747 (3977). **Fugitive from other state delivered up on
demand of executive.**—Any person, charged in any state or
territory of the United States, with treason, felony, or other
crime, who shall flee from justice, and be found in this state,
must, on the demand of the executive authority of the state or
territory from which he fled, be delivered up by the governor
of this state, to be removed to the state or territory having jurisdiction of such crime.

Morrell v. Quarles, 35 Ala. 544; Ex parte State, 73 Ala. 503.

4748 (3978). **Warrant of arrest issued by magistrate.**—A
warrant for the apprehension of such person may be issued by
any magistrate who is authorized to issue a warrant of arrest.

4749 (3979). **Arrest and commitment; copy of indictment
or other judicial proceedings conclusive evidence.**—The pro-
ceedings.for the arrest and commitment of the person charged
are in all respects similar to those provided in this Code for the
arrest and commitment of a person charged with a public offense,
except that an exemplified copy of an indictment found, or
other judicial proceedings had against him in the state or territory in which he is charged to have committed the offense, must
be received as conclusive evidence before the magistrate.

4750 (3980). **Commitment to await requisition of governor; bail.**—If, from the examination, it appears that the person charged has committed the crime alleged, the magistrate
must, by warrant reciting the accusation, commit him to jail for
a time specified in the warrant, which the magistrate deems
reasonable, to enable the arrest of the fugitive to be made, under
the warrant of the executive of this state on the requisition of
the executive authority of the state or territory in which he committed the offense, unless he give bail as provided in the next
section, or until he is legally discharged.

4751 (3981). **Bailed except in capital cases; condition and
requisites of bond.**—The magistrate must, unless the offense
with which the fugitive is charged is shown to be an offense
punished capitally by the laws of the state in which it was committed, admit the person arrested to bail, by bond or undertaking, with sufficient sureties, and in such sum as he deems

proper, for his appearance before him at a time specified in such bond or undertaking, and for his surrender, to be arrested upon the warrant of the governor of this state.

4752 (3982). **When discharged on bail.**—If such person is not arrested on the warrant of the governor before the expiration of the time specified in the warrant, bond, or undertaking, he must be discharged from custody on bail.

4753 (3983). **Jail fees paid in advance.**—No jailer is bound to receive any person committed under a warrant issued under the provisions of this chapter, until his jail fees for the time specified in such warrant are paid in advance.

4754 (3984). **Forfeiture of bail; proceedings; indorsement of magistrate as evidence.**—If the fugitive is discharged on bail, and fails to appear or surrender himself according to his bond or undertaking, the magistrate must indorse thereon "forfeited," sign his name thereto, and return it to the clerk of the circuit court by the first day of the next term; and a conditional judgment must be rendered thereon, and proceedings had, as in case of bonds or undertakings forfeited in that court, the indorsement of the magistrate being presumptive evidence of the forfeiture.

4755 (3985). **At expiration of time, discharged, bailed, or recommitted.**—At the expiration of the time specified in the warrant, the magistrate may discharge or recommit him to a further day, or may take bail for his appearance and surrender, as provided in section 4751 (3981); and on his appearance, or if he has been bailed and appear according to the terms of his bond or undertaking, the magistrate may either discharge him therefor, or may require him to enter into a new bond or undertaking, to appear and surrender himself at another day.

4756 (3986). **If prosecution pending here, surrender discretionary.**—If a criminal prosecution has been instituted against such person under the laws of this state, the governor may or not, at his discretion, surrender such person on the demand of the executive of another state, before he has been tried and punished, if convicted, or discharged.

4757 (3987). **Governor's warrant; directed to whom.**—A warrant from the executive may be directed to the sheriff, coroner, or any other person whom he may think fit to entrust with the execution of the same.

4758 (3988). **Executed where and how.**—Such warrant authorizes the officer or person to whom it is directed to arrest the fugitive at any place within the state, and to require the aid of all sheriffs and constables, to whom the same is shown, in its execution.

4759 (3989). **Authority of arresting officers, etc.** — Every such officer or person has the same authority, in arresting the fugitive, to command assistance therein, as sheriffs and other officers by law have in the execution of criminal process directed to them, with the like penalties on those who refuse their assistance.

4760 (3990). **Confinement in jail; when necessary.** — The officer or person executing such warrant may, when necessary, confine the prisoner arrested by him in the jail of any county through which he may pass; and the keeper of such jail must receive and safely keep the prisoner until the person having charge of him is ready to proceed on his route, such person being chargeable with the expenses of keeping.

CHAPTER 5.

HABEAS CORPUS.

4761 (4936). **Who entitled to writ; when the proper remedy.**—Any person, who is imprisoned or restrained of his liberty in this state, on any criminal charge or accusation, or under any other pretense whatever (except persons committed or detained by virtue of process issued by a court of the United States, or by a judge thereof, in cases of which such courts have exclusive jurisdiction under the laws of the United States, or have acquired exclusive jurisdiction by the commencement of suits in such courts), may prosecute a writ of habeas corpus, according to the provisions of this chapter, to inquire into the cause of such imprisonment or restraint.

As to jurisdiction of state courts to discharge enrolled conscript from custody of Confederate States' officer.—Ex parte Hill, 38 Ala. 458. Statutes on habeas corpus do not take away common-law right to the writ.—Kirby's case, 62 Ala. 51. Proper remedy when one sentenced to hard labor is confined in jail instead of being put to hard labor.—Kirby's case, 62 Ala. 51; Ex parte Pearson, 59 Ala. 654. Also, where justice of the peace imposes void sentence.—Ex parte McKivett, 55 Ala. 236. Also, where unauthorized sentence imposed for violating municipal ordinance.—Ex parte Moore, 62 Ala. 471. Also, where sentence is in excess of jurisdiction; but not where the sentence is irregular merely, and not void.—Ex parte Brown, 63 Ala. 187; Ex parte Simmons, 62 Ala. 416; Ex parte State, 71 Ala. 371. Not appropriate remedy in imprisonment for contempt.—Ex parte Hardy, 68 Ala. 303. Scope of inquiry where party committed by chancellor for contempt.—Ib. Not the remedy to test putative father's right to custody of a bastard child.—Matthews v. Hobbs, 51 Ala. 210. When lies by a father for the custody of his child. Ex parte Murphy, 75 Ala. 409. Although the writ is matter of right, it is not granted unless showing of party entitles him to relief.—Ex parte Campbell, 20 Ala. 89. The proper remedy to get case before supreme court when bail refused below.—Ex parte Croom, 19 Ala. 561. See note to section 4413. Not remedy in case of unauthorized discharge of jury.—Ex parte Champion, 52 Ala. 311. Nor for disqualification of presiding judge.—Ex parte State, 76 Ala. 482. Nor for failure of jury to ascertain degree of murder.—Ex parte Dover, 75 Ala. 40. When defendant not under indictment, may be discharged.—Ex parte Champion, 52 Ala. 311.

4762 (4937, 4938). **Application made by petition on oath; what petition must state.**—The application for the writ must be made by petition, signed either by the party himself for whose benefit it is intended, or by some other person on his behalf; must be verified by the oath of the applicant, to the effect that the statements therein contained are true to the best of his knowledge, information and belief; and must state, in substance, the name of the person on whose behalf the application is made; that he is imprisoned or restrained of his liberty in the county, the place of such imprisonment, if known, the name of the officer or person by whom he is so imprisoned, and the cause or pretense of such imprisonment; and if the imprisonment is by virtue of any warrant, writ, or other process, a copy thereof must be annexed to the petition, or the petition must allege

that a copy thereof has been demanded and refused, or must
show some sufficient excuse for the failure to demand a copy.

Sufficiency of petition.—Ex parte Champion, 52 Ala. 311; Gibson's case, 44
Ala. 17.   Not demurrable for failing to allege petitioner illegally restrained of his
own liberty.—Ex parte Champion, 52 Ala. 311.   Must be verified by affidavit.
Stibbins v. Butler, Minor, 121; Gibson's case, 44 Ala. 17.   Sufficient verification.
Gibson's case. supra; Ex parte Champion, supra.   Unnecessary averments, though
false, not subject of perjury.—Gibson's case, 44 Ala. 17.

4763 (4939). **'If name of party, etc., unknown, he may be
described.**—If the name of the person on whose behalf the
application is made, or of the officer or person by whom he is
imprisoned or detained, is uncertain or unknown, he may be
described in any way that is sufficient to identify him.

4764 (4940). **To whom petition must be addressed.**—When
the person is confined in a county jail, or any other place, on a
charge of felony, or under a commitment or an indictment for
felony, the petition must be addressed to the judge of the city
court, or to the nearest circuit judge, or chancellor, or to the
probate judge of the county where the person is confined; and
when the person is confined in the penitentiary, or under a sentence, judgment, decree, or order of the supreme court, the
chancery court, the circuit court, or the city court, other than
an indictment for felony, the petition must be addressed to the
judge of the city court, or to the nearest circuit judge or chancellor; in all other cases, it may be addressed to any one of them,
or to the probate judge of the county; and when the person is
confined in any other place than the county jail or the penitentiary, and on any other than a criminal charge, it may be addressed to any justice of the peace of the county, or to the probate judge thereof.

Section construed; when judge of probate has no jurisdiction; writ of prohibition to prevent him from acting.—Ex parte Ray, 45 Ala. 15.   In his county, probate judge has same jurisdiction as circuit judge or chancellor.—Ex parte Keeling,
50 Ala. 474.   Jurisdiction of circuit court; when action of circuit judge not restrained by prohibition from supreme court; presumption in favor of circuit judge's
decision.—Ex parte State, 51 Ala. 60.   When supreme court will issue writ.—Ex
parte Simmonton, 9 Port. 383; Ex parte Chaney, 8 Ala. 424; Ex parte Burnett, 30
Ala. 461; Ex parte Hardy, 68 Ala. 303.   Its jurisdiction is appellate only, and
confined to evidence adduced before lower tribunal.—Ex parte Brown, 63 Ala. 187.
When proceeding in its nature appellate, and when original.—Kirby's case, 62 Ala.
51.   Refusal of bail revisable on habeas corpus.—Ex parte Croom, 19 Ala. 561.
Application to revise action of circuit court.—Ex parte Cleveland, 36 Ala. 306;
Ex parte Hunter, 39 Ala. 560.

4765 (4941). **To whom addressed in absence of nearest
judge.**—When the petition is required to be addressed to the
nearest circuit judge or chancellor, and such judge or chancellor is absent, or has refused to grant the writ, or is incapable
of acting, it may be addressed to any other circuit judge or
chancellor; but, in such case, before the writ is granted, proof
must be made, either by the oath of the applicant, or other
sufficient evidence, of the particular facts which justify such
address.

4766 (4942). **Writ granted without delay; before whom
returnable.**—The judge, chancellor, or justice, to whom the
application is made, must grant the same without delay, unless
it appears from the petition itself, or from the documents thereunto annexed, that the person imprisoned or restrained is not,
under the provisions of this chapter, entitled to the benefit of
the writ.   When the person is confined in the penitentiary, the

writ must be made returnable before the circuit court of Elmore county, or of the county in which the convict is confined; when granted by a justice of the peace, it must be made returnable before the judge of probate of the county, or the judge of the city court, or the nearest circuit judge or chancellor; and in all other cases, it must be made returnable before the officer by whom it is granted.

4767 (4943). **Form of writ.**—The writ may be, in substance, as follows:

"The State of Alabama, ⎫ To the sheriff of ——— county ——— county. ⎭ (or other person by whom the party is imprisoned or restrained): You are hereby commanded to have the body of A. B., alleged to be detained by you, by whatsoever name the said A. B. is called or charged, with the cause of such detention, before C. D., judge of the circuit court (or other officer, as required by the preceding section), on ———, at ——— (specifying the time and place, or immediately after the receipt of this writ, as the case may be), to do and receive what shall then and there be considered concerning the said A. B. Dated this —— day of ———, 18—."

(Signed by the officer, with his official title.)

4768 (4944). **Not disobeyed for want of form or mistake.** The writ must not be disobeyed on account of any want of form, or any misdescription of the person to whom it is addressed; and it must be presumed to have been addressed to the person on whom it is served, notwithstanding any mistake in the name or address.

4769 (4945). **Notice to adverse party in civil cases.**—If it appears from the petition, or from the documents thereunto annexed, that the party is imprisoned or detained by virtue of any process under which any other person has an interest in continuing his imprisonment or restraint, the officer issuing the writ must indorse thereon an order requiring the applicant, or some one else for him, to give notice to such person, or to his attorney, of the issue of the writ, and of the time and place at which it is returnable, in order that he may, if he thinks proper, appear and object to the discharge of the party who is imprisoned; and if such notice is not given, when the party who is entitled to it is within fifty miles of the place of examination, the party who is imprisoned must not be discharged.

4770 (4946). **Notice in criminal cases.**—If it appears from the petition, or from the documents thereunto annexed, that the party is imprisoned or detained on any criminal charge or accusation, the officer issuing the writ must indorse thereon an order requiring the applicant, or some one else for him, to give notice to the solicitor of the circuit, or to the prosecutor, or principal agent in procuring the arrest, of the issue of the writ, and of the time and place at which it is returnable; and if such notice is not given, when the solicitor or other person entitled to it is within fifty miles of the place of examination, the party who is imprisoned must not be discharged. But if the party is charged with an offense which is bailable, and he waives an examination into the facts, the judge may fix the amount of bail, without notice to the solicitor or prosecutor; and, in so doing, must act on the presumption that the offense is of the highest grade.

4771 (4947). Procept to sheriff or constable.—At the time of issuing the writ, or at any time afterwards before the hearing, the officer issuing the writ must, on a proper showing, issue a precept, directed to any sheriff or constable of the state, commanding him to have the body of the person who is imprisoned or restrained before the officer before whom the writ is returnable, at the time and place at which it is returnable; which precept must be executed by any sheriff or constable into whose hands it may come, according to its mandate.

4772 (4948). Subpœnas for witnesses.—Subpœnas for witnesses must be issued at any time before the hearing, on the application of either party, by the clerk of the circuit or city court of the county to which the writ is returnable, or by the probate judge by whom the writ was issued, or by any justice of the peace of the county in which the witness resides; which subpœnas must be directed to the sheriff, or to any constable of the county in which the witness resides, and must be executed and returned as in other cases.

4773 (4949). Service of writ; by whom, and how made. The writ must be served by the sheriff, deputy sheriff, or some constable of the county in which it is issued, or in which the person on whose behalf it is sued out is imprisoned or detained, by delivering a copy to the person to whom it is directed, and showing the original, if demanded; and if such person cannot be found, or conceals himself, or refuses admittance to the officer, it may be served by leaving a copy at the place where the party is confined, with any person of full age, who, for the time being, has charge of the party, or by posting it in a conspicuous place on the outside of the house or building in which the party is confined.

4774 (4950). Return; when made.—The person to whom the writ is directed, after due service thereof, must make his return, if practicable, on the day therein specified; and if no day is therein specified, and the place to which the return is to be made is not more than thirty miles from the place where the party is imprisoned or detained, the return must be made within two days after service; if more than thirty, and less than one hundred miles, within five days, and if over one hundred miles, within eight days after service.

4775 (4951). Form and contents of return.—The return must be signed by the person making it, and be verified by his oath, unless he is a sworn public officer, and makes the return in his official capacity; and it must state, plainly and unequivocally, whether or not he has the party in his custody or power, or under his restraint; if so, by what authority, and the cause thereof, setting out the same fully, together with a copy of the writ, warrant, or other written authority, if any; and if he has had the party in his custody or power, or under his restraint, at any time before or after the date of the writ, but has transferred such custody or restraint to another, to whom, at what time, for what cause, and by what authority, such transfer was made.

4776 (4952). **Body also produced, with warrant, etc.**—At the time of making the return, he must also produce the person on whose behalf the writ was sued out, according to the command of the writ, and the original warrant, writ, or other written authority under which he was detained; but if, from sickness or infirmity, the party cannot be produced without danger, that fact must be stated in the return, and verified by oath, and, if required, established by other sufficient evidence.

4777 (4953). **Proceedings when body not produced on account of sickness, etc.**—When the party on whose behalf the writ is sued out, on account of sickness or infirmity, is not produced, the court, chancellor, or judge before whom the writ is returnable, if satisfied of such sickness or infirmity, may proceed to decide on the return as if the party had been produced; or may proceed to the place where he is imprisoned or detained, and there make the examination; or may adjourn the examination to another time.

4778 (4954). **Proceedings when body produced under precept.**—If the party is brought before the court, judge, or chancellor by virtue of a precept issued under the provisions of section 4771 (4947), the case must be heard and determined as if he had been produced in return to the writ.

4779 (4955). **Denial of return; examination, adjournment, bail, etc.**—The party on whose behalf the writ is sued out may deny any of the facts stated in the return, and allege any other facts which may be material in the case; and the court, chancellor, or judge may examine, in a summary way, into the cause of the imprisonment or detention, and hear the evidence adduced; may adjourn the examination from time to time, as the circumstances of the case may require, and in the meantime remand the party, or commit him to the custody of the sheriff of the county, or place him under such other custody as his age or other circumstances may require, or, if the character of the charge authorize it, take bail from him, in a sufficient amount, for his appearance from day to day until judgment is given.

4780 (4956). **Forfeiture of undertaking of bail pending examination.**—If the party fails to appear, as required by his undertaking, an entry of forfeiture must be indorsed thereon, signed by the judge or chancellor, and returned to the circuit or city court of the county in which the examination is had; and the same proceedings must be thereon had in such court, as if the undertaking had been taken in such court, the indorsement of forfeiture being presumptive evidence of that fact.

4781 (4957). **When party discharged; when remanded.** If no legal cause for the imprisonment or restraint of the party is shown, he must be discharged; but if it appears that he is held or detained in custody by virtue of process issued by a court or judge of the United States, in a case of which such court or judge has exclusive jurisdiction, or by virtue of any legal engagement or enlistment in the army or navy of the United States, or, being subject to the rules and articles of war, is confined by any one legally acting by authority thereof, or is in custody for any public offense committed in any other state or territory, for which, by the constitution and laws of the United States, he should be delivered up to the authority of such state or territory, or that he is otherwise legally detained, he must be remanded.

4782 (4958). **When bailed, and how.**—If it appears that he is charged with a public offense which is bailable, he must be admitted to bail, on offering sufficient bail; and if sufficient bail is not offered, the amount of bail required must be indorsed on the warrant, and the court to which he is required to appear; and he may be afterwards discharged by the sheriff of the county on giving sufficient bail in the amount so required.

4783 (4960). **Undertaking of bail returned to court; forfeiture thereof.**—All undertakings of bail taken by any judge, chancellor, or sheriff, under the provisions of the preceding section, must be transmitted by him to the clerk of the court before which the party is bound to appear, by the first day of the next succeeding term; and may be forfeited, and the same proceedings thereon had, as against other bail in criminal cases.

4784 (4961). **Judgment, etc., or commitment for contempt, not inquired into.**—No court, chancellor, or judge, on the return of a writ of habeas corpus, has authority to inquire into the regularity or justice of any order, judgment, decree, or process of any court legally constituted, or into the justice or propriety of any commitment for contempt made by a court, officer, or body, according to law, and charged in such commitment.

Merits of the case against a party committed by a magistrate may be gone into anew on hearing of application for habeas corpus; may demand hearing on all the evidence.—Ex parte Mahone, 30 Ala. 49; Ex parte Champion, 52 Ala. 311. Mandamus will lie to compel hearing on the evidence.—Ex parte Mahone, supra; Ex parte Shaundies, 66 Ala. 134. See Ex parte Champion, supra. Return presumed to be true, when no evidence produced on either side, and averments of petition not thereby admitted.—Ex parte Hunter, 39 Ala. 560. Not to be discharged unless witnesses previously examined against him are produced, if attainable; may be bailed.—Ex parte Champion, 52 Ala. 311. Order requiring party to give bond to keep the peace cannot be investigated.—Ex parte Coburn, 38 Ala. 237. Illegality, not error or irregularity, can be inquired into.—Kirby's case, 62 Ala. 51.

4785 (4962). **If under legal process, when discharged.**—If it appears that the party is in custody, by virtue of process from any court legally constituted, or issued by any officer in the course of judicial proceedings before him, authorized by law, he can only be discharged,—

1. Where the jurisdiction of such court has been exceeded, either as to matter, place, sum, or person.

2. Where, though the original imprisonment was lawful, the party has become entitled to his discharge by reason of some subsequent act, omission, or event.

3. Where the process is void in consequence of some defect in matter or substance required by law.

4. Where the process, though in proper form, was issued in a case, or under circumstances, not allowed by law.

5. Where the process is not authorized by any judgment, order, or decree, or by any provision of the law.

6. Where the person who has the custody of him, under any order or process, is not the person authorized by law to detain him.

If in confinement under final judgment of court of competent jurisdiction, not discharged on account of mere errors or irregularities, however gross.—Ex parte

Sam, 51 Ala. 34. If warrant and commitment good, irregularity of complaint no
ground for habeas corpus.—Ex parte McGlawn, 75 Ala. 38. Power of court to inquire into validity of order, when detention is claimed under civil process.—Mor-
row v. Bird, 6 Ala. 834. Party in custody under defective indictment will not, for
such defect, be discharged on habeas corpus.—Ex parte Whitaker, 43 Ala. 323.
Party held under valid process should not be discharged " by reason of some subsequent act, omission or event," unless the facts have the legal force and effect of
" former acquittal."—Ex parte State, 76 Ala. 482. See Ex parte Winston, 55 Ala.
422.

4786 (4963). **When remanded or committed for public offense.**—If it appears that the party has been legally committed
for any public offense, or that he is guilty of such an offense,
although his commitment was irregular, he may be remanded
to the custody or restraint from which he was taken, if the
person under whose custody or restraint he was is legally entitled thereto; and if not so entitled, he must be committed to
the custody of the proper officer or person.

4787 (4964). **After discharge, not again arrested.**—When
a person has once been discharged on habeas corpus, he cannot
be again imprisoned, restrained, or kept in custody, for the
same cause, unless he is indicted therefor, or, after a discharge
for defect of proof, is again arrested on sufficient proof, and
committed by legal process.

4788 (4965). **Penalty for refusal to discharge, or for re-
arrest.**—Any officer, or other person, who has the custody of a
party produced on habeas corpus, and who detains him after an
order of the court, chancellor, or judge for his discharge or enlargement, or afterwards arrests him without a legal and proper
cause, warrant, or other process, must, on conviction thereof,
be fined not less than fifty, nor more than five hundred dollars;
and is also responsible in a civil action for any damages the
party may have sustained.

4789 (4966). **Penalty for refusal to give copy of warrant,
etc.**—Any officer, who refuses or neglects to deliver a true
copy of the order, writ, warrant, or process, by virtue of which
he detains any prisoner, either to the prisoner himself, or to
any other person who applies for the same on his behalf, for
six hours after demand made, forfeits to the prisoner two hundred dollars, and is also guilty of a misdemeanor, on conviction
of which he must be fined not less than fifty, nor more than
five hundred dollars; but no officer is required to deliver more
than two copies of such order, writ, warrant, or process.

4790 (4967). **Penalty for refusal to obey writ.**—Any person to whom a writ of habeas corpus is directed, and who refuses to receive the same, or neglects to obey and execute it
according to the provisions of this chapter (unless sufficient
excuse is shown for such refusal or neglect), is responsible in
damages to the party aggrieved, and is guilty of a contempt,
and also of a misdemeanor; and, on conviction thereof, must
be fined not less than fifty dollars.

4791 (4968). **Attachment against person refusing.**—It is
the duty of the officer before whom such writ is returnable, in
case of such refusal or neglect on the part of the person to
whom it is directed, to proceed forthwith against him, by process of attachment, as for contempt, to compel obedience to the
writ, and to punish him for such contempt; and when such at-

tachment is issued against the sheriff, or his deputy, it may be directed to the coroner, or to any constable, and may be executed by such coroner or constable.

4792 (4969). **Penalty for eluding writ.**—Any person, who has in his custody, or under his control, a person who is entitled to a writ of habeas corpus, and, either before or after the issue of such writ, with intent to elude the service or effect thereof, transfers such person to the custody of another, or places him under the power or control of another, or conceals him, or changes his place of confinement, forfeits to the party aggrieved the sum of five hundred dollars, and is also guilty of a misdemeanor; and, on conviction thereof, must be fined not less than fifty dollars, and may also be imprisoned in the county jail not more than twelve months.

4793 (4970). **Penalty on defaulting witness; proceedings therefor.**—If any witness, duly subpœnaed under the provisions of this chapter, fails to attend as required, the judge or chancellor before whom the writ is returnable must indorse such failure on the back of the subpœna, and deliver it to the clerk of the circuit court of the county in which the examination is had; and the same proceedings must be thereon had as against defaulting witnesses in that court, the indorsement being presumptive evidence of such default.

4794 (4971). **Attendance of witnesses; how proved and taxed.**—Witnesses may prove their attendance before the judge or chancellor, as in other cases, and have the same taxed in the bill of costs, on the subsequent conviction of the party, where he is detained on a criminal charge.

4795 (4972). **Costs discretionary; how taxed and collected.** In other cases, the court, judge, or chancellor may impose the costs, or any portion thereof, on either party; and when the writ is returnable before a chancellor, or before a judge of the circuit or city court, the costs must be taxed by the clerk of such circuit or city court, and collected by execution.

4796 (4973). **Fees of officers; how taxed and collected.** The officer serving the writ is entitled to one dollar for such service, and to five cents for each mile in going and returning, to be proved by his own oath, before the judge of probate or clerk; and for issuing and serving subpœnas, the officers are entitled to the same fees as in other cases; which fees must be taxed in the bill of costs in the case provided for by section 4794 (4971), and in other cases collected by execution issued by the judge of probate.

4797 (4974). **Costs before probate judge; how taxed, etc.** When the writ is returnable before the judge of probate, he must tax the costs, and may collect the same by execution, except in the case provided for in section 4794 (4971).

4798 (4975). **Execution for costs, returnable when.**—An execution for costs, issued under the last three sections, may be made returnable at any day, not less than one month, nor more than three months from the date of its issue, except upon the conviction of a public offense.

4799 (4976). **Guards summoned when necessary.**—When the person, on whose behalf the writ is sued out, is charged with a public offense, the officer or person having charge of him may summon a sufficient guard to aid in conveying him before the court, judge, or chancellor, before whom the writ is returnable, and conveying him back again, if he is not discharged.

4800 (4977). **Compensation of guards; penalty.** — In the case provided for in the preceding section, the officer and guards are entitled to the same compensation as for removing any prisoner on a change of venue, to be paid in the same manner; and such guards are under the control of the officer summoning them; and any guard, who refuses to obey or violates the lawful instructions of such officer, is guilty of a misdemeanor.

CHAPTER 6.

CORONER'S INQUEST.

4801 (3991). **Process of holding coroner's inquest; jury of inquest summoned by coroner.** — When a coroner has been informed that a person has been killed, or suddenly died under such circumstances as to afford a reasonable ground for belief that such death has been occasioned by the act of another by unlawful means, he must forthwith make inquiry of the facts and circumstances of such death, by taking the sworn statement, in writing, of the witnesses having personal knowledge thereof; and if, upon such preliminary inquiry, the coroner is satisfied from the evidence that there is reasonable ground for believing that such death has been occasioned by the act of another, by unlawful means, he must forthwith summon a jury of six discreet householders of the county to appear before him forthwith at a specified place, and inquire into the cause of such death.

4802 (3992). **Oath of jury.** — When five or more of the jurors appear, they must be sworn to inquire who the person was, and when, where, and by what means he came to his death; and to render a true verdict thereon, according to the evidence offered them, or arising from the inspection of the body.

4803 (3993). **Witnesses and surgeons summoned.** — The coroner may issue subpœnas for witnesses, returnable forthwith, or at such time and place as he may appoint; he must summon and examine as a witness any person who, in his opinion, or that of any of the jury, has any knowledge of the facts; and he may also summon as a witness a surgeon or physician, who must, in the presence of the jury, inspect the body, and give a professional opinion as to the cause of the death.

4804 (3994). **Service of subpœnas; proceedings against defaulting witnesses.** — The sheriff or any constable must serve the subpœnas, or they may be served by the coroner; and if any witness, being subpœnaed, fails to attend, the coroner must indorse on the subpœna his default, sign his name thereto, and return the same to the clerk of the circuit or city court of the county, within five days thereafter; and such witness must be proceeded against in such court, in the name of the state, as if he was a defaulter therein; the indorsement of the coroner being presumptive evidence of the default.

4805 (3995). **Witness refusing to answer, misdemeanor.** Any witness, who refuses to answer any question in relation to the cause of such death, except on the ground that it may criminate himself, is guilty of a misdemeanor, and must be committed to jail by the coroner, unless he gives bail in the sum of five hundred dollars, to appear at the circuit or city court and answer such offense; and, on conviction thereof, must be fined not less than two hundred, nor more than five hundred dollars, and may be imprisoned not exceeding three months.

4806 (4004). **Coroner may administer oaths.** — Coroners shall have the right to administer oaths to persons on preliminary examinations provided for by this chapter.

4807 (3996). **Verdict of jury.**—After inspecting the body and hearing the evidence, the jury must render their verdict, and certify it by an inquisition in writing signed by them, setting forth who the person is, and when, where and by what means he came to his death; and if the death was occasioned by the act of another, by unlawful means, who is guilty thereof; and if the person, means, or manner of his death, or the person by whose act he came to his death, are not discovered by the evidence, the inquisition must so state; and if there is no evidence tending to show that the deceased came to his death by the unlawful act of another, the inquisition must also state that fact.

4808 (3997). **Inquest returned to court; witnesses recognized, etc.**—The inquisition thus taken must be returned by the coroner forthwith, together with the written statement under oath taken by him on the preliminary investigation, to the clerk of the circuit or city court of the county; and the coroner must also require all the material witnesses to enter into an undertaking to appear at the circuit or city court, if in session, and if not, at the next term thereof, and may require surety to such undertaking; and, on the failure of a witness to enter therein, may commit him until he enters into the same.

4809 (3998). **Warrant of arrest against supposed criminal; arrest, commitment, etc.**—If the jury find that the deceased came to his death by the act of another, by unlawful means, the coroner may issue a warrant of arrest for such person, which may be executed in the same manner as provided in chapter three, title three, part five, and the person, when arrested, must be brought before a magistrate of the county in which the inquest was held, who must proceed to examine the charge, and commit, bail, or discharge the defendant, as upon a warrant of arrest under the provisions of such chapter.

4810 (3999). **Money, etc., of deceased paid into county treasury; penalty.**—The coroner must, within thirty days after an inquest on a dead body, deliver to the county treasurer any money or other property which may be found on the body, unless claimed in the meantime by the legal representatives of the deceased; if he fails to do so, the treasurer may proceed against him for the amount or value thereof, on ten days' notice to him and his sureties, or against any of them served therewith, and recover the same, with twenty per cent. damages on the amount or value thereof.

4811 (4000). **Same; how disposed of.**—Upon the receipt of the money by the treasurer, he must place it to the credit of the county. If it is other property, he must, within three months, sell it at the court-house of the county, at public auction, upon reasonable public notice, and must, in like manner, place the proceeds to the credit of the county.

4812 (4001). **Same; paid to the legal representative of deceased.**—If such money in the treasury is demanded in six years by the legal representatives of the deceased, the treasurer must pay it to them, after deducting the fees of the coroner, expenses of sale, and five per cent. on the balance for the treasurer; or it may be paid at any time thereafter upon the order of the county commissioners.

4813 (4002). **Compensation of surgeons and physicians.** Any surgeon or physician, who, being duly subpœnaed, attends a coroner's inquest, examines the body, and gives a professional opinion thereon, is entitled to receive five dollars, with one dollar additional for each mile he may be compelled to travel in attending such inquest; to be collected out of the estate of the deceased, if solvent; and if insolvent, to be paid out of the county treasury.

4814 (4003). **When inquest held by justice of the peace; fees.**—If the coroner is absent from the county, or is unable to act, any justice of the peace may hold an inquest on the body of any deceased person, under the rules and regulations in this chapter prescribed; and is entitled to the same compensation for his services that is by law allowed to the coroner.

CHAPTER 7.

INQUISITION AND PROCEEDINGS IN REGARD TO INSANE PRISONERS.

4815 (1487). **Court orders to hospital defendant acquitted on account of insanity; expenses.**—When a person has escaped indictment, or been acquitted of a criminal charge on the ground of insanity, the court, being informed by the jury, or otherwise, of the fact, must carefully inquire and ascertain whether his insanity in any degree continues, and, if it does, shall order him in safe custody, and to be sent to the hospital; the state must defray his expenses while there, but may recover the amount so paid from his estate, or from any guardian or relative who would have been bound to provide for, and maintain him elsewhere.

4816 (1488). **Inquisition upon alleged insane prisoner; further proceedings; expenses.**—If any person in confinement, under indictment, or for want of bail for good behavior, or for keeping the peace, or appearing as a witness, or in consequence of any summary conviction, or by an order of any justice, appears to be insane, the judge of the circuit court of the county where he is confined must institute a careful investigation, call a respectable physician and other credible witnesses, and, if he deems it necessary, may call a jury, and for that purpose he is empowered to compel attendance of witnesses and jurors; and if it be satisfactorily proved that the person is insane, the judge may discharge him from imprisonment and order his safe custody and removal to the hospital. where he must remain until restored to his right mind; and then, if the judge shall have so directed, the superintendent must inform the judge and sheriff, whereupon the person must be remanded to prison, and criminal proceedings be resumed, or he be otherwise discharged; the provisions of the preceding section, requiring the state to defray the expenses of a patient sent to the hospital, shall be equally applicable to similar expenses arising under this and the following section.

One indicted and enlarged on bail not "in confinement," as meant by statute. Ex parte Trice. 53 Ala. 546. Jurisdiction vests in judge, not in court; notice to person affected indispensable; record must recite every fact, else judgment a nullity.—Ib. Fact of mental unsoundness of person on bail, endangering neighborhood property, gives judge no authority to confine prisoner in asylum.—Ib. Effect of insanity occurring after commission of offense.—See Jones' case. 13 Ala. 153; Marler's case, 67 Ala. 55. Admissibility of former evidence of witness who has since become insane.—Marler's case, 67 Ala. 55. Admissibility of record of proceedings under the statute.—Ib

4817 (1489). **Powers of county courts and justices in misdemeanors.**—Persons charged with misdemeanors, and acquitted on the ground of insanity, may be kept in custody and sent to the hospital in the same way as persons charged with crimes; and the county courts and justices of the peace have the same power in reference to persons charged before them with misdemeanors, as is bestowed upon the circuit courts in the two preceding sections.

CHAPTER 8.

IMPEACHMENT OF OFFICERS.

As amended, Jan. 21, 1879, p. 155, sec. 1.

4818 (4047). **Who may be impeached; grounds of impeachment.**—The following officers may be impeached and removed from office, to-wit: Chancellors, judges of the circuit or city courts, judges of probate courts, solicitors of the circuits, judges of the inferior courts from which an appeal may be taken direct to the supreme court; sheriffs, clerks of the circuit, city, or criminal courts, tax-collectors, tax-assessors, county treasurers, coroners, justices of the peace, notaries public, constables, and all other county officers, and mayors and intendants of incorporated cities and towns in this state, for the following causes, to-wit: Willful neglect of duty, corruption in office, habitual drunkenness, incompetency, or any offense involving moral turpitude while in office, or committed under color thereof, or connected therewith.

Ex parte Wiley, 54 Ala. 226.

Ib. sec. 23.

4819 (4069). **Disqualification a ground of impeachment.** Any of the officers named in the preceding section, who shall be disqualified by law from holding office in this state, may be impeached and removed from office on proceedings instituted and prosecuted in the manner herein provided.

4820 (4048). **Proceedings in name of state; upon whose information commenced.** — Proceedings under sections two and three of article seven of the constitution shall be instituted in the name of the State of Alabama, in the nature of an information, by the attorney-general, or circuit solicitor, or upon the information of such other persons as are by this chapter allowed to institute the same; and all such proceedings shall be conducted, and all process shall issue, in the name of the State of Alabama. Ib. sec. 2.

Seawell's case, 64 Ala. 225.

4821 (4049). **Five resident tax-payers may institute; must give bond.** — Any five resident tax-payers of the division, circuit, district, county, city, or town, for which the officer sought to be impeached was elected or appointed, may institute proceedings of impeachment, under either of the sections of the constitution above expressed, upon giving bond, with sufficient sureties, payable to the officer sought to be impeached, conditioned to prosecute the impeachment to effect, and, failing therein, to pay all costs that may be incurred; which bond shall be taken and approved by the clerk of the court before which the proceedings are proposed to be instituted. Ib. sec. 3.

4822 (4050). **Of the information.** — Such information shall be addressed to the court before which the trial is to be had, and shall specify, with reasonable certainty, the offense, offenses, or other grounds of impeachment, charged against the officer, within the provisions of section one of article seven of the constitution, and shall contain a succinct statement of the facts constituting the matters complained of, and an appropriate prayer for process and relief, and shall be signed by the attorney-general, or solicitor, or by counsel, as the case may be; and when such information is by tax-payers, the names of such tax-payers must be joined as plaintiffs with the state. Ib. sec. 4.

4823 (4051). **In supreme court; order, summons, and copy of information; continuances; precedence of cause.** If such information be filed under section two of article seven of the constitution, the supreme court, in term time, or a justice thereof, in vacation, shall make an order, requiring the officer proceeded against to appear at a place, and on a day, which may be either in term time or vacation, to be specified in the order, and answer the information; the clerk of the court shall issue a summons, in which shall be set forth a copy of the order, directed to any sheriff of the State of Alabama, which, together with a copy of the information, shall be served on the defendant; and if the summons is served twenty days before the day specified in the order, the defendant shall answer the information on the day specified, and if the summons is served less than twenty days before the day so specified, the court, in term time, or a justice thereof, in vacation, shall, on the day so specified, make an order setting another day, not exceeding twenty days thereafter, on which the defendant shall answer the information; and another day may be set, and other summons issued as often as may be necessary, and continuances may be granted in the Ib. sec. 5.

discretion of the court; but the cases herein provided for shall have precedence and priority over all other business in the court.

Ib. sec. 6. **4824** (4052). **Proceedings in supreme court.**—In all original proceedings commenced under this chapter in the supreme court, either party shall have compulsory process to compel the attendance of witnesses, to be issued by the clerk of the court, and served by the marshal of the court, or by any sheriff of the state ; and such witnesses shall be sworn and examined on the trial in open court; the examination of such witnesses shall be conducted, and defaulting witnesses shall be subject to similar proceedings and penalties, as in criminal cases in the circuit court; but, on the written consent of the defendant, the court, or a justice thereof, in term time or vacation, may appoint one or more examiners, whose duty it shall be, jointly or severally, as may be directed in the order of appointment, to take and certify, by such day as may be fixed in the order of appointment, the evidence against and for the defendant, on the several specifications contained in the information ; and the charges shall be tried by the court on such evidence so taken and certified, and such documentary evidence as may be offered ; and the court for the trial and impeachment may sit or continue its sessions at any time without reference to the terms as prescribed by law.

Ib. sec. 7. **4825** (4053). **Powers of examiners; and by whom their process issued.**—The examiner or examiners so appointed shall have power to issue subpœnas for witnesses, which shall be served by the sheriff of the proper county, or by any special constable appointed by such examiner or examiners, to compel the attendance of witnesses by attachment, and to punish for contempt by fine or imprisonment in the county jail, and to administer oaths to witnesses; and the oaths administered by such examiners shall, in all respects, be deemed and held to be lawful oaths.

Ib. sec. 8. **4826** (4054). **Proceedings before examiners.**—Either party shall have the right to appear before the examiner by himself and counsel, and, to this end, shall have five days' notice of the time and place of his sittings; each party shall have compulsory process to compel the attendance of witnesses; and from the rulings of the examiner on any question of the admissibility and legality of evidence offered, either party may reserve an exception, to be decided by the supreme court.

Ib. sec. 9. **4827** (4055). **When proceedings in circuit, city, or criminal court.**—If such information is filed in the circuit, city, or criminal court, the judge of such court shall make an order, either in term time or vacation, requiring the officer proceeded against to appear at a place, and on a day, which may be either in term time or vacation, to be specified in the order, and answer the information ; the clerk of the court shall issue a summons, in which shall be set forth a copy of the order, directed to any sheriff of the State of Alabama, and which, together with a copy of the information, shall be served on such defendant; and another day may be set, and other summons issued, as often as may be necessary, and continuances may be granted in the discretion of the court.

4828 (4056). **In case the sheriff or clerk is impeached.**—In all cases in which the sheriff is the party accused, all process relating to the cause shall be executed by the coroner of the county, and, if there is no coroner, then by such other person as may be appointed by the court, or the judge in vacation; and if the accused is the clerk of the court, then the court, or judge thereof, shall appoint a special clerk, who shall be some reliable and responsible person, and who shall perform and discharge all the duties of the office as to this particular case, under the direction of the court, or the judge thereof, until such case is finally determined, and shall be liable to all the penalties prescribed by law for any misfeasance, or malfeasance, or non-feasance, in the discharge of the duties of such office.

4829 (4057). **When cause stands for trial; trial by jury;** **precedence of cause.**—When the information is filed in the circuit, city, or criminal court, if the summons is served twenty days before the day specified in the order, such cause shall stand for trial on that day, and if the summons is served less than twenty days before the day specified in the order, then the court, in term time, or the judge thereof, in vacation, shall, on the day specified in the order, make an order setting another day on which the defendant shall answer the information, and the cause stand for trial; and the cause, if in term time, shall have precedence and priority over all other business in such court; and, whether in term time or vacation, shall be proceeded with in all respects as civil actions at law are conducted, with the right to either party to except to the rulings of the court, and to reserve such exceptions as in civil causes; and the defendant shall be entitled to a trial by jury on any issue of fact, whenever he demands the same; and if the trial is had in vacation, upon a demand for a jury, the judge of the court shall make an order requiring a jury to be summoned by the sheriff, in the manner provided for by law for summoning special juries in the county of the trial.

4830 (4063). **Time of trial.**—When such proceedings are in- stituted in a circuit, city, or criminal court, and the day specified in the order of the judge on which the defendant is to appear and answer is in vacation, a special term of such court shall be held on such day without further notice or order, and special terms of such courts shall be held on such day or days in vacation, which may thereafter be set, and to which such cause shall be continued, without further notice or order, unless a regular term of such court shall intervene, when the cause shall stand for trial at such regular term. Whenever any such cause stands for trial at a regular term of such court, and is not tried for any cause during such term, it shall not be continued to the next regular term, but the court shall make an order fixing a day in vacation for the trial of the cause, and for a special term of the court to be held on that day, at which special term it shall be tried, unless continued for good cause. At no special term of the court, held under the provisions of this section, shall any other business be transacted.

4831 (4058). **Verification of information when filed by tax-** **payers; costs.**—When the proceedings in impeachment are instituted by tax-payers, the information must be verified by the petitioners, or any one of them. The costs shall be given against the unsuccessful party, as in other cases, to be collected by execution.

Ib. sec. 13.   **4832** (4059). **Duties and liabilities of sheriffs, etc.; fees of clerk, etc.**—The sheriff, coroner, or constable, to whom process is issued under the provisions of this chapter, shall perform all the duties as sheriffs are required to perform them; shall be liable to all the penalties to which sheriffs, in similar cases, are liable, and shall be entitled to the same fees as sheriffs are entitled to for similar services. The examiners shall be entitled to such compensation as the supreme court may determine as fair equivalent for the services performed; and all such fees and compensation shall be taxed in the bill of costs; but no costs shall be adjudged against the state, nor against the successful petitioners on a return of no property found against the defendant, but may be paid out of the state treasury in all cases when the governor thinks it right to pay the same.

Ib. see. 14.   **4833** (4060). **Final record to be made.**—The clerk, or if he is the accused, the person acting as clerk, of the court in which the trial is had, shall make and preserve a final record of the proceedings, in all respects as clerks of the circuit courts are required to do of trials had therein; and all laws applicable thereto are made applicable to final records and proceedings under this chapter.

Ib. sec. 15.   **4834** (4061). **Appeals to supreme court.**—From any final judgment or decision rendered by any circuit, city, or criminal court, in proceedings under this chapter, an appeal shall lie to the supreme court in favor of the unsuccessful party; and such appeal must be taken within ten days after judgment rendered, and shall be taken to the first day to which such appeal can be made returnable, and not afterwards; and notice of appeals shall be given as in other cases. Such appeal shall have precedence or priority of all other appeals.

Ib. sec. 16.   **4835** (4062). **Security for costs.**—If the appeal be taken by the state in cases instituted in its name, by the attorney-general or solicitor, no security for costs shall be required. In all other cases, security for costs shall be required as in appeals to the supreme court in civil causes; and such appeal shall not suspend the judgment of conviction.

Ib. sec. 18.   **4836** (4064). **Amendments allowed; to what facts witnesses may testify.**—In all cases instituted under the provisions of this chapter, any and all amendments, necessary to a trial of the cause upon its merits, shall be allowed; and witnesses may testify to any facts or circumstances within their knowledge, which may show or tend to show that the accused has been guilty of any of the offenses or delinquencies charged against him, or is incompetent, as the case may be; and, in like manner, the accused must have a similar right to introduce like evidence to show that he has not been guilty of the offenses or delinquencies charged against him, or that he is not incompetent, as the case may be.

Ib sec. 19.   **4837** (4065). **Duty of clerks in certifying vacancy in office on conviction.**—It shall be the duty of the clerk of the supreme court, in all cases, when final judgment of conviction is rendered in that court, on appeal or otherwise, forthwith to certify the vacancy thus created to the appointing power, with a copy of the judgment; and, in like manner, the clerk of the circuit, city, or criminal court shall certify to the appointing power any final judgment of conviction rendered in such court, from which no appeal is taken.

4838 (4066). **Extent of judgment; liability of accused to indictment.**—No statute of limitations shall be valid as a bar to any of the proceedings provided for by this chapter; but the penalties in cases arising under the provisions of this chapter shall not extend beyond the removal from office, and the disqualification from holding office under the authority of this state for the term for which the accused was elected or appointed; but the accused shall be liable to indictment, trial and punishment, as prescribed by law. *Ib. sec. 20.*

4839 (4067). **Duty of grand jury; when report of grand jury transmitted to attorney-general.**—It shall be the duty of every grand jury to investigate and make diligent inquiry concerning any alleged misconduct or incompetency of any public officer in the county which may be brought to their notice; and if, on such investigation and inquiry, they find that such officer, for any cause mentioned in this chapter, ought to be removed from office, they shall so report to the court, setting forth the facts, which report shall be entered on the minutes of the court. If the officer so reported against is one of those included in section two, article seven of the constitution, the clerk of the court shall transmit a certified copy of such report to the attorney-general. If the officer so reported against is the presiding judge of the court, the report must not be made to the court, or entered on the minutes; and, in such cases, the report of the grand jury must be signed by the foreman, and countersigned by the solicitor of the circuit, who must transmit the same to the attorney-general. *Ib. sec. 21.*

Seawell's case, 64 Ala. 225.

4840 (4068). **Duty of attorney-general and solicitors.**—It shall be the duty of the attorney-general to institute proceedings under this chapter, and prosecute the same against any officer included in section two, article seven of the constitution, when the supreme court shall so order, or when the governor shall, in writing, direct the same, or when it appears from the report of any grand jury that any such officer ought to be removed from office, for any cause mentioned in the first section of this chapter. And it shall be the duty of the solicitor of the circuit to institute proceedings under this chapter, and prosecute the same against any officer included in section three, article seven of the constitution, when the circuit, city, or criminal court of the county shall so order, or whenever it appears from the report of the grand jury that any such officer ought to be removed from office for any cause mentioned in the first section of this chapter. *Ib. sec. 22*

4841 (4070). **Proceedings when defendant has removed, absconded, or secreted himself.**—If, in any case of proceedings for impeachment or removal from office under this chapter, the defendant has removed, absconded, or secreted himself, so *Ib. sec. 24.*

that the summons cannot be served on him personally, the sheriff, or other officer to whom the summons is issued, shall serve the same by leaving a copy thereof at the office of the defendant, if known, or at his last place of residence; and the sheriff shall forthwith publish in some newspaper, published in the county, or if no newspaper is published in the county, then in the newspaper published nearest thereto, a copy of the summons and notice to the defendant where a copy thereof had been left for him. The sheriff shall make return of the summons as in other cases, stating the facts; and such service shall be as valid, to all intents and purposes, as personal service on the defendant; and if the defendant fails to appear pursuant to the summons, whether served personally, or as provided by this section, the court shall cause the plea of not guilty to be entered for him, and the trial shall proceed as in other cases.

CHAPTER 9.

PROCEEDINGS IN CASES OF BASTARDY.

4842 (4071). **Reputed father of bastard arrested on complaint of mother; warrant.**—When any single woman, pregnant with, or delivered of a bastard child, makes complaint on oath to any justice of the county where she is so pregnant or delivered, accusing any one of being the father of such child, such justice must issue a warrant against such person, and cause him to be brought before him.

In absence of statutory provisions, father under no legal obligation to support illegitimate child.—Simmons v. Bull, 21 Ala. 501. Proceedings under this chapter partake of the nature of both civil and criminal proceedings; may be styled quasi criminal.—Hunter's case, 67 Ala. 81; Smith's case, 73 Ala. 11; Dorgan's case, 72 Ala. 173. Not a misdemeanor.—Ib. 173; Hunter's case, 67 Ala. 81; Satterwhite's case. 28 Ala. 70. Complaint must aver, or warrant must show, that woman was single.—Smith's case, 73 Ala. 11; Dorgan's case; 72 Ala. 173; Williams' case, 29 Ala. 9. Else justice has no jurisdiction; must also appear that woman was pregnant or delivered in the county.—Ib. 9. May hear evidence outside of complaint.—Ib. 9. Technical rules not required in proceedings like this.—Ib. 9; Austin v. Pickett, 9 Ala. 102; Dorgan's case, 72 Ala. 173; Crosby v. Hawthorn, 25 Ala. 221. Married woman cannot prefer this complaint, although her husband has left her.—Kerr's case, 17 Ala. 328. Statute in this case penal, and must be strictly construed.—Ib. Complaint before birth of child made in county of mother's residence; if after birth, made in county where child born.—Wilson's case, 18 Ala. 757.

4843 (4075). **Justice to summon witnesses.**—The justice of the peace must, on the application of the complainant, or the accused, issue subpœnas for witnesses.

4844 (4072). **Examination; if probable cause, held under bond to appear at court and answer.**—Such justice must then, in the presence of the accused, examine the complainant and her witnesses, and may examine also the accused and his witnesses, respecting the charge; and, if it appears that there is probable cause to believe that the accused is guilty of the charge, must require him to enter into bond, with sufficient surety, in a sum not exceeding one thousand dollars, to be approved by such justice, payable to the State of Alabama, and conditioned that the accused will appear at the next term of the circuit court of such county.

Justice no power to render final judgment.—Nicholson's case, 72 Ala. 176. His duties purely preliminary to ascertain probable cause.—Ib.; Smith's case, 73 Ala. 11. An examination and discharge do not preclude another examination.—Nicholson's case, supra. Nor can action of justice be pleaded in bar to second proceedings.—Ib. Mother of child may accept compromise, and dismiss prosecution Martin's case, 62 Ala. 119; Robinson v. Crenshaw, 2 Stew. & Port. 276; Ashburne v. Gibson, 9 Port. 549; Wilson's case, 18 Ala. 757; Merritt v. Flemming, 42 Ala. 234. Bond failing to require appearance at "next term" of court, is void, and proceedings under it *coram non judice.*—Seale v. McClanahan, 21 Ala. 345. Sufficiency of bond cannot be questioned, if defendant appears; when not invalid. Hanna's case, 60 Ala. 102. Formerly held that appearance bond should be made payable to governor and his successors, the statute being silent on this point.—Trawick v. Davis, 4 Ala. 328; Chaudron v. Fitzpatrick, 19 Ala. 649; Lake's case, 2 Stew 395.

4845 (4073). **Justice to return bond to circuit court.**—Such justice must return such bond and complaint to the clerk of the circuit court, by the first day of the term at which the accused is bound to appear.

Proceedings before justice become part of record.—Wilson's case, 18 Ala. 757. What necessary under this section to enable circuit court to take cognizance of the cause.—Hanna's case, 60 Ala. 102. Warrant may also be returned, and from its recitals jurisdiction may be sustained.—Williams' case, 29 Ala. 9. Formerly proceedings had in county and probate courts.—See Moore v. Maguire, 26 Ala. 461; Castleberry's case, 23 Ala. 85.

4846 (4074). **Reputed father imprisoned on default of bond.**—On the failure to give the bond as required, the justice must commit the accused to jail until he gives the same, or is otherwise discharged by law.

4847 (4075). **Clerk to issue subpœnas.**—The clerk of the circuit court, after the return of the bond, must, on the application of the complainant or accused, issue subpœnas for witnesses.

4848 (4092). **State and accused parties to record.**—The proceedings in bastardy are conducted in the name of the state as plaintiff, and the accused as defendant; but no proceeding shall be instituted under this chapter after the lapse of one year from the birth of the child, unless the defendant has, in meanwhile, acknowledged or supported the child.

Though the state, and not the woman, is a party, yet if state fails, she may be liable for costs; infancy of complainant immaterial.—Hanna's case, 60 Ala. 102. The female is merely the informer, not a party, and she recovers nothing.—Pruitt's case, 16 Ala. 707. The mother should not be made party to a writ of error, prosecuted by the father.—Trawick v. Davis, 4 Ala. 328.

4849 (4076). **Forfeiture of bond; conditional judgment and writ of arrest.**—If the accused does not appear, his bond is forfeited, and a conditional judgment may be rendered thereon, and the like proceedings had as in case of the forfeiture of bonds for indictable offenses; and the clerk must issue a writ of arrest, as in criminal cases on indictment found.

Appearance bond binding on all obligors until final disposition of case.—Trawick v. Davis, 4 Ala. 328. Defendant liable on bond for non-appearance, although not convicted.—Lake's case, 2 Stew. 395.

4850 (4077). **Re-arrest; defendant discharged on bond of one thousand dollars.**—The sheriff, on arresting the defendant on such writ of arrest, may discharge him on his giving bail for his appearance at court, in the sum of not more than one thousand dollars, to answer a complaint of bastardy; and if such bond is forfeited, a conditional judgment may be rendered thereon, a writ of arrest issue, and the same proceedings had as often as may be necessary.

4851 (4078). **On appearance, issue made up.**—The court, on the appearance of the accused, must, if he demand it, cause an issue to be made up, to ascertain whether he is the real father of the child or not.

Necessary to submit case to jury only when reputed father demands it.—Trawick v. Davis, 4 Ala. 328; Lake's case, 2 Stew. 395. And the only issue tried by jury was, under former statute, as to the paternity of the child.—Ib. 328; Ib. 395. Allegation that complainant was a single woman, is part of issue made up and tried.—Dorgan's case, 72 Ala. 173. Number of challenges of jurors not prescr bed. Ib. But see present statute. Defect in affidavit and warrant raised by motion to quash, not by demurrer; but motion must be made before justice, else too late. Smith's case, 73 Ala. 11. After appearance and trial, too late to object to recognizance taken by justice.—Wilson's case, 18 Ala. 757. After plea of guilty and execution of proper bond, etc., too late to object to defects in complaint or process before justice.—Pruitt's case, 16 Ala. 705. Objection to voidable, defective warrant must be made by motion to quash before regular appearance of defendant. Trawick v. Davis, 4 Ala. 328. Not required that evidence should prove guilt beyond a reasonable doubt; sufficiency of proof, etc.—Hunter's case, 67 Ala. 82. See Satterwhite's case, 28 Ala. 65. No statute of limitations; reason therefor.—Satterwhite's case, 28 Ala. 65. Now changed by statute. Action of justice not pleadable as former acquittal or conviction.—Nicholson's case, 72 Ala. 176. Release or compromise permitted, and ground for plea in bar, but not for motion to dismiss; but release by infant mother, if repudiated by her, is no bar.—Wilson's case, 18 Ala. 757. But compromise made or offered no evidence of guilt, if no admission of fact is made.—Martin's case, 62 Ala. 119. Relevancy of suspicious circumstances implying admission or consciousness of guilt.—Nicholson's case, 72 Ala. 176. Verdict affirming that defendant is real father of child sufficient.—Berryman's case, 9 Ala. 455.

Feb. 17, 1885, p. 187.
4852. Challenge of jurors.—On a trial of the issue before a jury, each party has the right to challenge six jurors peremptorily.

4853 (4079). **Either party may be examined.**—On the trial of such issue, the accuser and accused are each entitled to their oath.

Either accused or complainant a competent witness; and their testimony weighed like that of other witnesses.—Satterwhite's case, 28 Ala. 65. Misleading charge as to sufficiency of proof, when two witnesses of equal credibility swear against each other.—Dorgan's case, 72 Ala. 175.

4854 (4080). **On conviction, judgment for costs, and bond required to support and educate child.**—On the trial of such issue, if found against the defendant, judgment must be rendered against him for the costs, and he must also be required to enter into bond and surety, to be approved by the judge, in the sum of one thousand dollars, payable to the state, and conditioned to pay such sum, not exceeding fifty dollars a year, as the court may prescribe, on the first Monday in January in each year, for ten years, to the judge of probate of the county, for the support and education of the child, which bond must be recorded.

Correct construction of statute is, that accused be compelled to support child. not until it is ten years of age, but ten years from date of judgment.—Pruitt's case, 16 Ala. 705. Accused liable for costs if convicted.—Berryman's case, 9 Ala. 455. Form of judgment entry; what must show.—Smith's case, 73 Ala. 12. Erroneous judgment; what a misprision.—Wilson's case, 18 Ala. 757. Amendment of judgment allowed to require payments on first Monday, instead of first day of January, etc.—Williams' case, 29 Ala. 9. Under former statutes, judgment should be rendered in favor of judge of county court.—Brown's case, Minor, 208; Trawick v. Davis, 4 Ala. 328. But omission to state in whose favor it was rendered, would not reverse.—Yarborough's case, 15 Ala. 556; Seale v. McClanahan, 21 Ala. 345.

4855 (4081). **Judgment on failure to give bond.**—On failure to give such bond, the court must render judgment against the defendant for such sum as, at legal interest, will produce the amount directed to be paid yearly; and he must also be sentenced to hard labor for the county for one year, unless in the meantime he executes the bond required, or pays the judgment and costs.

See note to preceding section.   Sufficiency of judgment.—Austin v. Pickett, 9 Ala. 102; Berryman's case.—Ib. 455.   Imprisonment not unconstitutional.—Paulk's case, 51 Ala. 427.   Judgment not sustained by evidence of a bond; would not authorize execution.—Isaacs' case, 5 Stew. & Port. 402.

4856 (4082). **Execution on bond issues on failure to make payments.**—If such bond is given, on failure to make any of the payments required, to the judge of probate, on the first Monday in January in each year, execution may issue for such amount against all the obligors to the bond, on the application of the judge of probate, which, when collected, must be paid to him.

Must be a bond or evidence of a bond, to authorize execution.—Isaacs' case, 5 Stew. & Port. 402.   Direction in judgment that execution issue thereon for each default, held regular.—Trawick v. Davis, 4 Ala. 332.

4857 (4083). **Bond; when given after the adjournment of court.**—If such bond is not given before the adjournment of court, it may be given at any time before the term of imprisonment expires, and, in such case, must be approved by the judge of probate and recorded and filed in the office of the clerk of the circuit court, and execution may issue thereon from time to time, as under the provisions of the preceding section, and the amount, when collected, paid to the judge of probate.

4858 (4084). **Defendant discharged on filing bond, paying costs, etc.**—In the case provided for in the preceding section, the defendant must be discharged from imprisonment on payment of the costs, and the judgment against him is discharged.

4859 (4085). **Proceedings when defendant is not found.** If the accused does not appear, after the return of two writs of arrest against him "not found" by the sheriff of the county in which the court to which the complaint is returned is held, the facts stated in the complaint must be taken as admitted, and judgment rendered against the accused as provided for by section 4855 (4081); and at any time before the payment of such judgment, the defendant may be arrested by a writ of arrest thereon, directed to the sheriff, commanding him to take the defendant and deliver him to the proper authorities for the execution of the judgment.

Investigation of charge and judgment in absence of accused.—McClanahan's case, 21 Ala. 345; Trawick v. Davis, 4 Ala. 328; Yarborough's case, 15 Ala. 558.   Could be attached, if absent, and brought into court, and ordered to remain in custody until he gives bond required by statute.—Yarborough's case, 15 Ala. 556.

4860 (4086). **Discharged from imprisonment on paying judgment or giving bond.**—In the case provided for in the preceding section, the defendant can be discharged from imprisonment by the payment of the judgment, or executing the bond in conformity with the provisions of section 4854 (4080).

4861 (4087). **Money collected on bond applied to support of child.**—The amount collected on the forfeiture of any bond for the appearance of the defendant, and on the judgment rendered against him, must be paid into the county treasury; and the interest thereon, not exceeding the yearly sum directed to be paid by the court, must be paid to the judge of probate for the support and education of the child.

4862 (4088). **Such payment not made after giving bond.** But such payment must not be made after the defendant gives the bond required by section 4854 (4080).

4863 (4089). **Guardian appointed to receive child's money.** The judge of probate must appoint a guardian for such child, and, upon his giving bond and security as other guardians, the amount received by the judge of probate must be paid to him.

4864 (4090). **Death of child or marriage of parents; effect of.**—If the child is not born alive, or if, being born alive, it dies, or on the marriage of the mother and reputed father, on the ascertainment of such facts by the judge of probate, on motion to the circuit court, and proof thereof, an entry of record must be made thereof, and the bond be declared void, the judgment vacated, the defendant discharged, and the portion of such judgment paid into the county treasury must be paid, on the certificate of the clerk of the circuit court of the vacation of such judgment, to the defendant.

Death of child pending proceedings was held no ground for motion to dismiss, but good for plea *puis darrein continuance.*—Satterwhite's case, 32 Ala. 578. Not necessary, on appeal, that record should disclose that child was living at time of judgment.—Trawick v. Davis, 4 Ala. 328. Marriage of woman does not *ipso facto* abate proceedings.—Berryman's case, 9 Ala. 455. Nor is marriage inferred from change of name in subsequent proceedings.—Ib.

4865 (4091). **Complainant pays costs on verdict for defendant.**—In case the issue provided for by section 4851 (4078) is found against the complainant, judgment for costs must be rendered against her.

4866 (4093). **Either party may appeal; security for costs, execution, etc.**—Either party may appeal to the supreme court within thirty days after judgment. If the appeal is taken by the state, the complainant must give security for the costs of the appeal, if the judgment is affirmed; and the defendant, also, if the appeal is taken by him, must give the same security, to be approved by the clerk of the circuit court, the names of the sureties certified with the record to the appellate court, and execution may issue for the costs of the appeal against them from such court, if the judgment of the circuit court is affirmed. But when either the complainant or defendant makes affidavit that she or he is unable, after diligent effort, to make the appeal bond, they may appeal without any bond.

The security not required to be in any prescribed form; may be either a bond or simple acknowledgment in writing.—Satterwhite's case, 28 Ala. 68, explaining Williams' case, 26 Ala. 85, where the bond was held defective. Misdescription of judgment would be fatal; what omission may be supplied by comparison with clerk's certificate, or other parts of record.—Ib. 68. When supreme court will not reverse because evidence set out in bill of exceptions fails to show that complainant was a single or unmarried woman.—Dorgan's case, 72 Ala. 175.

TITLE V.

FEES, COSTS AND DISPOSITION OF FINES, FORFEITURES AND PRO-
CEEDS OF HARD LABOR.

CHAPTER 1.—Fees and costs in criminal cases.
      2.—Disposition of fines, forfeitures and proceeds of hard labor.

CHAPTER 1.

FEES AND COSTS.

ARTICLE 1.—Fees of attorney-general.
     2.—Fees and commissions of solicitors.
     3.—Fees of clerks of circuit and city courts.
     4.—Fees of sheriffs.
     5.—Fees of coroners.
     6.—Fees of justices of the peace.
     7.—Fees of constables.
     8.—Fees in county court.
     9.—Fees of jurors.
   10.—Fees of witnesses.
   11.—General provisions concerning fees and costs.

ARTICLE I.

FEES OF ATTORNEY-GENERAL.

4867 (5048). **Attorney-general's fees.**—In all criminal cases taken to the supreme court, if judgment is there rendered in favor of the state, the attorney-general is entitled to a fee of fifteen dollars, to be taxed and collected as costs.

ARTICLE II.

FEES AND COMMISSIONS OF SOLICITORS.

4868 (5047). **Solicitors' fees.**—Solicitors are entitled to the following fees, to be taxed against the defendant, on conviction, and if he is insolvent, to be paid out of the fines and forfeitures in the county treasury,—that is to say:

For each conviction under section 4055 (4208), or 4068 (4445)..$150 00
For each conviction under section 3942 (4144), 3932 (4169), ¹4075 (4222), or 3847 (4897).............. 100 00 ¹Feb. 17, 1885, p. 189.
For each conviction under section 4059 (4211), 4061 (4212), 4064 (4214), 4143 (4433), 3725 (4295), 3729

(4296), 3731 (4301), 3726 (4297), 3727 (4298), 3734 (4300), 3732 (4302), 3733 (4303), 3736 (4304), 3738 (4305), 3739 (4306), 3740 (4307), 3742 (4311), or 3780 (4346)..$ 75 00

For each conviction under section 4057 (4209), or 4058 (4210).. 60 00

For each conviction under section 4012 (4184), 4016 (4185), 4033 (4199), 4038 (4205), 4039 (4206), 3848 (4398), or 3849 (4399)... 37 50

1 Feb. 17, 1885, p. 161 ; Feb. 22, 1883, p. 140, sec. 22

For each conviction under section 4052 (4207), except when the defendant pleads guilty; and for each conviction under section 3775 (4109), 3776 (4110), 3777 (4111), 4032 (4200), [1]4041, [1]4042; and for each conviction of felony not otherwise provided for 30 00

For each conviction under section 4063 (4213), 3901 (4271), or [1]3986... 25 00

2 Feb. 12, 1879, p. 28.

[2]For each conviction of a violation of the revenue law, not otherwise provided for......... .... 30 00

In proceedings to vacate charter, or for usurpation, or forfeiture of office, if judgment is rendered for the plaintiff 100 00

For each conviction under section 4052 (4207), when the defendant pleads guilty; and for each conviction under section 3773 (4107), and for each conviction of an assault, assault and battery, or affray, where a stick or other weapon is used 15 00

On conviction in cases of bastardy, and for proceedings de novo in circuit or city court, as provided in section 4724 (1613), for violations of 4719 (1609), or section 4717.. 50 00

For each conviction of a misdemeanor, not otherwise provided for....... .... 7 50

1 Feb. 23, 1883, p. 173.

For each conviction in a case removed from the county court, or from a justice's court, the same fee as if the case had originated in the circuit or city court; [1]and for convictions in the county court, the same fees and emoluments that they are allowed by law for similar convictions in the circuit or city court; but they shall only receive one fee in cases that are convicted in the county court, and the defendant appeals to the circuit or city court, and is again convicted on the same charge.

1 Nov. 26, 1883, p. 72, sec. 3.

[1]For prosecuting a defendant charged with a criminal offense, whose case has been removed from any court of such solicitor's circuit into the United States court, to conviction in the latter court, or for making and successfully prosecuting motion in such court to remand the cause to the state court, the same fee as is allowed to him upon conviction in the state court for same offense; to be taxed and collected as such fee would be taxed and collected on conviction in state court. And any attorney appointed by him to appear for, and represent the state in such cases, in his stead, shall be entitled to same fees for like services, to be taxed and collected in same manner; but in no case less than........................... .... 25 00

On all forfeitures collected by the clerk or sheriff, five
per centum thereof.*

Entitled to only one fee when two or more indicted and convicted jointly.—Dent's
case, 42 Ala. 514; Brown's case, 46 Ala. 148.   Under indictment for assault to
murder with weapon, plea of guilty of simple assault denies the intent only, and
solicitor's fee is fifteen dollars.—Adams' case, 48 Ala. 421.   Where two counts
joined, and one nol. prossed, and conviction had under the other, solicitor's fee taxed
under latter.—Ex parte Tompkins, 58 Ala. 71.   Effect of repeal and re-enactment
of statute on provision fixing fees.—Caldwell's case, 55 Ala. 133.

ARTICLE III.

FEES OF CLERKS OF CIRCUIT AND CITY COURTS..

4869 (5041). **Fees of circuit and city clerks.**—Clerks of
the circuit and city courts are entitled to the following fees in
criminal cases,—that is to say:

For docketing each cause, to be charged but once........$	10
For issue of any writ, sci. fa., or notice......................	50
Each subpœna issued........	25
Each continuance by defendant................................	25
Taking undertaking or recognizance, and entering same	50
For each trial...............	50
Entering judgment against each defendant................. :.	25
Issue of each execution..	50
Each entry of the discharge of bail on surrender of the principal, to be paid by the bail........	50
Entering order of removal of trial, and the incidents of such removal..	1 00
Making transcript and certificate, for each hundred words.................	15
Entry of forfeiture against defendant......................	50

* On 28 February, 1887 (Pamph. Acts 1886–7, p. 161), an act was approved,
entitled "An act to pay salaries to solicitors instead of the fees which they now
receive, and to require said fees to be paid into the state treasury," which reads as
follows:
  "SECTION 1. *Be it enacted by the General Assembly of Alabama.* That instead
of the fees which solicitors are now entitled to receive for convictions procured
by them, every circuit solicitor, and the solicitor for the county of Montgomery,
shall receive an annual salary of three thousand dollars, to be paid them quarterly
out of the state treasury.
  "SEC. 2. All fees which are now, or hereafter may be by law taxed against defendants upon convictions as solicitors' fees, shall, when collected by any officer
authorized by law to collect said fees, be forthwith paid into the state treasury.
The circuit clerks of the counties in each circuit, and the clerk of the city court of
Montgomery, shall make quarterly reports to the auditor of the solicitors' fees
collected in their respective counties.
  "SEC. 3. All solicitors' fees which may be collected from convicts who are
hereafter convicted and confined at hard labor for any county, must, when collected, as now provided by law, be paid into the state treasury.
  "SEC. 4. Solicitors may appoint deputies to represent them in the counties whose
county courts are held, who shall prosecute all criminal cases before said courts,
and said deputies for such services shall receive five hundred dollars out of the
fees assessed in said county courts and paid into the county treasury, but in no case
shall they receive more than the fees assessed and collected; *Provided*, That the
surplus money paid into the state and county treasuries under the provisions of
this act, after the solicitors and their assistants have respectively been paid the
amounts herein provided for them, shall be paid into the fine and forfeiture fund
of the respective counties in direct proportion to the amount received from the
counties respectively; *Provided*, The provisions of this act shall not go into effect
until after the spring terms of the circuit courts are held in the several circuits of
the state in the year 1887."

Final judgment of forfeiture against defendant............$	50
Entry of forfeiture against witness or juror, each.........	25
Final judgment...	25
Issuing execution	50
Final record, for each hundred words	15
Record for supreme court, for each hundred words......	15
Certifying same..	25

¹ Jan. 23. 1888, p. 98, sec. 5.

¹For recording indictments and making certified copies thereof, under sections 4388 and 4392, to be taxed as a part of the costs in the case 25

As amended, Feb. 18, 1879, p. 73; Dec. 8, 1880, p. 52.

4870 (5042). **Costs; how taxed and collected.**—Of the fees specified in the preceding section, such as accrue on a forfeiture against a defaulting juror, witness, or bail, must be taxed as costs, and collected under execution against such witness, juror, or bail, unless excused therefrom by the court; and all other special fees for such services as are rendered in the case must be taxed as costs against the defendant, on conviction, or against the prosecutor, or the foreman of the grand jury, as provided by section 4355. (4779), and collected by execution; and in all trials in the circuit or city courts, or county courts, where the state fails to convict, or the indictment abates, or is nol. prossed, or withdrawn, the fees of the sheriffs and clerks of said courts shall be paid out of the fine and forfeiture fund; but said sheriffs and clerks must make affidavit before the circuit, city, or probate judge of the amount due them; and the right of said sheriffs and clerks to such payment of their said fees shall be postponed to the rights of state witnesses, as they now exist.

4871 (5024). **Clerks of city and criminal courts; how paid.** The legal fees of the clerks of the city and other criminal courts, in criminal causes, shall, at the termination of such causes, be paid to the clerks in the same manner, and to the same extent that clerks of the circuit courts are paid; and all laws now in force, or which may be hereafter enacted, providing for the payment of fees in state cases to clerks of the circuit courts are made applicable to clerks of city and other inferior courts.

ARTICLE IV.

FEES OF SHERIFFS.

4872 (5043). **Sheriffs' fees and allowances; sheriffs to file application for fees, when.**—Sheriffs are entitled to the following fees and allowances in criminal cases,—that is to say:

For executing search warrant by day........................$	1	00
For executing search warrant by night......................	2	00
For executing warrant or writ of arrest......................	2	00
For each bond or undertaking returned to court.........	1	00
For serving each subpœna or notice............,.............		50
For committing prisoner to jail.................................	1	00
For releasing prisoner from jail.................................	1	00
For summoning jury in capital case, or at any special court for trial of criminal.....	3	00
For attendance each day on such court...............	2	00

For execution of criminal, and all incidents, to be paid
  by the county.................... ....$ 50 00
For levying and making money on execution for costs..   1 00
[1]For feeding each prisoner in jail under charge or conviction for any indictable offense, to be paid by the
  state, for each day*...............................   30
But upon conviction, the fees for feeding such prisoner,
  though to be paid by the state, must be taxed against
  him as part of the costs to be collected by execution;
  and such fees, when collected, shall be paid to the
  clerk of the court from which the execution was issued, who shall give to the officer from whom he receives the same, receipts in duplicate, showing the
  amount, from whom, and the case in which the money
  was collected, one of which shall, within ten days, be
  forwarded to the auditor; and the clerk shall forthwith pay over the money so received by him to the
  state treasurer for the use of the state. In no case
  shall any defendant, on conviction, be sentenced to hard
  labor for the payment of the sheriff's fees for feeding
  him while in jail.
For feeding each prisoner confined in jail for contempt
  of court, or under attachment, or as a witness, or by
  virtue of any warrant or other process to keep the
  peace, or on account of insanity, to be paid by the
  prisoner, or by the state, if he is insolvent, for each
  day..,...............................   30
For feeding prisoner under bastardy proceedings, to be
  paid by complainant, or the defendant, according to
  the judgment of the court; or if the party adjudged
  to pay such costs is insolvent, then to be paid by the
  state, for each day...   30
For serving warrant on person charged with knowingly
  concealing or harboring person belonging to ship or
  vessel................................ ....   3 00
For levying execution, and making money on judgments
  against defaulting jurors, witnesses, bail and defendants, and on judgments confessed under section 4502
  (4454), the same fees as in civil cases.
For removing any prisoner in cases where there is no
  jail in the county in which the offense is committed,
  or the jail therein is insecure, to the jail of another
  county, and for returning him to the jail of the county
  from which he was removed, or to court for trial, for
  every twenty miles traveled, computed according to
  the route usually traveled, two and a half dollars for

[1] Dec. 11. 1882, p. 14.

---

* By act, entitled "An act to compensate sheriffs for feeding prisoners after they
are sentenced to be confined in the penitentiary," approved February 28, 1887
(Pamph. Acts 1886-7, p. 76), it is enacted: "That sheriffs shall be entitled to and
receive the same compensation for feeding prisoners confined in jail, under sentence of any court of competent jurisdiction, to be imprisoned in the state penitentiary, before removal to the penitentiary, by the proper officer, as they are now
entitled for feeding prisoners in other cases, and be paid in the same manner; *Provided*, That when any person or contractor has entered into any contract with the
proper authorities to work at hard labor any prisoner thus confined in jail under
such sentence, outside the walls of the penitentiary, then the compensation to
which the sheriff is entitled for the feeding of prisoners must be paid by such person or contractor before the prisoner is removed from the jail."

the sheriff, two dollars for each necessary guard, not exceeding two, and one dollar and twenty-five cents for the prisoner, besides usual fees for commitment, to be taxed against, and paid by such prisoner, on conviction, or, if he is insolvent, or is acquitted, by the county in which the offense was committed; but in no case shall the county to which such prisoner was removed be liable for such costs or fees.

[1] Feb. 17, 1885, p. 166.

[1]For removing any prisoner upon a change of venue granted in his case, or who is arrested and confined in jail in a county other than that in which he is triable, or arrested for contempt, for every twenty miles traveled, computing according to the route usually traveled, two and a half dollars for himself, two dollars for each guard, not exceeding two, and one dollar and twenty-five cents for the prisoner, to be paid by the state upon his sworn account therefor, accompanied by a certificate of the clerk of the court in which such prisoner is triable, that such fees have been reported to, and docketed by him; but no fee shall be allowed for any guard, unless the judge of the court making the order of removal shall state therein that, upon investigation, he believes such guard necessary, and shall designate the number thereof. If such prisoner is convicted, the clerk of the court in which the conviction is had shall tax the costs of such removal against him, and shall immediately, upon the adjournment of the court, issue execution therefor, and for the other costs, and deliver the same to the sheriff of his county; and such sheriff, upon the collection of the costs of such removal, shall pay the same to the state treasurer.*

4873 (5044). **Same; how taxed and paid.**—The fees specified in the preceding section, except where some other provision is made by law, are to be collected and paid in the following manner:

The fees which accrue against defaulting jurors, witnesses and bail are to be paid by them respectively, unless excused by the court.

---

* By act approved February 11, 1887 (Pamph. Acts 1886–7, p. 53), sections one and three of the act regulating the compensation of sheriffs for the removal of prisoners, approved March 1, 1881, are amended; and the sections, as amended, are as follows:

(1) "That for removing prisoners under order of a judge as herein provided, upon removal of trial, or when arrested and confined in jail in a county other than that in which he is triable, the sheriff shall receive for every twenty miles of the distance between the two places from and to which the removal is made, computed at the shortest distance between the two places by any route usually traveled, two dollars for himself, two dollars for each necessary guard, and one dollar for the prisoner; *Provided*, No guard shall be allowed for the removal of a prisoner charged with a misdemeanor."

(3) "That whenever any person, charged with the commission of a crime in any county in this state, shall be arrested and confined in a jail in a county other than that in which he is triable, it shall be the duty of the sheriff or jailer of the county in which such person is arrested and confined at once to notify the sheriff of the county in which he is triable; and upon the reception of such notice, it shall be the duty of the sheriff to apply to the judge of the circuit court, or the judge of the city or criminal court, or the judge of probate in his county, for an order to remove such person so arrested and confined in the jail of his said county."

The fees for services rendered in each criminal case must be taxed against the defendant on conviction, or may be taxed against the prosecutor, or the foreman of the grand jury, under the provisions of section 4355 (4779); and if an execution against either of them is returned "no property found," or if the costs are not taxed against either of them, such costs must be paid by the state, except when they are payable by the county.

[1] Unless otherwise provided, accounts due to sheriffs, which are payable by the state, must be proved in open court before the presiding judge of the circuit or city court, and certified by him to be correct, or be certified by the clerk of the circuit or city court, and sworn to before the probate judge; and, being so certified and proved, must be presented to the auditor, accompanied by the affidavit of the sheriff, to the effect that the same is correct, and that no part thereof has been paid; and, if found correct, must be paid by warrant on the state treasurer.

[1] Dec. 11, 1882, p. 14.

No sheriff must be paid out of the state treasury any fee or allowance whatever, on account of any prisoner who has escaped from his custody; but the commissioners' court may, in their discretion, pay such fees and allowances as are payable by the county, notwithstanding the escape of the prisoner, if satisfied that such escape was not caused by the connivance or negligence of the officer having charge of him.

4874 (5063). **Fees of bailiffs.**—Bailiffs shall receive two dollars per day while in attendance on the circuit, city, criminal, or probate court, to be paid in the same way that regular jurors are paid.

ARTICLE V.

FEES OF CORONERS.

4875 (5045). **Coroners' fees.**—The coroner is entitled to the following fees:

[1] For going to and returning from the place where he holds an inquest, five cents for each mile traveled.

[1] March 1, 1881, p. 118, sec. 2.

For holding an inquest...$	2 50
For summoning jury on inquest...............................	1 00
For each subpœna........	25
For each warrant of arrest...........	50
For each bond or undertaking returned to court	50

For attending post mortem examination, where no jury is summoned, and returning opinion of surgeon or physician, five cents for each mile traveled in going and returning, and $1.00; to be paid, to be returned to court, and to be taxed as costs in same manner as fees for holding inquest.

For money paid into the county treasury, when found on the body of a deceased person, five per cent., but in no case more than 5 00

For all other services performed by him, in cases authorized by law, the same fees that are allowed to sheriffs for similar services.

4876 (5046). **Fees for inquest, how taxed and paid; post mortem examinations and fees therefor; other fees.**—Fees for holding inquest shall be paid out of the county treasury, when, in the opinion of the court of county commissioners or board of revenue, the inquest should have been held; and such fees must be also certified by the coroner, to the clerks of the circuit and city courts of the county, and must be taxed as costs against any person who is convicted of murder or manslaughter by killing the person on whose body the inquest was held, and be collected like other costs in criminal cases; and, when collected in cases in which the county has paid the same, shall be paid to the county treasurer for the use of the county; and in other cases, to the coroner. But no fees shall be paid for an inquest when it is publicly known before the jury is summoned, who caused the death of the deceased, or when the slayer has been arrested for the homicide; but in such case, if the immediate cause of the death is uncertain, a physician or surgeon may be summoned to make a post mortem examination, who shall give his opinion in writing as to the cause of the death, which must be returned by the coroner as inquests are returned by him, and such coroner, physician, or surgeon, shall be entitled to the same fee and mileage, to be paid in the same manner, as for attending an inquest; such fees as accrue to coroners for services rendered by him in discharging duties of sheriff, must be taxed, collected and paid in the same manner that sheriff's fees for like services are taxed, collected and paid.

ARTICLE VI.

FEES OF JUSTICES OF THE PEACE.

4877 (5037). **Justices' fees**—Justices of the peace are entitled to the following fees in criminal cases,—that is to say:

For complaint made before him.................................$	25
For issuing warrant of arrest	50
For issuing search warrant.................................	75
For issuing a warrant in bastardy proceedings............	1 00
For taking examination in bastardy proceedings..........	50
For each bond or undertaking of the accused..............	50
For each bond or undertaking of witness...................	25
For issuing each subpœna or notice...........................	25
For order of commitment to jail	25
For each trial of misdemeanor.................................	1 00
For each order of continuance.................................	25
For each judgment on forfeited bond or undertaking...	50
For taking bond and certifying proceedings on appeal...	1 00
For each execution for costs.....................................	25
For issuing warrant for person knowingly concealing or harboring any person belonging to any ship or vessel, to be paid by the master.....................................	50
And for hearing the testimony and making necessary orders in such case, to be paid by the master............	1 00

4878 (5038). **Same; how taxed and collected.**—In prosecutions before a justice of the peace, where the case is not taken to the circuit or city court by appeal, or otherwise, the fees above specified, for such services as may be rendered in the case, must, unless otherwise provided, be taxed by him as costs, and collected by execution, as in cases tried in the county court; and, in all other cases, must be certified by him to the court to which the proceedings are removed, or to which the process is returnable, and there taxed and collected like other costs.

McPherson v. Boykin, 76 Ala. 602.

ARTICLE VII.

FEES OF CONSTABLES.

4879 (5039). **Constables' fees.**—Constables are entitled to the following fees in criminal cases,—that is to say:

For executing a search warrant by day.. ....$ 1 00
For executing a search warrant by night..................... 2 00
For executing any other warrant............................. 50
For serving each subpœna or notice issued by a justice
  of the peace............... 25
For serving each subpœna or notice issued by the county
  court 50
For carrying a person before a magistrate under a warrant of arrest, or to jail when committed thereto, for himself and each necessary guard, to be proved by his own oath, for each mile.................................... 10
For performing any other service under process from the county court, the fees taxed for those services under section 4881 (5035).
For carrying a prisoner to the jail of another county, when there is no sufficient jail in the proper county, the same fees that are allowed to the sheriff for similar services, to be paid in the same manner.
For serving warrant against person charged with knowingly concealing or harboring person belonging to any ship or vessel, to be paid by the master.............. 3 00

4880 (5040). **Same; how taxed and collected.**—In all criminal prosecutions, the fees specified in the preceding section, for the services rendered in the case, must be taxed as costs by the court or justice, and collected like other costs.

ARTICLE VIII.

FEES IN COUNTY COURTS.

4881 (5035). **Fees in county court.**—In prosecutions before the county court, the following fees shall be allowed for the services specified, and none other,—that is to say:

For taking affidavit of complainant and issuing warrant
  of arrest ....$ 1 00
For taking and approving bail bond 50
For issuing each subpœna or notice 25

For each order of continuance ....$ 50
For trial, entering judgment, and, when an appeal is
    taken, approving bond and certifying proceedings.....   5 00
For judgment on forfeited undertaking of bail............   3 00
For judgment against defaulting witness...................   2 00
For serving warrant of arrest when bail is given.........   1 00
For serving warrant of arrest when bail is not given,
    and carrying defendant to court or to jail...............   2 00
For serving each subpœna or notice.........................   50
The fees above specified shall be taxed against the de-
    fendant on conviction, or against the prosecutor under
    the provisions of section 4223 (4721), and, if not paid
    presently, may be collected by execution; but no fee
    shall be taxed for services not rendered.
The fees taxed for services performed by the county
    court, or by the judge of said court, belong to the
    county, and, when collected, shall be paid into the
    county treasury; and the fees taxed for all other ser-
    vices shall be paid to the officers by whom the services
    are performed.

4882 (5035). **Same; fees of judges to be paid out of county treasury.**—The judge of the county court shall receive no other compensation than the following fees, which shall be paid out of the county treasury,—that is to say:

If the warrant of arrest is issued by him, then for all
    the proceedings had before him in each case, including
    bond and certified copy of proceedings on appeal......$ 4 00
If the warrant of arrest is not issued by him, then for
    all services in each case...   3 00
For each judgment against a defaulting witness, or on
    forfeited undertaking of bail...............................   2 00

ARTICLE IX.
FEES OF JURORS.

4883 (5049). **Regular jurors' fees; proved by oath of juror; certificate of clerk.**—Regular jurors, grand and petit, are entitled to two dollars for each day's service, five cents for each mile traveled in going to and returning from court, and ferriage and toll, to be proved by the oath of the juror before the clerk of the court, whose duty it is to give each juror a certificate, stating therein the number of days he has served, the number of miles he has traveled, the amount of ferriage and toll he has paid, and the amount of compensation to which he is entitled; which certificate shall be receivable in payment of county taxes, and any other county dues, and payable out of the county treasury.

Jackson v. Dinkins, 46 Ala. 69.

4884 (5051). **Tales jurors' fees.**—Tales jurors summoned for the trial of a capital case, under the provisions of section 4320 (4874), and attending in obedience to the summons, are entitled to the same compensation for their attendance as regular jurors, and to be paid in the same manner; other tales jurors are entitled to the same compensation for each day's attendance as regular jurors receive, to be paid in the same manner.

4885 (5050). **Fees of coroner's jury.**—Jurors summoned by a coroner to hold an inquest are entitled to the same compensation allowed grand and petit jurors, to be paid in the same manner; the mileage to be estimated by the nearest route usually traveled from each juror's place of residence to the place where the inquest is held.

ARTICLE X.

FEES OF WITNESSES.

4886 (5059). **Fees and compensation of witnesses.**—Witnesses in criminal cases are entitled to the same fees and compensation as in civil cases.

4887 (4927, 4459). **How taxed and paid.**—The fees of witnesses, subpœnaed on the part of the state to appear before the grand jury, or before any court in which a criminal prosecution is pending, must be taxed against the defendant, if he is convicted, or against the prosecutor when the costs are imposed on him; but if the defendant is not convicted, and the costs are not imposed on the prosecutor, or if the indictment is withdrawn and filed, or the prosecution abated by the death of the defendant, or if the costs are imposed on either the defendant or the prosecutor, and an execution against him for the same is returned "no property found," or if no indictment is found by the grand jury before whom the witnesses appear, or if a nolle prosequi is entered in the case, such fees must be paid by the county in the manner specified in section 4889 (4460).

4888 (4928). **Only two witnesses allowed to same fact; exceptions.**—In taxing the cost, against either the defendant or prosecutor, under the preceding section, not more than two witnesses, who were summoned or examined to prove the same fact, shall be allowed; unless such witnesses were summoned or examined to assail or defend the reputation of a witness for veracity, or the character of the defendant, when put in issue; or unless the court, on a motion to retax as in civil cases, should determine that the facts of the case justified the summoning or examining of a greater number of witnesses.

4889 (4460). **Witness' certificate; how payable; clerk not entitled to fee for issuing.** — It is the duty of the clerk of the court to issue a certificate to each witness appearing on the part of the state, stating therein the amount of compensation to which he is entitled, and the facts which, under the provisions of section 4887 (4927, 4459), make it a good claim against the county, which certificate is receivable in payment of any debt due to the county for fines and forfeitures, and payable by the treasurer out of any fines and forfeitures in the county treasury; the clerk who issues the certificate hereinabove mentioned shall not be entitled to demand or charge any fee for performing said duty.

Certificate is primary charge on fine and forfeiture fund; need not be presented to commissioners' court for allowance.—Briggs v. Coleman, 51 Ala. 561. Failure of county treasurer to pay is breach of his bond for which action lies.—Ib. Clerk must authenticate by his certificate claims of witnesses before grand jury, although foreman is required also to give certificate of attendance.—Heer v. Seymour, 76 Ala. 270.   Sufficiency of certificate.—Ib.   Statute construed.—Ib.   Witness' certificates held to be transferable by delivery, etc.—Findley v. Wyser, 1 Stew. 23.

Feb. 23, 1883, p. 150.

4890. Fees of state witnesses when subpœnaed in more cases than one.—A witness for the state, attending in more criminal cases than one at the same time, shall only be entitled to fees in one case, to be selected by him while so attending; but if after the case in which he elects to claim his fees is disposed of, his attendance is required in the other case or cases, he shall, for such attendance, be entitled to claim his per diem in such other case, or if more than one, in the one in which he may then elect to claim his fees; and so on until all the cases in which he is required to attend are disposed of by trial, continuance, or otherwise.

4891 (5062). Witness' fees before justices of the peace.—In all criminal cases before justices of the peace, unless otherwise provided, witnesses are entitled to fifty cents per day, while in attendance on the trial, to be taxed in the bill of costs.

Article XI.

GENERAL PROVISIONS CONCERNING FEES AND COSTS.

4892 (5017). No fee charged unless expressly authorized. The law of costs must be deemed and held a penal law, and no fee must be taken but in cases expressly provided by law.

Statutes on subjects of fees and costs are penal, and must be strictly construed. Dent's case, 42 Ala. 514; Lee v. Smyley, 16 Ala. 773. See Caldwell's case, 55 Ala. 133. Motion to retax costs; appeal will lie from.—Dent's case, supra. Neither state nor county liable for costs incurred in prosecutions, except to extent and in manner provided by statute.—Greene County v. Hale County, 61 Ala. 72. State never taxed with costs.—Eslava v. Ames Plow Co., 47 Ala. 384; Pollard v. Brewer, 59 Ala. 130. County liable for costs on failure in action against bail.—Dover's case, 45 Ala. 244.

Feb. 22, 1881, p. 11, sec. 7.

4893. When prisoner deemed insolvent; return of execution.—No prisoner shall be regarded as insolvent without the return of "no property" upon execution issued against him, in the particular case; and no execution shall be so returned within less than thirty days from the time it goes into the hands of the sheriff.

CHAPTER 2.

DISPOSITION OF FINES, FORFEITURES AND PROCEEDS OF HARD LABOR.

4894 (4458). Fines to go to county, and judgment accordingly.—All fines go to the county in which the indictment was found, or the prosecution commenced, unless otherwise expressly provided; and judgment therefor must be entered in favor of the state, for the use of the particular county.

Judgment for fines must be in name of state, for use of the county.—Warfield's case, 34 Ala. 261.

As amended, Feb. 28, 1887, p. 146.

4895 (4461). Surplus of fund to pay officers.—Whenever there shall be a surplus of the fund arising from fines and for-

feitures in the county treasury of any county, over and above
the sum required to pay the registered claims of state witnesses,
the county treasurer of such county must pay the fees of the
officers of court arising from criminal cases in which the defendant is not convicted and the costs are not imposed on the
prosecutor, or in which defendants have been convicted, and
have been proved insolvent by the return of executions "no
property found," or in cases in which the state enters a nolle
prosequi, or where the indictment has been withdrawn and
filed, or the prosecution abated by the death of the defendant;
Provided, The provisions of this act do not apply to Butler
county.

Statute construed.—Herr v. Seymour, 76 Ala. 270.   Fees of justices not payable out of fine and forfeiture fund, as fees of officers of court are in certain cases.
McPherson v. Boykin, 76 Ala. 602.

4896 (4462). **Same; officer's statement under oath; when
to refund.**—In cases specified in the preceding section, the officers of court must make a statement under oath of the amount
of such fees due them respectively, setting out the style of each
case and the term at which judgment was rendered; and if at
any time such costs so enumerated, or any part thereof, shall
be paid to such officers of court by the defendants, under execution or otherwise, they must refund the same to the county
treasurer, who must place the amount to the credit of the fine
and forfeiture fund of the county.

4897 (4463). **Same; when indictment withdrawn, afterwards reinstated, and defendant convicted.**—When an indictment has been withdrawn and afterwards reinstated, and
the defendant convicted, the fees paid under section 4895 (4461)
shall be taxed against such defendant as a part of the costs; and,
upon the collection thereof, shall be paid into the fine and forfeiture fund.

4898 (4464). **Penalty for failure to make statement and
refund fees afterwards collected.**—Any officer of the court,
failing or refusing to comply with the requirements of the two
preceding sections, must pay fourfold the amount so withheld,
to be recovered by motion of the county treasurer in the circuit court of the proper county, on three days' notice to the
defendant.

TITLE VI.

FORMS OF INDICTMENT.

4899 (4824). **Following forms sufficient.** — The following forms of indictment, in all cases in which they are applicable, are sufficient; and analogous forms may be used in other cases.

Laws prescribing forms of indictment not prohibited; sufficiency of accusation; forms allowed abridging and simplifying common-law forms.—Noles' case, 24 Ala. 672; Elam's case, 25 Ala. 53; Burdine's case, Ib. 60; Sherrod's case, Ib. 78; Thompson's case, Ib. 41; Salomon's case, 27 Ala. 26; Schwartz' case, 37 Ala. 460; Bowles' case, 46 Ala. 204; Johnson's case, 46 Ala. 212; Bryan's case, 45 Ala. 86; Danner's case, 54 Ala. 127. Not sufficient to pursue form in Code, if form defective in description of the offense.—Bryan's case, 45 Ala. 86.

1. CAPTION, COMMENCEMENT AND CONCLUSION. § 4365 (4784).

The State of Alabama, ⎫ Circuit court, ——— term, 18—.
——— county.   ⎭

The grand jury of said county charge that, before the finding of this indictment, etc. (describing the offense as in the following forms), against the peace and dignity of the State of Alabama.   E. F. J., Solicitor of the ——— circuit.

2. ABANDONMENT OF FAMILY UNDER VAGRANT ACT. § 4047 (4218).

A. B., having a family in said county, and being able to contribute to their support by his means (or, being an able-bodied person, by his industry), did abandon and leave them in danger of becoming a burden to the public, against, etc.

3. ABUSIVE, OBSCENE, OR INSULTING LANGUAGE. § 4031 (4203).

A. B. did enter into or go sufficiently near to the dwelling-house of C. D., and, in the presence or within the hearing of the family, or a member of the family of the occupants thereof (or A. B., in the presence or hearing of a woman), made use of abusive, insulting, or obscene language, etc.

4. AFFRAY. § 3764 (4101).

A. B. and C. D. did fight together in a public place.

5. ALTERING MARKS, BRANDS, ETC. § 3831 (4404), § 4382 (4812).

A. B., with intent to defraud, marked or branded an unmarked horse, the property of C. D.

6. ARSON IN THE FIRST DEGREE. § 3780 (4346).

A. B. willfully set fire to or burned a dwelling-house of C. D., in which there was at the time a human being.

7. ARSON IN THE SECOND DEGREE. §3781 (4347).

A. B. willfully set fire to or burned an uninhabited dwelling-house of C. D., in which there was at the time no human being.

8. ARSON IN THE THIRD DEGREE. §3784 (4348).

A. B., under such circumstances as did not constitute arson in the first or second degree, did willfully set fire to or burn a building (or, as the alternative may be).

9. ASSAULT AND BATTERY. §3747 (4318).

A. B. assaulted and beat C. D.

10. ASSAULT WITH COWHIDE, ETC., HAVING PISTOL TO INTIMIDATE. §3748 (4315).

A. B. did assault and beat C. D. with a cowhide, stick, or whip, having in his possession at the time a pistol (or a bowie-knife, or other deadly weapon), with the intent to intimidate the said C. D., and prevent him from defending himself.

11. ASSAULT BY LYNCHING. §3750 (4317).

A. B. and C. D. did abuse, whip, or beat E. F., upon an accusation that he had been guilty of stealing, (or to force the said E. F. to disclose where he was on the night of the twenty-first of August, one thousand eight hundred and sixty-five or to leave the country, etc., as the case may be).

12. ASSAULT WITH INTENT TO MURDER. §3751 (4314).

A. B., unlawfully, and with malice aforethought, did assault C. D., with the intent to murder him.

13. ASSAULT WITH INTENT TO RAVISH. §3751 (4314).

A. B. did assault C. D., a woman, with the intent forcibly to ravish her.

14. ASSAULT WITH INTENT TO ROB. §3751 (4314).

A. B. assaulted C. D. with the felonious intent, by violence to his person, or by putting him in fear of some serious and immediate injury to his person, to rob him.

15. ASSAULT WITH INTENT TO MAIM. §3751 (4314).

A. B. assaulted C. D. with the intent unlawfully, maliciously and intentionally to cut out or disable his tongue, or to put out or destroy his eye.

16. BETTING AT CARDS, DICE, ETC. §4057 (4209).

A. B. bet at a game played with cards or dice, or some device or substitute for cards or dice, at a tavern, inn, store-house for retailing spirituous liquors, or house or place where spirituous liquors were at the time sold, retailed, or given away, or in a public house, highway, or some other public place, or at an out-house where people resort, against, etc.

17. betting at gaming table, etc. §4057 (4209).

A. B. bet at a gaming table for gaming; or at a game called keno, or roulette, etc.

18. bigamy. §4016 (4185).

A. B., having a wife then living, unlawfully married one C. D.

19. bringing stolen property into this state. §3793 (4368).

A. B. feloniously took and carried away, in the State of Mississippi, one mule, the personal property of C. D., and brought said mule into the county of Mobile, in this state, against, etc.

20. burglary. §3786 (4343).

A. B., with intent to steal (or to commit arson in the first degree, or other designated felony, as the case may be, or in the alternative), broke into and entered the dwelling-house, or a building within the curtilage of the dwelling-house, or shop, store, warehouse, or other building, of C. D., in which goods, merchandise, or clothing, things of value (or other stated article of value, as the case may be), were kept for use, sale, or deposit, against, etc.

21. burglary in railroad car. §3787 (4344).

A. B., with intent to steal (or to commit a felony, describing it as "murder," or as the case may be), broke into and entered a railroad car, the property of the Louisville and Nashville Railroad Company, a corporation under the laws of the State of Kentucky (or as the case may be), upon or connected with a railroad in this state, in which goods, merchandise, or furniture, valuable things, were kept for use, deposit, or transportation as freight.

22. burglarious instruments in possession. §3788 (4345).

A. B. had in his possession an implement or instrument designed and intended by him to aid in the commission of burglary, or larceny, in this state, or elsewhere, against, etc.

23. card or dice playing at public places, houses, etc. §4052 (4207), §4054 (4807).

A. B. played at a game with cards or dice, or some device or substitute for cards or dice, at a tavern, inn, store-house for retailing spirituous liquors, or house or place where spirituous liquors were at the time sold, retailed, or given away, or in a public house, highway, or some other public place, or at an out-house where people resort.

24. CARNAL KNOWLEDGE OF GIRL CHILD. §3739 (4306).

A. B. did carnally know, or abuse in the attempt to carnally know, C. D., a girl under the age of ten years.

25. CARRYING CONCEALED WEAPONS. §3775 (4109), §3779 (4809).

A. B. carried a pistol concealed about his person.

26. CHALLENGING TO FIGHT A DUEL. §3767 (4104).

A. B. gave, accepted, or knowingly carried a challenge in writing, or in words (or as the case may be), to fight in single combat, with a deadly weapon, against, etc.

27. COMPELLING WOMAN BY FORCE TO MARRY. §3743 (4309).

A. B. did take C. D., a woman, unlawfully, and, against her will, by menace, force, or duress, did compel her to marry him (or to marry one E. F., or to be defiled, etc., as the case may be).

28. COMPOUNDING FELONY. §4006 (4149).

A. B., knowing that one C. D. had been guilty of the commission of burglary, took, or agreed to take, from the said C. D. money or other property, to compound or conceal such felony, or to abstain from any prosecution therefor.

29. CONSPIRACY TO COMMIT A FELONY OR MISDEMEANOR. §4007 (4152), §4008 (4153).

A. B. and C. D. conspired together to unlawfully, and with malice aforethought, kill E. F. (or to assault and beat E. F., as the case may be), against, etc.

30. COUNTERFEITING GOLD OR SILVER COIN. §3856 (4334).

A. B. counterfeited a silver coin of the republic of Mexico, called a dollar, which was at the time, by law, usage and custom, current in this state.

31. COUNTERFEIT COIN IN POSSESSION, ETC. §3856 (4334).

A. B. had in his possession a counterfeit of a gold coin of the United States, of the denomination of ten dollars, which was at the time current in this state, knowing the same to be counterfeit, and with intent to defraud or injure, by uttering the same as true, or causing it to be so uttered.

32. DECOYING AWAY CHILD. §3745 (4322).

A. B. did take or decoy away C. D., a child under twelve years of age, with intent to detain or conceal the said C. D. from his (or her) parents (or guardian, as the case may be), etc.

33. DEFAMATION. §3773 (4107).

A. B. did falsely and maliciously speak (write or print, as the case may be), of and concerning C. D. in the presence of E. F., charging him (or her, as the case may be), with a want of chastity (or with having committed larceny, or perjury, as the case may be), in substance, as follows, to-wit: (Here setting out the substance of the words spoken, written, or printed, as the case may be).

34. DESTROYING PUBLIC BRIDGE. § 3886 (4418, 4420).

A. B. willfully destroyed, otherwise than by burning, a public bridge, erected by authority of law, on a road leading from Greenville to Andalusia, against, etc.

35. DISCLOSURE OF INDICTMENT BY OFFICER OF COURT OR GRAND JUROR. § 3969 (4134).

A. B., an officer of court, to-wit, a deputy sheriff (or a grand juror, as the case may be), disclosed the fact that an indictment had been found by the grand jury of said county against one C. D. before the defendant had been arrested, or had given bail for his appearance to answer thereto, against, etc.

36. DISTURBING WOMEN AT PUBLIC ASSEMBLIES, OR IN STEAMBOAT, CAR, ETC., BY PROFANITY, ETC. § 4032 (4200).

A. B., by rude or indecent behavior, or by profane or obscene language, willfully disturbed a woman at a public assembly met for instruction or recreation, against, etc.; or, A. B., by rude and indecent behavior, or by profane or obscene language, willfully disturbed a woman on a railroad car (steamboat, or in any other public conveyance, as the case may be).

37. DISTURBING RELIGIOUS WORSHIP. § 4033 (4199).

A. B. willfully interrupted or disturbed an assemblage of people, met for religious worship, by noise, profane discourse, or rude or indecent behavior, at or near the place of worship (or by fighting at or near the place of worship, as the case may be).

38. EXHIBITING FALSE SAMPLES. § 3849 (4399).

A. B. fraudulently exhibited a false sample of sugar, by means whereof one C. D. was injured.

39. EMBEZZLEMENT, ETC., BY BANK OFFICER. § 3796 (4383), § 3810 (4811).

A. B., an officer of the Central Bank of Alabama, a bank incorporated under the laws of said state, embezzled, or fraudulently converted to his own use, money to about the amount of five hundred dollars (or bank-notes to the amount of about one thousand dollars, as the case may be), which was in the possession of the said bank, or deposited therein.

40. EMITTING AND CIRCULATING CHANGE-BILLS. § 4143 (4433), § 4144 (4434).

Form for emitting.

A. B., without authority of law, signed, made, emitted, or countersigned, or caused or procured to be made, emitted, signed, or countersigned, a certain paper to answer the purpose of money, or for general circulation, in substance, as follows: (Here set out substantially the paper), against, etc.

Form for circulating.

A. B. passed or circulated a certain paper, the substance or tenor of which is as follows: (Setting it out in substance), the said paper having been issued without the authority of law, to answer the purposes of money, against, etc.

41. ENDANGERING LIFE BY BURSTING BOILER, ETC. ?4113 (4231).

A. B., being the engineer of a steamboat used for the conveyance of passengers or freight, and in charge of the machinery thereof, or of some of the apparatus for the generation of steam, from gross negligence, or from ignorance, created, or allowed to be created, such an undue quantity of steam as to burst the boiler, or other apparatus in which steam was generated, or some apparatus or machinery therewith connected, and thereby endangered human life.

42. ENDANGERING LIFE BY OVERLOADING STEAMBOAT. ?4115 (4233).

A. B., while navigating a steamboat for gain, willfully received on board thereof so many passengers, or such a quantity of freight, that by means thereof such steamboat sunk, or overturned, and thereby endangered the life of a human being.

43. ENGAGING IN OR CARRYING ON BUSINESS WITHOUT LICENSE. ?3892 (4274).

A. B. engaged in or carried on the business of (here state kind of business), without a license, and contrary to law, against, etc.

If the business be selling liquor without license, the town or place should be stated, as in the following form: A. B. engaged in or carried on the business of a retail dealer (or wholesale dealer, as the case may be), in spirituous, vinous, or malt liquors, in a city, town, or village of less than one thousand inhabitants (or of more than one thousand and less than five thousand inhabitants; or over five thousand inhabitants, as the case may be; or, if the place is not a city, town, or village, it may be described as "at a place not in any city, town, or village"), without a license, and contrary to law, against, etc.

44. ENTICING AWAY, INTERFERING WITH, ETC., SERVANT, UNDER WRITTEN CONTRACT. ?3757 (4325).

A. B. knowingly interfered with, hired, engaged, enticed away, or induced C. D., a laborer or servant who had stipulated or contracted, in writing, to serve one E. F. a given number of days, weeks, months, or for one year, before the expiration of the term stipulated or contracted for, such contract being in force and binding upon the parties thereto, without the consent of the said E. F., to whom the service was due, given in writing, or in the presence of some veritable white person, against, etc.

45. EXTORTION. § 3926 (4154).

A. B., being a justice of the peace of said county, knowingly took from C. D. five dollars for the issue of a search warrant, being a greater fee than was by law allowed for such service.

46. FALSE PERSONATION, OBTAINING PROPERTY BY. § 3814 (4376), § 4380 (4799).

A. B. did falsely personate C. D., with intent to defraud, and, in such assumed character, received one hundred dollars, intended to have been delivered to the said C. D.

47. FALSE PRETENSES, OBTAINING MONEY BY. § 3811 (4370), § 4380 (4799).

A. B. did falsely pretend to C. D., with intent to defraud, that he had ten bales of cotton packed and ready for delivery, and, by means of such false pretense, obtained from the said C. D. one hundred dollars (or ten pieces of cloth, as the case may be).

48. FALSE PRETENSES, OBTAINING SIGNATURE BY. § 3813 (4374).

A. B. did falsely pretend to C. D., with intent to injure or defraud, that (here set out the false pretenses), and, by means of such false pretenses, obtained from C. D. his signature to a certain written instrument, in substance, as follows: (Here set out instrument as near as may be), the false making of which is forgery, against, etc.

49. FORGERY OF WILL, DEED, NOTE, BILL, BOND, RECEIPT, OR OTHER WRITTEN INSTRUMENT. § 3852 (4340).

A. B., with intent to injure or defraud, did falsely make, alter, forge, counterfeit (or totally obliterate, as the case may be), an instrument in writing, in words and figures substantially as follows: (Here set out the instrument in substance), against, etc.

50. FRAUDULENT CONVEYANCE. § 3834 (4352).

A. B., with the intent to hinder, delay, or defraud his creditors, did make a conveyance of property to C. D.; or A. B. did accept from C. D. a conveyance of property, with the intent to hinder, delay, or defraud the creditors of the said C. D.

51. GRAND LARCENY. § 3789 (4358, 4359, 4360), § 3791 (4812).

A. B. feloniously took and carried away a horse, the personal property of C. D. (or a gold watch of the value of —— dollars), the personal property of C. D.; or,

A. B. feloniously took and carried away from a building on fire, or which was removed in consequence of an alarm of fire, a silver watch, of the value of —— dollars, the personal property of C. D.; or,

A. B. feloniously took and carried away from a dwelling-house a diamond breast-pin, of the value of —— dollars, the personal property of C. D.; or,

A. B. feloniously took and carried away from the person of C. D. one bank-note for one dollar on the bank of Mobile, of the value of —— dollars, the personal property of C. D.; or,

A. B. knowingly, willfully, and without the consent of the owner, entered upon the land of C. D. and cut and carried off timber (or rails, as the case may be), of the value of twenty-five dollars or more, against, etc.

52. HORSE-RACING ON PUBLIC ROAD. ₴4097 (4229).

A. B. unlawfully engaged in a horse-race on a public road, against, etc.

53. INCEST. ₴4013 (4187).

A. B., a man, being the father of one E. B., a woman, and within the degree of consanguinity or relationship within which marriages are declared by law to be incestuous and void, and knowing of such consanguinity or relationship, did have sexual intercourse with the said E. B., or did live with her in a state of adultery, against, etc.; or, A. B., a man, and C. D., a woman, being within the degree of relationship within which marriages are declared by law to be incestuous and void, to-wit., the said C. D. being the widow of one E. F., the uncle of the said A. B. and, knowing of such relationship, did intermarry, or have sexual intercourse together, or did live together in adultery, against, etc.

54. KEEPING GAMING TABLES. ₴4055 (4208), ₴4056 (4808).

A. B. kept, exhibited, or was interested or concerned in keeping or exhibiting, a gaming table for gaming.

55. KIDNAPPING. ₴3746 (4323).

A. B. unlawfully or forcibly inveigled, enticed, or confined C. D., with intent to cause said C. D. to be imprisoned against his will, or to be sent out of the state against his will, etc., as the case may be.

56. LIVING IN ADULTERY OR FORNICATION. ₴4012 (4184).

A. B., a man, did live with C. D., a woman, in the state of adultery or fornication; or, A. B., a man, and C. D., a woman, did live together in a state of adultery or fornication.

57. LOTTERIES. ₴4068 (4445).

A. B. set up, or was concerned in setting up or carrying on, a lottery.

58. MALICIOUS INJURY TO ANIMALS. ₴3869 (4408, 4420), ₴4382 (4812).

A. B. unlawfully and maliciously disabled or injured a cow, the property of C. D.

59. Manslaughter in the First Degree. § 3731 (4301).

A. B. unlawfully and intentionally, but without malice, killed C. D. by stabbing him with a knife, etc. (or by striking him with a stick, etc., as the case may be).

60. Manslaughter in Second Degree. § 3731 (4301).

A. B. unlawfully, but without malice, or the intention to kill, killed C. D. by negligently throwing a brick from the top of a house, etc. (or by negligently running over him with a horse, or by striking him with a stick, etc., as the case may be).

61. Mayhem. § 3735 (4312).

A. B. unlawfully, maliciously, and intentionally cut out or disabled the tongue of C. D., or put out or destroyed an eye of C. D., etc.

62. Murder. § 3725 (4295).

A. B., unlawfully, and with malice aforethought, killed C. D., by shooting him with a gun or pistol, etc. (or by striking him with an iron weight, or by throwing him from the top of a house, or by pushing him into the river, whereby he was drowned, etc., as the case may be).

63. Murder by Killing in Sudden Rencounter with Concealed Weapons. § 3727 (4298).

A. B. unlawfully killed C. D. in a sudden rencounter, by the use of a deadly weapon concealed before the commencement of the fight, the said A. B. being the assailant, and his adversary having no deadly weapon drawn.

64. Negligent Escape by Officer. § 3993 (4126).

A. B., while jailer of said county, having the legal custody of one C. D., who was convicted of grand larceny, negligently suffered the said C. D. to escape.

65. Obstructing Public Road. § 4122 (4249).

A. B. did obstruct a certain public road, known as the "Chickasabogue" road, by a fence, bar (or other impediment may be alleged in the alternative, but must be specified), without leave of the court of county commissioners first had and obtained, against, etc.

Johnson's case, 32 Ala. 583.

66. Perjury on Trial of a Criminal Case. § 3906 (4112, 4114), § 3908 (4813).

A. B., on his examination as a witness, duly sworn to testify on the trial of one C. D., in the ——— court of ——— county, under an indictment for the murder of one E. F., which said court had authority to administer such oath, falsely swore, etc.

(stating the facts), the matters so sworn to being material, and the testimony of the said A. B. being willfully and corruptly false.

67. PERJURY IN OTHER PROCEEDINGS OR CIVIL CASE. §3907 (4113, 4114), §3908 (4813).

A. B., on an application for a continuance in a civil action in the —— court of —— county, in which one C. D. was plaintiff and the said A. B. defendant, being duly sworn by the clerk of said court, who had authority to administer such oath, falsely swore, etc. (stating the facts), the matters so sworn to being material, and the oath of the said A. B., in relation to such matters, being willfully and corruptly false.

68. POISONING SPRING, ETC. §4076 (4240).

A. B. willfully or wantonly poisoned a spring of water in the yard of C. D., or a reservoir of water in the public square in the town of Tuskegee, etc.

69. RAPE. §3736 (4304).

A. B. forcibly ravished C. D., a woman, etc.

70. RECEIVING OR CONCEALING STOLEN GOODS. §3794 (4365, 4367).

A. B. did buy, receive, conceal, or aid in concealing, one watch of the value of —— dollars, the personal property of C. D., knowing that it was stolen, and not having the intent to restore it to the owner, against, etc.

71. REMOVING DEAD BODY FROM GRAVE. §4023 (4193).

A. B. removed from the grave the dead body of C. D. from wantonness, or for the purpose of dissection or sale.

72. RESISTING OFFICER IN EXECUTING PROCESS. §3974 (4137).

A. B. did knowingly and willfully oppose or resist C. D., the sheriff of said county, in attempting to serve or execute a writ of execution, called a fieri facias, issued by the clerk of the circuit court of said county (or as the case may be, describing the process generally).

73. RIOT. §3766 (4103).

A. B., C. D. and E. F., being unlawfully assembled, did demolish, pull down, or destroy, or begin to demolish, pull down, or destroy, a dwelling-house.

74. ROAD OVERSEER NEGLECTING DUTY. §4129 (4810).

A. B., an overseer of a road precinct, failed to discharge his duties as such overseer.

75. ROAD APPORTIONER NEGLECTING DUTY. §4129 (4810).

A. B., a road apportioner of an election precinct, failed to discharge his duties as such apportioner.

76. ROBBERY. §3742 (4311).

A. B. feloniously took a gold watch of the value of —— dollars, the property of C. D., from his person, and against his will, by violence to his person, or by putting him in such fear as unwillingly to part with the same.

77. SELLING, REMOVING, OR CONCEALING PERSONAL PROPERTY COVERED BY LIEN OR CLAIM. §383.; (4353).

A. B., with the purpose to hinder, delay, or defraud C. D., who had a lawful and valid claim thereto, under a written instrument, lien created by law for rent or advances, or other lawful and valid claim, verbal or written, did sell or remove personal property, consisting of one bale of cotton (or other property, as the case may be), of the value of ten dollars, the said A. B. having at the time a knowledge of the existence of such claim.

78. SELLING LIQUOR WITHOUT LICENSE, OR IN VIOLATION OF SPECIAL PROHIBITORY LIQUOR LAWS. §4036 (4204), §4037 (4806).

A. B., without a license as a retailer, did sell spirituous, vinous, or malt liquors; or A. B. sold spirituous, vinous, or malt liquors without a license, and contrary to law, against, etc.

Sills' case, 76 Ala. 92; Boon's case, 69 Ala. 226; Powell's case, Ib. 10.

79. SELLING LIQUOR TO MINORS OR INTEMPERATE PERSONS. §4038 (4205).

A. B. did sell or give spirituous, vinous, or malt liquors to C. D., a minor (or person of known intemperate habits, as the case may be).

80. SELLING OR GIVING LIQUOR TO PERSON OF UNSOUND MIND. §4039 (4206).

A. B., who kept vinous, fermented, or spirituous liquor for sale, did knowingly sell, give, or deliver such liquor to C. D., a person who was, or reputed to be, of unsound mind.

81. SELLING, GIVING, OR LENDING PISTOL, OR BOWIE-KNIFE TO BOY UNDER EIGHTEEN. §4096 (4230).

A. B. did unlawfully sell, give, or lend a pistol or bowie-knife. or other knife of like kind or description, to C. D., a boy under eighteen years of age, against, etc.

82. SODOMY AND BESTIALITY, OR CRIME AGAINST NATURE. §4020 (4191).

A. B., against the order of nature, carnally knew C. D.; or A. B., against the order of nature, carnally knew a certain beast, to-wit, a cow, against, etc.

83. STREETS OF TOWN OUT OF REPAIR; INDICTMENT AGAINST MUNICIPAL AUTHORITIES. §4118 (4248).

A. B., C. D., E. F., G. H., etc., corporate officers of the town of Gadsden, a town duly incorporated under the laws of this state, the inhabitants thereof being exempt from working on

the public roads, did allow a street therein, known as ———
street (or, if the street is not named, it may be described), to remain out of repair for more than ten days at one time, without
a reasonable excuse therefor, against, etc.

Nowlin's case, 49 Ala. 41.

84. SUNDAY LAW, VIOLATIONS OF; KEEPING OPEN STORE, ETC. §4045 (4443).

A. B. unlawfully engaged in hunting or shooting (or gaming,
or card-playing, or racing, as the case may be; or, being a merchant or shop-keeper, and not a druggist, kept open store, or
did compel his child, or apprentice, or servant, in the alternative, as the case may be, to perform labor not the customary
duties of daily necessity or comfort, or works of charity) on
Sunday, against, etc.

85. TRAMP. §4048.

A. B. was a tramp.

86. SAME; FOR ENTERING A DWELLING-HOUSE, ETC., OR THREATENING, ETC. §4049.

A. B., being a tramp, did enter the dwelling-house, or other
building of C. D., without the consent of the occupant thereof
(or did willfully or maliciously injure, or threaten to injure, a
person therein; or A. B., being a tramp, did injure, or threaten
to injure, the real or personal property of C. D., or did demand
of or order C. D. to deliver or surrender to him an article of
value, as the case may be).

87. USING FIRE-ARMS WHILE FIGHTING IN PUBLIC PLACE. §4094 (4228).

A. B., while fighting at a militia muster (or in a street of the
city of Mobile), or at a public place, used, or attempted to use
a pistol (or gun, as the case may be), not in self-defense, etc.

88. VOLUNTARY ESCAPE BY SHERIFF. §3990 (4125).

A. B., while sheriff of said county, having the legal custody
of one C. D., who was charged with burglary (or indicted for
robbery, as the case may be), voluntarily permitted the said C.
D. to escape.

89. VOTING ILLEGALLY. §4185 (4289).

A. B. voted more than once, or deposited more than one
ballot as his vote for the same office (or, not being twenty-one
years of age, unlawfully voted), at the last general election held
in this state (or the kind of election may be designated, as the
case may be), against, etc.

INDEX.

CONCEALING PROPERTY. See Fraudulent Secretion of Property. *Section*

CONCEALED WEAPONS. See Carrying Concealed Weapons.

CONFESSION OF JUDGMENT.

CONSPIRACY.

CONTEMPTS.

CO-OPERATIVE ASSOCIATIONS. See Mutual Aid Associations.

CONVICT SYSTEM.

ORGANIZATION, OFFICERS AND THEIR DUTIES.

INFORMATION.

INQUISITION. See CORONER'S INQUEST; INQUISITION AS TO INSANE PRISONERS.

INQUISITION AS TO INSANE PRISONERS.

INSANE PRISONERS.

INSOLVENT CONVICTS.

JAIL. See IMPRISONMENT IN COUNTY JAIL.

JEOPARDY.

JUDGMENT AND SENTENCE.

JURISDICTION.

PUBLISHING ANOTHER AS A COWARD. See DUELING.

PUBLISHNG FORGED INSTRUMENT. See FORGERY AND COUNTERFEITING.

PUNISHMENTS.

QUARANTINE. See HEALTH AND QUARANTINE.

RACING. See HORSE-RACING; STEAMBOAT-RACING.

RAILROADS.

ERRATA.

§ 3957. For "having made *the* sale," in second line, read "having made sale."

§ 4026. For "*relations*," in seventh line, read "*relatives.*"

§ 4058. For "except *for* charge," in third line, read "except *the* charge."

§ 4140. "*Individual*," in head or index line, though in original manuscript, should be stricken out, as the word was stricken out of body of section by the joint committee.

§ 4242. For "*county* court," in head or index line, read "*city* court." The error is in the original manuscript.

§ 4261. For "*any* officer," in first line, read "*an* officer."

§ 4309. For "*jurors* so drawn," in second line, read "*persons* so drawn."

§ 4330. For "fifteen, on trial for," in seventh line, read "fifteen, *when* on trial for."

§ 4359. For "expression of opinions," in seventh line, read "expression of *their* opinions."

§ 4401. For "*return*," in third line, read "*retain.*"

§ 4703. For "section, to obey," in twenty-second line, read "section, *and* to obey."

§ 4834. For "*or* priority," in last line, read "*and* priority."

In original manuscript, section 4005 constitutes a separate article, numbered ten, and entitled "Accessories after the fact;" but, in printing, it was made a part of article nine.

Lightning Source UK Ltd.
Milton Keynes UK
UKHW021108200721
387438UK00002B/251